PRESENCES

PRESENCES

A BISHOP'S LIFE IN THE CITY

PAUL MOORE

COWLEY PUBLICATIONS
Cambridge ∾ Boston
Massachusetts

Published in the United States of America by Cowley Publications, a division of the Society of St. John the Evangelist. No portion of this book may be reproduced, stored in or introduced into a retrieval system, or transmitted, in any form or by any means—including photocopying—without the prior written permission of Cowley Publications, except in the case of brief quotations embodied in critical articles and reviews.

Library of Congress Cataloging-in-Publication Data may be obtained by contacting the Library of Congress or Cowley Publications.

ISBN 1-56101-168-1 (alk. paper)

This edition published by arrangement with Farrar, Straus and Giroux. Cover design adapted by Vicki Black from the original design by Susan Mitchell. Frontispiece: Outside the Cathedral after being installed as Bishop of New York, 1972

This book was printed on recycled, acid-free paper in the United States of America.

Cowley Publications
28 Temple Place • Boston, Massachusetts 02111
800-225-1534 • www.cowley.org

To Brenda and to my grandchildren:
Finnian, Carrick, Amias, Rowan, Eli, Avery,
Quincy, Faye, Violet, Leonardo, Indiana, Jamie,
Eamon, Maeve, Nicholas, and Ruby

CONTENTS

Cowley Publications is a ministry of the Society of St. John the Evangelist, a religious community for men in the Episcopal Church. Emerging from the Society's tradition of prayer, theological reflection, and diversity of mission, the press is centered in the rich heritage of the Anglican Communion.

Cowley Publications seeks to provide books, audio cassettes, and other resources for the ongoing theological exploration and spiritual development of the Episcopal Church and others in the body of Christ. To this end, it is dedicated to developing a new generation of theological writers, encouraging them to produce timely, creative, and stimulating publications of excellence, and making these publications available widely, reaching both clergy and lay persons.

PRESENCES

INTRODUCTION

CERTAIN moments over the years have defined my life. I was born in my mother's bedroom in an enormous house in New Jersey staffed by butlers and maids. A three-hole golf course lay beyond the garden. There were guernsey cows for our milk, horses to ride or drive, chickens, pheasants, pigs, and purebred dogs for our pleasure. We spent the winter in another huge house in Palm Beach, Florida, the summer at a camp in the Adirondacks and at my grandmother's mansion on the sea on the North Shore of Massachusetts. The shape of the life that lay before me as I grew up was determined at birth; the day after I was born, my father entered me in St. Paul's School, where he had gone, and he expected me to attend Yale.

One evening at St. Paul's, I heard the words "Go in peace, the Lord has put away thine offenses, and pray for me, a sinner." As I rose from my knees, at the close of this first confession, I was overwhelmed with God's presence.

Some six years later, I rose to my knees to throw a hand grenade at a Japanese machine-gun nest and felt the scorching wound of a bullet in my chest. As I lay on the sand, my breath bubbling with blood as it escaped from the hole in my lung, I thought I was dying.

In the candlelight of a gypsy restaurant a few weeks after I returned from overseas, my hand touched the hand of a beautiful dark-haired woman, and I fell in love with Jenny. She later became my wife.

On December 17, 1949, I knelt before Bishop Washburn; as he laid his heavy but gentle hands on my head, I was made a priest. This changed my life forever.

One Maundy Thursday at my first parish, in Jersey City, after the beautiful evening liturgy of the Last Supper, I returned to the rectory and found a derelict sitting on the bench outside. He stank of vomit, urine, and stale wine. He looked up at me and groaned, "Why, Father? Why? . . . Why? . . . Why?" The next day I was to preach on Jesus' strange last words on the cross, "My God, my God, why hast Thou forsaken me?" It came over me at that moment that Jesus was staring through the bloodshot eyes of the man before me.

One cold night, we were having family supper in the rectory kitchen. We heard a tapping at the window and saw the face of a black boy, somehow deformed, looking at us. I went to the door to ask him in, but he ran away. He came back and ran away, night after night. Finally, he summoned the courage to come in. As we gave him a plate of spaghetti, his face lit up with a twisted smile, and he asked, "Does this mean I belong?"

Living among very poor people for eight years, I came to realize the agonizing burden borne by the poor in America and the need for Christ's love among them.

In 1950, I was run out of Groveland, Florida, for investigating a case of alleged rape. The sheriff, who was white, murdered three of the accused, who were black, on their way to trial a few weeks later. I felt the rage of racism penetrate to my very bones.

The night before I was consecrated bishop in January 1964, I was making my confession in the dim beauty of the Bethlehem chapel of the National Cathedral. As I acknowledged my sins, my weakness, my unworthiness, I was overcome by deep sobs.

In 1972, I was installed as Bishop of New York. I stepped forth onto the steps of the cathedral to bless the great city I loved and dedicated myself to fulfilling the role, to being a symbol of God's Church, a prophetic voice, and a pastor to the pastors of the diocese.

In 1973, my first wife died, and I faced the dark terror of her end, more fearful than the threat of my own.

A couple of years later, outside a hospital room where an old friend lay dying, I embraced his courageous wife, Brenda, and began to fall in love again.

In recent years, I have visited trouble spots around the world where people are being tortured, starved, and killed in flagrant violation of human rights. And always, in those places, I have found extraordinary courage and a wild, free spirit in the young men and women who struggle against this oppression. This thirst for freedom in the young is a token that every human person is made in the image of God.

A year ago, Brenda and I had an accident on the Thruway. When we smashed into the concrete median, I thought, "This is what it is like to die in an automobile accident." But here I am.

Over the years, I have seen, in the flow of history, what the Letter to the Ephesians calls Principalities and Powers. "For we are not contending against flesh and blood, but against the Principalities, against the Powers, against the world rulers of this present darkness, against the spiritual hosts of wickedness in high places" (Ephesians 6:12). These powers surface in different forms in different eras: the lust for national power, often disguised as patriotism; the ancient energies of revenge, handed down from one generation to another; the invidious and seemingly ineradicable disease of racism, woven into the very fabric of institutions and worked out in the desperate struggle for economic and social survival; and increasingly, in our times, the vast and evil force of greed. As these powers take hold, the victims and the perpetrators alike become fearful and paranoid, which in turn makes the dominance of the Principalities and Powers more vicious still. Worst of all, the struggles often become imbued with religious meaning: greed mixed with chauvinism and religion is truly a witches' brew.

But I also have seen another pattern continually emerging. The Marxist and the disciple of free enterprise look at the dynamics of history in economic terms; therapists see the world in psychological terms; sociologists and anthropologists see the principles of their own disciplines working themselves out over time. Some of these insights are valid. When I seek the meaning of history, however, I see the long process of redemption, not just the saving of individuals, but the redeeming, the making whole, of all of society—and perhaps, as Origen believed, the whole of Creation, the very sticks and stones. I see the sweep of ongoing Creation, the breaking of its perfection by human sin, the long and painful path of love and suffering by which God's Kingdom is renewed, and the final consummation of perfection.

Even now, you can sense that Kingdom breaking through the clouds of history. It breaks through at every celebration of the Eucharist, by which the pattern of the Kingdom is acted out for the particular time and place where it occurs and for the particular people who take part. It breaks through in moments of love, when in the passion of the flesh the lovers' isolation disappears in ecstatic union. It flashes open in moments of sacrifice, when all care of self is thrown to the winds and one person risks his life for another. It opens wide in the first cry of a newborn child. We can see the Kingdom in the rise of movements for justice, such as the civil rights movement, and in the unexpected breakthroughs of peace, such as the dismantling, stone by stone, of the Berlin Wall. In all these moments of glory, there is pain. Each, in this way, reenacts the death and resurrection of Christ.

Such an understanding of history has given me a clear sense of vocation, of the purpose for which I am here; it has shown me how to deal with suffering and shown me the meaning of love, whether in sacrifice or in the warm wonder of physical love. The Kingdom sustains me in the frustrations and failures of life, because in the chemistry of redemption often failure is not defeat but the path to a greater victory.

This book recalls these times: of the slow growth in my understanding of the mystery of being whom we call God, and of the divine presence encountered in suffering, poverty, loneliness, in joy and love, and in the ongoing struggle for justice, freedom, and peace.

A SILVER SPOON

I WRITE these memoirs gazing out of a window in Greenwich Village. We are on a quiet street of brick and brownstone houses. How fortunate I am to be here now. Looking back on my gilded childhood, I find it strange that my convictions—convictions that will not let me go—should have become part of me. And yet I can see some of the roots of these ideals of social justice in those early years, and I can trace from those roots the vocation that led to my becoming a bishop.

Memorial Day, 1929, Morristown, New Jersey. Early in the morning, bathed and scrubbed, I was fitted into the khaki severity of my Wolf Cub uniform. (A Wolf Cub is a junior Boy Scout.) I was nine years old, and I felt most important. My mother and my nurse made sure the neckerchief was straight, the shirt buttoned. The butler, who had served in the British Army in World War I, was summoned to cast his seasoned military eye over my appearance. Finally, I was presented as a young patriot for my father's approval.

The car was waiting. The chauffeur gave me an approving grin, and we drove up the driveway and downtown to the fairgrounds, where all the Scouts of Morris County were rendezvousing before the parade. My few little friends and I distanced ourselves from our mothers and tried to look nonchalant.

Soon, we heard the band warming up, the tubas pumping. Other troops fell in, and our scoutmaster, Mr. Pfeiffer, blew his whistle; we came to attention and were given last-minute instructions about saluting the reviewing stand and any flag we passed by. The band boomed out a great Sousa march, and we followed up the hill proudly.

The parade passed our school on Elm Street. Mr. Peck, the head-master, and Mrs. Peck waved solemnly as we went by. The column turned up South Street, past St. Peter's Church, to the war memorial. Here we stood at attention and recited the Pledge of Allegiance in front of the flag and, in the silence that followed, felt the great re-sponsibility that it bestowed.

The ceremonies continued. The names of those who had died in the service of our country were read, a prayer of thanksgiving for their heroic sacrifices recited. The climax was the singing of "The Star-Spangled Banner" by my friend David's mother, Mrs. Dennis, an understudy of the famous opera singer Dame Nellie Melba. As she reached the highest note, my young soul was moved beyond words.

The little boy in the Scout uniform was the product of a long line of Yankees who had migrated many times before my parents reached Morristown. My father's father grew up in Greene, New York, a village northwest of Binghamton, where he was a banker and justice of the peace. His grandmother, Rachel Beckwith, came from an old Connecticut family; one of her ancestors was an original Yale trustee, and another owned the land on which Yale built its first buildings in New Haven. The first Moore we know of in America was Alexander Moore, constable of New York in the 1730s and a member of the vestry of Trinity Church, Wall Street.

My grandmother Adelia "Ada" Small Moore's family lived in Maine, where Small Point still bears that name. In 1852, they moved to Galena, Illinois, a thriving Mississippi River town where my grand-mother spent her girlhood. She recalls President Grant, a friend of her father's, taking her on his lap at a dinner, and bidding him fare-well on his way to the White House. With the advent of railroads, Mr. Small left Galena for Chicago and the greater opportunities this growing city would afford an ambitious lawyer. My grandfather, mean-while, having attended Amherst College, traveled west to Puget Sound seeking adventure. In those days, the railroad ended in Kansas; from there, he had to ride on horseback. He entered the bar in Puget Sound and, after a few years, rode back to Montana, where he came to know Sitting Bull. The story comes down that Sitting Bull told him to leave, for there soon would be trouble with the white man—

and so he left for Chicago, where he joined Mr. Small's firm and married Small's daughter. Grandfather was most successful in business and moved to New York in 1900. His house, designed by Stanford White, still stands at 4 East Fifty-fourth Street in Manhattan.

My mother's family settled in New Lisbon, Ohio, in the early 1800s, having come from Vermont, where my great-great-grandmother, Rachel Hanna, is said to have held an entire pack of wolves at bay with her steadfast gaze as she hurried home from a neighbor's house. The family later moved to Cleveland, where the Hannas organized the successful mining establishment M. A. Hanna Company.

My father courted my mother on the porch of the old Oceanside Hotel in Magnolia on the North Shore of Massachusetts, attracted by her beauty, charm, and her championship tennis. He never kissed her until they were engaged. Soon after he graduated from Yale, they were married and moved to Morristown. I was born there in 1919 and grew up with my older brother, Bill, and two older sisters, Polly and Fanny.

In those days, Morristown was a small country town, civic-minded and proud of its heritage: George Washington had wintered there. Because of the beauty of the countryside and the convenient commute to New York on the Delaware–Lackawanna Railroad, in the early twentieth century several very rich families built elaborate English-style estates there. Our family was one of them.

When my grandfather died, in 1922, my father ceased practicing law in order to look after the family interests in the companies my grandfather had helped to found, including the National Biscuit Company, the American Can Company, Bankers Trust Co., and the Lackawanna Railroad.

I recount this family background because it instilled in me a faith in America and an old-fashioned kind of patriotism. In later years, when I became engaged in progressive movements, I never lost this deep trust in our country, nor did I ever wish radically to overturn the established order.

The books I read as a boy extolled the same simple patriotism— *The Rover Boys, Tom Swift, With Kit Carson in the Rockies, Davy Crockett*—as did the movies we saw. On Friday evenings, we children would go to the movies, accompanied by one of our nannies. We were each allowed a box of Charms as we settled down to *Pathé News*, *Felix the Cat*, a Laurel and Hardy short, and then the main feature. Our favorites were the Rin Tin Tin movies, which showed a brave police dog (as we then called German shepherds) fighting in the trenches of World War I with "our boys." The climax came when one of our soldiers went over the top to rescue a wounded comrade and was wounded himself; Rin Tin Tin sensed there was trouble and by barking and tugging at khaki trouser legs brought help. In the process, of course, the dog was also wounded. The moral was crystal clear: even dogs would risk their lives for their country!

Every night, before I went to sleep, my Scottish nurse, Jean Watson, would read me a story and listen to my prayers. "Now I lay me down to sleep, I pray the Lord my soul to keep. If I should die before I wake, I pray the Lord my soul to take. Our Father, who art in heaven . . . God bless Mummy and Daddy and Billy and Polly and Fanny, and make me a good boy." I believed God was right there. Jean also taught me the Creed and the Ten Commandments, and my mother took me to church every Sunday. How boring, I thought. But I prayed for our country, and I kept in mind the end of the Scout's law: "A Scout is brave, clean, and reverent." The Scout's handbook had a picture of a clean-looking Scout leaning against a pew in front of a stained-glass window. God and our country were all but indistinguishable.

In this way, I soaked up a political point of view: simplistic, conservative, unquestioning. Only in later years, when I first saw the ugly side of conservatism through the eyes of the poor people of Jersey City, did I become more liberal at heart. And it was not until I faced the reality of the war in Vietnam that my blind childlike patriotism began to disappear.

As a little boy, I was sick a good deal. All I wanted to do was lie in bed, where my Jean would wait on me and worry over her "poor, wee lamb." I was given beef broth, enemas—humiliating and painful— and, if nothing else worked, a dose of castor oil in a glass with orange juice, which did little to disguise the slimy stuff. Sometimes I had feverish dreams, in which a large, gray balloonlike cloud descended on me from above, repeating louder and louder: "I am the biggest thing in the world! *I am the biggest thing in the world! I am the biggest thing in the world!!*" Finally Jean would rush into the room to comfort me. I can still see her in her curlers and pink flannel nightgown. I knew my mother loved me, and she was soft and tender, but Jean I could always trust to be there when I needed her.

Jean told me often that she had given her life to the care of us children and never regretted it. She was great fun with her Scottish songs and her endless willingness to play games, but she worried constantly about us; if I was out late she would become so anxious that she would throw up. This obsessive attachment felt like prison.

My mother was a remarkable woman in many ways. Her guernsey herd was one of the finest in the country; her dalmatians were champions; she drove our champion hackney, Seaton Pippin, to best in show five times in Madison Square Garden. She was beloved by all who knew her for her charm and her good works, her enthusiasm and sense of humor.

Although I am sure she did not realize what she was doing, she imprisoned me as well. Mother was sick a good deal: she had neuralgia, what we would now call migraine headaches. I remember her lying on the sofa in her bedroom in a purple silk wrapper. Mother's room had a special smell, a lavender aroma from her perfume and from the sachets in her lingerie drawers. Twin canopy beds faced a fireplace. Large windows looked out on the garden on one side and the woods on the other, tall tulip trees in a stately grove through which you could see the lower pastures. On the floors were hooked rugs; the tables and a few chairs were American antiques of maple, pine, and cherry. Two easy chairs and a sofa were covered in chintz. I particularly remember her dressing table of tiger maple and the mirror above it, in which she placed the schedule of hunt meets for the season. Luster pitchers and cups stood in a corner cupboard and little china snuffboxes and ashtrays were on the tables. The room was large and sunny. By the time I was seven, my older sisters and brother had gone to boarding school; for all intents and purposes, I was an only child until I went to St. Paul's School at the age of twelve.

When Mother was feeling well enough, I would curl up beside her and she would read to me. The books she chose seemed magical: *Knock Three Times*, about a boy who entered another world by knocking on a tree; *The Princess and the Goblins*, about a little girl who followed a thread when she was lost in a cave; *Black Beauty*; *The Secret Garden*; and *Little Lord Fauntleroy*.

Sometimes, when nothing was planned for the day, she would say, "How about an adventure?" The word *adventure* held a special meaning, because that is what my storybook friends Uncle Wiggly and Jimmy Skunk were always having. Off we would go in the pony cart, a little two-wheeled red-and-black rig called a Meadowbrook, perhaps to Mr. Leible's nursery to pick up some pansies for the playhouse garden. Sometimes a cow blocked our path.

Thus were the silken threads of love woven around me. But with love came guilt. If these women who loved me so much gave their very lives to me, I had to pay them back by being a good little boy. I still find myself reacting in the same way, by being compulsively conscientious. I seem to need to pay something back to others, even to God. I suppose this tendency was a part of what drove me to the ministry and to the particular kind of ministry I chose to follow.

My friends and I played cops and robbers, kick the can, golf, and tennis, and all were great fun. But I was anxious and fearful when I played football or baseball; having been coddled so much as a child, I was afraid of being hurt. My brother attempted to toughen me up by teaching me to box. My sister Polly taught me to ride. I adored my older sister Fanny, but she went away to school when I was very young.

My father was home much of the time. I knew he loved me, but he was distant and rarely played catch with me or did other fatherly things. I never remember sitting in his lap. He sat in a big chair in the library, read, or listened to the radio. He drank a great deal but never seemed drunk; he would become slower in his speech, repeat his stories about salmon fishing or shooting a bull moose, then doze off. As I grew older, it was harder and harder for me to have a good conversation with him.

We were taught clearly what was right and wrong: never lie, never steal, don't bully, be generous, don't be a crybaby, cleanliness is next to godliness. However, the message we received about *social values* was confused. Charity was a good thing. Mother sat on countless charitable boards: the Visiting Nurse Association, the Women's Exchange, the Memorial Hospital, the women's auxiliary at church, the Audubon Society, the Society for the Prevention of Cruelty to Animals, and so on. My father established a fund to improve undergraduate teaching at Yale and gave generously to St. Paul's School. He was flattered that the austere rector asked to be called Sam; they would smoke cigars in the walled garden of the rectory, speaking of ways in which Dad could help the school.

Politics at home were rock-ribbed Republican. My mother's uncle was Mark Hanna, the GOP boss in the time of President William McKinley; Grandfather Moore was a prominent industrialist. Their Republicanism was not ideological (not "right wing" as we now understand it) but business oriented. My father believed that the success of our country depended on free enterprise and that the Republican Party was favorable to enterprise. He could not stand labor unions and was shocked when a Roman Catholic, Al Smith, ran for president. Once a year, the local head of the Republican Party would stop by our library and sit down nervously as Dad unloaded his views and negotiated his annual gift to good government—the Republican Party!

We were admonished to finish whatever was on our plate: "Think of the starving Armenians," we were told. Clearly, we were supposed to help those less fortunate than we, and yet not only did we live in a most extravagant way, but a real class system was part of our daily life. We had servants who worked for us in the house and on our "gentleman's farm." How we all ate our meals was symbolic. Mother's secretary was served on a tray in her office. She did not eat with the family nor with the servants. Our Scottish nurse and my sisters' French governess ate with the children and my mother when we had breakfast or lunch but never when my father was at the table. The butlers, maids, and cooks ate in the servants' dining room in the back hall. The cow barn, the farm, the chicken yard, and the vegetable garden each had hierarchies of their own, and the people who took care of them existed in a clearly understood but unspoken social structure. We grew up in this milieu and took it for granted that that was the way things were. We played with the children of the groom but, for some reason, not with the children of the herdsman. Perhaps that was his choice.

We became good friends with many of the help. One of the chauffeurs threw pop flies for me on warm spring evenings. The grooms tirelessly taught us how to ride—how to gentle our way with our ponies, how to sit straight with toes in, and, when we were older, how to jump. "Lean forward," Bob Christie would say. "Throw your heart over the fence and follow it."

The captain of our boat, "Cap" Lockwood, who was around in the winter in Florida and in the summer at my grandmother's house in Prides Crossing, Massachusetts, was something of a father to me. He must have figured out that I was overprotected, for he never missed a chance to get me out from under my nurse. He took me sailfishing off Palm Beach, for instance. I had bad luck for several years and never caught one of those great fish; nonetheless, day after day, we would troll across the purple Gulf Stream, watching the birds, seeing the flying fish, chasing a distant splash. Suddenly a great fin came up behind the bait. "It's a sailfish," Cap yelled. "Now be careful, don't jerk the line—wait till he strikes, and then let him run with it." I felt a sharp tug on the line. I let the reel run. Faster and faster the line went out. Cap shouted, "Okay, put on the brake. Strike him." The brake went on, the line went taut, and I was almost pulled out of the chair. I sank the hook and out of the water jumped an enormous fish, and then, even though the brake was on, he continued to run and jump and dance across the water—my first sailfish.

Fishing is still one of my passions; the water of the sea or of a stream, the washing of my mind by the wind, the lovely, wandering emptiness of my thinking, occupied enough not to stray into worry, but free enough to follow memories and fantasies, I love the sightings, the smellings, the feel of the wood of the boat or the rough surface of a solid rock.

Sometimes, the delicate balance between the family and those who worked for us broke down, such as the dreadful moment when my friend and I were having a fight with Charlie Benham, one of the sons of the herdsman, and I shot him with my BB gun. And Christmas was excruciating. In the afternoon, all of the help and their families would arrive at the house, all dressed up. Mother had a present for every person, every child. We Moore children, dressed up as well, stood awkwardly as Mother called off their names. Then we would hand out the presents to polite thank-yous and forced smiles. It was an agony of embarrassment. I am sure their children were as embarrassed as I.

I suspect my embarrassment arose from feeling that there was something not right about all this. All year long, everyone "stayed in their place" and did not come into the house unless their work brought them there, but on Christmas they were treated as equals, though not quite. Billy MacKenzie, the son of the groom, was one of my playmates. We climbed trees together, rode bikes, wondered about sex, smoked cigarettes I would steal from the silver boxes in the house—and yet here he was, in suit and tie, shaking my hand and respectfully thanking me for his present.

The adults treated me in a respectful but affectionate way. MacKenzie, the groom, was Scottish; Plowright, the butler, cockney English; Mr. Cowell, the farmer who always wore a tie even at work, country English; Tony, who took care of the vegetable garden, Italian; John Czap, the carpenter, Czechoslovakian; Mr. Creighton, the head gardener, Scottish and a man of some stature in the community. Some were called "Mr.," some by their last names, some by their first names, another subtlety of the hierarchy. As a small act of democratic rebellion, I called them all by their first name. For their part, most of them addressed me as "Master Paul." My grandmother's butler, Higgs, kept up this custom for years, *ad absurdum*: first I was Master Paul, then Mr. Paul Jr., then Lieutenant Paul, then Captain Paul, then Reverend Paul, and finally, Bishop Paul.

Thus was I introduced to the inconsistency of my own family's value structure. My mother unwittingly brought it to my attention. She would buy purebred guernsey cows, hackney horses, dalmatian dogs; she collected antiques and cultivated an exquisite garden—yet she always saved the ribbons from Christmas presents to use the following year. She would often say how guilty she felt "with all this" —sweeping her arm in a great arc, as if to sweep all this, all her guilt, away. My father, however, did not have a guilty bone in his body.

Although the people who worked on our place came from many different backgrounds, they were all white Christians. I only heard about Jews when my father made remarks about "the kind of people" who went to Miami. Before my first encounter with an African American, on a vacation to White Sulphur Springs, West Virginia, Mother said, "Now, Paul, on the train there will be men with black faces. I want you to be polite to them because they will be taking care of us." Even Roman Catholics were slightly suspect: they did not join us in the Lord's Prayer at school, and they went to a different church on Sunday. One time, when my friends and I were exploring an old sandpit on the edge of our place we found a huge cross. Someone explained it had been left by the Ku Klux Klan and had something to do with Catholics. I grew up with little overt prejudice, because we never were exposed to African Americans or Jews; yet I suppose an even deeper prejudice grew out of this invisibility.

Even a small boy could sense the economic chasm that divided us from society. In those days, one could have a car custom-made, and in the 1920s my father had a Rolls-Royce designed especially for us. A Mr. Fleischman came to see my father in his library and spread preliminary drawings on the table. Much conversation ensued concerning the leather upholstery, the maroon color with a cherry-red stripe on the door—our stables' colors. There would be a glass, which could be rolled up and down, between the front and rear seats so that the chauffeur would not overhear our conversations and a series of buttons for us to communicate with him: faster, slower, turn right, turn left, and so on. (There also was a phone, in case the message was complicated.) Whitewalls completed the design. I must say it was magnificent but not exactly inconspicuous. Once, when our chauffeur drove past the breadlines of Hoboken, I was so embarrassed to be riding in it that I hid on the carpeted floor.

Like most children, I had a rebellious side: being a "good little boy" was so confining that I had to bust out from time to time. One afternoon, for no particular reason, two of us took some bricks from their neat pile in the garden and smashed about fifty cold frames made of glass. The noise was sensational, and the sheer madness of it gave us a thrill. Another time, we repeatedly leaped on a beautiful boxwood hedge and ruined it. We were punished in due course, but that did not deter us in the slightest from other deeds of wanton destruction.

My best friends were Ned Ross and Prentice Smith. Our parents were friends, but more importantly, our nannies were friends. On many a sunny afternoon, they brought our baby carriages together at one of our houses and gossiped about how the chauffeur was flirting with the parlor maid or how shocking the younger generation had become with that terrible new music called jazz and those short dresses. Ned's nurse, Annie Fitzpatrick, was a staunch Roman Catholic; my nurse, Jean, was an equally staunch Presbyterian. They never had theological quarrels, even though Jean once whispered to me that Catholics worshiped idols—and to prove it showed me a statue of the Virgin Mary with a vigil light in front of it in the bedroom of my sisters' French governess.

One day, Ned, Prentice, and I had the great idea of forming a beagle pack. The make-believe beagles consisted of Laddie, my beloved golden retriever (who, being the largest, was the head dog), Ned's fox terrier, Dickie, and Prentice's two Scotties, Sandy and Laddie. We supplemented the pack with two of Mother's dalmatians, my brother's retriever, Polly's pair of West Highland terriers, and Fanny's French poodles. In our imagination, we were dressed in white breeches, shiny black leather boots, and bottle-green velvet jackets. In our minds' eyes, our miscellaneous gathering of canines became a beautiful pack of beagles, their tails feathering, trotting before us as we snapped our imaginary whips, blew our imaginary horns, and shouted "Tallyho!"

The first meet was duly scheduled at my family's house, an enormous brick mansion modeled on an English country house. The facade and front lawn provided the right atmosphere for this historic event. We had decided to hunt for rabbits up through a small patch of woods to the road and then have a "check," as the lingo went. (We had all gone to a real beagle meet a few miles away and so were conversant with the language of beagling.) We reached the edge of the woods in good order, but then the pack disintegrated. Laddie stayed by my side no matter how much I urged him to show a little leadership and plunge ahead into the forest. The terriers dispersed in every direction, and the poodles began playing French games with each other.

We three boys, however, decided to go right ahead through the woods. We had been in this small bit of woods many times, but each time the tall hardwood trees, the dense spruce thickets, and the occasional underbrush took on the character of the game we were playing. That day it was a stately English forest, and we were young

noblemen on a lordly hunt. Our fantasies had been inspired by the
English hunting prints that hung on the walls of our living rooms at
home.

We emerged from the forest onto the road with only three "beagles." Much shouting, whistling, and lordly cursing ensued. Some
twenty minutes later, with the pack reassembled, we decided to go
next door into the alien territory of Mrs. George Marshall Allen's
estate, an enormous Tudor mansion, where, in the downstairs play-
room, we had attended her grandson's splendid birthday parties, fea-
turing a magician *and* a movie. Venturing onto her grounds without
permission was somewhat daring, especially with our rowdy beagles.
We rounded the marble fountain of some long-forgotten Italian
nymph, who had found her way to this little corner of Elizabethan
England in New Jersey, and sneaked past the leaded panes of the west
wing, hidden by tall rhododendrons. So far so good. We surfaced at
the formal terrace, its deep-green turf surrounded by brown brick bal-
ustrades and crossed by brown gravel walks, immaculately raked. We
halted, in awe of this perfection. The dogs put down their ears and
looked at us as if to say, "What are we going to do now?" Just then,
out of the corner of the terrace sprang a rabbit. Prentice saw him first
and shouted, "Tallyho!" and the pack took off in a scramble of legs,
tails, ears, and barks.

But the rabbit had disappeared: to the right of some stone steps
leading down to a succession of terraces, there was a tile drain. "Oh,
for a ferret!" I cried. No one had thought to bring a ferret, and even
Sheila, a West Highland, could do no more than get her head and
neck down the opening of the drain, her little white bottom wiggling
away while the other dogs pranced around barking—except for Lad
die. Brilliant tactician that he was, he had rushed down the steps to
where the drain opened into a gutter. There he waited, ears cocked,
tail stiff and quivering. Sure enough, the benighted rabbit rushed out
right into his jaws.

"A kill! A kill!" I shouted. We were ecstatic. Laddie paraded
around with his tail up high; he had the soft mouth of a retriever,
and the rabbit was still alive. None of us knew what to do next.
Suddenly, Mrs. Allen's gardener showed up to see what all the fuss
was about, and we ran into the nearby woods and made our way
home.

By the time we got there, the rabbit was dead. I took it away from Laddie and, honoring tradition, held it up by the ears, dipped my finger in its blood, and smeared the foreheads of my fellow huntsmen and my own with the blood of our first kill.

Dogs were not our only pets. When I was about ten years old, my mother gave me a bantam rooster. I kept it in my own chicken coop near the house, next to a dovecote for the white fantail pigeons that decorated the lawn. The bantam had been bred as a fighting cock; his comb was trimmed flat. He was lean and svelte, his feathers shone bronze and iridescent in the sunshine. I called him Jim, and he sat on my shoulder wherever I went. Mother did not object to his indiscretions in the house. In fact, Mother did not mind animal indiscretions of any kind.

Naturally, Prentice and Ned were a bit jealous of Jim, so we set about trying to get a fighting cock for each of them. We asked Mother where she had found Jim. She told us Mr. Frelinghuysen had given him to her when she admired him as he strutted across the Frelinghuysens' lawn. "Do you think he has any others?" they asked. Mother called him up and learned he was delighted to give away some of his game chickens that roamed around his farm now that he no longer fought them. Apparently, when Peter Frelinghuysen's father, George G. Frelinghuysen, first owned the land, it was a center for cockfighting in that part of the world.

Early the next morning, we hopped on our bicycles and rode to the Frelinghuysens' place. The first thing we saw was a herd of prize jersey cows that turned their dark eyes on us as we went by with our chicken nets. Clearly bored with what they saw, they went back to chewing their cuds.

When we came to the chicken yard, we approached the chicken man with some trepidation. He seemed enormous; he wore a long, fearsome black mustache. "Sir," I said, "Mr. Frelinghuysen said it would be okay for us to catch some chickens, sir."

"Why you want 'em? They're too tougha to eat, too lazy to lay, not legal to fight. They makea de biggest mess. You wanna 'em, you take 'em."

"But where are they?"

"Theyse about a hundred acres here. You can find 'em anywhere but in the indoor tennis court."

I had brought Laddie, hoping that his bird-dog instincts would come into play. So I said, "Sick 'em, Laddie!" He took off. Laddie flushed a splendid silver-marked rooster out of a small haystack under the trees. The rooster started walking at first with some dignity, as was his wont, but when he turned his head and saw this fierce golden animal charging down on him, he took off into the nearest tree and stood on a branch squawking.

I looked up, and there was the intrepid Prentice climbing the tree, chicken net in hand. He had marked the quarry as his own. Ned and I stood back, aghast at his impulsiveness. Then we doubled up with laughter. Net at the ready, Prentice inched out on the rather flimsy branch where the rooster had taken his place. Closer and closer he came. The rooster was so preoccupied with Laddie's barking and our laughing that he did not notice the tremors of the branch. Prentice moved closer. Then, with a mighty lunge, he netted his quarry. But at the moment of triumph, he lost his balance, and he, the net, and the chicken dropped in a scrambled heap on the haystack below. "My God, he has killed himself!" Ned screamed. But when we found Prentice's face under the hay, it was wreathed in smiles, pink with joy to the tips of his considerable ears. "I got him," he cried.

Soon, Ned captured his cock, and we shifted into another fantasy: we became hard-boiled chicken fighters. But the last thing we wanted to do was hurt the chickens. I would not even think of letting Jim fight, so we returned to the Frelinghuysens' time and again until we each had a half dozen roosters. By now, Mr. Frelinghuysen, his chicken man, and even the placid jersey cows had had enough of the eleven-year-old monsters. But we had our stable of chickens.

Joe, who took care of Ned's horses, knew a bit about cockfighting. He suggested making boxing gloves to go over their spurs. Great. The nannies were immediately drafted to fashion chamois gloves for our new pets. We trained our roosters by throwing them up in the air again and again as our new mentor had instructed us. We fed them raw meat to make them fierce. When they were put on the ground, they actually went at each other.

How did it all end? Sadly. At this point, the father of another friend of ours suggested a real fight with steel spurs. Mr. MacDougall took us into his den, where the walls were adorned with trophies from World War I, including a tommy gun, a sword, and even the wheel of an old artillery piece. He reached into a drawer and pulled out real cockfighting spurs. These are strapped onto the cock's legs, and the birds fight until one of them is killed. He showed us the gleaming steel, stroked the spurs with his fingertips, and smiled in a strange way. He invited us to do the same. "See how sharp they are," he said. "Wouldn't you like to see your cocks fight with these? Wouldn't you?"

I felt scared. I did not want to seem a sissy, but something in his manner and the ominous tone of his voice, something in his suppressed excitement as he stroked the spurs, was unnerving. But I also felt excited. Like most little boys, I had a blood lust. My adrenaline was up now. I guess the others had the same conflicting emotions, but Mr. MacDougall convinced us we should have a "main," a cockfighting tournament, and offered his garage. Somehow, we never connected the idea of a real fight with our beloved pets' getting hurt.

The day came. We gathered in the MacDougalls' garage. The first fight was between one of my cocks and one of Ned's. We strapped on the evil-looking spurs, stepped in the ring, poked the cocks at each other to get them angry, then, at a signal from Mr. MacDougall, let them go. It was all over in a couple of minutes. My beloved rooster lay convulsing in a pool of blood on the ground while Ned's bird stood over him and let out a loud crow of victory. I do not remember much more. I took my dead rooster, put him in a bag, gathered my other cocks, and got into our station wagon. When we cleared the driveway, I burst into uncontrollable sobs.

Mr. MacDougall had fought in World War I. Somehow, the evil of war had invaded the innocence of our childhood.

Every year we moved from place to place at about the same time. In the spring, we would be on the farm in New Jersey, riding and driving our ponies, learning to play golf on the three-hole links on the property, riding our bicycles, rambling around the farm with its livestock, gardening at the playhouse, and going to the Peck School. We spent some time in New York at our apartment on Fifth Avenue, across from the zoo. About the first of July, we traveled in a private railroad car to Camp Otterbrook in the Adirondacks: fishing, boating, climb-

ing mountains, a tradition I have kept up every summer of my life.
From there, it was on to Prides Crossing on the North Shore of Boston to visit my grandmother. After Labor Day we went back to New
Jersey until the new year. At the end of January, we departed for
Palm Beach, where we had an elaborate place, complete with tennis
court, swimming pool, a tunnel under the road to our own beach,
and a lakefront with a fishing boat and speedboat tied to the dock.

Granny's magnificent white mansion, called Rockmarge, was set on
a slight rise, extending down from which were a series of lawned
terraces; beyond, the grass swept out to the sea. Down one side, a
willow walk provided a way to the beach in the shade. The lawn was
immaculately maintained. Once a week, we would watch a splendid
white hackney, recently retired from the show ring, trotting with high
steps from one side to the other, pulling a mowing machine. After
the cutting, a dozen young men on their hands and knees would dig
out the weeds and crabgrass with penknives.

Let me try to convey the style of her life there by describing a
particular evening much later: August 17, 1938, when we celebrated
Granny's eightieth birthday. As we gathered for the birthday party,
the evening shadows fell across the lawn, and in the distance the
islands glowed in the setting sun. A sailboat slowly made its way to
harbor, and the lighthouse on Baker's Island began to flash its white
and red light against the darkening sky. Granny's dress was what she
called a tea gown, long and flowing, with full sleeves like those of a
kimono. She wore her pearl necklace and a brooch in the shape of a
rose, which was my favorite because I had been with her when she
designed it. She had brought the precious stones back from India. I
remember her spreading them out on a black velvet cloth. She chose
a magnificent honey-colored cat's-eye to be the center of a wild rose;
then she surrounded the cat's-eye with ruby petals and emerald leaves,
set on a stem of platinum, with small diamond thorns.

Despite her beautiful dress and jewels, Granny was not in the least
pretentious. Her manner was that of a New England grandmother.
She smiled readily, wore pince-nez glasses, and had a nice twinkle in
her eyes.

At seven o'clock, the martinis were served in a silver vessel with
a spout, making it seem more like a teapot than a cocktail shaker.
Granny loved to tell stories about the past. "Children" (this included

my fifty-year-old father), "I want to tell you when I had my first martini. It was on a summer evening just like this. Your grandfather had been to Myopia." Myopia was a venerable golf club founded by three men who were nearsighted. "He drove home, as usual, in his yellow road coach with the four gray hackneys. Horace, the bugler, stood on the back in his livery bugling warning peals at every corner. Your grandfather did drive rather fast. A friend once told me that people stayed off the road around six o'clock because Judge Moore was on his way home. In any case, on this particular afternoon, he came in the door and said, 'Ada, I have just had a most delicious cocktail. It is called the martini. You put some gin and a little vermouth in something called a cocktail shaker. You shake it up and then you pour it out.' Well, we had our first martinis that night, and I have had one every night before dinner ever since."

And so the conversation continued until, at the stroke of seven-thirty, the doors to the dining room glided open, and Higgs, the butler, resplendent in his tailcoat and white tie, announced, "Dinner is served, ma'am."

Granny took my father by the arm and led us into dinner. The dining room glistened with candles and silver, a lace tablecloth, and crystal glasses. It was a lovely room: on the floor lay a blue-and-cream-colored Chinese rug. A Chinese screen hid the door to the pantry. Mirrored doors lined one wall, and over the mantle hung exquisite blue-and-white antique Chinese plates. The paneling was white, and the whole room was oriented toward a plate-glass window overlooking the lawn and the blue sea.

While we were eating, Higgs stood behind my grandmother's chair; the second man, in different livery according to his rank, stood behind my father; and the houseman, dressed up for the occasion, stood behind my mother. They were supposed to stand expressionless unless asked to do something, but Higgs pretended not to be able to contain himself whenever my grandmother said something funny. He would put his hand over his face to hide the smile and on occasion, if the joke was really funny, would have to leave the room.

We sang "Happy Birthday," and Granny blew out the candles, carefully leaving one to grow on. Champagne was served, and the sentimental toasts began, spoken sometimes with humor and sometimes with a tear or sniffle.

After dinner, the real fun started: watching Granny open her presents. The large table in the center of the living room was piled high with packages of all shapes and sizes. We clustered around and watched her become a little girl again. "Oh, gracious! There's one from the Chinese ambassador. How thoughtful of him." This turned out to be a jade snuff bottle.

"This package ain't a birthday present, but it just arrived from Egypt." Granny always insisted that "ain't" was a proper word. (I suspect it was in the 1860s in Galena, Illinois.) She unpacked a small box containing a second-rate imitation Egyptian bronze. She turned it over with hands shaking in anticipation and dug out some clay to reveal a hole in the base of the figure. Then she poured the muddy contents onto an ashtray. "Children, come see. These are precious blue lotus seeds I smuggled out of Egypt," she tittered. "Don't tell anyone. It's against the law."

The openings continued: a crayon picture from a great-grandchild, a Victrola record from one of her musician protégés, an ivory elephant from a maharaja, a marble statuette from an archaeologist at Persepolis, a birthday card from Helen Keller. "Children, did you know that when my friend Helen Keller comes to see me she just loves holding jade snuff bottles to her cheek. And, would you believe it, she can tell the color of each one by its vibrations."

After about an hour, Granny said, "Oh, pshaw! I can't open them all tonight, because I do want to have time to bowl a few balls before we go to bed." We insisted that Granny bowl the first ball. She took off her evening slippers, rolled up her right sleeve as best she could, made sure her glasses were firmly in place, took two steps, and sent the ball deliberately right down the center of the alley. As it rolled and rolled on its way toward the pins, we all started shouting, "Granny, that's great. It's going to be a strike!" The ball mowed down every last pin; Granny turned around, made a slight curtsy to her fans, who were clapping wildly, and, when the noise abated, announced, "I don't think I ever need to bowl again!"

Granny and I were good friends. Beginning when I was a small boy, eight or nine years old, whenever my parents were out for dinner, we would sit together watching the evening shadows lengthening across the lawn and the sea and have long, long talks. She recalled her childhood, her family, and her journeys. After Grandfather died,

Granny chartered an oceangoing yacht and, boarding at Rockmarge with a sister and a friend, sailed around the world. On her travels, she stayed with a maharaja, met Mahatma Gandhi, flew to Persia— one plane for herself and her friends, one for the maids, and one for the luggage. She even went up the Yangtze River. I remember her tales filled with wonder of her travels to far-off lands. She would tell me not only where she had gone, but the history and legends of those exotic places.

Occasionally Mother tried to vary the family routine. When I was about six, she decided it would be fun to travel to Florida by ship. So we boarded the *Croonland* in Hoboken: Mother, Dad, my two older sisters and brother; Kitty Burgoyne, Mother's maid; Plowright, Dad's valet and butler; Mlle. Ruell, the French governess; and Jean, my nurse (as well as five dogs, a canary, a parrot, and a goat named Dinty Moore). On the way down, we ran into a storm, and everyone became deathly ill. When we arrived off Miami, the temperature was well over ninety, and the swells lifted the tender, which had come along-side, up and down, up and down. We all were safely loaded on board when we saw some boxes slide down the swaying gangway and break open. They were cases of Dad's best bootleg Scotch. The porters, of course, made sure some of the bottles broke open as well, and they scooped the whiskey up with their hands. Meanwhile, the door to the parrot's cage flew open, and she started screaming for Plowright. My father never traveled with the family again.

My childhood was completely isolated from what was going on in the world. The only visible effect of the Depression was that Prentice's brother had to mow the lawn because they could not afford a gardener. From this rich cocoon, at the age of twelve, I was sent away to boarding school. I felt liberated.

ST. PAUL'S

THEN, as now, driving into St. Paul's School, just outside Concord, New Hampshire, was like entering a New England village. Elms arched over the street, and white wooden houses lined each side. At the bottom of a slight hill stood the handsome neo-Gothic chapel, surrounded by a lawn. The rectory, across from the chapel, was a rambling clapboard house. Across the Lower School pond, a fine stand of white pines gave way to hardwoods and wetlands along the shore. Further on, the granite library dominated another pond, from which a waterfall became a stream that wound through the school grounds beyond.

The school was fashionable, exclusive: no Jewish boys, no African Americans, no girls were then admitted. But that was true of almost all private college-preparatory schools in those days.

Going to SPS, as it is familiarly called, was a rite of passage in our family. My father had gone there; my brother was a senior, a sixth former, and captain of the hockey team. In New Jersey, we even had a St. Paul's School garden outside my father's library, with the school shield on its iron gate and the school symbol, a pelican, over a fountain. The pelican is an ancient Christian symbol; according to legend, it opened a wound in its neck and fed its young with the flow of blood. My mother liked that symbol; in a way, she thought of herself in that role.

I was open to accepting everything the school stood for. By the time I graduated, in 1937, its values had been deeply embedded in my soul.

Preparatory schools like St. Paul's had a pronounced influence on the country through their graduates, who, for several generations, were the leaders of the United States: Franklin Roosevelt, Jack Kennedy, Averell Harriman, the bankers of Wall Street. These schools were modeled on the so-called public schools of England as training grounds for future leaders. They instilled faith in a god who looked favorably on gentlemen and demanded no shift in social values from the status quo. This god did demand courage, loyalty, and patriotism. He was available to bless marriages and to give assurance at funerals. A rather simple, childlike faith remained with many St. Paul's boys throughout their lives, a faith that let them turn to this god for support in times of grief, danger, or pain; this god was there for them when they needed him. This religion had a touch of Calvinism to it, a tendency to believe that worldly success and position were blessings given to those who deserved them. But together with such a view of life went a strong emphasis on noblesse oblige. If you were blessed with privilege, education, and position, you were obliged, in return, to give service and leadership to your community and to be a steward of the wealth you had inherited or earned because of your advantages.

Understandably, the alumni of these schools were at their best in times of war. Most of them volunteered before being drafted, and many distinguished themselves through bravery and leadership. They fought for democracy against foreign foes but did not fight for justice and full democracy within their own land. They gave to the community chest, the hospital, the neighborhood house, and they volunteered in programs to help the poor. Social change to eliminate poverty, however, was thought to be dangerously liberal. Franklin Roosevelt was called a "traitor to his class," and in a minor way, later in life so was I.

The privileged prefer charitable giving to social action to empower the poor because charity makes the giver feel good and the receiver feel humbled; empowerment gives the poor a sense of dignity but threatens the advantages of the rich. For instance, if you give money to a settlement house for black people, where they can humbly beg for help when they are down and out, this assists them, to be sure, and it gives you a nice feeling inside. If, however, you help break the color barrier in your neighborhood, a black family buying a house will feel proud, but you will be criticized or even ostracized by your white neighbors. If you encourage a labor union to seek higher pay or better working conditions, you endanger the profit margin of your family's company and threaten investments.

At St. Paul's we received a sound education, for the most part, but the pedagogical methods of some of the masters were often eccentric. I remember our second-form (eighth-grade) science class, taught by Mr. Jeremiah Black, who wore a cutaway and spats to chapel on Sunday, emulating an older master. In the classroom, if you answered a question incorrectly or whispered to your neighbor, Mr. Black would throw a piece of chalk at you with unerring aim. Even so, we boys looked forward eagerly to the spring term, when he would teach us biology, culminating in a couple of sessions on sex, complete with diagrams. He opened the class with the bald statement, "If any boy in this class says he does not masturbate, he is a liar."

Mr. Beach White, who taught English, was keen to have us write as much as we could and enjoyed introducing us to the authors we were assigned. When we came to *Walden*, instead of having us write a book report, he told us to go out to a place in the woods and write down everything we saw, in the manner of Thoreau. I chose a knoll looking over a forest stream, sat down on the pine needles, and began to see how each was shaped. I examined the pattern on the bark of a tree for the first time, noticed the ants and the occasional beetle, the form of a maple leaf that had settled nearby, the smell of the woods, the sound of the stream. I was awakened in a way that changed my feeling about nature; whenever I visit St. Paul's, I try to return to that place.

Mr. White claimed that he graded our papers according to how much they weighed. He welcomed twenty-page childish scrawls, which he would correct meticulously for grammar and style.

We learned the values of the school in asides during courses in history or literature, and they were preached from the pulpit; but it was in the daily life of the place that we absorbed them most deeply. The phrase "a good attitude" was used. If someone was thought to have a bad attitude, he was said to have "bad att." At the opening assembly each year, the president of the sixth form, invariably a tall and ter-

rifying young man, told us in a gruff voice that anyone who did not
study hard enough would be put on the blue list, but if he was a rotter
with bad att, continually flouted authority, or committed a major
breach of discipline, he would be put on the red list, cast into outer
darkness, and he had better look out lest he be expelled.

At the heart of the system of student self-government was the principle that loyalty to the school superseded loyalty to a friend. This
attitude was brought home to me in a traumatic incident my first
night at school. We little boys lived in a huge hall, partitioned into
alcoves that contained only a bed, a bureau, and a chest. After lights-
out, total quiet was imposed. My brother happened to be the supervisor of the dormitory. He was having difficulty calming us down the
night we arrived. Finally, in a fierce voice, he said, "If anyone makes
another noise, I will take him out to the stairwell and paddle him."
I sneezed loudly. "I recognize that voice," he said, hauled me out of
bed, and took me by the scruff of the neck out to the stairwell. I was
terrified. Instead of paddling me, however, he told me to yell and
scream as if I were being paddled. We raised quite a ruckus. I went
back to bed, and my brother had no more disciplinary problems after
that.

This charade was the exception, though: the system was deadly
serious and made great demands on the boys. Every boy, whether he
held a position in the student government or not, was expected to
enforce the rules. If he found another boy smoking, he was supposed
to warn him, and if he found him smoking again, he was supposed to
report him, even though the smoker could be expelled as a result. I
found a friend smoking once and in a rather superior way told him
I would report him the next time. This did not feel right to me, but
I made myself do it.

In retrospect, I think such demands were too much to impose on
young people, and they set "good guys" against "bad guys." Furthermore, they undermined one of the most endearing natural virtues of
the young, loyalty to a friend.

I made many friends at St. Paul's, and those friendships have lasted
all my life. Prentice and Ned, my childhood friends, came to St.
Paul's. Walter McVeigh, a heavyset young man with curly hair and
deep-set eyes, became my closest friend, since he and I were most
affected by our conversion experiences in our last year. Bob Cox, a

rangy blond with literary skills unusual in a young man, was killed in the war, as were Peter Hazard and Bob Fowler. Tony Duke, our class president, has spent his life working with poor children. Watson Dickerman, my roommate the last two years, a young Cole Porter in his mastery of light verse, died of leukemia in his thirties. Our class treasurer, Charles "Shot" Warner, has kept us all laughing for over fifty years. He is a retired professor. And there was Ben Tilghman, with whom I roomed at Yale. We all loved the school and were deeply loyal to it. We loved the place so much, in fact, that a group of us bought a little cottage nearby to stay in when we returned to visit.

The school owned several hundred acres of farmland and woods. When the rigorous athletic season went slack in the early spring or on the rare holidays, we wandered the woods, skinny-dipped in the lakes, canoed down the stream, watched animals mating at the farm, and made hideaways in the woods, freeing ourselves from the rigid structure of the school. I recently found a letter I wrote my first year, which captures the feel of those days:

Dear Mother:
I had a swell time to-day going swimming in Little Turkey Pond. The water was cold, but all the same it was good. Saturday, we went all the way to Little T. in our canoe, the only trouble being it leaked horribly. As a matter of fact, we sunk. Coming down with the current on the way home was swell fun. I went with Ollie Vietor to Bishop Dallas's house in Concord, and had lunch. Gosh! He's a swell man. It's a little late but I hope that Fan [my sister] had a good anniversary.
Since there is no more news, I will stop.
Love,

Paul

I absorbed a variety of perspectives from masters outside the classroom. These informal contacts made a far deeper impression on me than what I learned in class.

In the spring, for instance, some of us would climb into Mr. White's Model T Ford and scour the countryside for nests or migrating birds. He was an ornithologist with the most complete collection of bird skins in New Hampshire. If he saw a bird not in his collection, he would bring it down with dust shot so fine it did not harm the feathers. On good days, we boys could skinny-dip in the river. When the snow was on the ground, we gathered in his hut in the woods, banded birds, roasted marshmallows, chopped firewood, and inhaled his cigar smoke. We read poetry aloud and talked about all manner of things. But whenever a flock of birds swooped down to the traps, each of us would pull the string we had been assigned and spring the trap on surprised woodpeckers, nuthatches, brown creepers, juncos, or sparrows. We then took out a carrying cage, brought the birds back to the hut, and, holding the quivering, warm feathered body on our hand with one leg carefully extended, applied a numbered metal band. One year someone set fire to the hut. We rushed out to see the damage, and there, in the snow, were the smoldering ruins of that magical place. We cried and swore, but Mr. White put us to work rebuilding it with better windows through which to watch the birds.

Mr. White's room at St. Paul's was full of objects he had collected on a trip to the Far East. There was an ebony table supported by storks, and Persian rugs on the floor and over the sofa, which resembled the famous couch of Dr. Freud. Mr. White was probably sixty years old at the time and had lived out his single life in that one room for nearly forty years. As a confirmed agnostic, he hated going to chapel, which was required of all the masters as well as the boys. He was fiercely anticlerical and could not stand the rector. Sometimes, in the midst of a conversation, he would jump up from the sofa and say, "Be quiet, be quiet. He's coming! He's coming!" He would then rush to the window, pretending that the rector was eavesdropping on our conversation. Of course, the rector was never there, but it gave us all a shiver of delight to believe that we were some kind of revolutionary cell implanted in the heart of the school.

This eccentric gentleman instilled in me a love of nature and poetry.

From different masters, we absorbed different and sometimes conflicting values. While Mr. White despised pretense and could sniff out a hypocrite a mile away, Mr. Wylie, our French teacher, was an elitist and implied that we not only had an obligation to assume leadership but a right to it. This noblesse required a high morality. One of his heroes was John Jay Chapman, who thrust his hand into the fire because he had struck a friend. Mr. Wylie was perhaps the most popular master with the older boys. Sometimes more than twenty of us, fresh from athletics, would crowd into his small room for tea. The combination of our sweat, Mr. Wylie's pipe smoke, and the smoke from the fire made for a heady atmosphere. Since some boys held responsible positions in student government, the affairs of the school were aired and Mr. Wylie offered guidance.

Willard Scudder was known familiarly as Chappy, I think because he would affect the English habit of calling the boys "chaps" and wore cutaway and chaps to chapel. As an avid Anglo-Catholic, he crossed himself, to the consternation of the other masters. He ran the choir and was a most faithful communicant. He prided himself on knowing all the alumni, who their parents and grandparents were, and where they fitted in society. His other great interest was rowing. He was the director of the Halcyon boat club and wore its red blazer with pride. He would stand on the dock each afternoon, red mega-phone in hand, and direct the crews as they launched and landed their shells. He died on the evening of a race day when the Halcyons had won, while chatting with some old friends in his small living room. We all felt that he deserved such a pleasant end.

The St. Paul's ethos was austere, rugged; the school sought to toughen us up, in the belief, I am sure, that we had been spoiled at home and were soft. You had to go out for a sport whether you wanted to or not. My first fall I was forced to play rugby even though I weighed only 110 pounds. We wore shorts. It was freezing cold. We never wore overcoats to class but sported scarves under our tweed jackets. We never wore overshoes; they were referred to as "sissy boots."

St. Paul's was a church school. Most of the boys were Episcopalians. Every morning all four hundred of us went to chapel for a hymn, a psalm, and a few prayers. We sat facing one another as if in a choir and sat in order of rank, the youngest in the front row, the sixth form and the masters in the back. Every evening we had family prayers before supper in the dining rooms. I enjoyed chapel, even before I became interested in the Church, and I think most of us did. Sunday Evensong was my favorite time. Sitting in a long, wood-paneled chapel with the afternoon sun throwing colored patterns through the stained glass after an afternoon of exercise, a shower, and some tea and cake at a master's house, I felt warm inside. The choir processed in, and the rector strode down the long chancel in his flowing robes, looking very much like God. We would begin with a gentle hymn, such as "Now the day is over, Night is drawing nigh, Shadows of the evening, Steal across the sky." Then the rector in his melodious bass voice would commence the Evening Office: "Let my prayer be set forth in thy sight as the incense, and let the lifting up of my hands be an evening sacrifice." It was a time when one felt at ease, at peace with the world. It was a time for beautiful thoughts and fantasies. It was a time to think of home, of memories, of hopes for the future. It was a time to think about the school and how much it meant to us.

Except for prayers and readings, which we hardly listened to, chapel had precious little to do with Christianity. (In fact, when I was asked to preach at the school as a young priest, I chose as my subject the difference between Christianity and the St. Paul's School religion. I was not asked to preach there again for twenty years!) Yet I believe the chapel did deepen the values the school stood for and perhaps elicited an occasional prayer. Alumni came to chapel when visiting the school, but because the atmosphere there was so different from that of a parish church, the majority of alumni were not churchgoers. In a way, you were worshipping St. Paul's School; and the rector, who lent his personality to the worship, was also your headmaster, not a strange priest with whom you might have little in common.

Religion was not very important in my life until the fifth form (eleventh grade), when some of us came to know Mr. Bartrop, one of the masters who was a priest. During long evenings in front of his fire or at pleasant tea parties in the afternoon, he would tell us marvelous and sometimes hilarious stories. Often, these stories were about heroic Christians: the French Jesuits who were burned at the stake by the Iroquois, gallant Anglican priests who served on the London docks at the turn of the century, St. Francis stripping himself of his rich clothes in the public square. I began to realize that being a Christian was not primarily about being dragged to church as a little boy, nor about feeling mellow in the chapel at school, nor about calling on old ladies. I was looking for heroes at that age, and these Christians fulfilled that need.

Mr. Bartrop also introduced us to the Catholic tradition of our

Church. He taught us the importance of Holy Communion and even went so far as to call it Mass. One snowy night, he drove us all the way to Christ Church, Portsmouth, where we encountered the Benediction of the Blessed Sacrament for the first time, replete with incense and bells. He encouraged us to make our confessions—a terrifying thought. He drew us into an understanding of the mystical nature of the Church. This Anglo-Catholic tradition had a forbidden quality in that it was not part of the religious life of the school. We felt slightly seditious on these ventures into strange rites and mysteries. It was exciting.

When a monk visited the school, Mr. Bartrop suggested I see him. Father Wigram was a Cowley father—a member of an Anglican (Episcopal) order of monks with their motherhouse in England. They kept the full monastic vows and cultivated a quiet holiness in their communal life. At St. Paul's, Father Wigram stayed in a visitor's suite, called the Prophet's Chamber, overlooking the waterfall. With some trepidation, I climbed the stairs and knocked on the door. I had seen him walking around the school in his black cassock and large black shovel hat. He looked gaunt, austere, ascetic. But he welcomed me into the little sitting room with a warm and gentle smile. I sensed about him a holiness I had never encountered before. He seemed self-assured and at peace.

He welcomed me in and asked if there was anything particular on my mind. I did not know where to begin. Finally, I blurted out that I wanted to talk about confession. Why should I tell my sins to a priest, I asked him, rather than just to God? Wouldn't God hear my confession of sin if I made it in private? Why should a man, even if he was a priest, come between me and God? What good did it do to confess a sin if you went right out and did it again? How could you know what was a sin and what wasn't, and how could you remember them all anyway?

"Well, well," he interrupted, "you do have a lot of questions. Let me try to take them one at a time." He explained that God does hear you when you confess your sins in prayer but that when you make your confession before a priest and he gives you absolution it is a sacrament, and you are *assured* of God's forgiveness because the priest has the authority to declare that God has forgiven you. He pointed out that the process of speaking your sins aloud and hearing the priest's prayer of absolution is the outward and visible sign of the inward and spiritual grace of forgiveness, in the same way that Holy Communion is a very special way of having Christ come to you, even though he also comes to you in prayer. So it is, he went on, that in the sacrament of penance God gives you a strong and powerful sense of forgiveness. He concluded by saying that it made sense, psychologically.

"How do you mean, psychologically?" I asked.

"Well, let's say you and a friend have a fight and you forgive him in your mind and heart, it isn't the same as asking his forgiveness and shaking hands. Shaking hands is a sign that you are reconciled. Does that make sense to you?"

"Sort of. I guess so. But, sir, I'm sort of scared. Do I really have to do it? I'd be so ashamed."

The conversation turned to other topics. I was making to leave when he said, "You know, Paul, I think God wants you to make your confession."

"He does? How do you know?"

He assured me that it would mean a great deal to me, since I was becoming serious about my faith. He said that it would help me on my way and bring me closer to God.

"But I don't know what to do."

He gave me a little folder and told me to go back to my room, to use the sins on the folder as a checklist, and to pray that I would remember my sins, especially those that I thought kept me from God's love.

Before I left, he prayed: "Almighty God, our loving Father, we thank you for bringing Paul here tonight. Help him search out his sins and come to you with a penitent heart so that, being forgiven, he can have a new life with you. Amen."

"Amen," I said, feeling sort of strange.

Promising to return in an hour, I went back to my room. Thank goodness my roommate was not there. I knelt down and prayed that I would do this thing right, and then began to examine the list of sins on the folder. It included sins such as "I have lied," followed by a blank where you were supposed to put how many times. That would have been okay had it not been my first confession—I couldn't begin to count the times I'd warped the truth a bit or been nasty to my parents. And so it was with the other sins. But I did my best with a grubby little pencil and wrote in 100 here, 50 there, and so forth. After a while I got to the tough ones: "I have had impure thoughts. I have done impure things alone or with others." I knew that meant sex, and you can imagine the embarrassment of a seventeen-year-old boy listing numbers after those questions.

At nine-thirty I returned. Father Wigram told me to kneel down by the chair he was sitting on. He put on a purple stole and told me to say the prayer on the form I held in my shaking hands.

"Bless me, Father, for I have sinned."

"The Lord be in your mind and in your heart that you may truly and rightly confess your sins unto Almighty God."

"I confess to God Almighty, to all the saints, and to you, Father, that I have sinned in the following ways." Out came the list, and blushing and sweating and stammering I got out all those shameful things. "For these and all the other sins I cannot now remember," I read from the form, "I ask pardon of God, and from you, Father, penance, counsel, and absolution."

I was astonished that Father Wigram did not seem shocked. He gave me some advice about prayer. He said if I prayed and folded my hands when I got to bed it would help with those impure sins. But mostly he told me how wonderful it was that I had had the courage to make my confession. He asked if I had any questions and then gave me the prayer of absolution, ending with the phrase, "And by his authority, committed to me, his priest, I absolve you from all your sins in the name of the Father, the Son, and the Holy Ghost, Amen. Go in peace, the Lord has put away your offenses, and pray for me, a sinner."

At that moment, the most mysterious, powerful, and beautiful sensation came over me. I was cleansed, I was filled with a presence I had never felt before, I was dazed, lifted up, filled with an extraordinary joy and peace. I got up from my knees, mumbled thank you, and stumbled down the stairs.

I walked back to my room through a misty night as if I were floating and went right to bed. The next morning I served the altar; Mr. Bartrop was celebrating Holy Communion. The chantry was silent. I knelt on the cold stone. Mr. Bartrop's familiar voice said the holy words, "This is my Body which is given for you . . . This is my Blood."

When I received the Sacrament, it was as if Christ entered my very being. It was as if I were making my Communion for the first time in my life.

This was a conversion experience, and although its intensity wore off, my life has never been the same since. I am sure that the great mystery of being whom we call God laid hands on me that evening in the little room by the waterfall. I was pointed in a new direction, and however badly I failed in the years to come, this calling, this vocation to follow where Christ seemed to be leading, became the center of my life. As I knelt before Father Wigram, my soul was touched, and the ultimate purpose of my life was determined. It was not only a change in direction—it was the coming into my life of a new presence. The transcendent joy and peace I felt as I walked back to my room through the misty night so many years ago have come to me again and again in prayer when I have opened myself to God, and whenever I have needed God's strength, it has been there.

I have often tried to analyze what happened that night. Theologically, it was a clear breakthrough of the Holy Spirit into my life, a life that was apparently ready. Some psychologists explain such events in terms of the unconscious; others might call it an adolescent hysterical episode. Such may well be the case, but that is no reason to deny that the Holy Spirit can and indeed does work through our unconscious. In any case, whatever the psychological or even neurotic roots of the experience, it was the most important moment of my life. God works through our weakness as well as through our strength.

I was not the only one who came under the influence of Mr. Bartrop and Father Wigram. Walter McVeigh became a Trappist and the abbot of his monastery. Another friend, Davis Given, became an Episcopal priest and spent many years with the Navajo. Tony Duke received the strength to build a creative camp and settlement house for poor children. Bob Cox was killed in Al-Alamein with St. John's Gospel in his pocket.

The first person I told about my conversion was my grandmother. She was a faithful Episcopalian who attended St. Thomas Church in New York, just across Fifth Avenue from where she lived, and in the summer, St. John's, Beverly Farms. Her travels, however, had widened her understanding and opened her to the insights of other faiths. In the time just after my conversion, I was fiercely dogmatic and self-righteous. Because of Granny's openness to Buddhism, Hinduism, and Muhammadanism, I worried about her orthodoxy. I thought about it. I prayed about it, and finally, one evening, screwed up my courage to bring it up. I told her I was a little worried about her seeming devotion to other religions. I asked her point-blank whether she believed in the Creed. She assured me she was a believing Christian, but that God, in his mysterious ways, somehow reached people who had never heard of Jesus.

I really did not know what to say to that, because part of me, in my deepest heart, agreed with her.

In later years, Granny and I looked back in amusement on my worry about her immortal soul, but I felt an affectionate regard that she took me seriously. I also realized that her religion was thoughtful and ran deep.

Taking my newfound faith outside the school's familiar setting was difficult, though. I went home for Christmas and could not find a midnight Mass to attend. After the presents were wrapped and everyone had gone to bed, I longed to be with Christ right then, rather than wait for the Christmas service in the morning. It was a cold, clear night. I went out into the woods, and there I knelt on the snow and worshipped under the stars. From that time on, I knew my faith would stay with me wherever I found myself.

Last Night finally came, the ceremony that marked our leaving St. Paul's forever. We filed into chapel as usual and took our places. It was a time of sweet sadness. I looked at the masters' faces, the lovely stained-glass windows. I smelled the musty odor of the wood. There was a special stillness that night. And then the rector's voice spoke the prayers, sounding more beautiful and mysterious than ever. We sang the Last Night hymn:

> *Savior, source of every blessing,*
> *Tune our hearts to grateful lays:*
> *Streams of mercy, never ceasing,*
> *Call for ceaseless songs of praise.*

Then followed our favorite prayer:

O Lord, support us all the day long, until the shadows lengthen, and the evening comes, and the busy world is hushed, and the fever of life is over, and our work is done. Then in thy mercy, grant us a safe lodging and a holy rest, and peace at the last, through Jesus Christ our Lord. Amen.

Tears filled our eyes as we lined up outside in the darkening cloister to say goodbye. Every member of the St. Paul's family filed by and shook hands with us, from the smallest first former to the rector himself. I cried and cried, I loved the place so much. It was at St. Paul's that I had come to know the Lord, there that my deepest friendships had begun, and there that I had been instilled with the instinct of institutional loyalty.

St. Paul's was over, but my life as a Christian was just beginning. The summer following graduation I visited Father Truman Heminway, a priest who had a farm in Vermont. His earthy mysticism was a healthy counterbalance to the school's High Church spirituality. I also was a counselor for two weeks at a summer camp run by the school in New Hampshire. I enjoyed it enormously and for the first time came to know and love city kids. They were street-smart, funny, tough, sometimes nasty, but lovable. They were Polish, Irish, Italian, African American, Latino. This was the first time I came to know people from other backgrounds, and I enjoyed it. I can still remember some of their faces, some of their names. We were told about the hardships they had endured in their family lives, but we did not feel sorry for them, because they did not feel sorry for themselves. Their resilience and courage shone through. I was drawn to that joie de vivre then and again and again through my life. The seeds of Tony Duke's Boys' Harbor were sown there, and perhaps, too, those of my own vocation to the work of the Church in the city, because I had already begun to consider becoming a priest.

YALE

I ARRIVED in New Haven in September 1937, having been preparing for this moment all my life. When I was a little boy, I would say good night to my father as he was dressing for dinner. His room seemed masculine. The walls were cream colored, the furniture polished mahogany. Formal photographs of his mother and father stood in silver frames on his bureau; one of my mother, beautiful in her wedding dress, adorned a table. On the walls hung a print of a Scottish golfer and several photographs in dark oaken frames: fifteen young men, black suited, stiff-collared, and very, very serious; an ugly, ivy-covered brick building, and over the door, a stylized wolf's head, carved in ebony. I wondered about these old things of his, and when I asked about them, he would say with a proud but secretive smile that they were Yale things: the fifteen men were members of Wolf's Head, his senior society; the building was their "tomb." These things were part of Yale, and my brother, Bill, and I would go there one day.

On the wall of our library was a yellowed document, old, wrinkled, and written in Latin. One day, Mother pointed to it and said, "If we ever have a fire, save this first." I asked why it was so important to save that, since we had everything from gold cups to Mother's jewelry in the house. "It is a Yale degree," she said, "which belonged to one of your ancestors, George Beckwith. He graduated from Yale in 1769. His name is on the degree in Latin. See, here it is, D. Georgium Beckwith." The rest of the day I hummed the funny name to myself, D. Georgium, D. Georgium.

George Beckwith's father was a trustee of the Yale Corporation when his son graduated in 1769. I was on the corporation when my son Paul graduated two hundred years later, in 1969.

My older brother, a great athlete, had some academic problems at school, and the family was worried that he might not be admitted to Yale. I remember the jubilation when he was accepted. My child's mind could not even imagine what would have happened had he failed. Father, uncles on both sides of the family, a brother, ancestors—all had gone to Yale. But when the time approached for me to go to college, I found that almost all my friends from school were pointed toward Harvard or Princeton. I really wanted to go to Harvard, but I did not even dare suggest going anywhere but Yale.

I often had difficulty talking to my father, but when he spoke of Yale, he brightened up. For him, college had been a most happy experience. "Paul," he would say, "Princeton is a good college, but it doesn't measure up to Yale. I have a lot of good friends here in New Jersey who went to Princeton, but you know, they never grow up. There are Princeton boys, but Yale men."

Knowing perfectly well what he would say, I asked, "What about Harvard?"

"Harvard men spend too much time going to debutante parties in Boston. All the clubs there are based on who your family is rather than on whether you amount to anything. Harvard is a very social place. They drink too much.

"Yale, however, is a male society working hard all week. There are no women at Yale to distract you, except on football weekends or the junior prom."

He would go on, reminiscing about wonderful courses in Browning and Tennyson given by the famous professor William Lyon Phelps and the jolly times he'd had with his friends in Alpha Delt, his fraternity. He would conclude by saying that Yale was the best possible preparation for life a man could have. Given my father's mastery of all this mythic material, I was not at all surprised to find out that his classmate Charlie Seymour was now the president of Yale.

When I left home, Dad sat down at his desk and wrote out a check for me. "This should get you through your first year," he told me. "You are to pay all your bills by the tenth of the month. You will pay your tuition and other expenses. Always keep a neat checkbook and check your balance with the statement from the bank."

I looked at the check and blushed. It was for two thousand dollars. I had never seen that big a check. "But what shall I do with it?"

"Oh, bring it to the bank at the bottom of the green and give it to Lou Hemingway, the president. He is a classmate. He will tell you how to open an account."

It turned out Dad guessed just about right. I only had to ask for another two hundred dollars in the spring. I never bounced a check off Mr. Hemingway.

Despite all this family preparation (or perhaps because of it), I was apprehensive about going to Yale. I was young for my class, not much of an athlete, no great scholar, nor did I have any close friends going there. The one time I visited New Haven, it had seemed a most forbidding place. The students looked like middle-aged men to me, each intent on some weighty business. The boys I knew at St. Paul's, for the most part, wore white shoes, tweed jackets, and gray-flannel trousers. These men wore suits and scraggly black or brown ties. Their collars were likely starched, not buttoned down; their shoes were black, unpolished. There were some prep-school types, but their loud laughs and athletic builds were just as threatening. And the city itself hung like a gray cloud around the campus: no dazzling skyscrapers, no friendly New Hampshire hillsides, just a flat, dismal, small industrial city. How could anyone be happy there?

Ben Tilghman and I took the train to New Haven together. He was a friend at St. Paul's (but we were not that close), and we would be roommates our first two years at Yale. Ben was older than I, bright, intending to major in science but a lover of poetry. We would have long discussions about the relative merits of my favorite poet, Edwin Arlington Robinson, and his favorite, Edna St. Vincent Millay.

When the conductor came through the car crying, "NooooHaven! NooHaven! NewHaven!" I felt goose pimples up my back. Soon we pulled up in front of Phelps Gate, the port of entry for freshmen. Phelps was a massive four-story tower through the bottom of which a pretentious Victorian Gothic entryway opened on the old campus. This was the oldest part of the university and consisted of a large, grassy space shaded by elms and surrounded by dark nineteenth-century-brownstone buildings, in front of which were flagstone walks and the famous Yale Fence. In the center stood the oldest building at Yale, Connecticut Hall, a modest three-story, brick colonial structure. A statue of Nathan Hale, portrayed as a slim, graceful, gallant-looking young man with long hair tied back in eighteenth-century style, stood prominently in front. On the pedestal below were engraved his famous words, "I only regret that I have but one life to lose for my country." He was the archetypal Yale man. It is hard to believe now, but in those days most freshmen took seriously the last line of the great Yale football song: "For God, for country, and for Yale." I felt that Nathan Hale probably would have regretted having only one life to give for Yale, since at that moment Yale seemed more important to me than country and more tangible than God.

Ben and I walked across campus to the corner building, and there, in the center of the courtyard on the ground floor was our room, 455 Wright Hall. It turned out to be in the very heart of the college, because the post office was in the basement. Across the way, we found Ned Hall, whom I knew from the North Shore of Boston, and his roommate, Johnny Carhart, both from St. Mark's School. Soon our two rooms became a preppy common room.

Drinking was de rigueur at college in those days, although none of us liked the taste. My only experience with alcohol had been drinking stingers at the old Pennsylvania Hotel while listening to Benny Goodman's orchestra. Someone suggested we try rum and Coca-Cola, a Cuba Libre. The political significance of the name completely escaped us. After two or three drinks the room would be too small to contain the party, and six, eight, or ten of us would romp across the campus, shouting up at windows, adding new recruits, breaking bottles, singing, wrestling, stopping at other rooms as we gained momentum. Ned Hall found a duck decoy on our first outing, so we christened ourselves the Duck Club.

Our lightheartedness did not last. One of our circle contracted a large gambling debt. His family was not rich, and his honor was at stake. I'll never forget the fear in his eyes as he threw the dice and lost a final roll for double or quits. Not long after, two others were almost killed in a car crash while driving drunk. The Duck Club disbanded before Christmas.

At Yale, you were expected to go out for a sport. I went out for rowing, practicing in the dirty harbor on frosty afternoons and in the smelly gymnasium all winter. We even came back early from spring vacation to practice among the ice floes of the Housatonic River. Knuckles were bruised, thighs scraped bloody, lungs almost burst in long sprints. But finally spring would come and with it the glorious moments when the boat would dart like a dragonfly across the sparkling waters and we would feel the thrill of the shell, while the birds sang on the shore. Beautiful, until Ed Leader, our fearsome coach, would scream, "Moore, you look like a hunk of shit on a barbed-wire fence!"

The main reason we were at Yale, presumably, was to study, and most of us studied hard. Night after night I'd fall asleep over Shakespeare or Virgil after a long workout on the river and an enormous dinner at the training table. Freshman Latin, Greek, and English were hard work and dull, for the most part. I do remember one Greek class with joy. My junior year, four of us persuaded Professor Harmon to invite us to his house one evening a week to read the *Odyssey* aloud. The language was so easy that we sailed along without translating; we could feel the wind and the waves and see the rosy-fingered dawn rising up across the Aegean Sea.

My awakening to the intellectual life came to me in another way, however. In my sophomore year, I took a course on Alexander the Great given by the well-known classics scholar Michael Rostovtzeff. He was a tiny, round man with Slavic features. Though at first his English was hard to understand and his delivery undramatic, he made Alexander glisten. The young king was brilliant, handsome, and spun visions far beyond reason: running behind his horse Bucephalus to show his men he was tireless; passionately embracing beautiful young women and young men alike; finding a soothsayer in the desert who proclaimed him divine. Statues gave him the aura of a young god. All my own romantic longings, my love of Greece, my adolescent hero worship broke forth in fascination with this glorious young man. But there was more in my awakening to history than that. Professor Rostovtzeff led us through the complex political and economic history of the Hellenistic world, from the beer industry of Egypt to the influence of Hellenism on the latter part of the Old Testament. He showed us the increasingly decadent beauty of Hellenistic art and literature so that we could see how the decline of vigorous cultures can be traced through their art. History—its movement, its power, its meaning—was mine to know.

I had come to Yale still in the first flush of conversion to Anglo-Catholicism. Mr. Bartrop had suggested that I attend Christ Church, New Haven, a large Victorian Gothic church on the edge of campus. Since I did not know much about the Church outside of St. Paul's and my little parish in New Jersey, Christ Church was full of surprises. The first time I went there I saw three women dressed as nuns kneeling in the rear of the church. I smelled incense and spied a statue of the Virgin Mary surrounded by vigil lights. Nearby were two confessionals. I hesitated, then went back outside and read the sign to be sure I was in an Episcopal and not a Roman Catholic church. Christ Church was a full-blown Anglo-Catholic parish, a product of the Oxford Movement of the previous century, which had revived the Catholic heritage of the Anglican Church, dormant since the Reformation.

I had been brought up with a distinct prejudice against Catholics. WASPs looked down on Roman Catholics as being superstitious, lower-class Irish, Polish, or Italians, with a few prominent families as the exceptions. Therefore, it was hard for me to feel at home in the Anglo-Catholic setting of Christ Church. Soon, however, even with all the other distractions of college life, I grew into the full power of the Catholic faith. I was a young man, full of energy and idealism, open to experience, but also beset with the conflicting feelings of adolescence—sexual drives, guilt, confusion, intellectual doubt, ambivalence toward my parents. I had no understanding of how the body, mind, and spirit were connected, nor had I ever heard of the unconscious. Into this confusion of thought and feeling poured all the beauty, depth, and wisdom of that ancient faith.

My friend Walter McVeigh had given me a crucifix that glowed in the dark. It hung over a prie-dieu in my bedroom. There I said my prayers morning and night; when I turned out the lights, I could still see Jesus, and Jesus, I felt, could still see me. In retrospect this seems sentimental, but at the time, kneeling before the crucified Christ led me into a serious effort in the life of prayer. Father Clark Kennedy, the rector of Christ Church and my confessor, gently told me that prayer could not always be as full of joy as it was in the beginning.

He spoke of the "dry periods" when God seems absent. But even when prayer was a bore, even when I did not *feel* God's presence, I continued to believe he was there.

No matter how drunk I was when I came home, I fell on my knees (if only for a minute), crossed myself, and told God I was sorry for being such a miserable sinner. The drunker I was, of course, the sorrier I would be. If I was sober, the prayer would be more orderly: a con-fession of sins, thanksgiving for the blessings of the day, and prayers for my family and anyone I knew who was sick or in trouble. In the morning, if I kept to my rule of life, I would say prayers of praise and dedicate myself to what lay ahead during the day. I also tried to make a daily ten-minute meditation. That was the time when the great, dark mystery of God lay before me. And yet, again and again, rather than probing the darkness or plunging into the cloud of unknowing, I would find myself preoccupied with an upcoming exam or crew race or just distracted with fleeting thoughts.

I would tell this to Father Kennedy, and he would urge me to be patient. He would say, "Paul, my son, trying to pray is prayer. The point of prayer is not what you get out of it but what you give God." Although his answer made sense, it was singularly unsatisfying for someone who wanted to be St. John of the Cross in a month or two. But I kept trying. I read countless little books on how to pray. I studied St. Ignatius of Loyola's *Spiritual Exercises* and St. Francis de Sales's *Introduction to a Devout Life*. Using de Sales's suggested method of meditation, I would dutifully read a passage from the Bible, picture the scene, and allow my affection to flow to Jesus as he stood in my imagination. Then I would promise to do something special for him that day and take away some saying or vignette to carry in my mind and heart. I came to know Christ that way and grew a little in faith if not in virtue.

And then there were times, especially on retreat, when a powerful insight or an unusually vivid sense of God's presence would come to me. It was all mixed up with my growing up, but it was a start. One spring evening I was meditating in the chapel at the Monastery of the Holy Cross, which stands high above the banks of the Hudson River. It was one of those times when all seemed well with my life, and I was praying out of joy, not pain or desperation. My eyes fell upon a statue of the Virgin Mary in a sunlit corner of the chapel. She was clad in the traditional blue and white and stood in a graceful pose, emanating a sense of peace, sweetness, and femininity. Three or four blue vigil lights burned before her, and a vase of fresh, white narcissi and a sprig or two of dogwood were at her side. I could not keep my eyes off her, and my prayers seemed to float her way. A flood of affection came over me; I felt taken care of, relaxed in mind and soul, and I found myself saying quietly, "Hail Mary, full of grace, the Lord is with thee. Blessed art thou among women. Blessed is the fruit of thy womb, Jesus. Holy Mary, Mother of God, pray for us sinners now and at the hour of our death."

A few years later, at seminary, I studied the theology of Mary: how she is to be venerated and honored but not worshipped as God is worshipped. I read of the abuses and superstitions of the cult of Mary in the Roman Catholic Church and of the high place she occupies in Eastern Orthodox spirituality, in which she is referred to as Theotokos (God bearer). We Anglicans scoffed at the idea that one had to go "through" Mary to get to Jesus—as if she were the first sergeant of a busy commanding officer. Yet that spring day I sensed within myself a pull toward the feminine in my worship, which up to then had concentrated on the male images of God the Father and God the Son. This experience helped me, many years later, to accept the language changes recommended in the new liturgy, and indeed the whole feminist movement within the Church. I came to believe emotionally what I had always known intellectually: that God is neither male nor female but somehow includes, in rich complexity, that to which our masculine and feminine natures respond; that God can be referred to with "she" as well as "he." I am convinced that the whole cult of Mary sprang from an intuitive sense among early Christians that God is not only male and from the longing to bring the soul in touch with the feminine in God, which I felt in the chapel that evening.

At other retreats, I gained other insights. It was as if I had to be quiet for a period of time in order to uncover some new understanding of God or of myself. For instance, I had recited the Creed since my boyhood without reservation and had known several happy Easters, but it was not until a retreat during my sophomore year that the vision of the risen Christ became real and a strong part of my faith. The image of the crucified Lord had been so powerful that somehow it had obscured the Resurrection in my prayer.

The Low Church liturgy of my home parish and St. Paul's School bored me, but the beauty of Anglo-Catholic worship drew forth springs of wonder. The plainsong, the vividly colored vestments, the incense, the ritual—all these reached the depths of my soul. I grew to love being in church. I enjoyed crossing myself, genuflecting, serving the altar as an acolyte, and knowing when to ring the Sanctus bell. Worship was no longer mainly an activity of the mind; it had become an action in which all my senses could take part. I was being drawn ever closer to the decision to become a priest.

In those days, my faith had little to do with social consciousness. Much later, I came to find Christ in others, in the poor, in the suffering. But at Yale my religion was individualistic, pietistic, concentrated on the spiritual life in the narrow sense. Of course, I knew a Christian was *supposed* to "perform good works." Out of a sense of duty, then, I volunteered to lead a Scout troop. The first meeting, already scheduled by my predecessor, was to include a visit to a funeral home. He really must have run out of ideas! The boys did not think there was anything particularly odd about this adventure, so who was I to be shocked? I had never been to a funeral parlor either.

We were met at the door by a particularly slimy mortician. "Now, boys, you are going to have a lovely time seeing our establishment. We are, if I do say so, the finest funeral home in all New Haven." The boys grew more and more nervous as we went from "slumber room" to "slumber room" viewing caskets. By the time we arrived at the embalming lab, with its sharp instruments and metal basins, some were giggling uncontrollably, others clinging to me. The mortician told us the home's motto was "Peace, perfect peace." At that point, one of the boys said loudly, "Peace on you, mister." I knew it was time to go.

I shall never forget the boys' nervous laughter, the emotional confusion that brought forth giggles at the mention of a dead mother, and their fear as they confronted the notion of cutting up dead flesh. I had begun to learn about the business of death: the cultural euphemisms, the slick salesman coaxing the family to the expensive casket ("I am sure you want the best for your dad"), the ambivalence toward death we have developed in America. As a priest, I have wrestled with this ambivalence time and again—urging those in the shock of grief to look death straight on, encouraging them to deal with it by going through the cross to the Resurrection, rather than avoiding the cold terror with words like "slumber" and the sickeningly sweet music of the funeral home. This means letting your emotion go, crying your eyes out so that you can find peace.

My sophomore year at Yale, I went out for football manager, a prestigious position. The competition for the spot was miserable; it consisted of doing all the dirty work for the players, including picking up their sweaty clothes while they were in the shower. (Gerald Ford, then in law school, was an assistant coach; I picked up the future president's jockstrap.) I was so inefficient, it became clear that I could not win the competition, but my father insisted that I see it through. At Yale, he reminded me, you did not quit.

Where did this ethos come from? Yale had Puritan roots, to be sure; it had been founded by Puritan divines in the eighteenth century, and the harsh theology of the likes of Jonathan Edwards molded its early life. In the nineteenth century, the Christian ethic of Calvin and the business ethic of America came together to give Yale a sturdy, hardworking chauvinistic spirit. Yale College was made the center of life: self-sufficient, claiming all loyalty in order to forge a serious, public-spirited young man who would take his place in industry, law, academic life, or public service.

The mystique of Yale in those days was undergirded by the presence of the strange and secret senior societies. For students prominent in any way, for the sons or grandsons of alumni, and for those who came from preparatory schools, being "tapped" for a senior society was the touchstone of success. Skull and Bones was the oldest and best known, but often by the luck of the draw, as it were, other societies attracted a more prominent delegation. The code of secrecy was such that, at the wedding of a member, the bride was inducted and made to promise that she would never divulge any society secrets her husband might let slip in pillow talk. Even though only ninety men were tapped, the life of Yale was affected by the austere presence of the "tombs." Skull and Bones occupied a massive square brownstone of

Egyptian design; Scroll and Key's was only a little less austere because of a small lawn in front; the relatively new Wolf's Head—which tapped me, as it had my father—met in a large Tudor mansion with all its windows bricked in, surrounded by a wall. Attendance at all meetings was compulsory. We met informally on Saturday nights, but the societies' formal gatherings were on Thursday night. The members wore black suits, stiff collars, black four-in-hand ties, and, pinned prominently on the tie, the gold emblem of the society. No member was allowed to speak to anyone on his way to the meetings, and the delegation marched home as a body, letting off each member at his room on the way. I remember, as a freshman, hearing the martial tread of the Bones men going by my window. Each member had to retire without speaking, unless his roommate was a member of the same society. Luckily for me, my roommate senior year belonged to Wolf's Head—Seth French, a splendid, cheerful guy who worked his way through Yale running the student suit-pressing concession.

To say that this behavior was sophomoric would be an understatement, although I did not think so at the time; nor did the elitism and exclusivity involved bother my underdeveloped Christian ethic. Even for those who did not join, the criteria of accomplishment for election to a society directly affected Yale undergraduate life. And those who spent their senior year in the tight camaraderie of the tombs found the experience worthwhile. Two evenings a week with fourteen other young men developed in most of us a respect for another's opinion, gave us a chance to share our inmost thoughts in complete confidentiality, and formed bonds that for many of us have lasted a lifetime.

Many lighter moments and less serious organizations were part of undergraduate life. One of these was the Haunt Club, the sole purpose of which was to have two huge bashes in the country each year. Thirteen "ghosts" made up the membership. The criterion by which one was elected to this elite group was quite simple: you had to be able to drink a lot. These rural bacchanals, rollicking around the countryside, would begin with gallons of milk punch and end with champagne.

On the way home from the fall meeting, a Harvard friend of mine, Shot Warner, a Yale friend, Flash Flaherty, and I stole a parking sign and put it in the back of the car. As we pulled up to a traffic light at the corner of the campus, an alert policeman spied the sign, asked us what we were doing with it, and ordered us out of the car. Shot was driving.

"Where's your license?"

"I don't have it."

"Where's your registration?"

"I left it at Harvard."

"Oh, so you're a Harvard boy . . . all the better! You are under arrest!"

Then one of the great lines: "You can't arrest me, you peasant, we have been drinking champagne!"

We were all immediately arrested and taken to jail, where we sang Christmas carols to the inmates. One of us was allowed a phone call. We decided Flaherty should have the privilege since he was already on probation. He called our favorite tailor, J. Press, from whom he had purchased many a tweed jacket. Early the next morning, we were arraigned and held on $500 bail. "You're kidding!" I said to the judge. He wasn't. At that point, up the aisle strode a very small man wearing an immaculate three-piece suit with old-fashioned lapels on the vest and a large gold watch chain across the front and a gray derby on his head. It was Mr. Press with our bail. (I still patronize J. Press.)

The most embarrassing part of it was that our names appeared in the newspaper, and soon after I reached my room there was a soft knock on the door. The room was a shambles. I was barely conscious. It was Father Kennedy, who had seen the newspaper article and was making a pastoral call. I learned from this awkward moment that people do not always want to see a priest.

The war was a distant cloud on the horizon until senior year, the fall of 1940, when it moved to the center of our thoughts. Some of my friends quit college to join the service, even going to Canada or England to be part of an army at war. We romanticized ourselves. At Harvard, my friends gave a Lost Generation party: "Eat, drink and be merry . . ." was an easy excuse for hard drinking, but we really thought some of us would die in the war, and many did.

I look back and wonder what happened to me during those four years at Yale. I began as a snobbish, spoiled boy from St. Paul's

School: tall and still growing, skinny, young for my class, entering an awesome place where I had to make good because Yale had meant so much to my family over the years. Now, I was about to graduate into a world in the midst of war.

I majored in English and acquired a rooting in the classics, from the grand lines of Marlowe to T. S. Eliot's tortured Christian vision. Professor John Allison of the history department led us through a course in historiography—the Old Testament, Herodotus, Plutarch, Marx, Toynbee—until we could see how much the writing of history depended on the perspective of the historian. The bits and pieces of my various courses came together: the Old Testament and Homer, the Crucifixion and Greek tragedy, Shelley and the Greek lyric poets. I absorbed the interaction of economics, politics, art, and religion. This may seem obvious; it is, of course, what a liberal education is all about. But I am talking about that great surge of light when suddenly you discover a whole new way of thinking of the past, or, in a flash, understand the present through a moment in history. I sometimes felt the way Keats felt when he first looked into Chapman's Homer and compared the moment to Cortez's sighting the Pacific "upon a peak in Darien." Much is said about the importance and usefulness of a liberal education but not enough about the sheer joy of the experience for an eager young mind. Such an education grounds you in a wisdom and perspective you never lose. Certainly, I had grown intellectually and had a firm grasp on the framework of English-speaking culture and the history of Western civilization. I could see the sweep of history. I could recognize the rise and fall of nations. I could trace the birth, flourishing, and disintegration of movements within society and within the arts. Classical and English literature became a part of me: the rough beauty of Homer, where almost every great hero was so human that he was destroyed; the searing tragedies of the dramatists; the beauty of Plato's Ideas, the rough and tumble of Socrates' searching questions, the easy and open relationships between the masters and the youths they taught; the games, the temples, white against the blue of sky and sea. I was enthralled by *The Canterbury Tales*, especially the religious characters; never again would I be shocked by the corruption of the Church, but I sensed Chaucer's good-humored compassion for those who strayed and his sense of real evil where it occurred. We read everything that Shakespeare ever wrote and went on to the beauty of the seventeenth-century poets, Donne, Vaughan, and Milton, who wrote of the darkness and the light of those years.

As at St. Paul's, all the teaching was not in the classroom. One beautiful spring evening, two professors, Robert Bates and Beekman Cannon, and three of us undergraduates drove in my open car across the New England countryside to an old inn. After a splendid dinner, where I learned the delight of a long meal and conversation, we motored back and talked till dawn in Bob Bates's apartment. My only memory of the conversation is of a long discussion of why Shakespeare used five "nevers" in a line from *King Lear*: "Never, never, never, never, never." In such moments, I sensed the joy of poetry and its mystery.

My spiritual life continued to develop. The rapture that had followed my conversion wore off, but the sense of God's presence in my life continued. I found prayer tough in retreat after retreat, as I tried to search deeper into the mystery. But I also found a steady, rocklike quality to my faith, even when I neglected it, even when I felt most unworthy. I am glad I began to learn about God in a secular place: in later years, I was never tempted to hide within the Church but always saw it as part of daily life, even during the war.

Although Yale was a men's place, longings for girls were in our thoughts and conversations. In those days, "nice" girls did not go all the way, and I was turned off by the women we occasionally picked up on adventures to the nearby amusement park. Our only outlet was necking, a wonderful but frustrating experience!

Graduation celebrations began with the New London Boat Races between Yale and Harvard, which filled the river Thames with all kinds of craft, from little outboards to enormous yachts: J. P. Morgan's *Corsair*, the *Nourmahal*, *Cleopatra's Barge*, and the *Constellation*, the latter two being beautiful schooners with crews in spotless uniforms. The only time I ever saw President Roosevelt was on one of these yachts. We looked at him through our binoculars and could see the jaunty cigarette holder and the famous smile.

My father lent me our rather modest powerboat, the *Beeswing*, for the weekend. We tied up at the dock near the railroad station. Friends from Yale and Harvard came and went. We had a glorious time. Unfortunately, Cholly Knickerbocker, a gossip columnist for the *Daily News*, wrote us up as "the golden youth of American society, rich boys, who threw beer cans at the townspeople, some of whose sons were already serving their country." That was a fabrication, but the name of the boat was mentioned. With great care, I kept the article from my parents' eyes until after graduation.

After the great bash at the old Griswold hotel near New London, we returned to New Haven, celebrated further in a last gathering at Wolf's Head, and, much the worse for wear, wobbled through graduation.

So ended those bright college years, as our whole generation faced war.

GOING TO WAR

ONE evening toward the end of August 1939, my mother and I were in Ireland, staying in a castle belonging to our friends the Henry Laughlins. After dinner, we sat by candlelight in the great hall, listening to the radio with an old Irish woman who was the housekeeper. Through the static, we heard reports of the mounting crisis in Europe. Hitler had invaded Czechoslovakia, and his troops were now massed on the Polish border. Great Britain had declared that the invasion of Poland would mean war. The world was poised on the brink of unimaginable disaster. Between broadcasts, the old housekeeper, in a world-weary tone I had never heard before, told us of the wars she had known: the Boer War, the Irish uprisings, the Great War, colonial actions throughout the empire. She had lost her father and her brother, and we saw the tragedy of her life on her wrinkled face in the wavering light of the candles. The ghostly images of thousands of splendid young men, slaughtered in India, Africa, and Flanders fields, passed before us.

The next day, we sailed home on the *Manhattan*. The dock was crowded with people desperate to escape from Europe on the brink of war. The ship departed on schedule even so, and we were served hot consommé on our deck chairs at eleven in the morning and tea and scones at five.

As a boy, I'd been taught that the Great War would end all wars. The papers were full of disarmament and the League of Nations; the war movies seemed as remote as the Crusades. Now I was eighteen, and I sensed that this war would be my war. As we sailed home, I allowed the broad Atlantic to wash the doom away. I was going home, where none of this could really happen. I would be safe again.

In Prides Crossing the morning after our arrival in the States, as I lay half asleep in my favorite room, my grandmother's butler opened the door with the news that Poland had been invaded and war declared. His solemn voice and faraway eyes reminded me that he had been a Tommy in the First World War.

From that moment on, the war in Europe became a dark backdrop to all our thoughts and plans. My parents began to relive the last war. Women took up knitting socks for "the boys in the trenches" (although there would be no trenches in this war). By the summer of 1940, some of my friends had enlisted. Organizations like Bundles for Britain gathered food and clothes for the English. The national debate on whether the United States should be involved intensified, but we sensed that war was inevitable. We had adolescent dreams of glory and a new sense of self-importance as we made decisions that would change our lives.

Walter McVeigh and I admitted to each other that we rather hoped we would go to war. We had romantic notions of battle, of courage, of seeing life in the raw. Yet I wondered whether in conscience I could be in the military. My faith had never interfered with my life before. All my friends were set to go, and the only conscientious objectors I knew were pale, pimply-faced youths who hung around Dwight Hall, the Christian center at Yale. I consulted Father Kennedy, my parish priest, who had been gassed in the trenches in the Great War and whom I deeply respected as a man of prayer. With great sadness, he told me that he felt going to war was the lesser of two evils. If Hitler conquered Europe, soon he would conquer the United States, and the whole world would be under Nazi rule. Civilization as we knew it would be over and done with. That was what I wanted to hear, and my conscience (such as it was) bothered me no longer. As it happened, the war was the most formative experience of my adult life. Finally I broke out of the sheltered world of privilege and met men from other places, men with other ways of thinking, speaking, and acting. I came to know and love them, and after a while we acted together as if we had grown up on the same block. I saw death and suffering, heroism and brutality, and learned that I had enough courage to be a Marine. Most important of all for me, my faith survived the crucible of the war.

In the winter of my senior year, the pressing question was what branch of the armed services to join. Most of my close friends were going into the Navy—a more gentlemanly life, so it seemed, than the muddy proletariat of the Army. But I could not make the Navy, with only high school plane geometry to offer. The more adventurous wanted to fly in the Army Air Force, but the thought of flying in war scared me to death. Then one sunny day, George Mead, a close friend who lived across the hall from me at Yale, and I saw a handsome young Marine officer driving around campus in a convertible coupe with whitewall tires and the top down. He wore an immaculate white cap on which shone a Marine emblem of silver and gold, and when he got out of the car, the crimson stripe down the side of his blue trousers flashed in the sunshine. That was all we needed. The next day, we stripped down in the recruiting office, were found to be breathing, and signed up for four years, beginning with an officers' training course in Quantico, Virginia.

First we had the summer off, and what a happy summer it was! My family threw a house party at our camp in the Adirondacks for my friends, including George and Jerry Knapp, who had signed up with the Marine Air Force, and my brother-in-law Jack Denison, who entered the ambulance corps of the American Field Service. We had some girlfriends along as well. My father took George and me out every day to practice rifle shooting in preparation for the Marines. George, Jerry, and Jack all would soon be dead, and when I go to our camp I always recall the happy faces of the summer of 1941.

The partying continued into August on the North Shore of Boston. I even was arrested for drunken driving in my grandmother's driveway at ten in the morning. The omnipresent Higgs appeared at the front door just in time; he winked and said to the police officer, "Mr. Paul could not possibly be intoxicated at ten in the morning."

In October, I went fishing in the Florida Keys with some other friends. Some St. Paul's classmates were already in the Navy, stationed in Key West. One night, they introduced us to what sailors and Marines do on liberty by showing us the red-light district. I was a virgin, and the thought of visiting such a place was intimidating. Already high on a good many beers, we crowded into a disreputable-looking house, ordered some more beers, and were immediately joined by women. The one next to me was singularly unattractive, yet she was acting sexy and patted me on the leg. I was more embarrassed than aroused and talked about the weather. One by one, I saw my friends go upstairs with their companions. I was the only one left. The woman with me said, "Come on upstairs."

I said okay. What else could I do? I was trapped. To say I was anxious would be an understatement. We entered a room whose only piece of furniture was a rickety-looking old iron bed; the paint was flaking off the bars, the brass balls were black with age, but the white sheet looked clean. I wondered how many sailors had used this bed. In the corner, my "date" was washing herself in a basin with strong soap. Then she came over to me, and I kissed her clumsily. We fell on the bed, and it collapsed. "You asshole!" she screamed.

"To hell with you. I'm getting outta here."

"Pay me!"

"For what?"

"My time, for Christ's sake."

I threw ten dollars at her and ran downstairs, her voice chasing after me: "You fucking cheapskate!" My friends were waiting, and we all left in a hurry, I with my virginity intact but without compassion for a woman eking out a living in a humiliating way.

On the first of November, George Mead and I went to Quantico. If you can believe it, we had been to Abercrombie and Fitch (at my father's suggestion) to buy boots, and we carted our golf clubs along as well.

George was a quiet, amiable, and most popular fellow. He managed the football team at Yale, a high office in the undergraduate hierarchy. He neither drank nor smoked and was most respectful to the girls he dated. He stood about five eleven, with brown hair, freckles, and a pleasant grin. Among all my classmates, he was the most respected. But he was not stuffy; he enjoyed parties and had many friends, one of the closest of whom was Jack Kennedy. He had money;

his family business was the Mead Paper Company of Dayton, Ohio. His father ran the price-control program during the war.

As soon as we got off the train at the Marine Barracks, a sergeant started screaming at us. For the next three months, sergeants would be screaming at us. So began the most miserable three months of my life, Marine Corps basic training. The idea seemed to be to make it so horrible that going to battle would seem like a relief.

We were toughened physically by the calisthenics, long marches with heavy packs through the scrubby Virginia woods and red Virginia mud. We drilled until our bodies reacted to commands before our minds understood what they were. We were toughened psychologically to kill or be killed. We ran the bayonet course, screaming obscenities at the top of our lungs: "Fuck you, you dirty yellow bastards. We'll stick you in the gut! Rip you open! Yow! Wyeee!" Screams from our guts, growls, howls, rebel yells. We stuck our bayonets into straw dummies with faces painted to look like Japanese and knocked their heads off with our rifle butts. If we ran the course under a certain time, we were given a badge. I did not qualify the first time—because I did not scream loud enough. "What's the matter, Moore, are Yale boys too polite to yell?" The strange thing was that after a certain point we got into it, let ourselves go, and actually enjoyed the wild violence. This was exactly what the bayonet course was supposed to do. Also, as I later learned on the battlefield, screaming tended to obliterate your fear and did indeed intimidate the enemy.

I was hopeless at close-order drill, and, because I was six foot four, the drill sergeant noticed every false move. I felt myself slipping away from the gold lieutenant's bar that awaited us three months hence. Finally, I asked to see our lieutenant.

"Private First Class Moore reporting, sir."

"At ease, Moore. What's your problem?"

"The rankings came out today, sir, and I am tenth from the bottom out of three hundred candidates and well below the unsatisfactory line. What can I do about that, sir?"

Lieutenant Reid put his prematurely balding head in his hands and was silent for a few moments. Then he raised his head, gave a deep sigh, and said, "Moore, you don't look like a Marine, you don't act like a Marine, you'll never be a Marine."

"But, sir . . ."

"Attention! Dismissed!" I performed a splendid about-face and left the office.

The pressure was enormous. My worst fears and insecurities came to the surface. I needed so badly to pass this macho test.

Then came the most important training of all, the rifle range. To my great surprise (and to the surprise of my commanding officer), I came within a point of qualifying as expert. My troubles were over; if you can shoot well in the Marines, it covers a multitude of gaffes. All those hours practicing with my father's deer rifle in the Adirondacks had made the difference.

We were told that all the agony of basic training would seem worthwhile at graduation, when we took part, shoes and brass brilliantly shined, in the massive liturgy of a full-dress parade. I must say that when the band sounded off with "From the halls of Montezuma" I felt a surge of pride and joy, marching smartly with my rifle on my shoulder, the Marine Corps flag and Stars and Stripes waving in the breeze up ahead. I could understand how the young men of Germany became Nazis.

In February we received our commissions and continued training as officers. We could go to the officers' club. We sported splendid green and even more splendid dress uniforms—a navy-blue tunic, bright-blue trousers with a red stripe down the sides, a shiny, dark Sam Browne belt, rifle badges, and a magnificent cap with a sparkling silver and gold Marine emblem over the visor. We stood very straight, were obnoxiously arrogant. We were Marine officers, just like the young man who had recruited us at Yale. We had become gentlemen.

Military training had imposed itself on my very soul, quickly erasing qualms of conscience that I thought were deep. Killing became a good, sensitivity a fault. Later on, in combat, I was thankful for this psychological armor. I was thankful that my men responded to commands immediately, without thought. When I saw my first bodies and faced fire for the first time, I was thankful that I was no longer a sensitive, protected preppy. It took me many years after the war to resensitize myself.

How could a young Christian be changed so quickly? I think I compartmentalized my thinking and feeling. I still prayed, I still went to Mass, but I did not feel any inconsistency between my changed personality and my faith. Our culture revered the image of the Christian soldier, whether George Washington or Robert E. Lee. The Boy Scouts mixed military and spiritual values: "A Scout is brave, clean, and reverent." Thus I felt comfortable being a Christian and a Marine, even though the violent brutality of the bayonet course and all it represented was blatantly unchristian.

This hardening of the heart was a necessity for a disciplined fighting force. But what has this done to the leaders of the world, many of whom were trained the same way and continued in the service? Was this part of the reason that presidents and prime ministers could so easily order young men and women to their deaths? Did civilian leaders (even women, such as Indira Gandhi and Margaret Thatcher) fall under the spell of the generals, admirals, and veterans who surrounded them? Some would say that the experience of war makes leaders less likely to support it. Colin Powell was reluctant to enter the Gulf War. Yet he went along with it because, as a military man, he had to obey his commander in chief.

Despite the shooting, the bayonet course, the maneuvers, it all still seemed a game, an extension of college, until December. I had gone home for my first weekend. What a relief to return to the luxury of linen sheets and breakfast brought to my room by Plowright. I reveled in the pride in my parents' eyes. For the first time, I felt almost superior to my brother, a civilian.

On that Sunday, December 7, we were sitting in the sun-filled living room—Mother and Dad, my sister Fanny, my brother, Bill, and his wife, Mouse—drinking martinis and nibbling hors d'oeuvres. I was filled with a sense of well-being. Plowright came in, presumably to take orders for another round of drinks, and the conversation quieted down. He said, "Excuse me, madam, but I thought you should know that the Japanese have just bombed Pearl Harbor." We rushed to the radio, and I felt a chill go down my spine. The Marines were no longer a game. After an emotional farewell from the family, my brother drove me to the airport. I was in uniform. As we drove out the beautiful bluestone driveway past the patch of woods in which I had played as a boy, Bill said, "If one of those little yellow bastards harms a hair of your head, I'll kill him!" This made no sense, but it felt good to have Bill say that, as if I were his little brother being bullied on the playground. He went into the Navy soon and had a distinguished career on a destroyer escort in the Atlantic. He received the Bronze Star for bravery when a German submarine crew boarded his ship.

At Quantico our training was accelerated, and George, myself, and many of our classmates were assigned platoons in the First Marine Division, stationed in a dusty tent city at New River, North Carolina. Being a rifle platoon leader was considered one of the most dangerous assignments, because, in combat, the platoon leader was in the lead. Scouts were sent out in front of the platoon, and the platoon leader would direct them with hand and arm signals. He would be in a position between the scouts and the rest of the platoon. I had asked to be a platoon leader, because I wanted to be in the thick of things, in a leadership role, not a staff position. Choosing to go into the Marines, choosing the infantry, and choosing a rifle platoon were all part of the same desire: as long as I was in the war, I really wanted to experience the essence of it.

My first platoon seemed skeptical of me—some of them were mere boys, others older and tougher. I called them to attention and found them perfect except for their rifle slings' brass buckles, which were dirty. In leadership training, we had been told to be strict at first. Here was my chance. I bawled them out in as tough a way as I could summon. Looks of astonishment passed over their faces. "Excuse me, sir," said my platoon sergeant with ill-concealed pleasure, "in the field we are not allowed to shine our buckles, because they would catch the sun and the enemy would see us." I was humiliated, and the fact that I lost one of my men on the first night maneuver in rubber boats hardly helped to build an image of competence. (He turned up before the night was over.)

It was a long journey to gaining the men's respect after that. But we did grow close, and strong bonds formed among us: Carl Trieglaff from Metropolis, Illinois; Charlie Sviatoha and Malcolm Kirshbaum from the Upper West Side of Manhattan; Sergeant Homer Skipper from southern Maryland, who liked to talk about making jelly; Gene Asche, who later became an undertaker; Steve Stypanzen and Howie Johnston, the shortest guy in the platoon; Bob Wallace, Jim Smith, Al Fiedor, Corporal Kelly. We came from many different ethnic backgrounds—except at that time there were no blacks in the Marines. We came to trust one another in spite of our differences, or perhaps because of them, and because we all had volunteered to be Marines. We knew that our lives would depend on one another.

That sense of interdependence is something I've never forgotten and perhaps was the emotional bedrock on which I came to understand the meaning of the Body of Christ—the Church—and why I found myself preaching with vehemence in later years that our very salvation could not be a solitary matter. In the same way that our lives were physically dependent on one another and that this dependence had to be based on some level of trust, of love, so, in the Church, we are spiritually dependent on one another, and this dependence is based on love, even for strangers.

From New River we soon boarded the *Wakefield* at Norfolk, Virginia, and sailed to destinations unknown. She was a sister ship of the *Manhattan*, in which I had returned, first class, from Europe. The same murals were on the walls (now called bulkheads).

The voyage through the steep green sides of the Panama Canal and the two weeks it took to cross the Pacific were a grand adventure. We ran through some tropical storms; we watched magnificent albatross soaring behind the ship on their long tapered wings and porpoises playing in the waves around the bow. At long last, we sailed between two massive, rounded green hills, under a spectacular rainbow, which arched over them, into the harbor of Wellington. We had instructed our men in the conservative culture of New Zealand. We told them it was not the custom to speak to a New Zealand girl unless properly introduced. I went ashore an hour after the men were released and, walking up the main street, saw that virtually every Marine had a girl on his arm! I never did figure out how there could have been five thousand proper introductions in less than an hour!

The people of New Zealand were deeply grateful for our presence. Their army was fighting in Africa; the Japanese were drawing ever nearer; the islands of New Zealand were vulnerable.

We were looking forward to several weeks of training in the small village of Paikakariki but were soon ordered back to Wellington to combat-load our ships for an amphibious landing at an undisclosed beach. None of us had a clue as to how to do this but soon became expert at lowering huge artillery pieces by crane into the narrow opening of the hold. It rained day and night, and we worked day and night. To make matters worse, most of us had severe diarrhea. Even so, I later found out that many of the ships never were combat-loaded and that as a result some essential equipment never got ashore.

One early morning in the hotel, I was shaving, stark naked, with the door to the bathroom open. In came the maid with my morning tea (they never knock when bringing tea because they do not want to wake you up). She took one look at me, let out a shriek, dropped the tea tray with a marvelous crash, and scurried down the hall as fast as her rather fat legs could carry her. We had not been indoctrinated about this particular part of New Zealand culture.

In about a week, we were loaded, and on July 22, 1942, we sailed north for the Solomon Islands. We had had a disastrous rehearsal on Koro, one of the Fiji Islands; many landing craft were wrecked on the coral reef, and our confidence was shaken considerably. No time was allowed for a second rehearsal, because the Japanese were close to completing the airfield on Guadalcanal. The high command had made the hard choice to send in green troops rather than forfeit the advantage of air superiority.

Each day on board our transport, the *Neville*, the tension mounted. We were given crude maps of the terrain and the operation plan as it applied to our unit. We went over and over our orders. We cleaned our weapons again and again. One night, while some twenty of us were stacked like sardines in our compartment, Tony Mazanek, a huge coal miner from western Pennsylvania, was cleaning his .45 automatic; he inadvertently fired a round that ricocheted from bulkhead to bulkhead. Yes, we were a little nervous.

You might wonder what men talk about the night before battle. I

spent that last evening on board ship being quizzed by George Ches-
ton, a Harvard friend, about what went on in Wolf's Head. He could
not believe I would hold back such irrelevant secrets the night before
I faced possible death.

D day came. We rose at dawn to see a vast armada of warships:
transports, destroyers, cargo ships, cruisers, battleships, aircraft carri-
ers, the great military might of the United States. It was a strangely
beautiful and moving sight.

In a landing operation, everything is timed back from H hour, the
moment when the first troops are to hit the beach. At H hour minus
one, we clambered down the side of the ship on the cargo nets, heavy
with equipment, fearful we would somehow miss the little boat heav-
ing up and down below. Once in the landing craft, we began to
rendezvous with other boats designated for our section of the beach.
Round and round we went in an ever widening circle, covered with
spray, as boats containing other platoons joined us. Meanwhile, on
Tulagi, where we were to land, shells from our cruisers and destroyers
were exploding in great black mushrooms of smoke, and dive-bombers
were dropping five-hundred-pound bombs on enemy emplacements.
Who could survive such a bombardment? At H hour minus twenty
minutes, the command came over the radio to head to the beach.
We kept low in the boat to avoid being hit by enemy fire, but there
was none. A hundred yards out, the Higgins boat crunched to a halt.
We leaped over the side, heavy with packs, weapons, and ammunition, and waded ashore. Not a shot was fired; we had taken the enemy
by surprise.

The first day, our company advanced through the jungle to secure
the west tip of the island. The beauty of the Solomon Islands in those
days was extraordinary. Along the coast, where the settlers had cultivated the land, stood coconut trees, which waved like grass on a
prairie when the great tropical winds came up. The jungle itself contained some impenetrable bamboo patches, but the great rain forest
was relatively free of undergrowth. Enormous trees of all kinds
stretched up and up to find the light. Vines like those on which
Tarzan traveled hung from the trees, and sometimes giant bushes resembling rhododendrons grew glorious pink flowers. Most amazing of

all were the birds. The moment we landed that first morning, I saw several large flocks of squawking red parrots fly overhead, and occasionally a white cockatoo with yellow crest perched nearby for a moment or two to eye us curiously.

The rain forest was beautiful, and I forgot why we were there until I heard a rifle shot. A Marine had come upon a Japanese soldier, and in their surprise a moment elapsed before either could comprehend that they were enemies. The Marine clicked into action first, firing rapidly, and bolted as fast as he could back to us. "I got one! I got one! I killed him! A great big Jap! Honest, right back there. Jesus! God! Whew!"

One guy said, "Stop the fucking bullshit, you didn't kill nobody."

Another asked, "You really did? You lucky bastard!" Then the sergeant took over the conversation. "It's a hell of a note when one Marine don't believe another Marine."

In a few minutes, we came upon the soldier at the side of the trail. We turned him over. His lifeless eyes stared up at us from a face like a little boy's; his small feet were clad in those Japanese sneakers split for the big toe. A violent shame swept over me. On the way back the next day, we saw him again, covered with beetles and beginning to smell.

I had never really dealt with death. The only person I ever knew who died was a friend, Jackie Schley, who'd been killed in a fire when I was ten. But this was a Jap, and we had been brainwashed into thinking that the Japs were not really human, that they were pure evil. How could a relatively sensitive Christian young man like myself, who, among other things, had read the life of the Japanese saint Toyohiko Kagawa, become so twisted by the most obvious military propaganda? I pulled down that curtain between myself and the fellow on the side of the trail.

We bivouacked in the jungle at the end of the island, setting up outposts around the perimeter of the company. During the night, we had heard the rat-a-tat of machine guns, the thumping of Browning automatic rifles, and the booming of mortars. Over the two-way radio came the familiar voice of my buddy Jack Doyle, from Greenwich, Connecticut, calling out orders to his 81 mm mortar platoon: "They're on their way up the hill now . . . We are under heavy machine-gun fire . . . We are pretty well cut off . . . We can't with-draw." At midnight the message came through that we had to go to the other end of the island and take over the attack at dawn.

We came up behind the lines that had formed on the top of a hill where the British colonial residence stood, a single-story, white clap-board house surrounded by a veranda. The forward company had se-cured the hill. I saw several Marines on stretchers, facedown, and as I looked, a fly crawled across the ear of the body nearest me. The Marine was dead. This was not a Japanese "half-human" enemy, this was a dead Marine. Death was getting closer.

We came upon a house where the British had lived only a few short weeks before, and my men showered it with bullets, then set it on fire. When the flames died down, they combed the ashes for sou-venirs: a samurai sword, a good-luck belt of a thousand stitches, a gold tooth from a dead Japanese. By nightfall the island was secure, and our men had calmed down. The island was secure, but out to sea we saw explosions and heard the sound of large naval guns. We learned later that four of our cruisers were sunk that night and that the freighters with our food and the transports with our gear had sailed off, since they no longer had protection.

Where we dug in was a pleasant spot. A cricket field lay below us, and beyond the palm-lined shore the blue sea stretched across to the distant mountains of Guadalcanal. I thought of my grandmother, cel-ebrating her birthday in the sunset by another sea. We spent two pleasant weeks there, swimming at a beautiful beach (although a friend said he missed the YMCA pool in Columbus, Ohio) and eating Japanese rice, coconuts, and palm roots. Every morning a Japanese submarine would lob a few shells in our direction, and Lou Diamond, an ancient gunnery sergeant, would try to sink it with his 81 mm mortar. One day, as we sat by our foxholes on the forward part of the hill, someone yelled, "There goes one!" Without a command, my whole platoon opened fire at this Japanese soldier scurrying across the cricket field like a rabbit. It was like target practice. He finally stum-bled and lay dead. Inside his pack we found snapshots of a beautiful Japanese family, the mother and daughters in kimonos, the father and son standing stiffly in dark suits. Again, I felt a twinge of guilt; this indeed *was* a human being.

·   ·   ·

On the first Sunday after we landed, the Roman Catholic chaplain celebrated Mass in the center of the cricket field. Hundreds of dirty men knelt down, leaning on their rifles. Mud and blood clung to their clothes. The musty smell of the tropics and the sweet smell of decaying corpses filled the air. Everything was rotten. Many men had had close friends killed. Most of the mussed bare heads were bowed, but when they lifted their eyes, they saw what they needed to see and felt what they needed to feel. The only clean thing on the island was the sparkling altar cloth. God in his purity was present in the midst of the filth.

On a moonless night two weeks later, we sailed across the sound to Guadalcanal on a destroyer converted into a small troopship, called an APD. No lights were allowed, so we gathered in the small officer's wardroom. An old friend, Heyward Pepper, was on board, and we reminisced about college days over real coffee, which tasted like ambrosia after the muck we'd had on Tulagi. Before long, we landed on the dark shore of Guadalcanal. As we came ashore, we were met by the Marines stationed on the beach. In the gray dawn I recognized a face, and I asked him about George Mead. "Oh, didn't you know? He was killed." I can still see the dark shadows of the helmets against the gray. I can still hear that husky voice. But I did not, could not, shed a tear. And so death came closer and closer.

The next day, I wrote this letter home:

August 25, (?) 1942

Dear Mother and Dad:

. . . You remember my last letter (incidentally the tear was where a bullet hit the box of stationery when in the storehouse) I had said that George Mead was okay so far as I knew. You see I'd heard that there had been very little fighting on Guadalcanal where he was. Well, when we landed here from Tulagi, the first thing I heard was that he was killed. You don't know what a feeling that was. He was such a superb person and so close. I'd been looking forward to seeing him for two weeks so we could laugh together about the various happenings. And God, to think of him, of all people, dead. I still can't believe it. . . . I haven't seen anyone to get the full story but it seems something like this. His company was fighting

some Japs for a village they held and was supposed to get some reinforcements. The other outfit never showed up so the battle was even and very
fierce. One of George's platoon was wounded up in front and George, as
was like him, rushed up to help him out. He bent over the wounded man,
and as he did the Japs opened up. It was instant death, thank goodness.
But *why* did it have to be George? . . .

Up to that time we had not seen any troops who had been exposed
to much action, but soon after we reached Guadalcanal I saw the
Raiders come straggling along the beach road from a terrible battle.
They were filthy, but what caught my attention was the look in their
eyes. They looked at you and did not see you. They did not walk so
much as stumble. They had seen horror and death beyond what we
had known.

We came to know this horror when we reinforced the same Raiders
against suicidal attacks by the enemy. It was all mixed up with the
smell of bodies. After the first night of the Battle of Bloody Ridge,
the colonel ordered all the foxholes to be filled with Japanese bodies,
as a way of frightening the enemy. By the time we saw them, the
bodies had blown up like balloons in the tropical sun. Death had
become very cheap—not just the deaths of our enemies but our own
deaths as well.

Between battles, we were located in a coconut grove near the
Lunga River, where we could go to bathe at the end of the afternoon.
Men would arrive in all sorts of costumes, including Japanese T-shirts,
carrying a rifle over one shoulder and an extra shirt over the other.
They undressed in a hurry and rushed into the river. The swimming
and frolicking made us forget in the sheer joy and relief the water
gave.

Not long after the Battle of Bloody Ridge, we went out on patrol
across the grassy ridges that separated the coast from the mountain
rain forest. The grass was so tall that sometimes even I could not see
over it. As we snaked along the ridge, without any warning, about
ten Japanese rose up from the grass and started running toward us,
waving their arms and shouting. My men opened fire, and all of the
enemy fell. We walked carefully toward them. My pistol was cocked.
We were not sure they were alive or dead. I looked down on a small
person lying there with a bare stomach. I took aim at his navel and

shot three times to make sure he was dead. It was needless slaughter, for it turned out they were unarmed laborers. But by this time, I felt no guilt, no remorse, no more than if I had stepped on a cockroach.

It seemed that no matter how close death came, it could not touch me now. I was insulated. But I had yet to see one of my own men wounded or killed, a man for whom I was responsible. Our platoon had been lucky. Our luck did not last.

General Alexander Vandegrift, who was in command of the operation, had decided to enlarge the beachhead protecting Henderson Field. The west flank was bordered by the Matanikau River, across which the enemy was dug in, a battalion strong. Colonel "Chesty" Puller (who later became something of a Marine icon, having received five Navy Crosses) was in charge of the detachment that was to take the mouth of the river. Puller had little regard for his own life and no regard for anyone else's. I could not stand him.

The mouth of the Matanikau, like that of most small jungle rivers, was crossed by wading over a narrow sand spit. The river turned to the left and flowed about a hundred yards between the bank and the sand spit and thence into the sea. Puller's plan was to soften the enemy with mortar and artillery fire and then, under the cover of heavy machine-gun fire, send a platoon across the sand spit to assault the dug-in battalion on the opposite bank. Five platoons went across, one after another. Five platoons were forced back with heavy casualties. Still Puller stayed with his foolish plan.

Our platoon was to go next. When the command to move out was given, we hunched over and ran as fast as we could along the ocean side of the sand spit and threw ourselves prone on the sand. Enemy fire was heavy, but I sent out two scouts, covering them with our Browning automatic rifles. One was a little guy named Art Beres. I watched him swim across. Art was a bright young kid from Long Island, barely tall enough to get into the Corps and cheerful no matter how bad things were. He and I used to go swimming together when we had a chance and talk about the South Shore of Long Island. I watched him go. He splashed all the way across and grabbed hold of a root that protruded from the overhanging bank. Then he turned around, and I saw that half of his face had been blown away. Blood was gushing from what was left of his mouth. I jumped into the river and swam after him. The water around me was showered with bullets.

I looked up to see grenades going overhead. I reached Art, grabbed him, and with the help of another man towed him back to safety. Then we rushed back into the river to lead the platoon in attack. Soon I found myself out of my depth, treading water. The firing increased. I looked to my right and saw three of my men lying motionless on the sand. But it had been drilled into us: Marines never retreat. What should I do? Should we all throw ourselves at the enemy and certain death? Or should we retreat, despite the mighty Marine tradition? Still treading water, I took out my pistol, fired two wild shots at the enemy, and decided we could not possibly make the other shore. With deep misgivings, I waved my men back. My sergeant and I bent over the wounded men as the sand around our boots was spattered with bullets. We turned each body over and saw the terrible expression of death on each familiar face. We left them and ran as fast as we could along the beach back to safety. I reported to Colonel Puller, who was sitting against the trunk of a coconut tree smoking a cigar.

"Lieutenant Moore reporting, sir."

No answer from Puller.

Louder: "Lieutenant Moore reporting, sir!"

Still no answer, no recognition.

"Sir, there is at least one enemy battalion well dug in on the other side of the river. There is no way a platoon can dislodge them, sir."

Still not so much as a nod of the head.

"Sir, can you hear me?"

No response at all. I stood there at attention for a full two minutes and then left. I still cannot comprehend the man's behavior. Maybe he just did not want to admit that he was wrong and that he had recklessly lost many men. Maybe he was angry that we had retreated rather than remaining to die.

I rejoined my platoon, and we sprawled out under the coconut palms on the edge of the beach looking out to sea. We were all in a daze. We still heard the rattle of machine guns and the explosions of artillery as yet another platoon was readied to cross the sand spit. Out to sea we saw a Japanese destroyer sink one of our destroyer transports. Thirty thousand feet overhead, the bombers were coming in, and the fighters trying to shoot them down left great white vapor trails against the blue. No Hollywood war picture could have equaled that amazing sight of land, sea, and air battles occurring simultaneously before our eyes.

Yet I could only brood about what had happened at the river. Could I have done something different so those beloved men would not have been killed? Now that I had been covered with the blood of my own men, now that I had looked on the lifeless stare on their faces, death grew even closer. In fact, death had come so close that it began to change its image, its character. I was so familiar with it now that it became less frightening. Somehow death had become so much a part of daily life that it had lost its strangeness, its terrifying thrust into my heart.

Looking back over those three terrible months, I realize that different people react in very different ways to the extreme pressure of the fear of death and the stress of responsibility for others' lives. Some of our men went along enduring what they had to endure, bitching and griping but keeping their sanity. (There is an old Marine saying that if your men are bitching don't worry, but if they are silent, look out.) Some of my men became more silent. Some cracked open completely. The fact that our company moved around so much made things worse. I found that if a Marine could stay in the same foxhole night after night, it became a kind of home. He would dig it deep and safe, line it with palm branches, fashion a small shelf for his canteen and a picture of his girlfriend or family. Overhead he might make a canopy of palm branches to keep off the sun. This familiarity kept him stable.

In any case, three of our men became psychotic. In the middle of a dark night on Bloody Ridge, I heard terrible screams from one of our foxholes. I rushed over. The man was writhing around, screaming, "They're going to get me. They're going to get me!" We gave him a shot of morphine and shipped him back.

A few days later, when we were marching up to the Matanikau for our first combat there, one of my men did not show up at the first checkpoint. He had been at the rear of the line, and so the corporal did not miss him. He was small, barely seventeen, and young for his age. He had to run to keep up with us. In the last few days, his narrow face had become grim looking. After being missing for two days, he came back to our area like a little shamefaced puppy, miserable that he had deserted, the worst crime a Marine can commit. I saw him, and my heart went out to him. The other men were looking at me, wondering what I would do. I wanted to take him in my arms and comfort him. Instead, I yelled at him and called him a dirty yellow bastard and put him on report to the captain. I can still see his face as he heard my words. I had to do that to prevent the other men from following his example when the going got even tougher.

A machine-gun section from the weapons company—the one John Hersey wrote about in *Into the Valley*—was attached to us when we were in our defense position. I found the sergeant one day, his back to a coconut tree, with a grenade in his hand and a wild look in his eyes. He was a Russian and known to be moody. A couple of my men were standing nearby, looking at him in a frightened way. As I approached, he said, "If any of you bastards come near me, I will let this grenade go. The pin is pulled out. If anyone reports me to Company, I'll blow the shit out of him." I stood staring at him for a long, long time. I did not know what to do. I froze, then gradually slipped away when he was not looking. I called the company command post. They sent two corpsmen, who quieted him down and led him off.

Toward the end I wondered how long I could hold out myself, and I sometimes felt that I was slipping inexorably to the edge of sanity. I kept praying to the lines of "A Mighty Fortress Is Our God." In another prayer, I pictured the bloody cross rearing up in the midst of battle; I would reach for it with both hands and hang on as the earth swayed and crumpled beneath me. The Cross seemed to belong in the center of all the harm, cruelty, and blood, in the misdst of men sacrificing their lives, a symbol of loving sacrifice as well as a symbol of human cruelty. My faith helped keep me together—and so did an ugly emotion, revenge. I wanted to kill "every yellow bastard" I could find because the Japs had killed George and my own men. Somehow, the prayer and the obscene feelings of revenge did not conflict in the crazy emotions of war.

About a month after our first battle at the Mataniko, I was sitting on a high, grassy ridge looking across the beautiful blue of the bay. It was peaceful, yet I was sad. The bay had been christened "Iron-

Bottom Sound," so many ships had been sunk beneath its waters. I had heard that Scotty McClennan and Jerry Knapp, my two Yale classmates, had been shot down. I had just taken the afternoon off a few days before to go for a swim with Scotty on Guadalcanal's white beach. I asked him how long his unit would be on the island. He said, in a matter-of-fact voice, "Till they shoot us all down." Jerry, a torpedo bomber pilot, had paid me a visit at our defense line in the jungle. Just a year before, we were together in the Adirondacks. John "Flash" Flaherty, my Yale jail mate, whose platoon happened to be next to mine, joined us. We were jealous of Jerry, he was to go home in a couple of days, but on his last mission, trying to sink a Japanese transport, he went down, too.

I looked to the right at Henderson Field: no airplanes. It had been bombed out of commission. Japanese warships cruised up and down the bay, firing at our positions at will. Far down the coast to the west, enemy troopships were unloading unmolested. Bombers were making their daily high-altitude run overhead, no longer threatened by our fighters. Suddenly, a small fighter came flying low across the top of the jungle toward us. We hit the deck and looked up to see large red circles on its wings.

That night it rained. In the jungle it was so dark we could not tell if our eyes were open or shut. We had strung a rope to guide us along the defense line. I held on to it as I stumbled from foxhole to foxhole inspecting our troops. Many men were shaking with fever from malaria. Morale was lower than low. Despair had set in. I was so exhausted I kept falling asleep on watch. A buzzing in my ears (from the quinine we took to ward off malaria) made it hard to understand the voices on the field telephone. Since the battle on the Matanikau, I had had an infection in my hand where a bullet had grazed it. In the tropics, the slightest scratch can become infected quickly and seriously. After one of those terrible dark nights in the jungle, I went to the aid station at battalion headquarters to have my hand attended to. Major Lew Walt, our battalion commander, saw me and asked, "Moore, what would you think if we were asked to go on the offensive?"

"Offense? No way. Sir, the men can hardly walk. We simply can't ask any more of them."

That day I tried to find out who was on the ragged edge. I would take a man aside if he seemed depressed, put my hand on his shoulder, look into his eyes, and ask, "How's it going with you?" Sometimes a word of encouragement was enough, a sign that I knew he was having a rough time. I asked that one or two be relieved for a few days.

Later that morning, the company officers were called back to the battalion headquarters. "Men, we have been ordered to launch an attack up past the Matanikau to push the enemy back beyond artillery range of the airfield," Major Walt told us. "There is one officer here who says we can't do it. I trust none of the rest of you feel as he does." Walt looked me in the eye as he spoke. I wanted to fade from sight.

That night we were shelled by 16-inch guns from a Japanese warship. This was more terrifying than bombing, because the shells went screaming overhead sounding like an elevated railway. (As a matter of fact, some of the enemy's ammunition came from the New York Sixth Avenue el, which had been sold as scrap to the Japanese.) Under the trees it was as light as day. Searchlights or flares from the warships lit up the night and the scurrying forms of Marines running to their foxholes. I did not even bother to get in my foxhole I was so tired. During lulls in the shelling, I could hear guys groaning and vomiting.

Of course, we did go on the attack the next day. The company was down to 50 out of the 150 we'd started with. At four o'clock in the morning, muster was taken, and our battalion took up positions across the river but about a mile inland. Over the next day we fought our way down to the beach with little resistance and cut off the enemy retreat, trapping them at the mouth of the river. All day, under a violently hot sun, we held the position, keeping Japanese reinforcements at bay with artillery fire, which I directed. Our shell would whoosh overhead; I would jump out of my foxhole, watch it explode, and duck back just as a fieldpiece we were trying to knock out was fired at the spot where I had stood.

We stayed in that position for several hours. We had no water, and our thirst became so unbearable that we drank from the slimy puddle that had collected in an old shell hole. I had somehow left my cigarettes in a place exposed to enemy fire. I craved a cigarette so much that I ran out to grab the pack at the risk of my life. Danger had become meaningless.

That night we pulled back from the shore to safer positions with the intention of fully securing the beachhead the next day. At dawn, on November 3, 1942, we advanced again toward the beach. The Japanese had occupied our former position during the night. Now the firing began in earnest. We advanced as a line of skirmishers, sometimes dashing from the cover of a log or a bush to the next cover, sometimes crawling ahead on our bellies. The enemy began to fire more frequently. We procured a 37 mm field gun armed with grapeshot. The battle became more and more violent. We were completely pinned down. I looked to my left and saw that two of my men had been killed. Sergeant George Ahoyt passed the word we had lost four more from a machine gun that was to our right, just in front of me. I located it, pulled the pin out of a grenade, stood up on my knees, and threw it. At that moment, I felt a piercing, burning stab of pain going into my chest on the left side. I fell to the ground and realized I had been hit. The air was blubbering in and out of a hole in my lung. I knew I was out of action. I called to Ahoyt to take over, then collapsed. I thought I was dying. I did not know what to think. I remember reading that your whole life passes before your eyes at such a time. Mine didn't. I thought, What a weird place for a person like me to die. Oh, I remembered, I should pray. "Father, into your hands I commend my spirit," I whispered without much conviction, and then fainted.

In a few moments, a most courageous corpsman crawled up, gave me some morphine, and before long I was dragged back to a stretcher and started toward the regimental headquarters aid station. I regained consciousness and heard a familiar voice. It was the regimental chaplain, Father Reardon, a Roman Catholic with whom I used to have long teasing discussions about whether we Anglicans were real Catholics or not. "So, Paul, how are you doing? Is there anything I can do for you?"

"Well, you'd better give me absolution, just in case."

"I already have, you darned Protestant." He leaned over me, put his warm hand on my head, and gave me a blessing. That felt very good: God's love and comfort channeled through the warm, strong hand of a priest who was also a friend.

I finally knew what it was like to die. Death had indeed lost her sting. Was it really that easy to die, or did it seem so because death had become so familiar? I never thought about whether I would go to heaven, come to Judgment, or simply fade away. In fact, it was not a "spiritual" experience at all. Would it have been different if I had died?

COMING HOME

I SPENT my last night on the island in a deep dugout at the division aid station. Men were stacked four or five deep on makeshift bunks around the dirt walls. The groans, screams, and sobs of the wounded filled the hot, stinking darkness. After two days, we flew out. The flight was painful for me because we had to fly very high to avoid the Japanese planes; I was wheezing away on one lung. We were delivered to a naval hospital of Quonset huts in the New Hebrides. Every night, I had terrible nightmares in which the Japanese would set up a field gun at the foot of my bed and start firing away. I awoke screaming.

A hospital ship arrived, the *Solace*, rumored to have clean sheets, ice cream, and nurses aboard. It was November 15, 1942, my twenty-third birthday. What a present! We could even see this beautiful white ship from our makeshift ward. The patients were carried out, one by one, until I was the only one left. The ward was totally silent. As I watched, the *Solace* sailed away. I never found out why I was left there another two weeks, until the *Solace* finally returned. This time, they hoisted me aboard by a derrick, which lifted my stretcher, and we sailed to Auckland, New Zealand. On Christmas, some New Zealand ladies sang us Christmas carols, and they showed us Bing Crosby in *Holiday Inn* singing "A White Christmas." I cried a little. After a few weeks, we sailed home to San Francisco on a troopship with special medical facilities. Mother came out to see me, and we went home together on the train. My father met us at Grand Central Station with a wheelchair and three redcaps. We went back to Granny's house for a splendid breakfast of scrambled eggs, bacon, sausages, and waffles, served, of course, by the inimitable Higgs.

I reported to the hospital at the Brooklyn Navy Yard. The young doctor, Dr. Childs, who examined me there, looked at my chart with a puzzled expression. "Is your grandmother Mrs. William H. Moore?"

"Yes, she is."

"My uncle, Dr. Paterson, took care of her. I took care of her butler."

Like all the doctors I had seen, Dr. Childs was surprised when he examined the entry and exit wounds left by the bullet. "Your heart must have been on the in beat when the bullet went by," he said. "On the way out, it missed your spine by two inches. You shouldn't be here!"

Again I wondered whether my living on borrowed time meant the Lord had something special for me to do with my life. I am not sure that is good theology, but the idea persisted and persisted.

About three weeks after I came home, I was sitting in our library telling my father about some of my experiences. All of a sudden, I felt a strange lump coming up from my feet, through my legs, through my stomach, and then into my head, where it burst into uncontrollable sobs. I sobbed and sobbed and sobbed for what seemed like half an hour. All the poison and all the grief and all the horror and all the dying that I had kept at bay for those long weeks came pouring out. These attacks of weeping came upon me every week or so, when with friends or drinking at a bar. I could not bear to go to a war movie. After a while, they came only every month or so. Once, years later, at supper with my family, when I was telling them about the war, one of my children made an inappropriate remark, and I broke down and ran upstairs, where I sobbed away what was left of the trauma.

The human psyche protects itself by allowing a person to experience only as much shock as he or she can handle. The reaction is so violent—a rape of the human spirit that it takes years to work out. My psychic wound is still there. It will never go away. And I thought I had become used to death.

I did not return to duty until the following summer. The sick leave was a strange time. I loved being home but could not stand it for more than a few days at a stretch. I felt claustrophobic when immersed in the love and the memories of childhood. When I needed to escape, I went to New York, stayed at my family's apartment, and every night went out with whomever was home on leave and with the girls (as we used to call them) who were around. I was drinking heavily, and from time to time the sobbing would recur. When I saw a Marine in uniform, even though he was a perfect stranger, I would go over and talk with him, feeling closer to this stranger than to my own family. This was the spring of 1943, and the casualties were beginning to mount. Almost every week Mother would come into my room as I woke up to tell me that one of my friends had been killed: Bob Fowler, sunk off Guadalcanal; Bob Cox, killed in the desert of Africa; Peter Hazard, who had guided us around Key West; Prentice Willetts, with whom I shared a sled at St. Paul's School; Billy MacKenzie, downed in a bombing mission over Germany; John Bonsall, executed as an Allied spy. And so it went, week after week.

My faith remained strong. I went to Holy Communion the first Sunday I was home. My father left me a note under the door, he who never went to church, saying he knew how much it would mean to me and wishing he could be with me.

Word came that I had been awarded the Silver Star for the Matanikau River battle and the Navy Cross for the battle in which I was wounded. George Mead and I used to look covetously at pictures of the medals and wonder if we would ever be decorated. Poor George received the Navy Cross as well, posthumously. I had become a "hero." But why? Those battles simply happened. We did what we were ordered to do, not wondering whether we were brave enough. Other men did brave things and were not decorated. And now I was being told I had been very courageous. Twice within a month, the Marines at the Brooklyn Navy Yard lined up in formation, and the colonel in charge pinned a medal on my chest, while my mother and father looked on. At the time there were very few returned wounded veterans, and I was much in demand for speeches. I addressed club dinners. I spoke at St. Paul's. I was even carted around to munitions factories, where I would tell thousands of workers gathered at their noon lunch hour to keep up the good work. At the Picatinny Arsenal,

I held up one of the hand grenades manufactured there and said, "With a grenade just like this, I knocked out a Japanese machine-gun nest." Cheers from the workers! I drank deeply of the adulation and became arrogant and offensive. Father Truman Heminway, a priest I had been close to, had the courage to write and tell me that I was not handling myself well. He was right.

One night shortly after my return, I took Jenny McKean out for dinner and dancing. About one o'clock, at a nightclub in Greenwich Village, the Russian Kretchma, we sat in candlelight amid the strains of gypsy music. Our hands touched as I lit her cigarette, and we fell in love. Jenny was tall and slim; her hair long, dark, and luxurious; her blue eyes large under long brown lashes. She had a whimsical humor and was Phi Beta Kappa at Barnard. Her parents and mine knew one another, and our grandmothers were great friends. We had spent a hilarious summer in the same group just before the war but had not fallen in love.

That spring we were inseparable. I visited her at her parents' place near my grandmother's in Prides Crossing; we rode bicycles and had picnics on the beach. We grew closer and closer until the tension became intolerable. I felt that we had to get married or split up, for in those days living together without being married was unacceptable. As a result, I took an assignment at the University of Washington in Seattle, training officer candidates who were going to college there in what was known as the V-12 program.

Seattle was glorious: my work was easy and great fun, and I was welcomed into the homes of many Seattleites. I managed to have three members of my Guadalcanal platoon assigned to my staff—Gene Asche, Carl Trieglaff, and Art Beres, whose face had been beautifully repaired. There were days of tennis and swimming, house parties on Mount Rainier, golf at the Highlands golf club, and many carefree beer busts. I even coached the Washington crew for a season, much to the consternation of my crew coach from Yale, whom I ran into one day on campus.

I wrote Jenny almost every day, and she came for an unsuccessful and frustrating week's visit in the winter, when there was nothing to do—I had lost my carefully hoarded gasoline-rationing stamps. Our long-distance romance went up and down. But on the way east on the plane, I decided that I would propose to her. A few nights later, at Fefe's Monte Carlo on the Upper East Side, after everyone else had gone home, I asked her to marry me. She said, "I don't believe you. You must be drunk. If you really mean it, call me in the morning."

The next morning, Mother came into my room and woke me up to tell me that my sister's husband, Jack Denison, had died from pneumonia in Africa. Fanny was in New York, and it was decided that I would go in to tell her. I had her paged at a restaurant, and she came back to the apartment. From the look on my face she knew at once what had happened. We fell into each other's arms and cried. She rushed out to the country to be with her sons. I will never forget seeing her sitting on the couch with her arms around those two little blond boys, telling them that they would never see their father again. (Jock Denison, the older of the two boys, told me recently that he had dreamed of his father's death the night before.)

I was so shocked that I forgot to call Jenny! In any case, we worked it all out, became engaged, and planned to have the wedding two weeks later.

I had been assigned to command and staff school in Quantico, Virginia, for three months. I asked the commanding officer if I could take off the half day's training on Saturday. He asked if it was an emergency. I said yes, that I was getting married. He denied my request, saying a wedding was *not* an emergency.

We were married in New York on Sunday, November 26, 1944, in a beautiful Nuptial Mass at the Church of the Resurrection on East Seventy-fourth Street. After the reception, we went to the airport and boarded the plane, trying to look like an old married couple. I took off my cap, and rice spilled all over the aisle. Cheers from the passengers, congratulations from the pilot! We spent our wedding night at a hotel in Fredericksburg, and I reported for duty at seven-thirty Monday morning, after a seventeen-hour honeymoon!

We stayed in a little house that had been the slave quarters of George Washington's brother's plantation in Fredericksburg, Virginia. We called him the uncle of our country. I carried Jenny across the threshold, upstairs, and dropped her on the bed, which broke. We were most embarrassed to admit to our landlady that we had broken the marriage bed. This was not the only problem: the house was freezing, and the only heat was from a small woodstove, the wood for which, damp oak, I had to chop.

When the school was over, I was given orders to report to the Third Marine Division in Guam. We flew to San Francisco, where we had only twenty-four hours to say goodbye and to celebrate the fact that Jenny was pregnant. We danced at the Top of the Mark, and the next morning, off I flew from the San Francisco harbor in an enormous seaplane.

As I look back on it, we were foolish to get married and conceive our first child just before I was due to go overseas again. But we had a romantic notion that if I were killed at least I would have left behind a child. That a resentment against an absentee father might build up in Jenny's psyche never entered our minds. When I was overseas, she sent me a picture of herself, standing on the sidewalk in New York, very pregnant. I thought it was great, even though it was August 1945, we were scheduled to invade Japan, and the odds of returning for the birth were not in my favor.

I wound up as a company commander with the Third Marine Division on Guam. Rumors had begun to spread about a strange new bomb that had been dropped on Japan. We thought it was scuttlebutt but hoped it was true. In any case, we broke camp and were told we would board troopships in a day or two. Then one night, we heard the distant firing of rifles and machine guns. The island was secure, no maneuvers had been planned. Had the Japs landed to counterattack? Unlikely. We were puzzled. The firing came closer and closer as each unit took it up. When the battalion next to ours began to fire, we heard shouting and cheering and the great words, "The war is over! The war is over!" We feared it was a false armistice, but there were those rumors that the strange bomb had been dropped on Japan a few days before. Maybe they were true.

They were true. We gathered at the officers' club. Lieutenant Colonel Meyerhoff, the battalion commander, tried to persuade me to stay in the Marines. I was not drunk enough to say yes.

.   .   .

One night on the long voyage home from Guam, we were sitting around in a crowded cabin when a sailor burst in: "Cable for Captain Moore!" Sudden silence, then apprehension. You just did not get cables on troopships. I wondered who had died. My hands trembled as the cable was given to me. My eyes filled with tears. Someone asked, "What happened? Is it okay?"

"My God, I'm a father!"

Someone ran out of the cabin and miraculously came back in a couple of minutes with a bottle of champagne. We drank the health of Honor Moore, born October 28, 1945. The world was opening up perfectly. I could not stand the delay of the stay in San Diego, nor the interminable train ride home. I sent telegrams to Jenny from every station: CAN YOU BELIEVE IT STOP STILL IN TEXAS STOP I CAN'T WAIT.

I arrived at our Manhattan apartment about three days after Jenny returned from the hospital. I was shaking as I rode up in the elevator. The door opened, and there she was, thin, in a white satin nightgown, long, dark hair flowing to her shoulders. A nurse hovered behind her. We embraced awkwardly, then walked arm in arm into the nursery. There was Honor, pink and healthy with a small mop of dark hair and squinty eyes. I thought I should feel something enormous, but I did not feel anything much.

The apartment was furnished attractively, with our wedding pres-ents placed here and there; but being newly painted and very neat, it did not seem like home.

The following night we had a terrible fight. Jenny became furious at me over nothing. I was hurt, shocked. I could not believe that this was happening to me on my second day back. Was this my wife, the woman I loved, the one I had dreamed of coming home to? I look back and see how predictable it was. I had been away while she was pregnant. She felt postpartum depression. We could not make love yet. I did not appreciate the baby or know how to act with her. I had been too self-centered to thank Jenny for all she had done.

By the time I returned from overseas, I had decided to go to seminary and become a priest. Other possibilities, such as teaching, did not feel right. This major decision had been slowly growing on me since my conversion experience at St. Paul's. The roots lay deep within me. I did not choose a priestly vocation as a means of helping others, nor out of a need to have a respectable life. I knew that my father was against it and that it would surprise all but my closest friends. In those days, people from my background rarely chose the ministry. Dad called our local minister "that little fellow at the church" and seemed to rank him just a notch or two above the local tradespeople.

The real reason for my choice was a longing to stand at the altar and celebrate the Eucharist. I felt that that was where I belonged and that whatever sacrifice might be involved could be an offering to my Lord. And lurking somewhere was the feeling that my surviving the war meant I should do something special with my life.

Beneath these conscious reasons, unconscious dynamics were pulling me inexorably toward a closer relationship with God. These pressures may have grown out of childhood, out of my feelings about my parents. Did I want more intimacy with a father? Possibly. Was the Church somehow a mother to me? Perhaps. In any case, when I returned from overseas, my mind was firmly made up.

When I announced my decision to my father, he was visibly upset. "But why didn't you talk it over with me?" he asked. I replied that the last time I mentioned it he had said he did not wish to discuss it ever again, that I should learn to make a living and then, if I still was interested in the ministry, I could take it up as a hobby. I think he presumed that I had given up the idea. However, he soon accepted my going into the ministry, and part of him, I believe, was proud of me. Mother, of course, thought it was lovely. She always backed her children's decisions.

The dean of the General Theological Seminary did not want anyone to enter in midterm, so I pursued a course of study at Columbia toward a master's in history while Jenny completed her last semester at Barnard.

I went to Yale for a reunion. Naturally, everyone, right after saying hello with great gusto, would ask what you were going to do. When I replied that I was going to seminary to be a priest, one friend put his hand on my shoulder and said, "Gee, Paul, I didn't know you had that hard a time in the war!"

Many of us felt at sea those first few months. Even if we had definite plans, the world we were entering did not seem real. If I saw a Marine at a bar, I still would leave my friends, rush over, and shoot the breeze. It was like meeting another American when traveling in the Gobi Desert.

Gradually, we made the transition. I cried from time to time, especially if I had had a few drinks. Jenny and I saw many old friends around town. There were weekends in the country and cruises on *Baruna*, a beautiful yawl belonging to Walter Taylor's father. We all partied a lot, as if we were still in college. We were in our twenties; we had not learned how grownups act.

TRAINING FOR THE PRIESTHOOD

O N Ninth Avenue, between Twentieth and Twenty-first Streets, stood the brick facade of the General Theological Seminary. When you entered the forbidding doors, you came upon a small enclosed campus with tall trees and grass so green it seemed to have come from a cathedral close in England. The faculty and students swept along the old flagstone walks in academic gowns. The great red-brick Gothic chapel, dominating the scene, rang its bells for Evensong. The place glowed with Anglican beauty in the late afternoon, when sounds of chanting came forth from the chapel and the roar of the city was muted beyond the walls. Jenny and I rented an apartment on West Twenty-first Street, across from the seminary close.

What happened to me at seminary laid the foundation, intellectual and spiritual, for the long years ahead. During the war, I had been exposed to suffering, brutality, danger, and death. I had fallen in love, married, had a baby, but I did not know the underpinnings of the intense personal faith that had carried me through so much.

I arrived at seminary as something of an intellectual snob. What could a small denominational seminary teach someone who had gone to Yale, who had sat at the feet of the great Chauncey Brewster Tinker, who had taken all the course requirements for a master's in modern history at Columbia and heard lectures by Jacques Barzun? I went to seminary because there was no other way to become a priest, but I really did not think I would learn much at that small, obscure school. Well, this presumptuous, rich, "cultured" Marine hero was overwhelmed by the intellectual impact of the place.

Dean Hughell Fosbroke's presence dominated the seminary; he was a tall, gaunt, slightly stooped man, who looked like an English earl played by Edward Everett Horton. He would peer at you through thick, horn-rimmed spectacles. On the first day, I was showing Jenny the close and saw the dean looming toward us. "Good morning, sir," I said. "This is my wife, Jenny."

He scowled, shook his head, and said, "Oh, Mrs. Moore. At the General Seminary we do not like women, but we will, I am sure, absorb you. Good day." In those days, only six of the students were married, and seminarians were not allowed to marry while in course.

We had engaged a nanny for Honor and were surprised to find that the faculty wives at the seminary soon were abuzz at our lifestyle. This was simply not the way we were expected to live. Indeed, the seminary was full of surprises. One young man in his academic gown swept by some mothers and their baby carriages, peeked into Honor's carriage, and exclaimed, "Oh, is that a baby?"

Of all the impressive teachers I had at seminary, Dean Fosbroke was the most memorable. In class, he was like an Old Testament prophet. He first took us to the ancient desert, where nomad tribes moved from place to place through blistering heat, sandstorms, earthquakes, and volcanoes. He brought us face-to-face with their warrior God, Yahweh, the Lord of Hosts, of whom the psalmist said: "He looks on the earth and it trembles: he touches the hills and they smoke." As he carried us along with his strong, deep voice and an occasional snort to emphasize a point, he seemed to become Yahweh. And he led us, as God had led the children of Israel, down the years. We accompanied Abraham on his mission to found a new people. We stood with Moses, trembling, before the burning bush, sensing the numinous presence of the god of Abraham, Isaac, and Jacob, in his confrontation with the holy, the total otherness of God. We marched dry-shod through the Red Sea and listened to the Ten Commandments read to a rebellious people from the tablets of stone.

As the weeks went by, we saw this primitive god transformed in the minds of his people from a being of raw power to a god of righteousness and love. We underwent, with the Israelites, bitter and traumatic events, reflected upon them through the prophets, and developed an ever-deepening, more sophisticated understanding of God. But the dean never let us forget the primitive Yahweh: "It is not easy to cuddle up to a volcano," he would say. He could not stand the sweet, blond Jesus with a fleecy lamb under his arm as an image of God. "Lambs are not clean," he snorted.

No course I ever had before or since has made such an impression. There had been the seminar on historiography at Yale. But the historiography I was encountering now gave me a way to bring history into the transcendent dimension; we were learning "holy history." Not only did events shape a people's comprehension of God, the historical process also developed in them a sense of who they were. Thus a doctrine of humanity grew out of their interaction with God: they were men and women made in the image of God, free to choose, to love, to hate, to develop into the fullness of humanity, yet fallen, twisted, distorted by their breaking away from God's love through centuries of sin. I had seen the glory of human beings in the heroism of war, and I had seen their depravity—the image of God in self-sacrifice, the laying down of a life for a comrade, and the rot of sin in the needless sadism and mindless, unfeeling slaughter of battle. With the study of the Old Testament, everything began to fall into place intellectually. I could see how my understanding of God and of myself unfolded from my own experiences. I had been arrogant, proud, and cruel in the Marines. I had found myself fragile and on the edge of an emotional breakdown. I had been insensitive to the prostitute in Key West. I had killed a Japanese laborer in cold blood on a grassy hill in Guadalcanal. And yet God did not forsake me and apparently was able to use me despite, or perhaps because of, my sinfulness.

Thus did this wonder-filled process of biblical revelation touch the deepest part of me. I came to understand the Bible not as an ancient book full of wise sayings but as a record of the dynamic, rough-and-tumble revelation of God to his people—in different ways, over thousands of years. The process continues, the uncovering of the mystery of being.

Dr. Marshall Boyer Stewart taught dogmatics. He was a quiet, gentle man with a pink, shining face and a cap of snow-white hair. In the spring, you could see him leaning over to smell the flowers along the borders. He lectured in a slight Southern accent, his blue eyes twinkling. From him we learned how Anglicans go about determining doctrine. As he traced the historic development of such teachings as the Incarnation, the presence of God in Christ, he would say, "Well, you can't quite say that he was just a good and saintly man, and you can't say he was God covered by a human body—it's somewhere in between." This summarized neatly four centuries of bitter theological debate in the early Church, culminating in the definitive statement of the Council of Chalcedon in 451 A.D.: "Jesus Christ at once complete in Godhead and complete in manhood, truly God and truly Man." He talked of faith: "You know you can't believe in God very much on a cold Monday morning."

One day, I picked up *The New York Times* and was shocked to read that the Bishop of Birmingham, England, did not believe in the bodily Resurrection of Jesus. I gathered some of my classmates, and we rushed to see Dr. Stewart. "Dr. Stewart, Dr. Stewart, what are we going to do? It says here that the Bishop of Birmingham does not believe in the Resurrection!"

He put his face in his hands for a moment and then, with a broad smile, said, "Well, someday the Bishop of Birmingham is going to die, and probably the next Bishop of Birmingham will believe in the Resurrection." We returned to our rooms, much relieved. Once, years later, after I had told this story at a parish coffee hour, a woman with a clipped English accent came up to me and said, "My Lord, I happen to be the daughter of the Bishop of Birmingham." I groaned and turned red with embarrassment. She went on, "Not the bishop of whom you were speaking, but his successor. You know, my father did not believe in the bodily Resurrection of Jesus, either!" We chatted further and determined that the present bishop did believe in the Resurrection. Thus do Anglicans deal with heresy.

Two splendid Anglican principles underlie this story. We believe that the mainstream of the Church flows strong and deep and is nourished week by week, year by year, through the liturgy, the scripture, and the ministry of love. The Latin phrase used by the early fathers, *lex orandi, lex credendi*, lies at the heart of Anglicanism; it means that the principles of belief grow out of the experience of prayer. Thus the prayer book is at the heart of Anglican doctrine. An occasional straying from the main line is not to be silenced, censored, forbidden; rather, it is discussed, and through that discussion a deeper insight into the truth will emerge. As Gamaliel said in the Book of Acts, "If this plan or this undertaking is of men, it will fail; but if it is of God, you will not be able to overthrow them. You might even be found opposing God!" (Acts 5:38–39). False teachings will wither away if they are not from God. The other principle is that great mysteries, such as the Resurrection, can be understood in several ways. The original descriptions of New Testament events were related by word of mouth. They were described by people of a different age and a different culture from ours, people who had a different understanding of the physical world than we do. Furthermore, the Gospel stories themselves are at variance. However, beneath these rather primitive and inconsistent accounts of the Resurrection of Jesus, lies the foundation of the Christian faith. Jesus acted out in his life, death, and risen presence the great cosmic rhythm of dying and rising: the flow of winter into spring, the healing following illness, the emergence of forgiveness after a quarrel, the deeper understanding of the link between love and suffering after the death of one you love, and, finally, the recurring hope of some kind of life continuing after death itself. This principle lies at the heart of the sacrament of baptism, by which one is made a Christian, dying to one's old life with Christ in his death and rising with him into the new life of a Christian. This principle also lies at the heart of the Eucharist, whereby the Christian is renewed again and again by offering his or her broken life on the altar and receiving that offering back as the presence of the risen Christ in the bread and wine. If you believe this in your very bones, it is possible to live through the most terrible human experiences with hope. Through this comprehension of the rhythm of life, you realize how the deepest insights into reality and the most profound strengthening of faith come out of times of sorrow and suffering; how love and pain, death and life are part of one reality. You do not understand much about God when life is floating along happily. In listening to Dr. Stewart, we learned to use our reason and common sense while maintaining a sense of the mystery of God.

Dr. Powell Dawley, who taught Church history, had the manner of an Oxford don; he was a large man who strode down the close like a ship in full sail and who seemed continually bemused by the antics of the Church over the years. His stories, vignettes, and images made the dusty tomes we read spring to life. We could see Anthony of Egypt writhing through his nightmares in the hot desert, we could hear the belly laugh of Henry VIII. We saw crowds of poor people listening with wonder to the preaching of John Wesley on a smoky hillside hard by a factory that had brought to them the misery of the Industrial Revolution. We learned little by little how God works through all kinds of people to shape the history of the Church and the world.

The New Testament was taught by Dr. Burton Scott Easton, a small, spry, neat, stiff-backed, white-haired man with a round face and pince-nez glasses. He lectured without notes, his hands folded carefully before him on the desk. To emphasize a point, he would bounce once or twice on his small posterior until his glasses wiggled and almost fell off. He was dry, a strict scholar who had no use for romantic or faddish notions. For instance, his scholarly analysis of *kairos*, the fullness of time, which described why Christ appeared at a particular moment in history, was a masterpiece: the Jews had completed their understanding of the nature of God and humanity; the Roman Empire provided the order, easy communication, common language, and transportation of the Pax Romana; the Greco-Roman culture had grown tired of the gods of mythology and was floundering around from exotic sect to exotic sect. The world was ready for Christ. Christianity brought the discipline and power of transcendent monotheism together with the cultic intimacy of the Eucharist.

And so it was, in that obscure, small enclosure in the middle of New York, that my mind was broken open to the intellectual impact of the Christian faith in the Anglican tradition. The genius of Anglicanism is its blend of faith and reason and its openness to a wide variety of theologies. Sometimes this openness blunts its impact. For those who need an emotional religion, Pentecostalism is more appealing. For those who need an authoritative religion, Roman Catholicism or Fundamentalism is more attractive. Anglicanism, we like to think, appeals to those who do not park their minds on the doorstep of the church, those who wish the same personal freedom in their faith as they insist on in their government. The gift of freedom of the mind is God given and should never be sacrificed in the name of God. This intellectual freedom within the faith makes demands on the individual and requires the courage to live with uncertainties, mystery, and continual exploration of one's belief.

The years following the war were a time of great change in theological thinking. The teachings of Marx and Freud caught the imagination of the postwar intellectual world and challenged Christian thought. Paul Tillich was the theologian of the moment. He set forth a theology based on God as the ground of being, which dug beneath both traditional theology and contemporary thought. By putting aside the metaphysical structures of St. Thomas Aquinas, on the one hand, and of John Calvin, on the other, he avoided some of the conflict between contemporary thinking and Christian theology. His systematics were obscure, but his sermons made his then-radical theology available to non-scholars, as in his best-known collection, *The Shaking of the Foundations*. I took a course with him at Union Theological Seminary and was disappointed: it was a course on Luther, in which Dr. Tillich let little of his own thinking intrude. But at least I came to know the great man.

Reinhold Niebuhr, also at Union Theological Seminary, was another religious leader. Jenny had taken a course with Mrs. Ursula Niebuhr at Barnard, which led to our spending many a fascinating evening with the Niebuhrs and their young friends discussing the affairs of the world. Reinhold Niebuhr's participation in political matters gave stature to the Church as a critical, prophetic force in the debate of national and international issues. I was delighted that a theologian was being consulted by congressmen, the President, and the Secretary of State, but I felt Niebuhr became too pragmatic in his views, too influenced by realpolitik. Thus, to some extent, he bolstered the thinking of men like John Foster Dulles that later became the ideology of the cold war.

Each seminarian was encouraged to take a summer of clinical training in order to become familiar with clinical psychology and the workings of hospitals. I was accepted at Greystone, an old New Jersey state hospital in Morris Plains. It was near my family's place in Morristown, and we decided to stay there so that Jenny could be taken care of while in the last month of pregnancy with our second child. Once more, we lived in luxury at home, but during the day I entered a terrifying world.

I had grown up with jokes about Greystone: if someone was eccentric, the quip would be, "Send him to Greystone." I had never seen the inside of the place and drove onto the grounds with trepidation. The main building, built in 1876, is a massive, overpowering hulk of gray stone. The grounds were neat, the institutional planting immaculate. A few patients could be seen sitting quietly on benches or aimlessly wandering around the lawn. This building contained the incurables, some of whom had been there for many years. When I first entered one of its back wards I felt I was diving into Dante's Inferno. The guard rattled his immense cluster of large keys and opened a massive steel door. I stepped in; the smell was overpowering, a repulsive mix of urine, sweat, bowel movements, and disinfectant. On the benches, set against the wall of a huge, high-ceilinged gray room, sat the patients in their dirty white gowns. Some were hunched over with their heads in their hands, immobile, deeply depressed; others looked out with unseeing eyes dazed from medication. Manics rushed up and down the corridors leading off this common room. A catatonic stood, seemingly paralyzed, leg back, about to kick an imaginary ball. Strangest of all were the hebephrenics, smiling away, murmuring phrases like "Thank you, Jesus. Thank you, Jesus." Locked in padded cells were the dangerous paranoids, some stark naked, having ripped off their clothes, others shrieking obscenities at whoever passed by.

We, however, worked with patients in another building who had been recently admitted, for whom some hope of cure remained, although hanging over them was the prospect of spending the rest of their lives in a back ward. We were assigned five cases, each with a different diagnosis, such as dementia praecox, as schizophrenia was then called, of various kinds (catatonic, hebephrenic, mixed); alcoholism; menopausal neurosis; manic depression. We studied their case histories and then entered the ward with no introduction to begin our first session. We made verbatim copies of the interviews and went over them with our supervisor. At the end of the summer, we submitted case histories of each patient.

We also were given lectures on psychiatry, attended diagnostic and discharge sessions, and watched shock treatments. We even witnessed an autopsy: when I saw a knife cut silently through the dead gray flesh, I almost fainted.

I remember my first interview. The nurse let me in and pointed out my assigned patient, whose name was Kenneth. He was sitting on a bench by himself, a nice-looking man in his early twenties, with blue eyes, light-brown wavy hair, and a fair, sunburned complexion. He reminded me of one of my Marines. His diagnosis was dementia praecox. I sat down next to him. He did not turn. "Hi, Ken. My name is Paul. I work here as a student and wanted to get to know you." No response. "Nice to see you." I put out my hand. It stayed there for a while. I looked at it and put it down.

"How long have you been here?"

"Long," he mumbled.

"Where are you from?"

"Long."

"Is it bad here?"

"Bad, real bad."

Such desultory half conversations continued, day after day, until I began to enter the strange world in which he lived. At home, he had kept tropical fish and talked endlessly about guppies and Siamese fighting fish. I learned that the best way to draw him out was to repeat the last word he had said. The process was like unsnarling a fishing line little by little, following a strand into the midst of the snarl as far as you could. In the process we became friends; he would smile when he saw me coming.

We students discussed our cases with one another and in sessions with our supervisor, glibly using terms we had recently learned ("psychotic break," "psychoneurosis mixed," "paranoid schiz"), but rarely did we delve into the way in which immersion in mental illness threatened the carefully structured academic theology within which we spoke of souls and free will. At seminary, we had not been told of the pressure on the free will by the so-called unconscious. If temptation came to us, we were supposed to be able to resist sinning; but here we were faced with men and women who seemed to have little or no control over their actions.

We were taught Freud's theories in our seminars. The doctors, by and large, were Freudians; Freud did not believe in God and taught that human actions were psychologically determined by the unconscious. Methodists believed that emotional religious experience was at the heart of our knowledge of God; for them to learn that such emotions could not always be trusted was alarming, to say the least. For young men and women brought up in the puritan atmosphere of the Methodist or Baptist tradition, Freud's teaching about sexuality also was threatening. We respected the doctors and yet could not accept the intellectual, seemingly atheistic hypotheses of their work. Some unsophisticated young Methodist students were so shaken that they left the ministry as a result of the program.

My Anglican theology held me in good stead; I could use Freud's insights but still retain the doctrine of God and humanity consonant with Christian theology. For instance, Freud was quoted as saying that God did not exist but was a projection of the father image. Well, to some extent a woman projects a father image onto her husband. This does not mean the husband does not exist. Thus, the suggestion that God is a projection of a father image does not prove that God does not exist. Freud's insight into the projection of images did not destroy my faith, rather it helped me understand the subtleties of the human mind.

Seeing mental illness in its extreme form assisted me later as a parish priest in detecting neurotic behavior in myself and others. These insights were helpful, for instance, when, screening postulants for ministry, I attempted to discern their understanding of God. Was he an angry father? Was God a gentle, forgiving mother? Did the answers to these questions reflect theological teaching or psychological history?

Despite and because of the experiences I had in the war, I believed that all human beings were created good, "in the image of God," but often turned violent and cruel. What I learned at Greystone helped me to understand how and why that image of God is deformed— that difficult childhoods, inherited genes, the use of drugs, or traumatic experiences could distort human nature and limit the freedom to choose the good. Further, one could trace the pathology in case histories back through earlier generations and discern the impact of society on mental health: poverty, racism, malnutrition, family disintegration.

After fifty years of cultural exposure to the theories of psychiatry, this all seems obvious, but it was not obvious then. This understanding seemed to bolster the theological proposition of Original Sin. Distortions of human beings, whom we believed were created good, in the image of God, occurred not only through disease and conscious individual sin, but also through Original Sin coming down through generations of a neurotic family or through society and its sometimes demonic institutions.

However distorted a person may be, I believed then and believe now that everyone can be reached by God. I looked on those who had left the world of reality, like Kenneth, as on someone in a coma. Such persons could not be held responsible for their actions. I believe God looks after them as if they were infants or in a state of unconsciousness. We were not allowed to carry on any direct ministry of prayer or the laying on of hands with the patients, but I always prayed silently for whomever I was with and sensed that the prayer somehow reached them. When Kenneth smiled at me for the first time, it was an answer to prayer: something had happened between us akin to love, and in that interchange I sensed the spirit of a loving God.

We learned the elements of good counseling: one should be as nondirective as possible. Rarely give advice, but let the client find his or her solution to a problem. Listen carefully not only to what is said but to the silences and to the tone of voice used. Watch for body movements as clues to what someone is upset about. Realize that the alleged reason for coming to see you is not necessarily the real reason. A woman may say she wishes to discuss the altar guild; when she comes into your study, she bursts into tears because her husband is an alcoholic. These and many other understandings of the pastoral role of a clergyman were more important than anything else I learned at seminary.

All this said, mental illness remained something of a mystery to me. Later, in my personal life, I was to come across this darkness again and again. I remembered the psychotic breaks of the Marines in combat. I have experienced intense depressions myself and have known, in a slight way, the powerlessness of the mentally ill. Toward the end of her life, Jenny slipped inexorably into a deep depression for which she was hospitalized. In retrospect, the experience of Greystone was one of the most important of my life. It helped me to be less afraid of mental illness, because I had some understanding of it.

.   .   .

At General, every morning and evening, the seminarians and the faculty in their academic gowns would file into chapel: sung Morning Prayer followed by the Eucharist at seven; Evensong every afternoon at six; day after day, week after week, month after month. We learned on our knees that worship was work, the work of God, *opus Dei*. The word *liturgy* comes from the Greek word meaning the work of the people. We offered it to God daily whether we felt good or not, whether we benefited or not, whether we believed or not. The Daily Office, as Morning and Evening Prayers were called, and the Eucharist were to be given to God each day as an offering. We believed that in this worship we participated in God's being through the spirit present in the services, the Holy Spirit. This tough liturgical life gave a foundation to our existence and would carry me through many ups and downs of my faith in years to come. Even though I often neglected to say the Office, and even though I sometimes missed the Eucharist, I knew the work of worship was going on in the Church and that I was part of it, whatever the state of my own faith might be.

We were required to do fieldwork in a parish on weekends. Dr. James Pike, who later became Bishop of California and a most controversial figure in the Church, asked Jenny and me to work with him at his parish, Christ Church, Poughkeepsie. He and his wife, Esther, later told us that they did not like our preppy image, but no one else was available. We, in turn, were not that excited about working in Poughkeepsie, two hours north of New York City. However, the four of us became great friends, and we found weekends with the Pikes exhilarating, even if it took us most of the following week to recover.

My assignment was the young people's fellowship. I had worked diligently in drawing up a course on marriage. Jim Pike thought the outline was great. The only problem was that the kids preferred Ping-Pong. No one at the seminary had taken the trouble to tell us how to handle teenagers. Besides the usual teenage restlessness, these particular boys and girls were depressed by living in Poughkeepsie, which they considered the most boring city in the world. I tended to agree but never said so. I finally gave up on the course on marriage and just tried to get to know them and to have them enjoy coming on Sunday nights and taking trips hither and yon on Saturdays. One of them, through no fault of mine, is presently a professor at General Seminary.

We also called on families. Walking up to the door of a house in which lived a family you knew nothing about other than that they were on the parish list was daunting. I would get out of the car, walk up the sidewalk screwing up my courage, ring the doorbell, and hope no one was home. I did not have anything to identify myself; who knew but that I was an insurance salesman? Sometimes a woman would answer the bell in curlers, speak through a crack in the door, and tell me she could not see me. I would blurt out, "I am from Christ Church and hope you will come there if you have not been recently. Here is a pamphlet about the church." Then I ran down the walk, vastly relieved. Sometimes I would be let in after a few moments, during which there was a great deal of scurrying around to put away a beer bottle or empty an ashtray. We might have a stilted conversation about the weather, or discuss her son who was in my group, or I would hear how terrible that Dr. Pike was with his out-landish High Church ideas. Sometimes I would pick up a little parish history. Occasionally, we would discuss religion in a sensible manner. Although I was not ordained, there were occasions when someone would pour her heart out to me.

Parish calling was not easy, but when I came back from these visits I had a sense of well-being. I found that what you talked about was not as important as just being there—a gesture that the church cared enough to call. And this is really the only way to know your people. You can tell so much about someone if you see the kind of house he or she lives in—the photographs, knickknacks, books, magazines. Also, if you have been to someone's house, he or she feels more at ease in calling on you for help if a problem arises later on.

After the last parish gathering on Sunday night, we would sit around the rectory and listen to Jim. He was a strange person in many ways: he had thought his way into the Episcopal Church from Roman Ca-tholicism and found the open Catholic tradition of our Church to his liking. He was always rethinking doctrine so that it would make sense to modern minds. And whenever he had an idea, he wanted to put it into practice. He taught us many things. He said people outside the Church were more important than people inside the Church; his attempts to reach the outsiders made him a burr under the saddle of the Church traditionalists and later led to what amounted to a trial for heresy in the House of Bishops. But by the same token, he was beloved by non-churchmen.

We learned a great deal from Jim. He showed us how hard you have to work to make a parish go, and he demonstrated by his example the intense pastoral concern a priest should show to the sick and those in trouble. He was exciting and fearless. He led a full-blown attack on the vapid, eclectic Protestantism being taught in the Vassar chapel, which caused a huge stir on campus and drew rebellious students to Christ Church, where they would listen eagerly to Jim. He put candles on the altar for the first time in that old, hidebound Low Church, much to the consternation of the older members. He was always in the midst of controversy and loved every minute of it.

Jim was fascinated by psychic phenomena. He became convinced that Christ Church was haunted, because for no visible reason the controversial candles kept going out during the service. Jim was sure that the ghost of the late Dr. Alexander Cummins, the previous rector and a militant Low Church man who had died a few years before, was blowing them out. One night he arranged for an exorcism. He asked Kilmer "Kim" Myers, who later worked with us in our first parish and followed Jim Pike as Bishop of California, to come up and bring his dog, because Jim felt dogs were more sensitive to ghosts than people. He also invited Dr. Cyril Richardson, an eminent scholar of ancient liturgies and exorcisms.

About eleven o'clock on this Sunday night, we all had a stiff drink and then, led by Jim, started over to the church through a cloister that joined the rectory to the back door of the parish house. It was a gusty, autumn night; the moon was full, and clouds raced over its face, hurled along by the wind. Leaves swirled around us as we crept through the cloister. We were silent; only the sound of the gusts of wind and the rustle of leaves could be heard. As we approached the large oaken door, Jeff, Kim's Afghan, began to growl. He stood before the door with raised hackles, his curled tail erect and quivering. "See! See!" whispered Jim. "Jeff smells Dr. Cummins!"

With that, Jim turned the huge iron handle and slowly pulled open the creaking door. Out flew a bat. "There he goes! There he goes!" he shouted. The candles never blew out again.

It was a joke, and yet Jim half believed that Dr. Cummins, in the form of a bat, had finally left the church. Tragically, later in Jim's life, this fascination with the occult led him to try to communicate on a television program with his dead son, who had committed suicide. This shocked and saddened his friends and family, although, in a way, it was consistent with Jim's philosophy: "If I believe something," he would say, "there's no reason to hide it." And so he felt that even as personal a thing as communicating with his dead son should be conducted in public.

For all his eccentricities, he was a stimulating presence in the Church for many years. I think my own willingness to be drawn into controversy from time to time was partly due to Jim's example.

Years later, Jim died in the desert of Judaea searching for the source of the Dead Sea Scrolls. As he lay dying in the hot desert, I trust he found the Lord whom, in his restless life, he had always been seeking.

In the winter of my middle year, the father of an old friend, William Lusk, Jr., asked me to lunch at the Century Club to meet the Reverend Philip "Tubby" Clayton. The Reverend William Lusk was the rector of the Episcopal church in Ridgefield, Connecticut, and had come to know Tubby on his trips to England. This was an exciting moment for me. I had never been to the Century and was awed by the stately academic charm of the place, and I had heard tell of Tubby Clayton as something of a World War I hero. He was a small, round man, with balding white hair, a Churchillian slouch, a ruddy English face, and large blue eyes behind thick, horn-rimmed glasses. He muttered his words, often without removing his pipe, and gave off the stale aroma of fine tobacco.

Lunch in the book-lined dining room was a delight. Tubby told story after story of World War I, during which he had ministered to the English lads at the front. There, at Poperinghe on the Western Front, he provided a place of comfort and love for the shaken young men emerging from the trenches. He called it the Upper Room, after the place where Jesus had the Last Supper with his disciples. Tubby, scarcely more than a boy himself, was able to make the Lord's presence known in the dark intimacy of the Eucharist and provided a place for the young men to find healing for their shattered spirits and a release from the terror that had taken hold of them. My own experiences of combat came back to me as he spoke; I wished I could have done the same for my young Marines at Guadalcanal. He told us how he established a fellowship of these veterans after the war, called Toc H, a kind of Anglican YMCA for lonely estranged veterans.

These were not ordinary war stories. Tubby's fanciful imagination would construct what England would have been like had she not lost the leaders of a whole generation. "Young Lord So-and-So," he would say, "probably would have been Foreign Minister, George Such and Such, Chancellor of the Exchequer . . ." As he spoke, it was as if these figures held a parliament in the sky.

In World War II, Tubby founded a chaplain's corps for freighters and, although well along in years by then, served on a tanker. His present mission was to gather steel for his bombed-out church, the historic All Hallows on Tower Hill in London. He traveled with much paraphernalia. An amateur archaeologist, he brought along maps of Roman London, based on excavations near his church. There were photographs of his dog, Roman bricks, and Roman nails he had dug up, similar to the nails that impaled Christ on the cross. To assist him, he enlisted students whom he called aides-de-camp. They carried all this stuff, bought his tickets, and generally took care of him. These young men were invariably wellborn and often rich, but they would take time off to be with Tubby. They usually only lasted a few months, and then, worn out, would fall by the wayside. This happened once in Texas, at a fund-raising party, so Tubby grabbed an unsuspecting young Texan and asked him for a ride to the station. The fellow was still with him a year later and subsequently became a priest. Tubby's magnetism was irresistible. If he was driving along a highway at noon, he would stop the car, kneel down at the side of the road, and, in the midst of the roar of traffic, proceed to say noonday prayers: "Blessed Savior, who at this hour hung upon the cross stretching out your loving arms, grant that all the peoples of the earth may look to you and be saved, for your mercy's sake." This demonstration embarrassed whomever was with him, but Tubby was never embarrassed by his Lord.

A few days after this luncheon, Tubby summoned me to his room at the seminary. "Paul," he said, "would you be good enough to do me a favor?"

"Of course," I replied, not then realizing what a favor to him might entail, thinking he needed some tobacco or whatever.

"Yes, old boy, I would like you to recruit forty or fifty young men and women from across the U.S., raise the money, and take them to London next summer to relieve some of the priests who have not had a vacation since the war."

I was speechless. "B-b-but I'm just a middler."

"Awfully good of you, old chap. Now run along, I have to make some phone calls. I'm going to Pittsburgh tomorrow to see Mr. Mellon about some steel for All Hallows."

Over the next weeks, telegrams came in from all over the country: MOST IMPRESSED WITH PADRE CLAYTON STOP SAYS YOU HAVE DE-TAILS OF HIS PROJECT STOP WHERE SHALL I SEND FIFTY TENTS FOR THE VOLUNTEERS, or, I HAVE SIGNED UP WITH TUBBY CLAYTON FOR NEXT SUMMER STOP PLEASE SEND ME THE PLANS. Of course, I had no idea how to respond.

Although Jenny and I did not go to England because of our young children, the project succeeded and later became known as the Winant volunteers, named after our beloved wartime ambassador to the Court of St. James's, John G. Winant. The exchange continues today, with English men and women called the Clayton volunteers coming to the States as well.

On his last trip to this country in the 1960s, I called on Tubby in Washington. I had just been made a bishop. I entered his messy hotel room, and the old man immediately knelt down and asked for my blessing. As I placed my shaking hands on that embattled head, I could hardly speak for the tears.

He inscribed a book of his sermons to me as follows:

My thankfulness tonight is deeply due to having your hands laid on my white head. From 1947 until today, you've been the lamp which has relit my life, and now at last I came again beneath the mystic friendship and the tragedy of Gilbert Winant's brokenhearted state. Had it not been for you and Jenny and Ledlie [Laughlin] and Coit Johnson, I should have gone home blinded by despair. Your presence and your friendship upheld me. Tubby.

Gilbert Winant had committed suicide; he once was a teacher at St. Paul's School. Some providential grace seemed to have been at work: I had met Mr. Lusk, who introduced me to Father Clayton, at St. Paul's. We were planning to go to London but instead went to St. Peter's Church, where my lifelong commitment to urban ministry took shape. It all seemed to fit together. Such a confluence of places and people at moments in one's life seems more than coincidence. Without my freedom of choice being compromised, I was nudged along in a way that determined the direction of my life.

Tubby Clayton and Jim Pike each gave me a vision of what the priesthood could be if you broke the bonds of convention and followed your heart with courage. Each was a person with many faults who allowed himself to be used by the Lord, and each saw his ministry as extending far beyond the walls of the church. Tubby once described himself to me as an old, blunt penknife in the hand of God.

Having chosen not to go to England with Tubby but having no other plans, Chris Morley, a classmate, Jenny, and I decided to do in New York what we would have been doing in London. Kim Myers, who had been with us at Jim Pike's, was an instructor at General and the priest in charge of St. Peter's, Chelsea, a half block from the seminary. He agreed to have us work there. This turn of events was to shape my future.

"Chelsea for Christ" was our motto that summer. With romantic enthusiasm, we roamed the streets and picked up idle kids for baseball games and trips to the beach. We launched a vacation Bible school. We put banners outside the church and held services on the sidewalk. We called on the parents of children we knew and had many adventures.

One day, I climbed to the top floor of a tenement to call on a Mrs. Jones. I knocked timidly on the door at first, then I knocked louder. The door opened a crack. "Who are you?" asked a black woman I took to be Mrs. Jones. Her face was suspicious.

"Er, ah, I'm from the church where Tommy comes."

Long pause. Whispering to someone else behind the door. Finally, "Come in."

A young white man in a suit and tie stood nervously beside Mrs. Jones. She introduced us. "This is Mr. Alonzo, the Communist. This is Mr. Moore, the Christian."

Mr. Alonzo excused himself, and I proceeded to tell Mrs. Jones what a nice boy Tommy was and how I hoped he would come to our church on Sunday as well as during the week. "We'd like you to come, too," I added, tentatively. Mrs. Jones grunted. We were still standing. I did not have the courage to ask to sit down, much less to suggest I say a prayer, so I left.

I hurried back to the church to report my first encounter with godless Communism! The Party was active at that time in poor urban areas. A few days later, Chris Morley and I were walking down the street with a bunch of kids hanging all over us, hot and sweaty. A well-dressed, nice-looking fellow stopped us. "Excuse me," he said, "but are you trying to make these kids Christians?"

It had never occurred to us that that was what we were trying to do, so we stammered, "I guess so."

"My name's Jim Brown. I would like you to make me a Christian. I have been watching you over the last few days and have seen the way you treat the kids." It turned out that Jim had grown up in the Orthodox Church and had later become a Communist. He had been bitterly disillusioned. Now he turned to us. We shook hands and made a date for him to come by the church for instruction. We were thrilled. "You see it works, it works! Just show a little love, and people are drawn to Christ and the Church."

That was a heady summer. We talked and talked and talked. We read books about the worker-priests in France and how they reached the proletariat, as they called the working class. These priests had been in concentration camps, where they came to know working-class men with whom the primarily bourgeois Church had lost touch. These young priests sought to bring them back by working side by side with them in the factories and living as they did in the slums.

Often they would go for a year before letting on they were Christians and additional months before admitting they were priests. By that time, they had gained the confidence of the workers. Soon they were celebrating Mass on the workbench and organizing the men around the issues of labor, housing, and so forth. Cardinal Suhard, the Archbishop of Paris, took them under his wing and would often stay with them in their squalid quarters. It is said that Francis Joseph Cardinal Spellman of New York, known for his conservatism, persuaded the pope to stop the movement, because it was too close to Communism.

We read again about the Anglo-Catholic priests on the docks of London at the turn of the century. They too had been accused of being Communists. Kim Myers introduced us to the monthly newspaper *The Catholic Worker* and the thinking of Dorothy Day, its co-founder, who later became a good friend. We also learned about the National Association for the Advancement of Colored People and began to sense that in the United States, Negroes, as they were then called, were the equivalent of the European proletariat.

Night after night, as we talked, we began to visualize a strategy for putting these ideas to work in the Episcopal Church. Then one day, when Jenny and I were walking down the close, Kim Myers leaned out of his window and said, "Why don't we get some bishop to give us a church where we can work full-time?"

And so the search for a parish was on. We wrote the bishops of several urban dioceses. Bishop Washburn, the Bishop of Newark, having started his own ministry at Grace Church Chapel in a poor area on the East Side, responded with enthusiasm and offered us Grace Church (van Vorst), Jersey City. I was ordained a deacon in June at the Cathedral of St. John the Divine, and was ready to go on to this, our first parish.

JERSEY CITY

THE temperature was 95, the humidity at least 159. The four
of us sat in the kitchen of the rectory: Bob Pegram's bald
head was glistening and covered with pink splotches, Kim's
two-day beard made him look like a mad poet. God knows what I
looked like. We all had on our black trousers, black shirts, black
socks, and black shoes. Jenny, very pregnant, was in a sloppy house-
dress. On the white, tin chipped kitchen table were four cold beers
to relieve the letdown we'd felt following our arrival. The moving
van had left, and the sparse furniture was in place. We did not dare
discuss what our first step would be. This wilted group was the "val-
iant crowd," as one bishop who turned us down had called us, ready
to redeem Jersey City if not the entire world.

As we sat there, sweltering over our beer, we could see the lych-
gate through the kitchen window. (Prior to a funeral, in English country churches, the coffin could rest under the lych-gate until it was
time to bring it into the church.) The arch of our lych-gate was
adorned, in Gothic lettering, with the motto ENTER HIS GATES WITH
THANKSGIVING, but immediately beneath this eschatological welcome was a black iron gate with a formidable sign that said KEEP OUT.
Our first official acts had been to remove that sign and cart away the
carcass of a dead dog from the yard.

As we were talking, I noticed an old lady walking along the sidewalk. She paused a moment, opened the gate, and sat down heavily.
"A caller!" I exclaimed. We jumped up, torpor gone, put on our
clerical collars, and flew down the walk to greet her. She was a little

startled but not overwhelmed by this press of clerical attention. "How do you do," we chorused, and introduced ourselves.

"Pleased to meet'cha," she replied.

"How are you?"

"Hot," she said.

"Oh," we said. "What's your name?"

"Cherry. Cherry Armstrong."

"Do you belong to this parish?" Bob asked.

"What?"

I tried, "Do you belong to this church?" pointing to the building.

"Oh, that. I guess so. Jesus, it's hot!" She kept fanning herself with a newspaper. She was rather disheveled: sweat dripped from her wrinkled, round face; damp wisps of thinning brown hair lay on her brow; she wore a rumpled, black dress, and a pendant on a frayed ribbon hung from her neck. But when she looked up at us, her eyes were sharp.

"It sure is hot. The paper says it's hot."

"It does?"

"Yeah. Say, would you like something cool to drink?"

"I could use it."

"Jenny!" I shouted. She had been watching our "evangelism" from the porch. "How about some lemonade!"

We sat for a while discussing the heat and the humidity. Jenny came out.

"This is Mrs. Moore," I said.

"Pleased to meet'cha." Just then the tray broke and the pitcher of lemonade spilled on Cherry's lap.

"Oh my goodness, I'm so sorry," Jenny exclaimed. "Somebody get a rag, get a sponge, get something!"

"Don't bother. I ain't been so cool all day."

Cherry became a fixture in our lives. She would come by almost every afternoon for Evensong and sometimes stay for supper. She lived alone in a room and did not seem to have any friends. Her behavior in church was splendid—she said what she thought in a loud voice, fanning herself with a comic book all the while. One afternoon, the psalm was announced: "Psalm 119, verses 33 through 38 and 105 through 120."

Cherry spoke up. "Jesus Christ, we'll never find that one."

Another time, when Bob bogged down in the middle of a chant so that he had to begin again, she commented, "What the hell is the matter with him today?"

Beneath her sassy humor were loneliness, poverty, and uncertainty as to what the next day would bring, yet her pride and toughness kept the surface of her personality warm and gave laughter, not gloom, to those who came to know her. She died the following summer and was not found for three days.

Two old neighbors and I were at her burial in a weedy part of a cemetery next to a six-lane highway overlooking the Jersey swamp. The heat was merciless, the grave diggers anxious for us to finish the prayers so they could go home. The solemn words of the burial office were drowned out by the roar of trucks and trailers going by. That is where we left Cherry Armstrong, R.I.P. But there had been for her, in her last days, the Church. And now, perhaps, the Lord in all his glory.

When we came to Jersey City, we had two ambitions: to reach the people of the city with the love of Christ by ministering to their needs, both personal and social; and to halt the trend in the Church at that time of closing down a parish when Episcopalians left the area. I believe we had a great deal to do with convincing the Church at large that we should and could reach the people who lived near the church, whatever their background, and that this could be accomplished by living there and ministering to their needs.

Except for the great African-American parishes, the Episcopal Church at that time was thought of as an upper-class organization. Most society weddings took place in Episcopal churches. Upwardly mobile families often joined the Episcopal Church as a way of meeting prominent members of the community. Elite preparatory schools like St. Paul's, Groton, and St. Mark's were Episcopalian. We did not resent our Church's ministry to the rich, but we felt strongly that as a Catholic Church it should and could reach out to poor people as well. In the nineteenth century, wealthy churches like Trinity, St. Thomas, Incarnation, Grace Church, and St. James in New York established chapels in poor areas to work with immigrants. These people were not encouraged to become part of the mother churches.

It was a ministry to the poor rather than with the poor. We thought such an arrangement was well motivated but condescending. Our idea was to live with the people to whom we ministered and to identify with their lives as much as possible. I believe we did have an impact on the Church at large and helped prepare for the turmoil of the 1960s.

If you walked down Erie Street toward the church from Newark Avenue, where all the main shops were located, you passed a furniture store on the corner, which had had a POSITIVELY MUST GO SALE sign in its window for two years, then a barbershop run by two quiet brothers who came from uptown. A little further on was the cleaners, where, every spring, they would put up a sign reading, EASTER IS HERE. RESURRECT YOUR GARMENTS! Dominick, who ran it, was a cheery fellow. "Hi, Father!" he would call. His presser was usually silent, but if he had had a few drinks, you would find out he'd once studied for the priesthood. His dreams, like so many in the neighborhood, had been broken many years before.

Down the street, past the high stoops of furnished rooms, where the old men sat, we would see Harry, who used to work for the circus. He came for a sandwich one day and offered to sweep the church. He kept coming for a sandwich and kept sweeping the church. "Hi, Poppy!" Like our children, he called Jenny and me Mommy and Poppy. We found Harry in a rage one day, following an infusion of cow manure from my mother's cows for shrubs in the yard. "What on earth is the matter, Harry?"

"It's that manure!"

"It doesn't smell good, I know that," I said, "but it's real good for the plants."

"I know, I know," he said, "but I could have got you all the elephant manure you would want from the circus, and it's twice as strong!"

I pictured a herd of elephants backed up against the iron fence doing their thing for Jesus. Harry claimed to know Roy Rogers and said that Trigger, his horse, always "whinnered" when Harry went by.

Further along, Erie Street looked like a village street, lined with maples and little front gardens enclosed by privet hedges. In one of them was a shiny black-and-chrome baby carriage, real fancy. The inside was upholstered in white Naugahyde and contained a rosy-faced baby with jet-black hair. Her mother would lean out the window and wave.

The next corner was occupied by a funeral parlor, with a dying fern in the window. An old man sat next to the fern, dreaming of the five-car funerals of yesteryear. Next to it was another cleaners and another old man's face staring out the window, Sol. His wife had died three years ago. There they were, these two old men, quite alone. A stained-glass window of a previous Bishop of Newark was directly across the street from Sol. He thought it was a saint and from time to time said his rosary with his eyes on the window. Other times, when the children around the church became too noisy, he would scream at us, "You're just a bunch of phonies! You're no real priests. Phonies! Phonies!"

On the opposite corner of Second Street stood the church, surrounded by a fence and some overgrown grass. The building dated from about 1850, brownstone, Gothic, nicely proportioned with a squat tower in the center and a sloping green copper roof. We painted the door that faced the street a bright red. At the end of the church was the lych-gate, a yard, and a tall, brownstone Charles Addams–style rectory. On the other side of the yard from the church, the blank, brick wall of a tenement house stretched up four stories.

The immediate neighborhood was clean and quiet. The people, for the most part, were Italian, Polish, and Irish. In fact, directly across Erie Street was St. Mary's, a huge Irish Roman Catholic church of yellow brick. The parish held bingo every night, including Good Friday. Across Second Street stood another Roman Catholic church, St. Boniface, originally German. Behind us, on Third Street, was an Italian Roman Catholic church.

Two blocks down Second Street, and scattered here and there all over this lower part of town, were black and Hispanic neighborhoods. These parts of town were dirtier, and the buildings were generally in a state of disrepair. The landlords repaired the buildings as seldom as possible; the sanitation department rarely swept the streets. About half a mile away was a large public-housing project called the Booker T. Washington, all the tenants of which were black.

.   .   .

We prepared for the first Sunday with enthusiasm. We mopped the church, shined the brass, buttered up the altar guild of two elderly ladies, and carefully assigned the liturgy among ourselves: Kim Myers, as the senior clergyman, was to preach, Bob Pegram would celebrate the Mass, as we then called the Eucharist, and I was to read the lessons. We waited until eleven-fifteen. I looked out of the sacristy and counted fourteen people including my mother, a parishioner from St. Peter's, Chelsea, and eight children, two of whom, we were delighted to note, were black.

After the service, there was much shaking of hands and smiling at the door, as, properly attired in cassocks and birettas, we met our tiny flock.

Mrs. Flynn was there, a doughty, white-haired lady who dared to be a Republican and a Protestant in lower Jersey City, despite her name. I overheard her giving directions to someone on the sidewalk one day. He asked which of the two churches on Erie Street was the Catholic church.

Mrs. Flynn said, with a toss of her white hair, "That," pointing to St. Mary's, "is the Roman Catholic church. This," pointing to Grace Church, "is the Holy Catholic church."

There was Mrs. Mentzer, who had sewn all the vestments for the church over the years, and Chris Kelly, who said, "Father, I'm so glad you kept the resoived sacrament. I couldn't live without the resoived."

The Gilligans were there: Jim, Irish, alcoholic, and Kay, his long-suffering wife. One of their sons, who had been an altar boy, had died the year before and was buried in his acolyte's vestment. Kay showed us a picture of him in his coffin. "He looked just like an angel," she kept saying. "He looked just like an angel." Their other son, David, played the guitar and was our only acolyte. All of us tried our pastoral skills on the Gilligan family; we even hired Jim as part-time sexton. But they continued their hand-to-mouth existence year after year.

After the last old lady left, we came back to the rectory and had a slug of Christian Brothers sherry. We had decided nothing stronger than sherry or beer should be served in the rectory. All of us were discouraged by the small turnout, but soon, with the help of the Christian Brothers, we agreed that the fewer the better if we were going to create a new kind of mission.

During our long discussions at the seminary about a strategy for urban work, we had agreed on certain principles, mostly gleaned from the writings of the French worker-priests and from Abbé Georges Michonneau's *Revolution in a City Parish*. We should identify with the people whom we served, live in the same neighborhood, and share, as much as possible, their hardships and suffering. We knew we could never fully identify with, let's say, a black mother on welfare living in three rooms with nine children. Nor could we experience the despair of feeling that we would never leave the inner city, would never fight our way out of its loneliness, fear, and insecurity, because we could leave at any moment and, because of our education, we had resources of a totally different sort from our people. Yet we tried to live closely to them. The rectory was simply furnished with second-hand furniture from Goodwill Industries, its door was always open. People and kids of all kinds streamed in and out of our kitchen. Our children played in the yard with other children from the church and neighborhood. My son Paul's two best friends were black and Hispanic, Ralphie and Evaristo, known as Mounty for Mount Everest.

Bishop Washburn had agreed to ordain me to the priesthood on December 17, 1949. This was a moment to which I had looked forward since the days at St. Paul's. Mother gave me a set of beautiful Eucharistic vestments, with a pelican as the symbol on the chasuble. Father Truman Heminway accepted an invitation to preach. I had visited him often in Vermont during school and college, helping with the farm he took care of and worshipping in his beautiful mission church. His theological depth, his Catholic discipline, and his solid, earthy spirituality grounded my faith in those early days. I can still see him with his graying beard and deep-set eyes. In his sermon, he told me my first duty as a priest was to my family.

The small congregation made great preparations; friends and family came from afar. Much to my embarrassment, my grandmother arrived in her Rolls-Royce. Jim Gilligan remarked on it. I sputtered, "She rented it for today. You know she is a very old lady."

"Funny," he said, "the chauffeur said he had been with her for thirty years."

When Granny opened the door of the car, some of the children, wide-eyed, jumped in. Granny was delighted, the kids were happy. My cover was blown.

The service was moving. The hands of the bishop on my head and his deep voice pronouncing me a priest in the Church of God have stayed with me all these years. I celebrated my first Mass at midnight, Christmas Eve.

One of my ongoing problems of conscience during those days was how to handle my money. Here we were in the midst of poverty, and I had access to a large trust fund. Even if I had had the courage to give it all away, I felt doing so would have been irresponsible toward my children. Finally, after much agonizing and prayer, Jenny and I made a decision. We would live the comparatively simple life we had chosen and give away whatever was left over of our income. I also took some of the capital and established a foundation with a separate name so that I could give money anonymously to the Episcopal Church and other causes. This was, I think, a sound solution, but it has taken me many years to feel comfortable about it.

As at St. Peter's, Chelsea, we started moving into the neighborhood by getting to know the kids through baseball, trips, and vacation Bible school. Before long, they began to hang around the church. Even these early steps were not easy, however. One of our first recruits was Bruno Gussey, named after Bruno Hauptmann, whom his father thought innocent of the kidnapping of Lindbergh's baby. I had called on him and his eccentric father—they were on some parish list. Bruno sat, surly, in a big chair. The father told me he hated priests. I thought the visit a complete failure. A few days later, however, I was praying in the church, when Bruno came and knelt down beside me. I thought maybe he wanted to make his confession, but I respected his privacy and said nothing. After a minute or two, he nudged me, "Hey, Father, how about the baseball gloves? You know, the ones you talked to my stupid old man about?"

I remembered then that I had suggested starting a baseball team. Still kneeling, we discussed the team at some length. After a while, I realized we were not praying, so we got up and continued the conversation. I put Bruno in charge of raising money for the gloves. He stole it.

The last time I saw Bruno, we were summoned to the director's office of Children's Village, a private institution for disturbed kids. Mrs. Gussey and his sister Clara came along. Apparently, he had done some stealing there and seemed incorrigible. The director, his mother, and I tried to talk to him. He became more and more sullen and backed into a corner. We followed, until we actually cornered him. Suddenly, he broke past us to the large desk of the director, picked up a heavy crystal paperweight, and threw it through the plate-glass window behind the desk. As the window smashed, Bruno ran out the door. I never saw him again. We continued to see the family. One sister, Fidelis, fell in love with Kim. Clara, one Christmas Eve, tried to cut her wrists in the back of the church.

Through the kids, we came to know their families and began slowly to build the congregation. But the tension between their world and ours was always around us and within us.

Before long, we were receiving complaints from the neighbors. They even sent a petition to the bishop, which I still have.

August 7, 1950

Your Excellency Bishop,

We wish to bring to your attention, Sir, the conditions that exist since the new priests have taken over the fine church of Grace Church. Most of us have lived in the neighborhood for 10 and 20 years and we were proud that this was the best, cleanest, quietest section of downtown Jersey City. Now, groups of children have taken over. Just last week a 15-month-old baby was hit on the head with a baseball. The priests were approached and in reply told us that the conditions will exist further and that they hope to double the size of the group. We believe that everyone should go to church to ask the blessings of our Lord but that is where it should end and not to have gangs hanging around and make it into a playground. At the rectory, there is music and dancing. The children seem to come from all parts of the city and draw other groups to them.

Please, Sir, make an investigation. Grace Church was always known to be a clean and beautiful place of worship and we know that with your help it shall again become a place of worship and respect.

Respectfully yours,

Alexander Jalombrowski
259 Second St.

(Thirty-seven signatures follow.)

I can certainly understand the neighbors' point of view in retrospect, but we were so self-righteous that we gave them short shrift. The bishop answered the letter politely but was delighted that our presence was being felt, even in this painful way.

We ourselves had difficulty adjusting to the environment. When we came back from a day off, for instance, the contrast was stark, and we treated one another gently at such times. I remember coming home one night, after having been mesmerized by a ballet in New York. Far, far had my mind wandered with the movement, the music, first watching, then caught up and swept away in a world of delicate form and beauty. When the lights came on, I sat in a daze, as people pushed past me on the way out. All the way back on the Hudson Tubes, I lived on in that other world, until I walked up the steps of the rectory and found a dirty, ragged man covered with vomit, lying unconscious on the floor of the porch. I stepped over him, closing my eyes and my nose to his presence. It was too much. Oh, I knew he was more important than the fantasy world I'd come from. I knew Christ dwelt in him, that indeed he was Christ to me. And yet I could not face him, the stench of his vomit, nor my own priesthood, which bound me to him.

I came into the kitchen, and Bob Pegram was sitting at the table. He sensed my mood. He did not mention all that had happened that day at the parish, all that had gone wrong: Johnny, one of our acolytes, had been picked up and beaten by the police; Mary Drayton, a sweet-spirited member of the altar guild, had learned she had terminal cancer; a meeting on which we had counted for starting a new program had been a dismal failure. He did not mention any of this but asked, "How was the ballet?"

"Wonderful, wonderful," I replied. He said he would deal with the man on the porch and let me go up to bed. With this kind of sensitivity, we helped one another through the continual insult of living in two worlds. Thoughtfulness and trust were at the heart of our community.

The concept of Christian community was another principle we adopted. The community had two centers: the table that was the altar, where we believed our risen Lord came into the flesh and blood of all who received, binding us together in his body through the Sacrament of the Bread of Life; and the kitchen table, where we broke ordinary bread, cried, laughed, and made friends with those whom we tried to serve.

These principles, so theoretical at the seminary, soon became the stuff of everyday life. The Eucharist was so real there. It fed us, strengthened us to go out and love the people we met; it inspired us to try as best we could to bring the justice of God's Kingdom to the broken city in which we lived. By learning the pattern of God's Kingdom in the liturgy, we could discover its shape in the world around us. That pattern is one of offering, being broken open as Christ was on the cross so that the love of God can enter into your being, and then, having been made one with him, rising out of the pain you have shared together into a new life. In the Eucharist, you are taught to find peace in suffering and to live in a different state of being when your life leads you through dark times. This is not book learning; this is acting out the drama of Redemption with other human beings time after time.

We found the Kingdom of God present in unusual places. One day I went to visit Mary Drayton, who was dying of cancer in the hospital, and I met her husband, Joe, in the hall. Joe was six foot five, black, and weighed over 250 pounds. I put my hand on his shoulder and said, "Joe, this must be a terrible, painful time for you."

He turned and smiled at me with tears in his eyes and said, "No, it's the most loving time we've ever had."

As I came to know the ward where Mary lay, I realized that she had made it a community of love. It seemed that Joe's love for her, God's love for her, and her own long years of being with Christ spread to the other patients. After giving Mary her Communion, I always said a prayer with each of them. Instead of dreading those visits, I came to look forward to them and left her ward refreshed by the peace and even joy I found there.

Another principle of Christian community as we understood it was social action. We believed that this action should grow out of the needs of our people: if the children had nowhere to play, find a way to provide a playground; if housing was a problem, lobby all levels of government to provide better housing; if police were unnecessarily roughing up your boys, lodge a formal complaint. This may seem

obvious, but even today few churches have programs of social action.
Many minister to the victims after they are wounded, but few seek
to prevent the wounding. Again, we believed this grew out of the
Eucharist, which demonstrates the equal value of every human being
in that Christ gives himself in the bread and wine to everyone who
comes to the altar, a pattern of justice for all. On a practical level,
we decided to start our social action with modest projects so that
success in a small program could build enthusiasm for something more
ambitious.

The children of our neighborhood had no playground, and yet
there were many vacant lots full of rubbish. We organized cleanup
squads and had a reporter take a picture of us in our clerical collars
raking up the garbage. We wanted to start a movement and came up
with the brilliant idea of a float covered with artificial grass, carrying
a shiny red swing set. In huge letters, a sign proclaimed our motto,
VACANT LOTS FOR TINY TOTS. Well, we rehabilitated one lot, and
before a week was out, the swings had all been broken.

After that catastrophe, we became more realistic and decided to go
to city hall to persuade the mayor to erect sturdy playground equipment maintained by the city in such vacant lots. We formed a human
relations council and enlisted some other Christians, Jews, members
of labor unions, the head of the YMCA, the NAACP, and so forth.
Armed with this formidable group, which even included one intrepid
Jesuit, we made an appointment to see the mayor. We came to the
anteroom, high ceilinged and furnished with beat-up leather couches
and brass spittoons. We waited, and waited, and waited. Finally, we
were ushered into the mayor's office. Behind his desk sat Monsignor
McWilliams, the pastor of a nearby Roman Catholic church. "Good
afternoon," he said. "The mayor was unable to be here and asked me
to speak for him." I do not remember whether we just left or sputtered
out our concern about the needs of the city's children. On the way
home, we passed McWilliams's church and saw city bulldozers re-
making his school's playground. So much for the separation of Church
and State! Needless to say, the playgrounds never materialized. About
that time, I was asked to write an article on urban social action. It
was titled "Suddenly, Nothing Happened."

The Roman Catholic churches did much to help their parishioners
but never confronted the corruption of city hall. We were angry that

the mayor had asked a nonelected priest to represent him in a matter of community concern. Uncritical support of the political machine allowed them privileges like the use of city equipment for parish projects.

The next problem we tackled was housing. Several of the children who came to our vacation Bible school lived at 209 Second Street, a miserable, broken-down tenement. In the basement apartment, a family of seven occupied three rooms with dirt floors. One potbellied stove was used for heat and cooking. The bathroom was an outhouse in the backyard with a door hanging on one hinge. The conditions in the other so-called railroad flats were not much better. We visited each family and invited them to a meeting, where, with prodding from us, they agreed to a rent strike. The landlord reacted swiftly and evicted the family in the basement, several of whom came to live with us. So much for inept do-gooders. We brought the landlord to court and lost the suit. We went to the public-housing authority and found that, in practice, black families were being admitted to only one housing project, the Booker T. Washington. We took our case to the federal government, and finally, more than two years later, through pressure from our senator and congressman, all the projects were opened up to black families.

Changing the system is a long, arduous Sisyphean task. However, even when we did not succeed, after a few years the word began to spread that we cared. More and more people in distress found their way to the kitchen door. Some of them joined the Church. Somehow these pathetic efforts gave people hope. Gradually, Grace Church became known as a loving place.

In 1951, the depths of racism were burned into my understanding in Thurgood Marshall's hotel room in Orlando, Florida, where I had gone with the NAACP Legal Defense Fund. I will never forget the look on Thurgood's face. We were having coffee together. The phone rang. Thurgood picked it up: "Oh, my God, no! They were?" When he put down the phone, he turned to us. I saw his face, ashen, dazed. "They shot them," he told us. "They shot the boys. Sheriff Willis McCall was bringing them down for the trial. He said they tried to run away. He shot them, dead."

I was part of a group consisting of a professor and myself from the North, and a professor and clergyman from the South, all white men. We were accompanied by members of the NAACP legal team: Thurgood Marshall, Robert Carter, and Jack Greenberg. Carter and Marshall were black, Greenberg, white. Our mission had been to interview citizens of Lake County, Florida, in order to establish the need to change the venue of the trial for the alleged rape of a white woman by three Negroes, as African Americans were then called. The verdict of guilty in the first trial had been appealed and overruled by the Supreme Court. We were to testify at the second trial. There was no way the three men could get a fair trial because all the local papers had virtually tried them and found them guilty.

You may wonder how I ended up there. As with most of my adventures, I came to this one through a curious route. Because of the injustice we had found against African Americans in Jersey City, and because of reading done in those early days of my learning about discrimination, I had sent a large donation to the NAACP Legal Defense Fund. Walter White was so surprised at the size of the contribution coming from a previously unknown source that he called me up and asked me to come by his office so that he could thank me personally. I suggested we have a drink together. He said he would rather have me come to his office. He was then head of the NAACP and one of the best-known Negro leaders in the country. I saw a man sitting behind the desk, but he was white; in fact, his face was pink-cheeked, round. His blue eyes sparkled, alert behind his steel-rimmed glasses. I was about to ask where Mr. White was when he introduced himself. "I'm Walter White. I want to thank you for that magnificent gift." Another man came in. "This is Roy Wilkins." Walter then insisted on giving me a drink of bourbon out of a Lily cup. I was embarrassed but gulped it down. We became friends, and he came to speak at Jersey City a few months later.

Not long after that, they needed a clergyman to be part of the investigation of the Groveland case and asked me to come. Though apprehensive, I was honored, excited, and I agreed to go. I had no training in the law. They said no legal training was necessary for this venture; we were just to ascertain whether the persons we interviewed had already made up their minds about the guilt of the accused.

On the train to Orlando, Thurgood was greeted with great gusto

Our family's houses in
Palm Beach . . .

. . . and in New Jersey

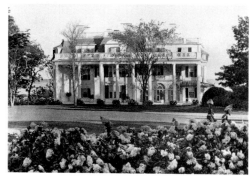

My grandmother's house in Prides
Crossing, Massachusetts

Camp Otterbrook in the
Adirondacks

My grandfather William H. Moore, dressed for the country

My grandmother (top center) and her entourage at the Pyramids

The family at poolside in Palm Beach

With my father in Palm Beach (*left*); on my pony Jupiter in New Jersey (*above*); fishing in the Adirondacks (*right*)

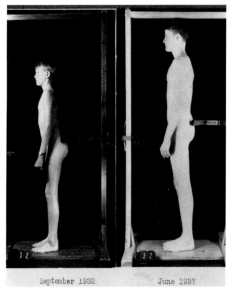

September 1932   June 1937

Entering and leaving St. Paul's

Father Wigram and Dr. Drury, 1936

With friends in the Adirondacks

With my parents the day I was awarded the Navy Cross

Addressing the workers at the Picatinny Arsenal, 1943

A cartoon for the service newspapers depicting my military exploits

On vacation with Jenny, 1945

Jersey City: My first Eucharist, Christmas Eve, 1949

With Robert Pegram
and Kilmer Myers

Out in front of the church with some of our kids

The artist Alan Crite caught the spirit of our life in Jersey City

Bishop's Gift to
Grace Church (Van Vorst)
Jersey City

Church School
Advent Offering
1950

by the waiters in the dining car; he had been such a waiter himself years before, while earning his way through school. An uproarious raconteur, he regaled us with story after story of his life, and even when the stories were of his own oppression, he would laugh and laugh, mostly at himself. (The last time I spoke with him, he told me a tale of his son's being asked in a Southern town, where he was serving as a federal marshal, whether he was related to the "Communist nigger" on the Supreme Court. The son answered, "Who, me?" Roars of laughter from Thurgood.)

In Florida we had to stay in separate hotels, of course, but we would gather each morning for a briefing and each evening to report. One day we drove out from Orlando through rows of the glorious orange-dotted, shiny dark-green trees of the citrus groves to the place where the rape allegedly had taken place. Groveland was an ugly little village with a broad main street, some buildings in need of paint, a few stores and beer joints. Having just driven through the beauty of the orange groves, I was reminded of that Victorian hymn, "From Greenland's icy mountains . . . where every prospect pleases, and only man is vile."

We parked. Two black lawyers and one white Jewish lawyer in suits and ties, a tall, gangly WASP in a black suit with round collar, and a professor with long white hair. We looked about as foreign as Zulus in Siberia as we walked down the main street of Groveland. A large red-faced, beer-bellied, curly-haired monster of a man soon confronted us. "What are you folks doin' here with dem niggers?" He pointed to Bob and Thurgood. "You must be Yankees. What are you doin' here? Trouble, I expect. Trouble."

Professor Ralph Harlow said, "Sir, we are here to interview some people about what they think of the trial of the Negroes who were accused—"

"I mighta' known it." He called over to some other men who were watching from the side of the street. "Did you hear that, guys? These Yankees and their niggers want to talk about that rape case." Ralph tried again: "Did you consider that these boys had a fair trial?"

"Those black bastards don't deserve no trial. Shoulda been lynched." The other men nodded. A crowd had gathered by now.

"Why, then, did the Supreme Court . . ."

"Listen"—now he raised his voice—"if you all don't get your black and white asses outta here in five minutes, we'll put you on a rail and ride you out. Do you understand?" The crowd began to close in. We looked at one another in a tense moment of silence, turned around, and got back to the car as quick as we could. A couple of them banged the roof as we skidded off in a cloud of dust.

That night we were shown the depositions of the accused. Here is a sample of testimony from one of them, referring to the night the alleged rape occurred:

> The cops came up in front of my house right by my brother-in-law in the same car that we had been driving the night before. One of the men, not in uniform, said something to Sammy, who had got out of my brother-in-law's car. He made an attempt to hit him and said, "That's the son-of-a-bitch, I remember the son-of-a-bitch." Pretty soon the policeman called me over and shoved me into the car. They drove me out and parked along the woods on a clay road. Told us to get out of the car. One short guy in plain clothes that had a pistol belt grabbed me and hit me with his billy a lot of times across the head. He held me and a lot of the others started hitting me with billies and fists, knocking me down, pulling me up, and knocking me down again. This continued for twenty minutes or so until blood was all over me.
>
> When they were beating me they said to me, "Nigger, you the man picked up this white girl last night?" I said to them, "What white girl?" They said, "Well, you might as well tell us you're the one did it 'cause we gonna beat the hell outta you until you tell us you did it."

And so it went until they put him in jail. You can imagine the fear, the terror, of that world. I could not begin to deal with it. This was the United States of America. This was the country that I fought for because I believed in our democracy, our freedom. And here we were in a place that felt like a police state. This was a turning point in my life. Never again would I trust the American system when it was dealing with African Americans.

They finally beat them with a rubber hose, and when they were on the edge of unconsciousness, the men confessed, a confession never used in the trial. They were judged guilty in the first trial; two years passed before the Supreme Court ordered a retrial and we came down to seek a change of venue. We were told later the boys were sure they would be acquitted. On their way to the courthouse, they were shot dead in cold blood.

The Groveland case radicalized me on the subject of race, or, rather, began to make me see reality. I would never be the same again. The combination of having become close friends with many poor black people, being with them in sickness, fire, death, despair, prison, and having them live in our house for long stretches of time made this cold-blooded racist murder something that entered the very depth of my being.

The chasm between white and black is so deep, the distrust so ancient, the arrogance of whites and the anger of blacks so built into their very being that many feel racism can never be overcome. Old-fashioned though it may sound, I believe love can eventually heal this fissure in our common humanity. I am not speaking of sentimental feelings. This will need to be a long love, a patient love, and, on the part of African Americans, a painfully forgiving love. Nor would I blame them for not wishing to make such a painful, psychic sacrifice. This forgiveness cannot be asked for, however, until society changes substantively.

The pain of forgiveness is symbolized by the cross; this is the kind of price we whites ask of African Americans. What price are whites asked to pay? Higher taxes, neighbors who seem strange at first, an understanding of the heavy load that people of color carry, pressure on federal, state, and local government? Little enough, little enough!

There are those who say the war on poverty failed. It barely got started. How could three years of anemic assistance wipe out three hundred years of systematic discrimination, humiliation, lynching, un-employment, starvation?

We soon found that race was a far deeper and more intractable barrier between people, even in Jersey City, than we had imagined. I had grown up without ever knowing a black person and hardly ever seeing one other than those working as porters and waiters on trains. Under Kim's tutelage we began to read about race. Gunnar Myrdal's An American Dilemma: The Negro Problem and Modern Democracy had come out a few years earlier. Ralph Ellison's Invisible Man was a best-seller. Langston Hughes was at his peak: I learned much from his early, small volume of short stories The Ways of White Folks. We began to see ourselves as if through the eyes of black people, adopted a liberal attitude, and learned about stereotypes, such as Uncle Toms. But when we started to deal with race, the neat phrases, even when true, did not help much. I learned the depth of my own prejudice when I found a kinky hair in my comb and had a momentary feeling of annoyance. One of the kids had used our bathroom.

We tried to teach our children to treat everyone the same, but they picked up other attitudes from the white kids next door. One day, we were in the kitchen entertaining a black woman, the first who had come into our house. We were thrilled that at long last a person of color had come to visit and were on our best behavior, as was she. After a few stilted, nervous attempts at conversation, we began to feel at ease. Just then, the door flew open and Pip, as we called our three-year-old son, Paul, rushed in, sobbing hysterically.

"What on earth's the matter, Pippy?" I asked, as I held his shaking little body.

"Some fucking nigger stole my truck!" he cried.

Luckily our visitor had a sense of humor, and we all burst out laughing. In fact, we persuaded her to come to church and bring her friends some Sunday, for at that time no black adult ever ventured into the eleven o'clock service of this "white" church. She came, breaking the ice, and, despite the grumbling of one or two whites, our black membership began to grow.

In 1950, Kim suggested we all join the NAACP. Soon I was asked to chair the local chapter's committee on housing. I was honored and set about trying to integrate the public-housing projects as much as possible. Our efforts met with some success, and I came to know several black ministers quite well. I invited Walter White to speak at our church, and he accepted. We were excited; we distributed fliers to all the black churches in town and around the neighborhood, expecting a huge crowd. Not one black minister showed up, and we had an embarrassingly small turnout. We were baffled. I think we were perceived as a threat to them, or perhaps they thought it inappropriate for Mr. White to make his first visit to Jersey City to appear at a church with white priests. Race relations was not an easy business.

We began to realize how very deep were the divisions between blacks and whites, how different our cultures. One evening in the parish house, I asked a black teenage boy to take off his hat while dancing. I had been brought up, of course, never to wear a hat indoors, much less when you were dancing. He almost hit me. Hats were a sign of manhood.

A British cabinetmaker whom we had come to know volunteered to run a carpentry class for the neighborhood boys. He was most British and most polite. One hot night, he came running up from the parish house basement where he held his class and said, "The boys are fashioning short iron pipes. I asked them what they were doing. They said they were making axles for their autos. I must say, I find that hard to believe." We found it impossible to believe. After some grilling, the boys admitted they were making weapons for an expected gang war.

It turned out such a war was indeed brewing. A few weeks earlier, I had been supervising a teenage dance in the parish house. A bunch of rough-looking black kids with turned-down hats clustered in the corner. I did not know any of them. Suddenly, with a war whoop they burst onto the dance floor and started beating up our kids. I was alone. I ran up on the stage in my flowing black cassock and shouted at the top of my lungs, "I just called the cops!" Thank God they believed me and scattered. It was rumored that they would strike again.

We notified the police and tried to get in touch with the gang leaders. No success, but we did organize with the advice of our boys. It was all a little bizarre—a council of war with teenage kids to defend the rectory. We decided we needed some scouts, so we asked two of the little kids to watch for any hostile activity a block or so away from the church. I felt like I was back in the Marines. A few nights later, one of the little boys who had been recruited as a scout ran in. "Father! Father! At least a hundred kids from the Hill are coming down Second Street! They have weapons," he said. Kim went out to meet them. I was to stay in the rectory to guard our place. By some miracle, Kim persuaded the leaders to come to the rectory for a peace conference. We carried it off, and the tension died down.

Out of this encounter, Kim started a small discussion group with black teenagers, during which they opened up somewhat about their personal lives.

However, I never felt completely accepted until one of the last nights before leaving Grace Church for Indiana, when Bob Hall, a young man to whom I felt especially close, took me out on the town in New York. We both wore jeans and T-shirts. Starting with a beer in Greenwich Village, we worked our way uptown, through Times Square, having a beer at every stop. These were joints of various kinds—some had floor shows, some just music; some were nothing but a dark place to swill beer. Bob and I talked and talked. He had changed his name a few years back, and I never knew why, but he told me that night. Apparently, when he tried to enlist in the Air Force, he needed a birth certificate. He visited city hall and learned there was no Robert Caldwell registered on his birthday. He went back a year to the same date and found a Robert Hall registered at his old address. He discovered that he was a year older than he'd thought and had been fathered by a man he'd never known. We compared notes about the service. I told him how it felt to be in combat. He told me that in the service he would earn a few bucks by making himself available to his captain. He explained how he never could keep a job, because he could not get used to the regularity and did not really feel right having a steady income. This made him angry, until he finally picked a fight and was fired.

By about three o'clock, we were leaning on each other as we weaved down the sidewalk. Our last stop was at the White Rose Café in Harlem. By that time, we were hardly verbal, but Bob put his arm on my shoulder and said, "You know, you're a damn good nigger." This was high praise. I had arrived. In the years to come, I would be in the middle of many civil rights struggles and have many black friends and colleagues, but that beery night on the town with Bob was never equaled.

Bob married a beautiful and good young woman who sang in our choir, but he was too tempestuous for the marriage to last. He lived and died alone in a furnished room.

Beneath the surface of almost all children who grow up in the poor sections of an inner city lies a deep anger. We ran into it again and again, anger such as that seen in the explosion of Bruno Gussey or in Bob Hall's inability to keep a job. Sometimes the anger would express itself in what seemed to be inconsistent ways, such as when the kids stole our car and we had to go to the very police whom we had accused of beating up the kids to report the theft. "So, Father, one of your little angels made off with your mother's fancy station wagon, huh? Maybe we should have beat 'em up more." Humiliated, we were at their mercy and felt the very powerlessness that made the kids so angry.

One young man of about twenty told me about a rage so strong that it would wake him up in the middle of the night. One night he got out of bed, dressed, and ran as fast as he could through the streets to wear out the emotion that was almost choking him. He ran and ran and ran until he found himself at the church. He tried to open the big red door, but it was locked. (We had to lock up at night for fear someone would wander in with a cigarette and set the place on fire.) He pounded on it and finally fell exhausted on the steps, rolled over, and sat against the door. The rage eased away after a half hour or so, and he went home to bed. This kind of grace, this invisible ministry, was usually unknown to us.

Christmas often brought hostilities to the surface. It is strange that a holy day commemorating God's tender, humble love as found in the Christ child should be a time of anguish for so many. The Norman Rockwell–like Christmas pictures of white, nuclear families gathered around a tree with presents strewn about, the advertisements for expensive Christmas gifts—these images obscure the story of the poor Virgin Mary with her homeless child. That God's grace should be present in a cold stable with a poor family can comfort the desperate, whereas the commercial images drive them to despair. The life idealized in these images, absolutely unattainable by our people, made them feel unworthy and increased their self-hatred. They struck out at the world or at themselves. One of our best altar boys was shot in the stomach while robbing a store on Christmas Eve. He had never been in trouble before, but his family needed food. Another year, some boys and girls were hanging out on the sidewalk just outside our house. A girl, new to the church and exceptionally pretty, was vamping one of the boys. His girlfriend flew into a rage and pulled the new girl's hair. A beautiful wig came off. At this, the now bald girl rushed at her assailant, bit her above the eye, and spit out the eyebrow she found between her teeth.

Of course those kids were angry: angry because they were black or Hispanic, or angry because every time they tried to climb the slippery walls of their imprisonment, something happened to shove them back down again—an eviction, a sick mother, a fire, a drunken father, an unwanted pregnancy. With each frustration, the anger grew. Some avoided it, I am not sure how—probably because they had been loved dearly by someone early on.

Despite the anger, we came to love most all of them, although a few seemed singularly unlovable. Often those few were the very ones who would cling to you until you wanted to run away from them and wipe your hands. But we tried. And I believe most of the ones we knew well came to love us. And that was, after all, why we were there, to be channels of God's love and to receive love in return from the kids and from their parents.

As I read this, that kind of love sounds sentimental and obvious, but it goes very deep. Such love is found at the bedside of a dying person, in the hug of a prisoner, or in the confused distress of a child. You pour love in, and because Christ dwells in those who are in pain, you receive his love from them. Such love is a mystery, and it is what keeps me a believer.

Such love can bring pain, too. When your lover, your spouse, your child wounds you, the depth of your pain is measured in proportion to the depth of your love for that person. When you speak to someone who has lost a beloved, tell her this, when the time is right. Tell her that you know she would not give up an ounce of her love to ease the pain of the loss. Somehow, in the midst of the mystery of pain and love stands the cross. When you look up and see Jesus Christ hanging there, you know that underneath the injustice and despair and absurdity of it all there must be a profound order, which is the substance of eternity.

It was through the mystery of love that we tried to understand the people whose lives we entered when we went to Grace Church: the "porch set" (as we called the derelicts who came for coffee), the kids who were so loving and yet who got into trouble so often, the girls with their strange notions about sex, the young men who were so angry they could not keep their jobs, the lonely old shut-ins, the eccentric religious types who were drawn to us, the friends of ours from New York who came when they were down on their luck. And we tried to understand how the grace of God touched their lives, even when they did not realize it. Through it all, I was deepened in my own faith that God in Christ was present in the flesh and blood and sex and suffering of his people and that all that came together at the altar, in the Mass.

Kim Myers left Jersey City first, to undertake the same kind of work on the Lower East Side of Manhattan. He was replaced by James Parks Morton, later the dean of the Cathedral of Saint John the Divine in New York. Jim's wife, Pamela Taylor, was an extraordinarily patient, wise, and witty woman. She and Jenny, on their way to the Tubes one day, saw one of the "porch set" urinating on the side of a building, and Pam said, "And to think that it's our soup!" Jim, like Kim, was an idea man, full of energy and creativity.

Bob Pegram, to his great surprise, fell in love, married, and moved to another church. When he left, Ledlie Laughlin arrived fresh from seminary but a veteran of many summers at Grace Church. He married Roxanna Dodd, a bright and beautiful summer volunteer. And so the community changed and grew.

Grace Church had an impact on the Episcopal Church far beyond the New York area. Not only did the parish itself continue to thrive under the leadership of Jim and Ledlie, but its influence spread throughout the Church. In the years after the war, seminarians, college students, and many clergy were looking for a different kind of ministry. Mission to the poor, an idea as old as the Church itself, had fresh appeal when clothed in the theology of the worker-priests of France. The notion that the "upper-class" Episcopal Church could reach people from other backgrounds took hold. This was not just social service in the name of Christ—it was social action. This was a gospel spelled out in civil rights, integration, and improved housing, in meeting the needs of poor people by empowering them to change the system that oppressed them.

We tied our social action to the liturgy, changing our liturgical practices in the church so that the people participated more than in the old style of liturgy. This emphasis was part of the liturgical movement, which swept across the whole Church and was essential to the changes in the Roman Catholic Church brought about by the Second Vatican Council a decade later. The priest celebrating the Eucharist from behind the altar so he faced the people rather than before it, the intercessory prayer becoming a litany, the kiss of peace acted out in the congregation, the dismissal at the end of the service to go forth into the world to love and serve the Lord—all these changes later were incorporated in the new prayer book.

A movement began. We organized a group we called the Urban Mission Priests and began to hold meetings and rallies to spread the word. We were joined by such great black priests as Shelton Hale Bishop of St. Philip's Church, who had been working along these lines for many years but had not been invited to work with white parishes. Some clergy in Boston started a similar ministry there. A black priest from Philadelphia brought a busload of parishioners to our rallies. Each summer we asked seminarians and college students to join us and expand our work with the children: rallies, street processions, field days that included baseball games with other churches, pet shows, races, booths for cake sales, and bus trips to Jones Beach. By reaching hundreds of children, we broadened our base for the rest of the year, helped the children have a good time, and exposed eager young college and seminary students to the realities of discrimination and poverty.

I vividly remember a rally in New York in 1956. It began outside All Souls Church on St. Nicholas Avenue just north of Central Park and processed up 110th Street to the Cathedral of St. John the Divine, from which the procession stretched as far as the eye could see. Bishop Donegan, vested in cope and miter, stood on the cathedral steps to welcome us in. Father Shelton Hale Bishop preached a fiery sermon decrying the "cotton curtain" that spread across 110th Street, separating the white churches of New York from the black.

We sent hundreds of children to camp. The sisters of St. John the Baptist administered the camp program and year in and year out tended to the needs of our people. They also gave spiritual depth to our community by their quiet, disciplined prayer life.

My old childhood and school friends lent a hand. Tony Duke was developing Boys' Harbor on Long Island. Some of us had helped him start it before the war. He resumed the work after the war with a handful of kids from our church. It now has grown into a massive and superb organization and celebrated its fiftieth anniversary in 1996. One of the Grace Church boys, Lonnie Williams, was the director for many years. Freddy Bradlee, brother of Ben Bradlee of *The Washington Post*, came out and started the Grace Church Players. His magic made the kids think they were on Broadway. He sent them flowers on opening night in our beat-up parish hall. "Dahling! You look gorgeous!" We had a wonderful mix of people; the rectory was full of laughter and tears, as we encountered one catastrophe after another.

From time to time, we led conferences and held retreats. I visited colleges and in the process helped guide some wonderful men toward the priesthood and work in the cities. I shall never forget one Harvard retreat. The chaplain, "Red" Kellogg, brought some bourbon for a fishing trip we were to take the next day, as well as Communion wine. The student who prepared the altar for the Eucharist put the bourbon in the cruet. When I received from the chalice after the Consecration, I tasted Jim Beam. What to do? Start all over again? I decided the Lord would understand, but when the students received from the chalice there were some startled faces.

The parish grew, slowly and steadily. We began in 1949 with a parish list of around fifty, and through our outreach eventually grew to more than five hundred. New leadership developed with our people. We branched out and established social-action cells in other parts of the city. We held Bible classes in the public-housing projects. I even conducted a Bible class in Spanish with the help of an English Bible, a Spanish Bible, a dictionary, and a bilingual teenager. Soon there were enough Hispanic people to have a Mass in Spanish.

The house was chaotic. One of our principles was to have an open rectory so as to live out the Christian virtue of hospitality ("Let all persons be received as Christ"). One afternoon Dorothy Day, the great co-founder of the Catholic Worker movement, paid us a visit. The dishes had not been washed, two of the children needed their diapers changed, three kids from the parish were racing around the table, some men were at the door asking for soup. Jenny turned to Dorothy and wailed, "What can I do?"

Dorothy replied calmly, "Lower your standards." That became a motto.

.   .   .

Our family grew. Paul, born when I was still in seminary, followed Honor, and Jenny was pregnant with Adelia when we went to Jersey City in July 1949. Two years later, Rosie was born in Jersey City. When the labor began, I rushed Jenny to the hospital, dressed in my black suit and round collar. As we entered the elevator, a nun stepped on. She looked Jenny up and down, then, focusing on my priest's outfit, shook her head and turned her back. Once in the labor room, Jenny was given an anesthetic, and Rosie arrived.

I returned to the rectory at about three in the morning, fell into bed, and did not wake until the alarm went off at seven. I learned later that one of our parishioners died in the night. I was called to give him the last rites, but I never answered. I cannot forget that strange juxtaposition of birth and death; in serving the one, I lost the other. I do not worry about the immortal soul of the man who died, but I know how anguished he must have been at the end not to have the Sacrament, for he was a devout Christian. He and I had been close during his illness.

When Paul came down to breakfast the next morning, and I told him he had a baby sister, he burst into tears and screamed, "God lied!" He'd been praying for a brother.

Jenny next became pregnant with George and decided to go to an obstetrician in Morristown, near my family's place. Dr. Charles Woodman was a pioneer in the movement for natural childbirth. Jenny reveled in the idea, but it made me nervous. I really preferred the "You will have your baby at ten on Tuesday" approach. Dr. Woodman was convincing, though, and even I bought the program hook, line, and sinker. Jenny did her exercises; we read the books, and I was informed that the husband had an important role. The doctor received reluctant permission for me to be present at the birth—the first time it had been allowed at that hospital. He was a senior doctor, my family had given a wing to the hospital, and I was a priest. The authorities crumpled before this temporal and spiritual power, and I was to be allowed to witness the event. There was to be no coming in on Tuesday night this time. He said to just wait until the contractions got rolling.

"But, Doctor," I said, "we are fifty minutes from the hospital. What if the baby comes on the way?"

"Not to worry. Just be sure you have some sharp scissors and a white shoelace for the umbilical cord," he explained.

I pictured myself pulled over on the side of the Pulaski Skyway at three in the morning in the pouring rain with my scissors at the ready. I wondered if Abercrombie and Fitch had a nice leather packet with the appropriate instruments. Maybe I could have one made with my initials on it.

We arrived at the hospital in time, I stayed with Jenny during the preliminaries, and into the labor room we went. I held her hand as tightly as I could and prayed hard. The doctor, the nurses, and I formed a cheering section, "One, two, three, *push!*" Jenny made a Herculean effort, and out slithered the baby, covered with what looked like cotton batting. The doctor held the child up, and there was his penis. Another boy: Paul would be pleased.

I remember having a vivid dream of being a father, even before Jenny was pregnant the first time. I can still see the baby boy in my dream image, in a child's screen bed, looking over the edge. The primordial thrill of having a child, of seeing a child arrive in the world, is indescribable, traumatic, joyful. I looked forward to happy times playing with them, taking them fishing, teaching them about life, showing them off to grandparents. I never pictured the heart-aches—how things could go wrong, the particular pain a parent can give a child and a child can give a parent, often without knowing it. Although it never reached the crisis of *King Lear*, I could identify with the old king and how he suffered through his daughters. Like romantic love, like marriage, the deeper the love goes, the sharper the pain when things go wrong. Anger builds up. Should a parent swallow his anger to keep the waters smooth, or should he let it all out? The WASP way, of course, is to swallow it; the new way is to let it all out. My kids and I do a little of both. I think letting your children know how you feel is healthy in the long run, but what courage it takes when you know that what you say will make them even angrier before a final clearing of the air is possible.

Each child, in his or her way, has given me great joy over the years. How fortunate I am to see them grow up into adults, find their creative, productive vocations, produce beautiful grandchildren, and be my friends.

By the time we arrived in Jersey City, the starched nurse had long since departed. All we had to help was Mrs. Johnson, a tiny, cross-eyed, tough, high-spirited Irish woman with a wisp of scraggly hair always hanging over her face. When we took a day off, an extraordinary Norwegian woman named Agnes Weickert came and held the fort. She was full of love and would hold the children on her generous lap, giving them the affection they needed and did not always receive from us, preoccupied as we were with so much else. We also had kids in the parish baby-sit. One boy sexually abused Honor, as she recounts vividly in a poem. She never told us about it at the time for fear he would be arrested. We sent them to the local public school but transferred Honor and Paul to St. Luke's School in New York as they grew older and needed better instruction. Our friends and family thought we were taking great risks in Jersey City, but despite some painful incidents, my children look back with happiness on those years. Honor loved the activity, the scores of people who came in and out of the house and sat around the kitchen table: poor parishioners; transients; black families burned out of their homes who came to live with us for a while; young, old, gay, straight; sophisticated friends from New York; musicians, artists, bankers, servicemen; refugees from Hungary; social pioneers like Dorothy Day and Walter White.

Paul attributes his being totally comfortable with people of color to those early years when his best friends were black and Latino. How much harm was done by incidents like Honor's abuse or by our involvement with so many other people, I cannot know. At the time, the children seemed healthy in mind and body and in retrospect feel that the attention given them by so many people made up for Jenny's and my preoccupations. It may be that exhaustion exacerbated Jenny's postpartum depressions.

Honor had a deep religious experience one Good Friday, identifying with the suffering of the cross, which we were afraid might have been too much. On another day, I remember her coming in and announcing she was king of the world. Adelia and Rosie have happy memories as well.

While in Jersey City, I continued to see my grandmother. She was in her nineties by then and almost completely blind; she was no longer able to go to church, so I brought her Communion every month. One day, when I arrived, the nurse told me that Granny was quite ill and in a deep sleep, perhaps even comatose. Usually, when she was unconscious, I would go into her room quietly, say a silent prayer, and lay my hands on her in blessing. For some reason, on this particular day, I decided to give her Communion, or at least attempt to. When I came into the room, I spread a small linen cloth on her bedside table, placed the pyx containing the Sacrament on the linen, and began the Communion prayers. The service in the old prayer book always began with the familiar Collect for Purity:

> Almighty God, unto whom all hearts are open, all desires known, and from whom no secrets are hid: Cleanse the thoughts of our hearts by the inspiration of thy Holy Spirit, that we may perfectly love thee, and worthily magnify thy holy Name; through Christ our Lord. Amen.

Since I knew the prayer by heart, I watched Granny's face as I spoke and saw her lips begin to move as if she were repeating these beloved words with me. I continued, and she followed the other prayers. Finally, I took the small Communion wafer and said the words: "The Body of our Lord Jesus Christ, which was given for thee, preserve thy body and soul unto everlasting life." She opened her mouth and received the Host. While I was folding the linen cloth and putting away the pyx, she spoke, clear as a bell: "Paul, may I make my own thanksgiving?"

"Of course, Granny," I said, and she began to thank God for her childhood, her father and mother, her marriage, her children. Indeed, her whole life passed before us as she prayed a most beautiful, simple thanksgiving. She came to the end, smiled, and closed her eyes. I gave her the blessing: "Unto God's gracious mercy and protection we commit you. The Lord bless you and keep you; the Lord make his face to shine upon you and be gracious unto you; the Lord lift up the light of his countenance upon you and give you peace, today and forevermore." Just at that moment, the chimes of St. Thomas Church began to ring. I had the most intense sense of the peace of God, which passeth all understanding.

A few weeks later, I visited her again. This time she was dressed and sitting in her favorite chair in the library. "Granny, it's great to see you so well. Was your last bout difficult?"

"Well, I don't remember much about it, but I did have a very vivid dream. I was up at Rockmarge, walking in my garden." (I could just see her in her flowing white dress and large summer hat, cane in hand, walking past the lotus pool, smelling the heliotrope and lavender.) "It was a lovely dream—the flowers never looked more beautiful. I strolled through the garden to the edge of the woods. As I went deeper and deeper into the woods, it became dark and I realized I was lost and I became frightened. Just then, you came and took me by the hand and led me home."

I then asked her if she remembered my bringing her Communion, and I told her how I had come, how she made her beautiful thanksgiving, and how the bells sounded a hymn as she went back to sleep. She was silent for some time, and then she leaned forward and said, "That was my dream."

At the end of her life, it was as if she dwelled in two worlds. The world of space and time was becoming less and less distinct. Another world, of eternal truths, was becoming clearer. She was a bit frightened of that other world, or so it seemed, and yet she found beauty there and peace.

Somehow her Communion had bridged that chasm between the worlds and perhaps had brought her back to this one for a time. I never understood the mystery of it, nor did I ever try to explain it. Enough that our love for each other over so many long years and the faith in which we both believed had brought her peace and had brought to me an experience of the chemistry of divine and human love that passes understanding.

After seven years at Grace Church, my health began to give way. I had spells of fatigue, depression, and a couple of bouts of pneumonia. Also, we had six children by then and the rectory was tight. Furthermore, the Mortons, the Laughlins, and the Sisters of St. John Baptist formed a solid base for the future. We were ready to move along.

One winter night, Paul Musselman, a friend on the staff of the National Church, came by and asked, "How would you like to go to Indianapolis?" He was referring to a position as dean of a downtown cathedral in Indianapolis, where I could use my urban experience in a different way. Jenny and I burst out laughing; all we knew was that the Indianapolis 500 car races were there. But after a few months we decided to go.

Once or twice a month, I lunched with Bill Johnson, a black lawyer who had been drawn to Grace Church because of our social-action program. We were close friends, and I leaned heavily on him for advice and support. When I told him our plans, he did not seem surprised. He had thought we would move along some day. He naturally expressed regret. Together, he and I planned how I would make the announcement in church the following Sunday.

That Sunday morning, however, he stormed into the kitchen, where Jenny was getting the children's breakfast. This calm man was very disturbed. "I knew we weren't good enough for you," he said bitterly. "We're just a bunch of niggers."

Bill did not really mean it—but on some level he did. His remark has always stayed with me. I promised myself that wherever I went I would remember it and try to stand against the terrible effects of racism and poverty.

Jenny later wrote a beautiful book about our time there, *The People on Second Street*. She was a legendary figure in the parish, and was still remembered vividly many years afterward. One woman told our son Danny, "All the women in the neighborhood talked about what she had given us and what a great woman she was."

On May 4, 1997, Grace Church celebrated its 150th anniversary with four former clergy—Fathers Jim Morton, Ledlie Laughlin, John Luce, and myself. I celebrated the Eucharist. The church was full. Many old parishioners, among them some of our Sunday school students—now grandparents—came up to me with tears in their eyes to say how much we had meant to them, how we had opened up the world to them.

On my last Sunday, I climbed the steps of the pulpit with my remarks prepared. "We have loved you," I said. "You are wonderful people. You have taught us so much by your courage and love. Keep up this great work of Christ. We will never forget you. But it is time for us to leave." When I looked down on those faces and that beloved place, I burst into uncontrollable tears.

The next day, the moving van came lumbering down Second Street, where so much had happened, and all of our belongings were carried out through the lych-gate, a symbol of death and new life.

INDIANAPOLIS

WHAT first struck me about Christ Church Cathedral in downtown Indianapolis was how clean everything was. The pews were shiny, the entrance hall to the parish house was covered with maroon wall-to-wall carpeting, and the paneling, a glossy tan, was decorated with pictures of former rectors, uniformly framed. The church even smelled clean. Into this spotless space on that first Sunday came the boys' choir, ready to process into the church, vested in sparkling white cottas, their white faces shining with the scrubbing to which they had been subjected that morning. What's more, it was five minutes to eleven. We were on time! Part of me was delighted to have a functioning parish like this; part of me wanted to dirty it up as quickly as I could. No blacks or Latinos, no ill-fitting cassocks, no latecomers rushing in and disrupting the choir's solemn entrance, no reflection of the turbulence of city life! I missed Grace Church already.

Christ Church Cathedral is set on Monument Circle, the very center of Indianapolis. The monument itself is a stone obelisk over a hundred feet high. The base is surrounded by sculptures of charging horses, cannons, Civil War soldiers, and limestone flags. Water gushes forth from this Wagnerian display, giving it the appearance of a four-sided Roman Trevi fountain. Meridian Street runs straight north and south from the circle; avenues named after states go off at angles—a mini-Paris with the Civil War monument its Arc de Triomphe.

The cathedral occupied a position of ecclesiastical prominence as well. The church was relatively small but handsome, built of Indiana limestone in neo-Gothic style in the 1840s. Next door to us on Monument Circle was the prestigious Columbia Club, and because our parish house was small, the Sunday school classes met in the club's private dining rooms. The kids would scurry through the two-story lounge, much to the consternation of the old businessmen sitting in large leather chairs.

The previous dean and rector, John Craine, had just been elected bishop coadjutor of the diocese (assistant bishop with right of succession when the diocesan bishop retired). When he had been called to be rector of Christ Church some eight years before, the parish had been sliding downhill. He instilled energy and pride, increased attendance, doubled the giving, renovated the building, and persuaded Richard Kirkhhoffer, the diocesan bishop, to make it the cathedral of the diocese. Christ Church lost its Victorian ethos and regained its confidence. Bishop Craine first interviewed me in his New York hotel room in the winter of 1957. He was a tall, long-faced handsome man of great inner dignity and spoke with authority and conviction. He told me how he had revived the parish with a dedicated group of laypersons; now he wanted me to make it the center of a vigorous urban mission. The more we talked, the more excited I became. Before we parted, he said he would nominate me to the vestry as the next dean and rector of Christ Church Cathedral. The church had money, leadership, confidence, and enthusiasm. Urban mission was my specialty. How could we go wrong?

I felt as though I was being given a brand-new Cadillac; the trouble was that I was used to driving a beat-up secondhand Ford. My strategy for an urban mission would threaten the very people who had helped John Craine rebuild, and I had little understanding of the deep cultural differences between Indianapolis and the East Coast.

In the early spring of 1958 Jenny and I went to Indianapolis for an interview with the vestry. I was forthright in stating my views. I spoke of the Church's mandate not only to serve the poor, but also to change the conditions that led to their poverty; not only to perform social services in the name of Christ, but also to encourage poor people and blacks to join the Church. I stressed that I belonged to the NAACP and believed in racial justice. Perhaps the bishop persuaded them that I was the man for the job; perhaps they had never heard of the NAACP; perhaps my youthful enthusiasm charmed them (I was just thirty-seven). After just a few minutes, I was called in and congratulated with great enthusiasm on being called as dean and rector of Christ Church Cathedral. Insofar as I would be the priest in charge of the parish, I would be rector; insofar as the church functioned as the bishop's cathedral, I would be dean.

They said they would like to meet Mrs. Moore. I rushed next door to the Columbia Club, where we were staying, and found Jenny in the bathtub, worrying about our move. She dressed in a rush, and we presented ourselves, a shining young couple, ready to do the Lord's work "with all you wonderful people."

We began to have reservations about accepting the call when we visited one vestryman's home for drinks and found the rumpus room decorated with fishnets and naked mermaids. It never occurred to us that we were being narrow-minded and snobbish in finding this in bad taste. Furthermore, some of the men and women present seemed not to understand our talk of urban mission, even though they nodded politely. And Jenny and I were bewildered when we were shown the house where we were to live. The deanery was a large, pretentious neo-Tudor mansion, set back from the still-fashionable Washington Boulevard by a well-tended lawn and shade trees. To one side was a formal terrace with a stone birdbath in its center. What a contrast to Jersey City's Charles Addams–style rectory, with its gloomy stone facade, its peeling gray paint, and the laundry lines strung across the backyard! Inside, a formal staircase swept into the front hall flanked by an enormous living room lined with French windows and dominated by a baronial fireplace and a formal dining room opening onto a glassed-in porch. The floor above contained five spacious bedrooms, the third floor three maids' rooms.

We were appalled. As soon as we found a moment alone, we said as one, "We can't live there!" Our whole effort in Jersey City had been to present the church as a friend of the poor, with the face of the poor. Our rectory there had been furnished with furniture from Goodwill so that the people of the neighborhood would feel comfortable. Here, the grandeur of the house was part of John Craine's effort to make the parishioners feel important and to impress visitors with its richness and prestige. We were guilty, too, of a reverse snobbism against what we felt were the bourgeois values of Indianapolis.

Where would we live, if we felt we could not live in the deanery? We decided to get hold of Father Frank Carthy, another imported

Easterner, who was more radical in his views than we. He was a rotund, humorous black-haired Irishman who grew up in the labor movement. He, too, had read Dorothy Day and the worker-priests. Frank was rector of an Anglo-Catholic parish in a poor neighborhood and had been provided with a modest house. We envied him.

We asked him to drive us around the neighborhood in search of less pretentious quarters. He understood, but he warned us that the bishop would be upset and that the vestry would climb the walls if we did anything but delight in the deanery. Furthermore, there were no residential neighborhoods near the church; the deanery could not be a drop-in center for the poor. We realized that we did need a large house for our seven children and knew that the vestry would deeply resent a change, so we took a deep breath and decided to move into the deanery.

Indianapolis was a patriotic town. Up Meridian Street from the Civil War monument stood the World War I Memorial, a massive stone building with a pyramidal roof. An ongoing issue was whether the local chapter of the American Civil Liberties Union should be allowed to meet in its auditorium, theoretically open to the public. The trustees apparently felt that the ideology of the ACLU dishonored those in whose memory the monument had been erected. Across a broad plaza from the memorial stood the national headquarters of the American Legion, and on the west side was the massive Scottish Rite Cathedral of the Masons.

Our first caller in Jersey City had been poor old Cherry Armstrong. Our first caller here was someone altogether different. One afternoon, Paul came running into the house and cried, "Hey, Pop, the fellow who runs the drugstores is here. He came in a Rolls-Royce!" "The fellow who runs the drugstores" was our senior warden, Mr. Eli Lilly, of Eli Lilly and Company, the enormous pharmaceutical corporation that dominated, in benign wealth and power, the city of Indianapolis.

I put on my collar, rushed downstairs, called Jenny. The doorbell rang, and Mr. and Mrs. Lilly came in, stumbled over a bicycle on the steps, and sat down stiffly in our large living room. In appearance, the Lillys were an unpretentious couple. He was rather short, with a comfortable frontage, round-faced, and balding. He peered through very thick, rimless spectacles with what could be arresting intensity. You would not notice him in a room, but at a meeting you'd sense his quiet presence. Mrs. Lilly, who had been his assistant, had a pleasant countenance and was modestly dressed.

Our conversation was polite, but we did not exactly rattle along like magpies. Mr. and Mrs. Lilly were shy. They tried hard to converse; Jenny and I tried even harder. Finally, Jenny said, "Would you like to see the house?" She blurted out the invitation without thinking. The tour proceeded well until we came to our bedroom in which there was no bed. It had been sent out to be rid of the Jersey City bedbugs, which had come along for the ride to Indianapolis. The Lillys were startled by this great expanse of emptiness, and Jenny mumbled something about the bed being broken. That did not sound very good either, so we hurried on to the children's rooms, which were in chaos. The Lillys exchanged a knowing glance, apologized for bursting in on us, welcomed us again to Indianapolis, and sped off in their gray Rolls-Royce, which, incidentally, had been parked in front of the house where the John Birch Society had been founded.

Mr. Eli (as he was familiarly called to differentiate him from his brother, J. K. Lilly) was an unusual person to be the leading citizen of his city. Besides having developed the company founded by his grandfather, he was an accomplished cabinetmaker, an amateur historian who had written the history of Christ Church, the leading expert on the Indian mounds of Indiana (about which he had made the authoritative study), and a former champion sailboat skipper of the Midwest. Mr. Eli was conservative, politically and economically, but because of his deep Christian faith he was absolutely clear and strong on social issues such as civil rights. The employees at Eli Lilly and Company were so well taken care of that no union could ever organize them. My labor friends saw this as paternalistic, but for Mr. Eli it was the right and just way to run a company. In any case, he and I became fast friends, although his manner always remained formal. He had never had a son; to some extent, I think I occupied that role in his life.

At the bishop's wise suggestion, I decided to take it easy with the congregation. I realized most of them were conservative—socially, liturgically, and politically. In Jersey City, the more radical your views and actions, the better the people liked it. The opposite was true in Indianapolis.

I preached pastorally oriented sermons from the biblical text rather than speaking to social justice issues. One day, when, because of some fuss in the parish, I wanted to preach a *very* mild sermon, I preached on peace, which at that time, before the Vietnam War, was a non-controversial issue. However, on the way out of church, an old lady said, "My goodness, that was a courageous sermon!"

I was taken aback. "Why?"

"Well, you said you approved of the United Nations."

By and large, the people were polite, but not overly friendly. As a boy, I had visited cousins in Cleveland, who entertained us with open, warm gusto. I expected the same in this Midwestern city. So the Hoosier standoffishness was disturbing. With the exception of the Lillys and one other family, for instance, no one asked us out to dinner during the whole first year we were there. What was wrong? Did we threaten the people within the parish with our Eastern ways? Had we somehow offended? As the years went by, we came to realize that Indianapolis was a reserved town that did not welcome strangers easily. Some said that this was because of the heavy German ancestry of many Hoosiers, others that it came from their farming background. We did notice a sense of inferiority about their town on the part of almost everyone, an inferiority with which we did not agree. Indiana University was one of the finest in the nation. A nationally known seminary was there. A friend of ours, Evans Woollen, had helped design a splendid new symphony hall. It was a city to be proud of. But many called it "Indianoplace." Who knows why they, our parishioners, were so hard to get to know. But that's the way it was. Once they opened up to you, though, they were loyal. A letter or two from Eastern friends helped us to find a social life outside the parish. These were liberal-minded people, many of whom had gone to college in the East. We had a splendid time together, fighting for the things we believed in and having family picnics.

We gradually adjusted to Indianapolis. My oldest daughter, Honor, was just entering her teens. Here are some excerpts from an address she gave to her twenty-fifth reunion at Radcliffe.

> When I was eleven, we moved to Indianapolis. The only black person in the house was our maid, Mrs. Lee (Leesy, as we called her). The girls at school wore matched sweater sets and circle pins, a far cry from St. Luke's School in New York. Worse, my first friend on my first day of school said to me as we looked out our classroom window, "I don't believe it, a nigger at our school."
>
> Her remark cut through me, a word only lynchers used. Should I protest to the only girl who had befriended me? I was paralyzed with fear. This was hostile territory, a place where I could not say what I thought. I said nothing, but my heart was broken. By not speaking up for the boy in the school yard, I betrayed the part of myself that I loved.

Honor went on to Shortridge High School, where some of the racial barriers broke down. The school had a vigorous drama club, where she found a place with like-minded people and from which she went on to become the first woman president of the Harvard Dramatic Club.

Paul, my second child, wrote a short note:

> Highlights: reading the Christmas lesson from the beginning of Genesis at the Christmas Eve service; playing football in the front yard; straight As junior year.
>
> Lowlights: Percy [our spaniel who bit the postman whom we all despised] being put to sleep without your telling us it was to happen; car wreck Christmas Eve; racial conservatism; we were not allowed by you to join a segregated club where all our friends went to swim.

Some of the worst hurts we give our children come from inadvertence. Paul might well have been the president of his class at high school in Indianapolis, but we moved to Washington, where he was lost, friendless, and lonely in a huge suburban school. It never entered our heads, or his, for that matter, that he could have stayed on and lived with a friend in Indianapolis. It pains me every time I think of our obtuseness. He did well, despite that, and went on to graduate from Yale, where he was an officer of the *Yale News* and a leader of the undergraduate resistance to the Vietnam War.

Here are some of the memories of our third child, Adelia, who was eight when we arrived in Indiana.

> Crowds of kids in the yard; playing rover red rover; climbing trees. Family prayers before a prayer desk with cross and candles in the living room; we each would pray and then sing a familiar hymn together, like "Now the day is over." Church a happy, secure place. Eli Lilly's huge swimming pool. Memories of Kennedy's assassination as the only Democrat in my class. Great time at Shortridge with fine teachers, music, plays.

Adelia was elected freshman homecoming queen and almost won the state spelling bee in a dramatic photo finish in the war memorial.

Rosemary, age six when we moved, had a close friend, Debbie, who was the daughter of the Unitarian minister, Jack Mendelssohn. I overheard this conversation one day as they came in the front hall, where there was a picture of Jesus. Debbie asked, "That's Jesus, isn't it?"

Rosie: "No, that's God."

Debbie: "No, it's Jesus."

Rosie: "Well, it's the same thing."

Debbie: "I never heard *that* before!"

Ecumenical dialogue at an early age!

As with the other children, the contrast of the move was profound for her. Rosie was a real street kid. I found her crying one day in the Adirondacks on the dock of this magnificent lake. She sobbed, "I miss the fire hydrant." Living in a house surrounded by trees and a lawn with no one playing on the sidewalk out front was upsetting. She says she always felt a little different. Here is a verbal collage of our life in Indianapolis through her eyes.

> So different from Jersey City; I never recovered. [Was this because, more than any of the children, people made a fuss over her twinkling face?] Indianapolis: a giggling club, baseball at the corner playground, being told to be nice to an unattractive boy next door. Holiday dinners with guests who would have been lonely. Visiting priest from India who played a trick with a banana. Christmas customs: during Advent, each of us could have the picture of Jesus in our room one night and get breakfast in bed; unwrapping presents all Christmas afternoon with Pop keeping the list of aunts' and uncles' presents. Poems by James Whitcomb Riley. Trips to Brown County for apples. Fainting when I sang in the choir. Cuban missile crisis. JFK assassination. Seven bathrooms in the house. [We had one in

Jersey City.] Wonderful family Fourth of July picnics on the lawn. Catholic families. Jewish families. Jokes about the differences. Agony of trying to stand up for my political views. Birthday party [February 29!] come dressed as a President or come dressed as you were when the phone rang. No one admitted answering the phone naked.

George, an artist, replied characteristically with a blueprint of the house and neighborhood annotated with comments about where major events in his life occurred.

The deli on the corner where I learned about change. The porch where Mom told me she was pregnant [with Patience]. Place where we burned the old Christmas tree. Spot where the milkman dropped a bottle of milk. Johnny Sluss's house . . . he was a bully. Kennedy funeral on TV with the horse Blackjack with the boots turned around. This is where a visiting artist taught me to draw a nose. Pop's dresser where I stole his change. Driveway where we built a Roman chariot on the old Chevy for the parade. The Chevy was named Arlene, after the bishop's wife, whose car it had been.

Marian recounts the happy memories of a seven-year-old: she remembers making mud pies in the woods; Peter Lawson, my assistant, without his trousers, in jockey shorts; first seeing the Beatles on TV; mirror-writing on the wall so Mom would think Danny did it, since he had a mirror-writing problem; being confused at church about whether Pop was God.

Danny was only five when we left, but he had some memories too, especially of Leesy, our housekeeper who loved and cuddled him so much. He remembers great picnics, but also being hit by a baseball bat so that he had to be rushed to the hospital for five stitches. He wrote: "I absorbed much spiritual 'juice' at church. I remember the dark foyer of the church as a redolent place with many people coming and going. Tricycles on the sidewalk. Planting pansies with Pop. Going to my first movie, *King Kong and Godzilla*. We all took bottles to bed: George got chocolate, Marian strawberry, I got banana."

We all counted on going east each summer to the Adirondacks. Our camp there is a magical, mythical *On Golden Pond* kind of place, which has become a deep part of our family life as we return, year after year. In 1922, my father and some friends bought a large tract of land that had been burned over a few years before and therefore had lost its value for lumber. The previous owner, Seth Low, at different times the president of Columbia and mayor of New York, and his family had a vision of local industry for the economically depressed area. There was a lumber mill and even an iron foundry that made wood-burning stoves. He also built a camp on the shore of an exquisite mile-long lake, surrounded by low mountains. On a sunny day the lake sparkles blue in the sun, and in the evening wisps of mist cover the black water. Loons cry their strange calls, and ripples appear on the surface from the rising of the fish or the wake of a beaver. The camp itself seems part of the natural landscape, so mellow has it become over almost a hundred years. The brown shingled living room, above the boathouse, contains a huge fireplace over which hangs the head of a stately moose. It is furnished with faded chintz-covered sofas and golden-oak furniture. Along a boardwalk is a row of white and brown cabins overlooking the lake; beyond them a small sitting room adorned with stuffed animals, a seedy-looking beaver, a molting black bear, and deer heads. Next door is the dining room and large kitchen. Up behind the kitchen are outbuildings, a barn, and a tennis court. The boathouse is full of sleek Adirondack guide boats, which glide through the water like canoes.

One of my earliest memories is of my father walking across the lobby of the St. Regis Hotel with a smile on his face and a strange long object in his hand, my first fishing rod. Dad used to charter a whole Pullman sleeper or a private car to carry us all to Horseshoe, the flag stop that was our station. I would wake early and peek through the window of my berth. Sometimes I saw a deer drinking in the misty depths of a swamp. We were met by the guides, served hot coffee and doughnuts, and trundled in Model-T station wagons over the five-mile dirt road to Camp Otterbrook. "There's the lake," someone would cry, and soon we rolled down the hill into camp.

Year after year, summer after summer, generation after generation, we drove that long road. My daughter Rosemary says it is like driving into your unconscious. Strange what happens there: we all regress to childhood, including myself. Rituals are meticulously observed: supper on the pine-clad island with charades in front of the open fire; picnics at the mossy slide, where we pin on diapers and slide on our fannies into a mountain pool; prisoner's base around the flagpole in the dusk; family tennis and Ping-Pong tournaments. One summer, we were there for three weeks, and it rained every single day. Three of the children were in diapers—old-fashioned cloth diapers. Luckily a teenage goddaughter, Elaine Dickerman, was there to lend a hand as diapers steamed in front of every fireplace.

Sometimes there is friction, as people live out ancient sibling rivalries, and sometimes the buried hurts surface with tears and anger. But for the most part our stays there have been full of joy and laughter. Cousins become friends, Granpop (me) tells stories, Brenda (my present wife) teams up with the younger grandchildren to scare the rest of us as we have cocktails overlooking the evening glow of the lake.

My father visualized a place for future generations to gather, to learn to love the woods, to deepen family ties, to have fun. He would be pleased.

Mother called me in Indianapolis the day after Susanna was born, December 15, 1959, asking me to come back East immediately. My father, who had been ill for some time, had taken a turn for the worse. I arrived in time for dinner and had a good visit with him in the library before he went to bed. In the middle of the night, Mother woke me. By that time, my brother and sisters had come. We gathered in Dad's bedroom, where the pictures of the days at Yale still hung on the wall. The doctor arrived and said he would not last much longer. He was unconscious by then, and after a while he slipped away. I said the prayers for the dying, those strong reassuring prayers, and gave him a final blessing. My sister Fanny leaned over the bed, hesitated, and then kissed him.

I celebrated a Requiem for the family in the morning, and the local rector took the funeral in the afternoon in our family church, Grace Church, Madison. So many old friends, so many memories. My father had a hard time expressing emotion, but I knew he loved me.

I brought two associates to Indianapolis: Herbert Bolles, an ex-Navy officer, a faithful and effective canon pastor; and Al Rountree, from the deep South, who had worked with us in Jersey City as a seminarian. Bishop Craine encouraged me to have a weekly Eucharist together with the other cathedral canons and the inner-city clergy. He celebrated the Eucharist, and then we had breakfast and talked at length. This was the cathedral chapter, and it became the group we relied on for support and stimulus. Frank Carthy regaled us on occasion with hearty labor-union songs. Henry Hill was there, a quiet black priest, rector of the only Negro parish in the diocese, St. Philip's. (Over the altar at St. Philip's was a ghastly mural depicting a scene from the saint's life: a black eunuch kneeling at the feet of a white St. Philip.) Malcolm Boyd, who had been a partner of Mary Pickford's in Hollywood and who later became known as the "espresso priest," came as rector of a nearby inner-city church. A few years later, he was driven out of the Diocese of Michigan because on television, in an effort to emphasize the humanity of Jesus, he'd said that Jesus had arms like you and me, a nose like you and me, and a penis like you and me. Luckily, he did not say that in Indianapolis.

John Craine and I had become good friends. He supported me strongly even when I did things that upset the diocese, and he took my side against some of his former parishioners when we had a show-down about race at the cathedral.

This was the inner circle. Here we exchanged ideas, kidded one another, laughed, and comforted one another when things went wrong. Out of these weekly conversations grew the style and spirit of our ministry there.

After a couple of years, we had formed ourselves into a coalition of inner-city congregations. The cathedral was the mother church, alone amid the tall office buildings of downtown. The other three were small parishes in comparison and located in poor residential areas. St. Philip's was in a black neighborhood. All Saints, Father Carthy's church, was in the process of founding an Episcopal social agency. Malcolm Boyd was trying to bend his Hollywood ways to the blue-collar membership of St. George's Church. The cathedral bought an old house and put Al Rountree in charge of work in an Appalachian community a few blocks away. The Jersey City ministry continued to be my model; I saw the need for each of these places to have a strong neighborhood program and believed that they would grow because of it. However, such programs needed money.

The finances were a stumbling block until one day I had lunch with Mr. Eli at the Columbia Club. After asking me his usual questions concerning the church's program, music, and so forth, he took out an old envelope (on which his most important aide-mémoire seemed always to be scribbled) and asked: "Do you think I could give more money to the church without hurting the giving of other people?"

I had *never* been asked *that* before. "Well, sir," I sputtered, "I guess we could work something out."

"You go ahead and put your ideas together for our next meeting. I have to go now."

Imagine the excitement this caused at the next cathedral chapter breakfast. Through the general good feeling, Carthy mumbled something about capitalism; Boyd thought this could fund a television documentary; the bishop, who had already received an endowment of over a million dollars from Mr. Eli for the work of the diocese, showed a mix of satisfaction, puzzlement, and deliberation on his long-jawed face. How much should I ask for? I timidly suggested a hundred thousand dollars. Everyone thought that was a great deal, but why not?

At my next lunch with Mr. Eli, we had hardly spread the big linen napkins on our laps, when he asked, "You have a plan for my new stewardship?"

"Yes, sir, but we had no idea how much you had in mind. Would a plan for spending"—I took a deep breath—"one hundred thousand be too much?"

"I'm not talking about chicken feed," he mumbled. "Prepare something for a million dollars."

So it was that the Talbot Fund (named after a former bishop and rector of Christ Church) was established to finance work done by the church in the city of Indianapolis. The money could not be used for Christ Church parish except in a dire emergency. We were on our way in a substantive outreach to the city.

It was 1957, and in many ways Indianapolis was a Southern town. The Klan had been strong here. The John Birch Society thrived. Up to that time, out of a membership of about seven hundred, the parish had only two black members: Alexander Moore, the principal of Crispus Attucks (the black high school), and his wife. I do not remember how, but Father Rountree befriended three black children, who began coming to Sunday school. At first, this upset no one, because they attended the nine o'clock service with the younger, more liberal families. Before long they asked to be baptized. The ceremony of baptism, according to a policy established by Bishop Craine, always took place at the eleven o'clock service. I was thrilled, anticipating a breakthrough. The day arrived, and into the church came the three children—the girls in starched dresses, the boy in a brand-new blue suit—each accompanied by two parents, several grandparents, and three godparents. Thus when the time came for the baptism itself, at least twenty black adults surrounded the font at the front of the church. I caught the eye of Nate Gore, our sexton, who was black. He smiled nervously, as if to say, This is great, but look out!

The baptisms went off beautifully, and my euphoria was such that I did not notice the scowls on the faces of many parishioners. The greetings at the door of the church that morning were less than fulsome, the newly integrated coffee hour sparsely attended.

That took place in 1957, just after the Little Rock school integration conflict arose. I had avoided preaching on social justice issues because I wanted to come to know the people before upsetting them with controversy. But I could not be still when the headlines were blaring out this crisis in American life, a crisis that had to do directly with Christian principles.

A month or so later, the vestry suggested we have an overnight conference at the diocesan camp. I was excited. I said to Jenny, "Imagine the vestry suggesting a conference. I certainly underestimated these guys." Plans were made, and the conference got under way. After supper the first night, I celebrated an informal Eucharist and preached about the Gospel story of Jesus washing the disciples' feet as a paradigm for the ministry of the cathedral. The next morning, we prayed and then I called the meeting to order. Mr. Eli, the senior warden, had not been able to come. So the junior warden rose to speak. "Wait just a minute. We want to tell you why we are here."

"Aren't we here to plan the coming year and our mission to the city?" I asked.

"Yes, but first we want to talk about those nigras you baptized a few Sundays ago." My heart sank, but they were off. I unconsciously took the role of group therapy leader and asked each member to express his feelings frankly. Their remarks were along these lines: "We have nothing against Negroes, but they have to have their own place. They have St. Philip's to go to, and we give them money each year. You know our daughters come to church, and what would happen if one of them made a pass at one of our girls? Would you want your daughter to marry a Negro?" And on and on. "People are already talking of leaving the parish, after all the work we have done," one vestryman said. "Bishop Craine preached about civil rights, but he never talked about integrating our parish." Another said that he heard I was sent out there as an undercover agent of the NAACP. Only the youngest and newest member of the vestry, Chuck Orban, spoke in my defense.

I responded carefully to each argument and concluded by asking what Jesus would say. Perhaps it was a cheap shot, but that was really what the controversy was all about, wasn't it? At the end of the day, I said, "I have something funny to tell you: it so happens that to-morrow, for the first time, we will have three black kids in the choir." In another twist of fate, my assistant, who was to preach at the ca-thedral the next day, had chosen as his subject Christian courage, using Althea Gibson, the famous black tennis player, as an example. I tried to disappear through the carpeted floor of the sanctuary as I felt the gaze of the vestrymen upon me, as if I had prompted the subject matter to further stir up controversy.

Two days later, Mr. Eli came to see me. "Sorry to bother you," he said, "but I want you to know that as long as I am senior warden there will never be a Little Rock on Monument Circle, and if you want to paint the church green with pink polka dots I will back you all the way. Good day, sir." I'd been shaken by the vestry conference, and it was wonderful to have such unsolicited support from him— not just because he was rich and powerful, but because of his deep Christian conviction in these matters. With Eli Lilly for you, few would dare be against you!

The war was not over, though. I tried and tried to win the recal-citrant members over. I played golf with them, showing up in dirty sneakers and with a set of old clubs from college. I told them I had not played much lately. They were kindly and condescending as they produced their shiny leather bags. To our mutual surprise, I shot a thirty-nine on the first nine. Or I would have a few drinks in their company and unburden my soul to them. But the surly underground rebellion continued, until I did not dare bring up anything controversial at the vestry meetings unless I had my majority of one. One morning in the sacristy, the warden of the acolytes said to me, "Father, you are good with poor people, you are at home with rich people, but you don't give a damn for the likes of us middle-class folks." He was partly right.

After a while the conflict turned mean, and I heard the dissidents were having unauthorized rump vestry meetings and were even working on our treasurer, who was dying of cancer in the hospital. As time went on, I became so obsessed with the conflict that I had insomnia and Jenny began to complain.

The turning point came when my secretary, Emily Craine, who was the bishop's sister, asked me whether I wanted the leaders of the dissident group on the vestry. I told her I did not but that the elections were a democratic process. She said, "Never mind, that's all I need to know." She passed the word to the younger members, who came to the meeting in force and elected a slate of splendid young vestrymen. God bless you, Emily Craine!

As I look back on it, the issue had to do with power within the Church. These men were on John Craine's team but never felt they were on mine. They understood his aims and approved the building up of the institution. They did not understand my aim, shared now by Bishop Craine, of using the institution to reform society even at its own expense. And underneath it all, of course, was a racism so deep-seated as to be unconscious. The Negro community of Indianapolis was conscious of it, of course. I preached two sermons on Negro history, which were published in the local paper. The Negro response was overwhelmingly positive. In a sense it was sad that they should have been so grateful for so little.

I continued to enjoy the work of a parish priest. Preaching every Sunday was fulfilling. Sometimes, when the congregation was particularly attentive, I would find myself saying things I had no idea were inside of me. The congregation, by its expressions, was drawing words from my depths, and it felt as if the Spirit were preaching through me. This was a thrilling experience. Preaching is a dialogue between the preacher and the people. On their part the dialogue is unspoken, but expressions, body movements, or sudden silences convey their feelings to the preacher, who in turn can pick up these signals and respond. Anglican preaching tends to be too bookish; sermons sound like lectures. A sermon should be sound in its content and be able to teach, but its basic purpose is to inspire, to fill the people with the Spirit. If a preacher reads his or her sermon, there is no chance for the Spirit to enter the process, no chance for the Word to come alive.

Visiting the sick was also an important ministry. Often, just your presence is important. I always offered to say a prayer, an offer rarely refused, and I was often surprised at the depths of faith I would discover. I remember one older woman who had come regularly to the early service each Sunday, but whose faith seemed merely conventional. I visited her when she was nearly comatose, but something urged me to give her Communion. When I placed the bread in her mouth, she presented her palms in the position of one receiving Communion. Even in an unconscious state, her being responded to the Sacrament.

Despite all the issues and conflicts, our steady work of ministry continued.

THE WIDER CHURCH

Sometimes one can understand what is going on in a culture by observing the changes in a particular institution such as the Church. As we did our best in Indianapolis to convert our sloppy, radical inner-city style to the sedate rhythms of that time, that city, that parish, the Episcopal Church at large was looking beyond the immediate problems of the poor to the sources of the problems in American cities at large. It was a time when *planning* was in vogue. We had many conferences on the techniques of planning, as if we could plan our way to utopia. The trouble with planning was that everyone used it to avoid tough problems: the more we planned the less we did.

In the early 1950s, concerned for the Church's impact on the cities of America, the Lilly Endowment (at the behest of John Craine) began a program to establish ministries in problem places, experiment with techniques, and then reproduce successful ones elsewhere. The ministries flourished because of the attention they received, but reproducing the techniques elsewhere did not really work out. I suspect churches are too idiosyncratic to be replicated. My strategy has always been to think of particular churches as organic entities that grow in different ways. They cannot be planned out like businesses but need to be tended like gardens: cut back here; water there; take inside for a winter's rest somewhere else. Some parishes need funding, some new leadership, some closer supervision, some therapy for the rector, and some need to be allowed to wait out a change in demographics before beginning a new ministry.

With the Reverend Morris "Ben" Arnold, rector of Christ Church Cincinnati (the equivalent in that town to Christ Church Cathedral in Indianapolis), I formed a group of downtown rectors, called the Church and City Conference, to discuss the problems of old parishes in the commercial areas of their cities. These problems were very different from the problems of inner-city parishes. The churches usually had endowments, but fewer and fewer people attended services. Their lay leaders were often influential in the economic and political affairs of the city, and we took advantage of this to lobby for an ongoing national urban program (to replace the Lilly program, which had terminated). We won a political battle in the Program and Budget Committee, and the new national urban program was begun, with my former Jersey City colleague Jim Morton as its executive. The program sponsored large conferences around the country in which the conferees played leadership roles in an artificial city, known as Metabagdad, to find out how city government, industry, and commerce—the city power structures—affected the daily lives of the people who lived there, especially the poor. This tactic was more sophisticated than dumping garbage on the steps of city hall to draw the city fathers' attention to the filth in the streets, but I am not sure it was more effective. What it did do was draw the attention of the Church at large to the problems of the city, explore the dynamics that brought them about, and insist that all citizens, including those who lived in the farthest suburbs, were responsible. We began to glimpse the reality of economic and political power and to think of how to change it.

Our basic difficulty was persuading businessmen to work against the bottom line. Social change to benefit the poor—whether within a corporation in terms of higher wages, or in the political arena in terms of higher taxes—usually goes directly against short-term business interests. I could appreciate the decency of Christian men and women caught in this bind but unable to change the system in which they worked. However, I believe that in the long run a just social order will stimulate sound economic development. What annoys me the most are the minor humanitarian gestures corporations make for the sole purpose of improving their image.

One of my attempts at a dialogue between the Church and the business community backfired. I persuaded some Episcopal business leaders to come to an overnight conference on business ethics led by the Reverend Joseph Fletcher, who was well known for his theory of situational ethics. Joe charmed them all, and I felt we had made some progress. However, a new reporter for the *Indianapolis Star* had just arrived from Boston, where Fletcher was considered a radical. The reporter headlined his report, "Radical Priest Leads Businessmen's Conference." The son of the *Star*'s publisher, Eugene Pulliam, Jr., had attended, and I learned through the grapevine that he heard from his father in no uncertain terms.

This all sounds like a wholesale condemnation of the free-enterprise system. In a way, it is. But socialism does not seem to foster political freedom. Is it possible to have economic justice and political freedom? So far, no large nation-state has been able to attain both. Why not? It seems so simple: retain the energy engendered by the self-interest of free enterprise and provide an effective safety net for those who are left out. But human greed and the drive for profit keep the powers that be from establishing a safety net that really works, and the competition from foreign corporations with far lower overhead and wages pushes local companies to economize in every way possible at the expense of their employees' welfare. Another contemporary difficulty is the pace of change. Just social structures take time to build; the rate of modern social and economic change is so rapid that structures cannot change fast enough to keep up. The body politic becomes discouraged and votes out of naked self-interest or sheer frustration rather than out of a vision for the nation.

Since working for social change was such an uphill fight in Indianapolis, once a month a small group of ministers, priests, and rabbis met to bewail the conservatism of the town, among them Ray Bosler, a progressive Roman Catholic who published the diocesan paper; Jim

Armstrong, who later became a Methodist bishop and president of the National Council of Churches; Roe Johnston, leader of the Athletes for God movement in the Presbyterian Church (and a former all-American football player, as I remember); Jack Mendelssohn, the Unitarian pastor; and Rabbi Maurice Davis, later the founder of a deprogramming process for former members of the Moonies and other cults. This was a strong group from a variety of theological backgrounds, but we felt totally united in seeking to bring about social justice in Indianapolis. We all had the same problems with our people, but because of one another's backing we did not lose courage.

The Church could not function by itself, so we established a human relations council, made up of churches, synagogues, labor unions, and other nonprofit groups, to work toward eliminating racism in the city. We lobbied city hall and worked with other groups. I believe we had some effect, and at the very least, our efforts lifted the morale of the Negro community.

What I missed in the battle for justice in Indianapolis, however, was the exhilaration of the Jersey City days, when we were on the streets with the people, in the jails, the emergency rooms of the hospitals, the police stations, the tenements. In Indianapolis, working for justice took the form of infighting within the parish, lobbying the legislature against the chamber of commerce, and trying to turn around the business community.

As the years passed, we realized that under the surface of the placid 1950s major forces were stirring. We felt the brunt of McCarthyism. We came to know the deep conservatism of the Midwest. The Korean War came and went without our realizing that it was the precursor of a far more crippling war. Then, the electricity of the election of President Kennedy sent a thrill of excitement through the country.

We still believed that a better world could be brought about by proper planning, plain speaking, and vigorous action without social disruption. The idea of planning, of cooperation—of what is now called networking—began to grow. Postwar society was taking shape, and as the country prospered, the underlying conflicts came closer and closer to the surface.

In 1955, when Rosa Parks refused to move to the back of the bus and the Montgomery bus boycott began, the Church had already begun to feel the power of the emerging civil rights movement. The Episcopal bishops of Alabama criticized Martin Luther King, Jr.'s tactics. During the following years, the Church's struggle to come to terms with racial justice took many forms. In 1958, the Episcopal Society for Cultural and Racial Unity was founded, under the vigorous leadership of the Reverend John Morris. In 1960 the presiding bishop appointed a prestigious committee on intergroup relations whose membership included Dr. Kenneth Clark and Thurgood Marshall. The presiding bishop, Arthur Lichtenberger, at first reluctant to speak out, made a highly publicized statement in 1963 asking for "an unmistakable identification of the Church, at all levels of its life, with those who are victims of oppression." He also spoke out against the growing practice in the South of founding Episcopal parochial schools as a means to avoid the integration of public schools.

Even in the quiet and prosperous suburbs, one sensed that all was not well. Books like *The Organization Man*, by William H. Whyte, and *The Suburban Captivity of the Churches: An Analysis of Protestant Responsibility in the Expanding Metropolis*, by Gibson Winter, pointed out the problems beneath the surface. The Church grew and prospered, but there was a "crack in the stained glass window."

The cold war was gaining momentum, too. When Russia launched *Sputnik*, a shudder of dread went through the country. I preached a sermon in which I tried to reassure the cathedral congregation. We were told to prepare for a nuclear attack by stocking our cellars with provisions.

I had not really worked through my views on war in the atomic age. In Indianapolis, my war record was a plus, and I did not disguise it. Some of my friends were pacifists, and I began to find the peace movement appealing now that I had started to think more seriously about the social implications of the Gospel. But how could I repudiate the military, to which I had given four years and almost my very life? How could I repudiate what had seemed at the time to be a gallant fight for justice? Those were hard questions—and I put them aside until one day in 1963, when, almost without thinking, I accepted an invitation to preach at the National Cathedral in Washington for the annual celebration of the Marine Corps' birthday.

As I prepared my sermon, I was forced to ask myself what I thought.

What a bewildering sensation, to stand in that great marble pulpit for the first time and look down on the glittering stars of the commandant of the Marine Corps and his fellow generals!

I acknowledged the honor of being there and the irony of preaching to the commandant, when once I did not dare address a sergeant. I spoke of the complexity of the issues facing a Christian in war. What about the deliberate hardening of mind and spirit, running screaming through the bayonet course, being taught to hate? What about the merciless discipline that produces the hardening of the spirit? What about patriotism turned into blind nationalism? I wondered, though: Without this hardening, could tender American boys have endured the screams in the darkness or seeing their best buddy blown to pieces in front of their very eyes? Did this hardening lessen the guilt of casual killing, the state of mind in which death has ceased to have any real meaning? I confessed that I had shared in this, that my hands were bloody, too.

I spoke, with a lump in my throat, of the bravery and extraordinary sacrifices I had seen there, far beyond what I had ever seen in civilian life. I added that most men are forever wounded by this experience. It may come out months or years later in uncontrollable sobbing. Or it may come out in compulsive drinking, mental illness, a broken marriage, or a broken life.

In the confusion of a world like ours, perhaps all we could do was to come to the altar and ask forgiveness from him who also screamed in the darkness of Calvary and had nightmare visions on the cross.

I had thought then that it was all clear: the United States was right, the enemy was wrong. Yet our enemies were now our friends.

I ended by saying that I wished we all would fight as hard for our country's ideals of freedom and justice for all, for civil rights, for tolerance, so that whatever sacrifice a Marine might make in the future would be made, in truth, for the finest way of life yet known to man. For the fight had not ended at Hiroshima, nor at the Yalu River, nor at the moment a red-hot bullet put me out of action. Our fight had to continue ceaselessly against the enemies of justice in our nation and against hatred within our hearts.

"I am a priest now, not a Marine; my work is different," I concluded. "And I do not think the Church can just bless the military establishment, even our beloved Marine Corps, casually. But I do think that the Church can say to all men everywhere that our Lord is with them and that he expects them to act according to their conscience. And we know that God is a forgiving and a loving God who once shared and in a sense still shares in all the sufferings, the doubts, and the complexities of life."

That was the best I could do then, but as the years passed, my revulsion against violence increased until the movement for peace became one of the principle purposes of my life.

When in Indianapolis, from time to time I was asked to give retreats. Over the years I had tried to be faithful in saying the Daily Office of Morning and Evening Prayer, receiving Communion regularly, making my confession, going on retreats. Keeping a regular life of prayer is not easy. Often days or even weeks go by when it is a tiresome business. Then something will happen—an event in your life, a word spoken to you in confession, a sudden insight when on retreat—and the attempts to be with God deepen and become exciting again. Also, as I grew older, I found that prayer soaked into my daily life and was not something reserved for those times when I was alone and consciously giving all my attention to it.

What is it like to pray, beyond asking God's help for yourself or others, thanking God for blessings, confessing the constant weaknesses of sin? What is it like to try to penetrate the ultimate darkness? Sometimes prayer is just that—trying, trying, trying, with all the concentration you have. But then you realize you cannot reach "up" to God, you need to relax, to stop trying so hard, to let God come to you, or better, to realize that God has been with you all along.

The saints and others have had visions, and they have written accounts of them. I have never had a vision, but a few times in my life I have been overwhelmed by a sense of God's presence. Ever since my first confession at seventeen, I have always believed, indeed have always *known* God to be present with me and known that I could be in touch with his presence. Prayer is like a human friendship. It varies in intensity; on rare occasions, a conversation breaks through into the recesses of your soul. At other times, there is silence between you, or casual conversation, or demands for help. If you realize that prayer can be all these things, the need to strain lessens, and you become aware that God is present with you even when he seems far away.

As I was typing these very words, the phone rang. A friend called to report on someone we both loved who had been diagnosed with a brain tumor. She had asked me and many others to pray hard. We did. On the phone she told me that the tumor was not there now. A misdiagnosis? Or the power of prayer?

I have never thought of myself as an authority on prayer. Perhaps this reluctance stems from my being something of a skeptic and trying never to say something I do not believe just because it is written in a book. Sometimes, when I am giving a retreat, when people have had a chance to quiet down and open up, when we have had some prayer together, I sense some other source for what I am saying. I have an outline for what I am to say. I begin to talk. We go deeper into the subject. I look at the intensity of concentration on the faces before me, and I hear myself saying things I had not intended to say. It is as if I were a channel. Do not mistake me. I am speaking not of "voices" but of something simpler. It is just me talking in my own way, but the words and ideas come from somewhere inside me, ideas more profound than what I had thought of saying beforehand, and I can sense the words reaching into the depths of the souls of those who are listening. This is a thrill. It is a feeling that I am doing what I have been put on earth to do—to open others to God.

Our family grew in Indiana. Susanna and Patience were born there, fulfilling what Jenny had wished when Adelia was born—that we have nine children. Indianapolis was an almost perfect place to bring up children. We had that huge house with a beautiful lawn in front and a good backyard with swings, a jungle gym, and a garden. The public schools were excellent, and no one sent their children to private schools unless the child had a problem or the parents were extremely snobbish. Our local high school, Shortridge, was one of the finest in America. What's more, it was integrated. Beneath this benign exterior, there was racism, however, a deep problem for us and for our children, who were torn between the racism their friends had picked up from their families and the understanding of racial equality they had absorbed at home and in Jersey City. But we all were happy there. Our house was full of the children and their friends. Jenny and I were busy and engaged with the community. It was a good time.

But something was missing. I worked hard within a conventional parish and the larger Church for the ideals we had formed in Jersey City. For a long time I did not dare admit it to myself, but I found the structures too confining. When I thought of the ultimate aim of the Church, the redemption of the world as part of the Body of Christ here on earth, the quarrels of an altar guild or the lobbying of the General Convention seemed irrelevant. I was a priest, and I believed in the priesthood: I enjoyed and was fulfilled in my work. And yet, in my darkest moments, the constrictions of Christ Church and the mores of Indianapolis were so confining that I began to question my vocation to the priesthood itself. I asked myself, should I, could I, let all this go for something else, some other vocation, as yet unclear? Would entering political life make more of a difference? Had my father been right—would being a powerful and rich businessman, able to give more to charity, enable me to make a greater impact? During the last years in Indianapolis, these questions lurked in the back of my mind. And then, with the election of Jack Kennedy, many of my own generation were in power in Washington. And there I was, running a parish in Indiana.

I had come to be known beyond the Diocese of Indianapolis because of my articles in Church papers, my participation in groups such as the Church and City Conference, my service on committees in the National Church, and my role in the General Convention. Inquiries began to come to me about whether I would allow my name to be placed in nomination for bishop.

Any priest in good standing in the Anglican communion is eligible to become a bishop. Different provinces (national churches in communion with the Archbishop of Canterbury) have different systems of appointing bishops. In the Episcopal Church—the Anglican Church in America—bishops are elected. When a diocese needs a bishop, a convention is called. A nominating committee selects several names. These and nominations from the floor are presented to the convention. To be elected, the nominee must secure a majority of the clergy of the diocese who are voting and a majority of the lay representatives of the parishes of the diocese. As in a national political convention, ballots are voted on until the required majority is secured. If there is a deadlock, the convention is adjourned and another convention called several months later. After a diocese elects, a majority of diocesan bishops and standing committees of the whole church must approve its choice of bishop.

I began to receive inquiries from several dioceses. When Springfield, Illinois, asked, I refused—it was a small, theologically conservative diocese; they presented my name anyway, and it was a deadlocked convention. When Pennsylvania inquired, I said yes.

I was excited. Pennsylvania was a large, ancient, and important diocese with many urban parishes. In those days, campaigning for office oneself in any overt way was frowned on, but those who were backing a particular candidate campaigned for him with energy. My backers in Pennsylvania arranged a large luncheon of influential clergy and laity at a downtown club to hear an address from me on the urban church. This was a thinly disguised opportunity for the movers and shakers of the diocese to look me over. I knew a good many of the clergy and some of the laymen from St. Paul's School and Yale connections. I was introduced in glowing terms as a great authority on the urban Church; mention was made of St. Paul's and Yale and my Marine Corps combat record. I stood up to speak in the vast dining room before almost a hundred people and delivered what I thought was an entertaining, occasionally humorous, intelligent address on the problems of the urban Church and the need for us to address them. My thesis was that the Church had to change in order to draw poor and minority people to its doors and that we had a moral and biblical obligation to fight injustice head-on. When I began to talk about the NAACP, however, I caught sight of Jesse Anderson, a leading black priest, sitting in the rear of the room, motioning to me wildly. He half stood up and waved his palms across his face in a clear message to tone down what I was saying. Despite his warnings, I continued to speak my mind.

Thank goodness, I lost to the then suffragan bishop. Perhaps the reason was my openness; after all I had nothing to lose, and although Pennsylvania attracted me I was happy enough where I was. Perhaps it was, as I afterward heard, that many who did not know me, and did not attend the luncheon, thought I was black because Jesse Anderson nominated me. I will never know.

Other inquiries surfaced, some serious, some not, some attractive, others less so. And then came Washington. It was the summer of

1963. Our family was in the Adirondacks, but the news of the great civil rights march was in all the papers and I felt the urge to go. Many thought it might be dangerous, and so, in what seems now to have been an old-fashioned sexist way, I told Jenny and my daughters it was too risky for women to go. But I did bring my son Paul, then just sixteen.

At that time, a political battle was lining up in the Diocese of Washington around the election of a suffragan bishop. The social justice crowd was pitted against the pastoral, psychological crowd—to oversimplify the issues. Bill Wendt, now the rector of a vigorous inner-city parish, St. Stephen's, led the urban caucus and was pushing my name. When I called him to say Paul and I were coming to the march, he invited us to stay in his rectory. We arrived to find the place swarming with marchers who were going to spend the night as best they could in the parish hall. I saw many old friends and comrades in arms. It felt like Jersey City. Indeed, Bill Wendt had worked with us at St. Peter's, Chelsea, while a seminarian, and later with Kim Myers on the Lower East Side of Manhattan. Paul and I spent the evening at the rectory, and I was looked over, questioned, and given many beers by the urban social action caucus. Paul and I shared a restless night on the floor of the rectory. I guess I passed muster, because they affirmed Bill's suggestion, and we all were united the next day in that historic march. If I had any doubts about wanting to be a bishop in Washington, they disappeared as Paul and I paraded down Constitution Avenue and stood before the Lincoln Memorial to hear the great dream of Martin Luther King, Jr. The future was bright. We were all together. Oh, to be part of this movement that would change America forever and to be part of it here in Washington!

A few months later, I attended a conference of the Episcopal Society for Cultural and Racial Unity (ESCRU) in Atlanta. I was in my room resting when there was a knock on the door. It was John Morris, the director of ESCRU. He solemnly said, "I have the honor of informing you that you have been elected a bishop in the Church of God."

WASHINGTON

WHAT better place, what better time to carry out a ministry of social action than Washington in the fall of 1963? A man of my generation was President, and many of my friends were at his side. The country was full of hope. Young, idealistic men and women from all over America had flocked to the capital to join the administration. Even the British ambassador was a young friend of the President. It really did seem like a new frontier.

In September, soon after my election as suffragan bishop of Washington, Jenny and I traveled to the city from Indianapolis to look for a house and schools for the children. We went to a party at Cord Meyer's (he had been an usher at our wedding) and met Barbara Gamarekian, who worked at the White House. She volunteered to get us an appointment with the President.

I knew Jack Kennedy socially; when I was with my family in Palm Beach right after the war, Jack came to dinner. Mother sat him next to her and was completely charmed. "You will go a long way, young man," she said. I also knew his sister Kick, who died in an airplane crash during the war, and we had many friends in common, including McGeorge Bundy, Chuck Spalding, who was on his staff, and George Mead, who had died on Guadalcanal. I had gone to college with Cyrus Vance and Steuart Pittman, now in the Pentagon. John Lindsay, whom I knew from St. Paul's, was in Congress. Ben Bradlee, then Washington bureau chief for *Newsweek*, had been a childhood friend.

Two days after our dinner at Cord Meyer's, Jenny and I were ush-

ered into the Oval Office. The brilliant sun of an Indian summer
morning poured into the room. The polished desk, the silver ashtrays,
the brass souvenirs glistened in the sunshine, and it seemed that the
President himself was shining. "Where are the children?" he asked,
before even saying hello.

"Back in Indiana—we will bring them by next time." We were so
naive that we did not realize how hard it was to get an appointment.
Steuart Pittman, when we told him we had been to see the President
at the White House, said a little bitterly, "I wish I could get to see
him."

The President was warm and exuberant as he showed us the office
and took us through the French doors to the terrace. We talked of
old friends, of the war, and of how he thought things were going. As
we looked out on the Washington Monument and sensed the beauty
and the power of the city, it seemed that anything was possible and
that we would have a hand in bringing in a time of real peace and
justice to our country and the world. We had fought a war for freedom. Kennedy and I and many others had almost been killed. We
had paid our dues, we had done our apprenticeship in our respective
vocations. Now the time had come for our generation to lead. I felt,
under the excitement, a weight of responsibility beyond anything I
had known before.

Two months later, I was in bed with the flu in Indianapolis when
Jenny called out: "The President's been shot!" Then followed those
awful, agonizing moments when it became more and more clear that
the wounds were fatal. I cried as much in anger as in grief. Our hope,
our generation's leader, was gone. The family gathered in my bedroom
to watch the dreadful unfolding coverage of the blow the nation and
indeed the world had sustained. In retrospect, we are more aware of
Jack Kennedy's faults, of his macho posture on foreign policy issues,
of the dalliances in his personal life. But at the time he was the king
of Camelot, and, even with all his faults, I believe the world would
now be a far better place had he lived. He had begun the war on
poverty, he had stood down Khrushchev in the Cuban missile crisis
without a shot being fired. He had brains and a sense of history. Now
all that was gone. Thank God we did not yet know of the tragedies
still to come.

. . .

For an Episcopalian, becoming a bishop was far more than a promotion. I knew I would never be the same. I thought my consecration would be a little like being ordained a priest, which really had made me different and had given me a spiritual power I was conscious of when visiting the sick or celebrating the Eucharist. What would this new power feel like? Our doctrine said it was indelible: once a bishop always a bishop. For almost two thousand years, the so-called apostolic succession had furnished bishops for every generation of the Church. When the original apostles grew old, younger men took their place and were given the titles *episkopos* (the Greek word for bishop, meaning overseer) and *presbyteros* (meaning elder). These terms were interchangeable early on, but before long the Church leaders who had jurisdiction over several congregations were called bishops, and the term *presbyter* was used to designate a man who led a local church. As time passed, the bishops assumed greater authority and spiritual power, and eventually only they could ordain elders, deacons, and other bishops. The rite of ordination included the laying on of hands by a bishop; through it (and it is to this that the term *apostolic succession* refers) bishops are thought to be direct spiritual descendants of the apostles themselves. Priests are presumed to take their authority from the bishop. Besides the overt authority it granted, the office held a mystique, a sense of hidden power.

The apostolic succession became the essential earthly structure of the Church. Even though, over the years, bishops have functioned in many different ways—as administrators, teachers, prophets, warriors, monks, feudal lords, and humble rural pastors—their spiritual authority and power have remained unchanged, as clearly stated in an early saying, *Ubi episcopus, ibi ecclesia*: Where the bishop is, there is the Church.

So being made a bishop was no light matter. I had known many bishops: kindly Bishop Benjamin Washburn of Newark, courtly Bishop Horace W. B. Donegan of New York, the austere but friendly Presiding Bishop Henry K. Sherrill, who once surprised me by leaving his desk to sit next to me when I paid him a courtesy call (he had known my grandmother and mother). And of course there was Bishop William Creighton, who would be my immediate superior as Bishop of Washington, an extremely modest man who had a peculiar strength as well. In those days, my old friend Bishop James Pike of California was always in the news, a maverick with an extraordinary feel for public relations; he seemed to be ahead of the other bishops in his views, roiling the Church but popular with those outside the Church, to whom he dedicated himself. Yes, I knew these and many other bishops; they all seemed different men, somehow, after they were ordained to the office. This was true of even my close friend Kim Myers of San Francisco and my seminary classmate Jim Montgomery of Chicago. I suppose the closest analogy is the sensation many people have that they are made different people by being married.

In any case, in order to prepare for consecration, I went on a retreat in New York, at the House of the Redeemer on Ninety-fifth Street, just east of Fifth Avenue. I was alone in that old mansion, except for the three sisters who took care of the place. On retreat, your outer shell falls away and your inner self becomes exposed and vulnerable. How could that inner thing we call the soul, the psyche, the self receive a change of spiritual state? What is the soul? Does anything really happen at the consecration of a bishop, or is it a product of your imagination and a projection of others? I thought about these matters and prayed about them. I knelt in the chapel in front of the Blessed Sacrament, watching the vigil light flicker, sensing our Lord's intimate presence. I opened myself as best I could to the Holy Spirit. What was being a bishop really about? What was I to do with the office? Was I to try to be prominent, a leader for social justice, or should I just serve people quietly, take care of my family, and pray? After a day of this questioning, I felt exposed and uncertain.

The afternoon of the second day, I went for a walk down Fifth Avenue on the park side, looking at the trees and hearing the rush of traffic. After a few blocks, I came to the astonishing white spiral of the Guggenheim Museum; I crossed the avenue and decided to go in. I was surprised to find that an exhibit of the painter Francis Bacon's work was on view. Bacon was a close friend of Ted Wickham, the Bishop of Manchester, who had started Industrial Mission in England after the war. I admired Ted, and he had told me of Bacon's power and insight into the human condition in postwar Europe. Taking the elevator to the top, I began to saunter down the Guggenheim's descending spiral ramp past the paintings. Suddenly I came upon four large portraits of a Renaissance pope. In each, a figure sat in ecclesial garb on an episcopal throne; but his face was twisted in agony. They seemed demonic. I could not tell if the popes were screaming forth the suffering of the world, or writhing in their own guilt and horror over corrupting so great an office, or shouting out an evil spiritual command in the voice of possession. I ran down the ramp and out into the street. Would my face look like that if I became a bishop? Were the temptations of spiritual pride so corrupting? I knew something of my own weakness; I wanted to have life both ways: to serve the poor but to enjoy a comfortable life with my family; to preach social justice and yet benefit from a portfolio of securities, including companies whose activities caused economic injustice; to seem as if I were always working for the good of the Church, when I was also ambitious to be in a position of power. In the end, would I resemble Bacon's screaming popes? I was chastened.

The consecration was to be on Saturday, January 25, the feast of the conversion of St. Paul. Although he is my patron saint, and I find his theology profound, I have never really liked Paul's personality. He seems to have been something of a misogynist, and although he spoke as if humble, he boasted a bit much about his sufferings for Christ, or so it seems to me. The day was appropriate for another reason, though: I had been confirmed exactly thirty-one years earlier, on January 25, 1933.

Our house was not ready, so our old friend Peter Frelinghuysen, then a congressman from New Jersey, and his wife, Beatrice, invited our whole family to stay with them in Georgetown—truly an act of charity given the size of our family!

The night before the service, I made my confession to Father Frank Carthy, who had become a good friend in Indianapolis. We met in the darkened beauty of Bethlehem Chapel in the crypt of the great cathedral. Frank sat on a chair in the sanctuary, and I knelt at the altar rail. "Bless me, Father, for I have sinned"; and I began the dreary litany of my sins of thought, word, and deed. This completed as best I could, I sensed that the inchoate sense of sin I had felt on my retreat needed to be articulated in some way, but I could not find the words. I paused and in that dark silence felt tears begin to well up from my innermost soul; I broke into uncontrollable sobs of desolation and unworthiness. I do not remember what I said to communicate the depth of the feeling of sin that overwhelmed me. Finally I pulled myself together and concluded with the set form: "For these and all the other sins I cannot now remember, I am truly sorry and purpose amendment of life, and I ask forgiveness of God and of you, Father, penance, counsel, and absolution."

Frank assured me that, whatever weakness and sin I might have, God would work through me; that, on the other hand, my strength or virtue, however great, could not carry out the task, only God's grace could. Not only did Frank's words console me—so did his affection, our long friendship, and my knowledge that he understood the sins of the clergy as well as anyone. I felt the deep cleansing of the sacrament.

I stayed on in the chapel and drank in the love and mercy of God that had come to me again, as it had when I made my first confession at St. Paul's so many years before. I felt a great peace and, finally, a readiness to become a bishop. Christ seemed to be saying to me, "We are in this together, fear not."

The next day, a bright winter sun glistened on the walls of the resplendent cathedral as we climbed the stone steps to the Gothic porch. People greeted me, congratulated me, ushered me into the sacristy. The great nave was full of the clergy and people of the diocese of Washington. A planeload of friends from Indianapolis were there, sporting MOORE FOR BISHOP buttons. A group came from Jersey City. My brother, sister, and mother were there, as well as friends from St. Paul's and Yale.

Bishop Lichtenberger, the presiding bishop, was to be the chief consecrator. The poor soul was in the advanced stages of Parkinson's disease and could hardly speak. But he had come down for the occasion because of his affection for me. He wrote in the Bible given to the new bishop as part of the ceremony, "To Paul Moore. This is only the beginning." Another gallant old bishop was there—Bishop Angus Dun, the retired Bishop of Washington, who, because of diabetes, had a wooden leg and had lost two fingers. Bishop Creighton of Washington and Bishop Craine of Indianapolis were the other consecrators. Kim Myers was to be the preacher, as he had been when I was ordained deacon.

Of all the clergy there, the one that meant the most to me was Fred Bartrop, reinstated as a priest, around whose fireplace at St. Paul's School I had first become excited about the Church. He was one of my priestly presenters. When an Army chaplain, he had been dishonorably discharged from the service because, after a few drinks one night on a beach in New Guinea, he had made advances to a soldier; he had survived years of alcoholism and several stays in mental hospitals. Even after he was deposed, he carried on a ministry of caring for those around him, whether fellow patients at Central Islip State Hospital or young male hustlers when he was on a binge in Times Square. He was reinstated as a priest and took up a ministry on Welfare Island. When he had been deposed, he gave me a handsome old silver traveling Communion set. When he was reinstated, I had it engraved and gave it back to him. When he died, not long after I became bishop, he left it to me in his will. So many strands of my life came together that day.

The procession, the glorious music, the solemn liturgy, Kim Myers's fiery sermon telling me to get out of the cathedral and onto the streets built up to the singing of the "Veni Creator." The congregation stood and I knelt down alone as they sang, "Come Holy Ghost our souls inspire / And lighten with celestial fire . . ." A collect was said, and then came the climax of the consecration itself. I felt Bishop Lichtenberger's trembling hands on my head, followed by the weight of the hands of the other bishops on top of his. And the great words were spoken: "Receive the Holy Ghost for the Office and Work of a Bishop in the Church of God, now committed unto thee by the Imposition of our hands; In the Name of the Father, and of the Son, and of the Holy Ghost. Amen. And remember that thou stir up the grace of God, which is given thee by this imposition of our hands; for God hath not given us the spirit of fear, but of power, and love, and soberness." These were words I would try to live up to as the years passed.

After the service, crowds came up for a blessing: my wife and children, my mother, friends and parishioners from all over, even Higgs, my grandmother's butler, a staunch Anglican. I almost cried when I placed my hands on his shiny, bald head.

.   .   .

Although my pastoral responsibilities lay in the field of social concerns and the Department of Missions, which supervised new and poor parishes still under the control of the diocese, I also performed the traditional roles of bishop—counseling the clergy, dealing with disputes in congregations, and making visitations to the parishes each Sunday. During a visitation, the bishop usually confirms members of the parish who wish to make a mature commitment to follow Christ. The visitation is when most people see a bishop and one of the only opportunities he has to communicate directly with the people, to find out about the nature of each parish and its community.

My first visitation, the morning following the consecration, was to St. Paul's, K Street, in Washington. St. Paul's prided itself on being Anglo-Catholic in a diocese that was Low Church, or more Protestant, in its style. Never before had a Bishop of Washington worn a cope and miter. They were thrilled as I performed the full Catholic ritual—incense, bells, holy water, genuflections, numerous signings of the cross.

During the singing of a hymn to the Holy Spirit, I took my place in the bishop's chair in front of the altar. I sat there in my regalia surveying the congregation and knew what it must feel like to be a king! The solemn examination of the candidates for confirmation having taken place, their promises made, the prayer for the Spirit said, the first confirmand came up and knelt before me. I laid my hands on the head of this youth and felt his hair, his warm scalp, and I sensed the Spirit flow into his young life. I thought of the moment thirty-one years earlier when Bishop John T. Dallas had laid his great hands on my young head and spoken the same words in his inimitable Scottish accent. I thought of Bishop Lichtenberger's trembling hands on my head the day before. I thought of the hands of bishops going back over the ages, through whose simple human touch the Spirit had been passed down. I thought of the hands of Christ laid upon the heads of the apostles, the first bishops, twenty centuries ago.

Since that day I have made more than twenty-five hundred visitations to parishes of all sorts, and I suppose I have confirmed over twenty thousand people, but each time I lay my hands on a person's head, I look down upon him or her, wonder where and how that life will be led, and pray that the Holy Spirit will be within the person always. If I have done nothing else as a bishop, that is enough.

My vineyard was no longer a conservative Midwestern city but the capital of the nation, and, in a sense, of the world. Metropolitan Washington was really three cities: the most visible, symbolized by the sparkling white buildings and monuments, was the government and all who were connected to it; arrayed around it to the north, east, and west were black communities, some of them prosperous and middle-class, others made up of people who lived in abject poverty —wounded, angry, rejected beneath the shadows of the pretentious white symbols of liberty and justice; then there were the white native Washingtonians, many of whom were culturally Southern. This last group ran the banks and the businesses of the city and controlled the committees of Congress that exercised jurisdiction over the municipal government. The diocese also included the rural areas of southern Maryland, stretching down the east bank of the Potomac, a land of tobacco farmers and watermen who harvested oysters, crabs, and muskrats. The interaction of these communities during the volatile 1960s posed a complicated ministry for someone who believed deeply in integration and in the Church's mandate to work for social and economic justice.

My first venture into the black community was for a rally at Howard University, the principal speaker at which was a young black man, who looked as if he were barely eighteen years old. He stood on a platform on the edge of the football field; his boyish figure and strong high-pitched voice held the crowd's attention. I asked who he was.

"Reverend Walter Fauntroy," I was told.

"But he is so young."

"Well, he is not as young as he looks, and he has become an important leader in Washington. He's a close colleague of Dr. Martin Luther King."

I soon got to know Walter Fauntroy, who later became the first nonvoting representative of the District of Columbia in Congress. He and I worked together for many years on the problems of Washington. Because there was no viable, integrated organization to address social

concerns in the city, we founded the Coalition of Conscience, recruiting as many liberal clergy and community leaders as we could.
Our first action was to picket the office of the Attorney General,
Robert F. Kennedy. I had met Bobby once or twice at social functions,
but I did not know him well. He was difficult to talk to, not at ease
with small talk. I liked him, though; his presence was magnetic. At
this point, he was not as fully impassioned on behalf of the poor as
he later became. As a senator two years later, he said the nation
needed "to change every facet of our society; and that we begin in
our urban ghettos . . . which stand as a blight on our cities and a
disgrace to our souls."

Our protest was my first such adventure in Washington, and I was
ignorant of the protocol, as it were, nor were the officials used to
seeing a bishop on the picket line. The purpose was to persuade Kennedy to put pressure on Senator Robert Byrd, the chairman of the
Senate Appropriations Committee for the District of Columbia, to
change the ruling whereby if a man was in the house a welfare mother
could not receive Aid to Dependent Children. Mary Ethridge, a welfare mother, had been found dead on the streets with her children.
Although conditions for the poor are far worse now, we sensed, even
then, the forces of reaction on a local level. We were confident that
with pressure from people of goodwill, conditions would improve and
a just society would come into being.

Senator Byrd himself was unapproachable. He had pulled himself
up from abject poverty, and he felt others could do the same. As
chairman of the Senate Appropriations Committee, which oversaw
the budget for the District of Columbia, he was virtually mayor of
Washington, even going so far as to ride in police cars.

When we finally saw Bobby Kennedy, he was courteous, with the
special graciousness Roman Catholic laymen give the clergy. We laid
our case before him. He listened and expressed sympathy. The policy
did not change, however. I felt ill at ease picketing Kennedy since I
had known him socially. I did not come on in as confrontational a
manner as I would have with a stranger. It is advantageous to know
officials because it means you can usually gain access to them, but it
makes one hesitate to question their sincerity.

·   ·   ·

"Potomac Fever" is the term for the intoxication of living in the midst of the power that ebbs and flows through our capital city. Our family caught a severe case of it as soon as we arrived. We were already fascinated by politics and with the way one could try to influence the government, whether in a ward in Jersey City or in a casual conversation with the President of the United States. Through our friends in government, we caught glimpses of the way decisions are made.

Two of our closest friends were Ben and Toni Bradlee. He was then chief of the Washington bureau of *Newsweek* and later became editor of *The Washington Post*. Ben and I had grown up together on the North Shore. His older brother Freddy, an actor and author, was also a close friend. Toni was an artist and one of the most beautiful women I have known; I used to dance with her in the old days at New York parties. Ben had been one of Jenny's first boyfriends. Ben loved the rough-and-tumble of official Washington. He was a born journalist, soaking up every bit of information or gossip he could lay his hands on, willing to risk his entire reputation on a story like the Watergate break-in. When we had supper with them, we always picked up some juicy inside story, and he was interested in our insights into the civil rights movement and the affairs of the city. He was hearty, an avid sports fan, and had a fine ability to make friends. He and Toni had been intimate with President and Mrs. Kennedy; Ben and I had long, introspective conversations about the dangers and advantages of a journalist being that close to power. Toni's first husband was Steuart Pittman, assistant secretary of civil defense under Kennedy. Our association with the Bradlees was fun and exciting.

Beneath the glitter, however, lurked darkness. Toni Bradlee's sister Mary, also an artist and an extraordinary beauty, had been married to Cord Meyer. Cord lost an eye as a Marine during the war, and when we were both home on sick leave we had seen a great deal of each other. Cord later became the first head of a world government organization called the United World Federalists and was also active in the founding of the American Veterans Committee, a new-style veterans' association. Despite these liberal credentials, Cord apparently became convinced that the fate of the world depended on our struggle against the USSR. He joined the CIA and together with James Jesus Angleton, a Yale classmate of mine, forged much of the agency's cold war strategy. I have often wondered what changed this brilliant, liberal idealist into a cold warrior.

In the fall of 1966 I was away at a General Convention when Bradlee called. From the tone of his voice I knew something terrible had occurred. He told me Mary Meyer had been shot.

"My God, Ben. She's dead?"

"Yeah, she's dead. Toni would like you to take the funeral."

How? Where? This beautiful, talented woman with the world at her feet, shot? Why? Why? Why?

Mary had been jogging along the canal towpath early one morning and was killed. No motive could be found. She was in her running outfit and had no money or jewels on her. An alleged assailant was prosecuted, but many people still believe that there were darker forces at work, because Mary had been a mistress of President Kennedy as well as the ex-wife of a leading member of the CIA. Furthermore, the authorities confiscated her diary right after she was shot. Why would they have done this, if she had just been mugged by a passing robber?

The service was held at the cathedral. I spoke a few words about Mary and the tragedy of it all and asked them also to pray for the murderer. That upset many who were there, but I was sure Mary would have wanted it that way.

The civil rights conflicts in Washington were part of the larger struggle for civil rights going on around the country. At the beginning of my first summer in D.C., in 1964, the eyes of the country were on the South. Since I'd gone to Groveland, Thurgood Marshall had become a Supreme Court justice; Martin Luther King had begun his crusade; the Little Rock crisis had brought the federal government into the desegregation struggle; the Student Nonviolent Coordinating Committee (SNCC) was conducting sit-ins; Episcopal bishop Dan Corrigan and the head of the National Council of Churches, Eugene Carson Blake, were arrested for breaking the color line at an amusement park in Maryland. (A picture of Dan in the papers showed him sitting on a bench reading The New York Times and holding a carefully folded umbrella. He did not look as if he were endangering the government.) Mrs. Malcolm Peabody, the wife of an Episcopal bishop and the mother of the governor of Massachusetts, and Mrs. John Burgess, who was black and the wife of Bishop Burgess, the black suffragan bishop of Massachusetts, had been jailed in Florida for breaking a segregation law. (It is said that the governor of Florida called Governor Peabody and said, "Hey, Chubb, I got your Mom in the slammer!")

The country was hotting up. I had continued to work for racial justice in Indianapolis and read and heard about these developments. Some of my friends had conducted a Prayer Pilgrimage, a kind of clerical freedom ride, traveling through Southern states and ending at our General Convention in Detroit in 1964. A new organization in the Episcopal Church was formed, the Episcopal Society for Cultural and Racial Unity. The National Council of Churches, under the leadership of Blake and his brilliant tactician Robert Spike, was organizing the churches for the struggle. Little by little, I was absorbing the weight and complexity of the fight against racism. The issue became part of my life. Every time the race barrier was broken, people felt a special thrill; black and white people made it a point to hug one another, as if pressing white skin to black skin would somehow erase the difference. I felt this was a deep part of the doctrine of the Incarnation; Jesus took on human flesh, all human flesh, and in Christ there was neither black nor white. We sang lustily:

> Join hands then Brothers of the Faith,
> Whate'er your race may be!
> Who serves my Father as a son,
> Is surely kin to me.

Yet civil rights advocacy could be dangerous, and I was torn about whether to go south and join the struggle. Three civil rights workers had been killed in Mississippi. In 1964, I had a wife and nine children, plus a new job in Washington.

Then one Sunday morning, I attended Mass at St. Stephen and the Incarnation Church, where Bill Wendt, my friend from seminary days, was rector. The Gospel was the account in Luke of Jesus' telling his disciples to go back out into the lake, even though they had not caught any fish that day. Jesus said, "Launch out into the deep and let down your nets for a catch." "Launch out into the deep . . ." The phrase struck me square in the face. The Lord had answered my question about whether to go south; I would go out into the deep. I am not saying that Jesus himself leaned down and whispered in my ear. All I am saying is that that particular phrase at that particular moment catalyzed my dilemma and became the moment of decision. A few days later, I boarded a flight for Jackson, Mississippi.

The ministers project in Hattiesburg, where I arrived first, was run by a plump, easygoing Presbyterian minister named Bob Beach. It was the only point of communication between the black and white communities there. Bob deployed the clergy—creaky denominational executives; eager, romantic young firebrands; respectable, suburban middle-aged pastors; rabbis; and returned overseas missionaries. Laid out like sardines on mattresses on the cement floor, this motley assortment of the ordained would snore the night away with visions of rednecks dancing in their dreams.

After a few days, we moved to McComb. We drove up to a little white house, the headquarters of COFO. But something was wrong and looked sort of queer. My Lord, it was the living room, you could see the inside of it from the street! It looked like a doll house where the front is taken off. The fellow who was driving, seeing my expression, said, "Yeah, that's where the dynamite went off last week."

An interesting spot it was, combining the feel of a college dormitory, an urban church summer program, and a Marine Corps command post. The talk ran its course through the ecumenical movement, back to Homer, then Edward Albee, and on to *race*. Every discussion always ended with race. In the background someone was strumming a guitar and humming a freedom song.

At the sink, a black neighbor who had volunteered to help was washing up. She did not look brave, but she was, just to be there. Three men had already lost their lives. Fifteen churches had been burned down. The twenty or so young people there knew what the stakes were, but they too had smelled freedom. It had sort of busted open from inside them. The movement possessed them, and their lives were given over to it. Christians they were, some of them. A great many were Jewish. Many were proud agnostics. Thank God the Church was there. The National Council of Churches' recruits humbly served as minister counselors under the leadership of the students and the local people.

One night we went to the basement of a black church on the outskirts of a small nearby town for a dramatic reading of Martin Duberman's *In White America* by some local black teenagers. The play is a series of dramatizations of Negro history that had a long off-Broadway run in New York City. We arrived in time for the second act. The Civil War has been won, but the battle continues in the Senate. Up stands Senator Tilghman of South Carolina to describe the imagined horror of the rape of a white girl in the backwoods of the South by a Negro. The speech is melodramatic in the high rhetoric of the period and ends with rage overcoming the father of the girl and his shout, "KILL KILL KILL!" The part was taken by Johnny, a fifteen-year-old black Mississippian. And because somewhere in his depths he found the power to reenact this part with violent feeling, a great moment of theater occurred. Equally moving was a scene from Little Rock: a quiet, clear-voiced girl approaches the soldiers for protection and finds cold steel. A local girl played this part, knowing that before long she too might meet cold steel for participating in this innocent evening. The scenes were interspersed with freedom songs, and we closed, as always, with "We Shall Overcome," hands joined across our chests, bodies swaying together, eyes wet with tears, and a prayer given above the humming of the Negro national anthem.

Those of us who went down there hoped that we could help black people find freedom, even if our contribution was small. We were accepted by most on that basis. Strangely enough, though, it was we who found the freedom. I had fought for freedom in the Marines, but I'd never *felt* freedom until I swayed back and forth to a freedom song in the basement of a Negro church that summer.

What was the Church doing there? The movement would have gone on without the organizational involvement of the Church. In some cases, the clergy contributed protection from the violence of local groups, in some cases a steadying word of advice, in some cases much-needed man power. But our true role, I think, was symbolized by a celebration of the Eucharist the last Sunday I was there. The altar was an old ironing board, the reredos a blasted-out side of the Freedom House, the congregation assorted Roman Catholics, agnostics, Episcopalians, Protestants of various descriptions, lay and ordained, and some courageous black neighbors. Barefoot kids ran around in the dirt. The Gospel for the day was the account of Jesus weeping over Jerusalem: "And when he was come near, he beheld the city and wept over it. If thou hadst known, even thou, at least in this thy day, the things which belong unto thy peace, but now they are hid from thine eyes." We were there to weep with him.

More deeply, though, we were there to celebrate with him the glory of his Kingdom as it appeared around us in courage, in patience, in love, in fire, in faith. We were there to say this is the Church, these purposes are of God. Through these young people, through the brave local leaders, the Holy Spirit was working, whether they knew it or not. For when all the registrations were counted, the most important thing was that together, black and white, Jew and Gentile, gave a shout for freedom, and freedom lived in the house and dormitories, freedom traveled in the cars with the two-way radios, freedom stood naked in the sun as a couple of canvassers trudged down a hot, dusty, weary road.

I arrived at the Newark airport from Jackson to read in the papers of a riot in Jersey City the night before. I drove to my mother's house in Morristown, where Jenny was staying. I wanted so much to collapse in that luxury for a few days, but naturally we called John Luce, who was the pastor at Grace Church in Jersey City, and he told us to come right over. They needed all the help they could get.

After catching up at the rectory—how strange it seemed to be there again—John and I walked over to Grand Street, with Jenny staying behind to watch over the rectory. Grand Street is where the riot had been, and more rioting was expected that night. As the summer sun set over the Margaret Hague Hospital—named after the notorious mayor Frank Hague's mother, and the hospital where our daughter Rosemary had been born—the young men began to gather. I had never experienced a full-blown riot and had no idea who might tear up the streets and confront the police. Then one of the young men came over. "Hey! Father Moore. Great to see you. How you doin'?"

Before long, a whole group of our kids from the parish gathered around, and we reminisced about the baseball teams, the field days, the processions at Grace Church years before. Everything was quiet and friendly. Then a police car drove down Grand Street, followed by another and another. The police were in battle dress and looked grim. One of the old Grace Church kids picked up a Coke bottle and lobbed it at a police car. Soon, the air was full of Coke bottles, then a brick or two. The police drove by again, sirens screaming. No change. A third time they drove by. Each time they went by exacerbated the situation, which we, under the leadership of Bob Castle, another old friend and Episcopal priest, were trying to calm down. This time, one of the boys ran over to the lead police car, jumped up on it, and waved to the crowd as if he were a bathing beauty, while the cops, powerless, grim-faced, drove him down Grand Street.

What began almost good-humoredly, became, to a large extent because of bad handling by the police, a vicious and fearful experience. Over the years, the people of the neighborhood had grown more and more resentful because of numerous acts of unwarranted brutality by the police. The situation had blown open the night before when a policeman arrested and allegedly roughed up a drunken black woman. The night I was there, the violence and terror were made worse as the police repeatedly charged the crowd, waving their nightsticks, needlessly harassing innocent bystanders, and firing their pistols, all while the mayor disregarded a highly responsible delegation of young people, clergy of all faiths, and civil rights leaders, who sought to be mediators early on.

Bob Castle went down to city hall, where there was a meeting scheduled with the mayor and the chief of police. The mayor's imaginative response was "We will meet force with force." Meanwhile, back on Grand Street, the police had got out of their cars and were firing their pistols into the air. John Luce was in a glass phone booth, and I saw him duck down.

We decided to join the group at city hall, since things were deteriorating so fast on the street and our presence was doing no good. As I remember, we persuaded the mayor to call off the cops, and the rioters gradually cooled down as we tried to talk them out of their anger by joking and suggesting ways to channel it into political action. On our return, a summer worker asked us why we had been there. The answer was the same one we had given in Mississippi:

these were our people, our friends. We moved freely and without fear among the rioters, because they trusted us. This was the Church. This was where its clergy must be, as at a deathbed, which it nearly was, or at a baptism, which, in a sense it was, too.

The long hot summer came to an end, and I gladly resumed my work in Washington. But the struggle for racial freedom was not over. Officials from the National Council of Churches had decided the Church should remain in Mississippi. They organized the Delta Ministry to continue the work of the summer project and asked me to chair its board.

We purchased a small college campus, Mount Beulah, which became a hospitality center and a headquarters for the movement. When it was going strong, Mount Beulah was a great rallying point. Major figures like Fannie Lou Hamer were involved. Warren McKenna, the first director, was joined by Art Thomas, both white, and later Owen Brooks, who was black. As with the summer project, many people came and went. They held a sit-in at the local Army Air Force base to claim that empty barracks should be used to house the poor. I was against this (being a conservative on their spectrum), because I thought opposing the federal government so frankly would set back the movement. But they did it, once again putting their needs before the public in a dramatic way.

Even though it sponsored the Delta Ministry, the National Council of Churches continually pressed us to justify our presence and our methods in Mississippi. White churchmen were anxious about confrontation. In a report in 1966, I finally made clear to them where we stood:

> We feel true reconciliation between unequal and alienated groups is not possible without justice. . . . We [the Delta Ministry] engage in a ministry of reconciliation by helping the poor to gain enough self-confidence, articulateness, and power to negotiate on a basis of equality of person with the powers that be. We feel that true reconciliation between unequal and alienated groups is not possible without justice. ("Crying 'Peace, Peace' when there is no peace"). Despite heavy criticism that we are agitators, we continue to feel that [our] understanding of reconciliation is truly biblical.

I was usually wrong when I became timid; history seemed to be on the side of boldness. The civil rights movement could not just be talked about—it had to be acted out in a great liturgy of events. In retrospect, I wonder whether, with a little more courage, I might have become a true leader of the movement and not merely an effective presence. I was never willing to risk losing my position as bishop or risk being considered a flake by moderate people of goodwill. A few times I pushed the edge of the envelope of liberal behavior, but by and large I felt my greatest influence would be within the system.

When Martin Luther King was planning the Selma march in 1965, he called our Coalition of Conscience into action. A series of out- rageous events in Selma, Alabama, so inflamed the conscience of America that thousands answered Dr. King's call for a great march from Selma to Birmingham, the capital of Alabama. People poured into Alabama from all over the United States: men, women, children, nuns, bishops, ministers, civil rights activists, liberal politicians. Few if any business leaders appeared. The morning the march began, po- lice were stationed at the bridge leading out of Selma to block its advance. Dr. King and his thousands of followers were forced back by dogs and fire hoses. It was clear that unless something were done bloodshed would occur when Dr. King resumed the march. In the meantime, Walter Fauntroy and I, together with George Wiley (chairman of the Welfare Rights Organization) and other leaders, had organized demonstrations in front of the White House. When pictures in the news showed Dr. King and his followers being beaten, hosed, and attacked by dogs, the crowds swelled until, on the day we had set for the major rally, they filled Lafayette Square.

The purpose of the demonstrations was to persuade President John- son to send National Guard troops to protect the marchers from the Klan and local police. The thrill of seeing so many citizens, black and white, exerting their power directly on the President was intoxicating. The rhetoric of the speakers matched the occasion. Fannie Lou Hamer took the crowd by storm. A very large, very black woman in her fifties from Rulesville, Mississippi, she had gained prominence through her great courage and leadership in the voter registration drive there. The crowd cheered her on with "Amens," "Right Ons," and "You tell 'em, Fannie Lou, you tell 'em." And tell 'em she did, in a voice of power that made you feel that all the thousands of black women and men from the cotton fields of the deep South were speaking forth in anguish over the ancient wrongs done to their people.

When Fannie Lou finished, it was my turn. I had prepared a reasoned Anglican address on the righteousness of the Selma march, but as Fannie Lou shouted out her message, I tore up my manuscript and prayed to God to give me utterance. I stood up and spoke from my heart, moved by the multitudes. This tall, skinny WASP was no Fannie Lou, but I did hear a few amens.

The following day, giving in to pressure and the importunities of some of his staff, President Johnson agreed to see us. About twelve of the leaders of the demonstration were chosen to enter the White House. We took our seats around the Cabinet table, and in a few minutes the President entered. The first thing that struck me was his size: he was a large man with an aura of power about him. He greeted us courteously and asked each of us to say what was on his mind. We tried to convey the frustration of the civil rights people and of black America at the apparent lack of sympathy on the part of the White House and to build the case for federal troops to protect the Selma march. When we were through, we expected Johnson to make a remark or two and then leave. But an hour later he was still talking. He told us that when pressure was put on him, "like from all of you, I feel like a mule in a hailstorm. I put my head down, hunch up, and let it rain." He told of his courtship of Lady Bird and of the old, good days in Texas. He said he was deeply sympathetic to the plight of the "Negras." At one point, he wanted to quote Scripture, so he called to Bill Moyers: "Bill, that's your department. Get me a Bible and find that passage from Isaiah, 'Come let us reason together . . .'" The next day he sent troops to Alabama.

We also visited Vice President Hubert Humphrey. He was gracious and seemed embarrassed that the administration had not done more for civil rights. I said, in no uncertain terms, that he and the civil rights movement had come to a parting of the ways. I was criticized in the press for being rude.

·   ·   ·

An amusing collision of two aspects of my ministry occurred during the Selma demonstrations. I had been scheduled to address the ladies of St. John's Church, Lafayette Square (in those days they called themselves "ladies"), at noontime on a Wednesday during Lent. It was to be a quiet, meditative way for them to meet the new bishop. As it happened, that Wednesday we were in the midst of the demonstration and were set to have a strategy meeting at noon in the St. John's parish house. I told my colleagues that I would be late to the meeting because of this service with the ladies.

I donned my vestments, combed my hair, and, exactly at noon, entered the church. About thirty ladies, in rather formal, churchgoing ensembles—white gloves, hats, and all—were quietly waiting, in Lenten dignity, for the service to begin. I was about to say "The Lord be with you" when I saw the back door of the church open and heard some loud voices. "Come on, Brothers and Sisters, we're going to pray with Brother Moore." The picket signs reading PROTECT SELMA, FREE ALABAMA, and SEND THE TROOPS were placed against the yellow walls behind the spotless white pillars of the church porch, and in they came, about fifty strong, dressed in bib overalls and T-shirts. Most of them were black, some with beards. They came up front, apparently feeling right at home. The ladies looked around in surprise and anxiety. I put away my careful Lenten meditation, gulped, and tried to explain to each part of the congregation how glad I was that we all had a chance to worship together. My words were received amicably. The ladies nodded demurely. The brothers and sisters uttered a few halfhearted amens. I said some prayers for Selma and for the ladies of the Diocese of Washington, gave a blessing, and walked to the back of the church. The ladies sidled out, careful not to knock over the picket signs, and the brothers and sisters stayed on for a strategy meeting.

This incident symbolized the internal struggle within the diocese between traditional Episcopalians and those caught up in the social action of the Church.

Benjamin Bradlee put together a cover story on activist clergy, and I was to be on the cover. I have the cover framed, but it never ran. I was bumped by the first man, a Russian, walking in space. However, the story itself did run, and it was sympathetic to our cause and to the recent activism of the Church. Many letters of criticism came in though, and I began to wonder if we had gone too far.

As we continued to work on the problems of the city, it became clear that without home rule Washington would remain an impoverished town. The liberal establishment in Washington had long been in favor of home rule—of making the district a state—but the discussions had been largely speculative, conducted in Georgetown living rooms or in the offices of Capitol Hill, and nothing substantive had been accomplished. The residents' interests in better schools, more affordable housing, sufficient welfare benefits, and a police department more sensitive to race all depended on their being able to elect their own officials, who in turn would direct tax revenues toward their needs. The tax-free status of all the property of the federal government impoverished a city that was virtually without any industry. It was to the advantage of the business community to keep things as they were, for home rule might well have brought stiffer taxes upon them. The people's slogan was "No taxation without representation."

And so again we ran up against the issue of money and political power versus human rights. This conflict is even more ominous today, when, more than ever, our country's domestic policy and our foreign policy alike are driven by corporate interests. The root of the problem, it seems to me, is that business is no longer run for the employees (if it ever was) but for the managers and those who hold stock in the company. Thus a fairly profitable enterprise in the Midwest, employing thousands, will close down a factory and move it to the South, or to South America or Asia, to make even higher profits. I do not blame the managers—they will be dismissed if they do not produce large profits or if they do not compete with other firms. Yet, a factory closing often tears apart an entire community and throws thousands of people out of work. Many of them will have to go on welfare.

Downsizing factories was not the problem in Washington, but the same dynamics obtained. The district's commercial interests successfully lobbied for low taxes; the government held back on subsidies in lieu of real estate taxes; and public schools, housing, and welfare resources deteriorated. We believed that these conditions could not change, unless the district attained some measure of self-government.

As a strategy to organize an impoverished people against the government of the United States and the Board of Trade, in 1967 several local leaders and myself conceived the Free D.C. movement. Marion Barry, later mayor of Washington, and I were its co-chairmen. At the time Marion was executive of PRIDE, a war on poverty program to help young people get jobs, and he was something of a rough diamond. He did not adopt the dress or manners of the black bourgeoisie that liberals were accustomed to dealing with. Rather, he talked and dressed like the poor black people he served. He understood their hurt and their anger since he himself had grown up on the streets; already he was beginning to form the constituency that later returned him to the mayor's office after he had served a prison term on a narcotics charge.

The later split between blacks and whites in the civil rights movement was as much a matter of class as it was of race. Marion and leaders like him threatened most white liberals with their rough language and unorthodox strategies.

The Free D.C. movement opted to attack the Board of Trade, which gave money to the political campaigns of congressmen on the committees for the district and thus induced them to favor the business community at the expense of ordinary people. This is why the capital of the richest nation in the world has shameful, desperate urban conditions for the very poor. Free D.C. representatives (most of them young people from Marion's PRIDE) were to canvas the stores in the district and put FREE D.C. stickers on the windows of those that were not members of the Board of Trade. They would encourage people to boycott those that were members. Some of the young canvassers, in their zeal, asked the merchants to contribute to our organization as well as sever ties with the Board of Trade. This kind of shakedown was illegal. Naturally, the press got wind of it, and one morning the lead editorial in *The Washington Star* read, "Bishop Moore Blackmails Merchants."

An explosion followed. Bishop Creighton and I had been trying for three or four years to gather the wardens of the parishes together, with little success. Well, that editorial galvanized the lay leadership to organize a huge meeting of wardens, with the aim of censuring the suffragan bishop. It was no coincidence that many of the wardens had business interests in the district. I was not invited to defend myself, despite the fact that Felix Kloman, the rector of the parish church next to my office, hosted the gathering. Nor was Bishop Creighton present. I would have liked to have had the opportunity to explain the dynamics and validity of the Free D.C. movement and to apologize for the illegal zeal of my young colleagues. Luckily, enough of my supporters were present to vote down a move to censure me, and the crisis passed.

One of the high points of the Free D.C. movement was the day Dr. King arrived to help us mobilize the community. This was in 1968, and by then he was one of the most famous people in America. I had never had the chance to meet him, but he was a close friend of Walter Fauntroy. The Free D.C. leaders gathered in his hotel room in the morning. Walter and Marion Barry were there. Dr. King was a reserved man, formal in manner, and although we spent much time together that day, I did not feel I came to know him personally.

We had hired a flatbed truck and planned to drive around the district making speeches for home rule in strategic places in the black community. When we pulled up to an open space, a parking lot or school yard, a crowd would already have gathered. When they glimpsed Dr. King, they roared and applauded. Marion Barry introduced each speaker. When my turn came, I spoke of the bizarre situation then extant that, in the capital of the world's richest country and its leading democracy, many citizens lived in desperate poverty and did not even have the civil rights they'd have had in a prison colony. Indeed, D.C. was known as the plantation where the black folks lived who were the servants in the white households of the district. I spoke of the neglect of schools, housing, unjust law enforcement, and all the other social ills of the city. I came down hard on the limited funding given us by Congress in return for all the tax-free federal property, pointing out how conservative, mostly Southern legislators controlled our destiny. Yes, there was plenty of material to crank up a good speech, and I did enjoy haranguing the multitudes, as I had done, years before, at munitions plants during World War II.

I stood there with hundreds of eyes on me; I saw upturned faces waiting expectantly for words they longed to hear—words that explained their feelings of hurt and anger, words that spoke of justice

and compassion, words that told them what they could do to make
things better. I felt that these were righteous words, words a prophet
might have spoken had he been alive that day, and it seemed, in a
sense, that God was speaking through me. I know that sounds pretentious, and yet I deeply believe that the Church does, from time
to time, speak the word of God through her members, both clergy
and lay. Of course, you cannot be sure that God wants a particular
organization, such as the Free D.C. movement, to succeed. But you
can be sure that God, as we know his will through the Bible, desires
justice for his people.

When Dr. King was introduced, the crowd shouted greetings: "Tell
it like it is, Brother. Amen, Brother. Welcome to Washington!" Here
was a real prophet—a national hero coming to speak to them in their
neighborhoods. And he was black. And he was a Baptist minister,
like the ones they had grown up with. He was their own. They would
follow him anywhere. I can still hear his voice, beginning quietly and
then with ever greater resonance climbing to a crescendo of power.
The fact that his leadership in the North was not successful, and that
weaknesses in his character were revealed many years later, cannot
take away from his passion for justice.

That night Walter Fauntroy, his wife, Dr. King, and I led a great
march on the White House for home rule. Such actions and contin-
uous lobbying, combined with the temper of the times, did lead to
changes, and before long the district had its first black mayor, named,
appropriately, Walter Washington. Even today, however, the local
government is financially beholden to Congress.

There was action for a more liberal leadership in the diocese as well
as in the city. Bill Wendt and his colleagues ran a slate of liberal
candidates at the diocesan convention, and a great deal of politicking
went on to assure their election to influential offices. By coincidence,
in an editorial for the diocesan newspaper I had declared that politics
was a good thing in the Church—that no democracy, which the
Church claimed to be, could function without political activity. Well,
Wendt's group won the election. That was a Saturday. Late that night
I had a call from Bishop Creighton. He wanted to see me the next
morning.

"But, Bill, tomorrow's Sunday."

"I know it. I want to see you at seven-thirty. A very serious matter has come up."

Such a peremptory summons was totally out of character for Creighton. I could not imagine what had happened.

When I arrived, he sat me down without even a "Good morning." He said he understood that I had been subverting the diocese: my article had shown that I was behind the political campaign that had won the election, and a bishop's meddling in diocesan politics was a most serious breach of ethics on my part. What did I have to say for myself?

I explained that my article had not been tied to the politicking and that I'd had nothing to do with the activities surrounding the elections. God bless him, he believed me. It must have been very hard for him to defend me. It was the only time he had ever dressed me down.

The incident showed me the power of the conservative wing of the diocese, but I also realized the strength of those concerned for social justice. They had won the election, after all.

Over the years the Church, when healthy, has been at the center of various controversies over social issues. In the 1930s, the issue was whether the Church should take a stand on the labor movement; in the early 1960s, it was civil rights. In the late 1960s, the peace movement within the Church did battle with those who supported the U.S. role in the Vietnam War. In the 1970s, the freeze movement took on the cold war hawks. The dynamics underlying these struggles in the Church were the same as the dynamics in the world generally: a resistance to change, and the political views of the middle and upper-middle class, which tend to be conservative. Those who have power and financial security want to keep it. The upper classes resist change. Conservatives tend to be sympathetic to the military and the whole paraphernalia of patriotism; liberals represent minorities and workers, who stand to gain economically from a more progressive system.

Conservatives generally do not approve of the Church's getting involved in what they consider politics, unless it is to bless the status quo. This is due in part to a misunderstanding of the separation of Church and State. The purpose of the notion of separation is not only to prevent the State from forcing any religion upon the people, but also to protect the Church's freedom to criticize the State. I saw this freedom jeopardized in a small way in Jersey City, where the Roman Catholic Church was so beholden to city hall that its priests would not speak out against municipal corruption. I have read of it in Nazi Germany, where the virtual silence of the Lutheran and Roman Catholic churches allowed a totalitarian regime to seize power. (Martyrs to the cause of justice, such as Dietrich Bonhoeffer, acted too late.) It can be argued that the Church's silence about the grinding poverty of serfs and workers contributed to the Russian Revolution. The same could be said of the Roman Catholic Church in prerevolutionary France. And I suppose a more alert Anglican Church could have warded off the American War of Independence.

To carry on the work of social action, progressives in the Church needed not only coalitions with secular institutions like the Coalition of Conscience, but also interfaith coalitions. One such group met every Tuesday morning at Diocesan House. The Reverend Philip Newell, a Presbyterian minister with Episcopalian leanings who loved the rough-and-tumble of social action, chaired the group. Channing Phillips, a black United Church of Christ minister, was another important leader. He was handsome, tall, thin, light-skinned with aquiline features, a mustache, and a ready smile. Channing was bright and deeply involved in the politics of race. He kept us honest. (Incidentally, he was the first black to be nominated at a convention for the Vice Presidency of the United States.) Several Jewish organizations were represented by Isaac Frank, executive vice president of the Jewish Community Council, but I do not think this rather conservative Jewish layman ever felt at home in our freewheeling group. Gino Baroni was there too, a Roman Catholic priest, pastor of a black parish, and one of the most dedicated Christians I have ever known. Gino was roly-poly, rumpled, funny, sensitive always to what you said to him, as he fixed you with his sharp, brown eyes. He came from a poor Italian family who worked in the coal mines of Pennsylvania, and his passion for justice and his commitment to the poor were evangelical. When Black Power ushered us whites out of civil rights organizations, Gino founded a movement to celebrate the ethnic her-

itage of Italian Americans and other ethnic groups within the Roman
Catholic Church. Without realizing it, he was one of the first pro-
ponents of the multicultural philosophy that has since replaced the
melting pot as the social ideal of America.

We met each Tuesday and planned ways to deal with issues as they
arose. We organized a food service to help the people who were victims of the summer 1968 riots. Suburban churches collected food and
clothing and dropped them off at inner-city churches where they were
distributed to those who had been burned out or who had lost their
jobs. With the same network, a year later we fed the people of Resurrection City, who had encamped near the Lincoln Memorial to
protest poverty and racism. By then Resurrection City—a dream of
Dr. King's—had become a sea of wretchedness, petty crime, and mud.
Perhaps he could have redeemed it had he lived.

Whenever possible, I like to work ecumenically. I have never been
much interested in the theological niceties that divide the people of
God. The older I get, the less important they seem. Again and again
I have felt closer to men and women of other faiths who are dedicated
to God's agenda of justice and peace than to members of my own
Church who seem to block these movements. In moments of human
crisis, the denominational barriers fall.

One weekend in the late 1960s, a group of Roman Catholics and
Episcopalians were making a retreat together, and we spent an entire
evening bemoaning the fact that, because of doctrinal differences over
the meaning of the Eucharist, we could not receive Holy Communion
at each other's altars. We concluded that this deprivation was a necessary sacrifice on the road to complete unity. The next morning,
however, I received word that my friend Bob Hall from Jersey City
days had been found in his rented room, three days after he had died.
I celebrated the liturgy that morning, and I devoted my homily to
Bob. As I told the others of his life—his personal struggles, the slings
and arrows of racism and poverty, and the way he and I had tran-
scended our differences of race and class at Grace Church—I broke
down and cried. When the time for Communion came, everyone,
Roman Catholic and Episcopalian alike, came to the altar rail. The
intellectual gymnastics of the previous night fell away in a simple act
of love.

LIVING THROUGH CRISES

ALTHOUGH social crises arose, I spent most of my time ministering to the parishes of the diocese. The southernmost parish in the diocese was St. Mary's Church, St. Marys City, on the tip of the peninsula separating the mouth of the Potomac River from Chesapeake Bay. Like in so many other southern Maryland parishes, the church was a graceful brick building erected in the eighteenth century. In some ways not much had changed since then. I came to know some of the watermen who worked the river. I was surprised, early on, when one of the senior wardens told me he farmed tobacco in the summer, fished for oysters in the fall, and trapped muskrat in the winter (a far cry from Eli Lilly!). I suppose I had a prejudice against white Southerners because of my work in civil rights, but it went away as I came to know the people of southern Maryland. I realized once again how people from various cultures all fit into the Episcopal Church. Full of native dignity and quiet loyalty to the church, each parishioner was every inch an Anglican. My honorarium from St. Mary's was a quart of fresh oysters.

Further north, at St. Mary's, Aquasco, I had another surprise. During the service, the rector welcomed me and then asked for volunteers to harvest God's acre. In a custom going back over a hundred years an acre of parish property was set aside for tobacco, to be cultivated and harvested by volunteers; the profits helped to pay the rector's salary. Less than a mile from St. Mary's was St. Philip's, Aquasco, a black church. The cinder-block building was modest, to say the least, and there was no plumbing. Since St. Mary's had fewer than thirty parishioners and St. Philip's nearly a hundred, I thought it would make practical sense—and be in the spirit of the times—to have them merge and worship together at the beautiful old church of St. Mary's. I was most diplomatic in bringing up the subject, but the mere mention of the idea was anathema to *both* congregations. Live and learn! The St. Philip's people felt they would lose their identity if they joined St. Mary's—that the leadership of the united parish would be white; the St. Mary's people simply did not want to socialize with blacks. (Years later I had the same problem in Yonkers; this was not a Southern issue per se.)

Immediately surrounding the city and in the outer reaches of the district were many large and medium-sized parishes, varying in style with their socioeconomic area. In the city itself, many Episcopal churches were filled with Southern-oriented old Washington families, as well as many government people and others who had stayed on in Washington. The vestries were generously sprinkled with generals and admirals. (In St. Marys City, for instance, Major General Robert E. Hogaboom served as warden. I had last seen him when he instructed me in map reading in the Marines. We got on famously, despite my pacifist tendencies.) Although many of the parishes had a few black members, the diocese also included several all-black parishes. For the most part, they were made up of middle-class professionals who were torn between their native conservatism, their identification with the goals of the civil rights movement, and what they considered the rude, even outlandish methods of militant young blacks.

When an old-time parish tried to become more involved in its neighborhood, friction always resulted. At staid old Christ Church, Capitol Hill, for instance, a new young rector, Don Seaton, began to minister to the hippies who lived nearby. They came to meetings and even started a commune in the rectory. Don was delighted; the parishioners were not. They complained to me. I defended Don but advised him to cool it. Then one day an elderly member of the altar guild rang the bell of the rectory looking for paper towels and was warmly welcomed by a stark-naked woman. That was the last straw. Don left in a hurry and later became the rector of a large parish in Oakland, California, while Christ Church resumed its old ways.

·　　·　　·

Although I enjoyed these visitations, they had one serious drawback: I was away from my own family all day Sunday. Jenny and the children attended St. Stephen and the Incarnation Church in the inner city, but one by one the children fell away from the Church. It must have been dreary for Jenny to keep going with them, alone, Sunday after Sunday, and I suppose they resented the Church for keeping me away from them and for its other disruptions of their lives. Teenage children's falling away from the Church is almost inevitable, unless they pick up a lively faith of their own outside the ambience of the family, as I did. My children have kept our concern for social justice and have developed their own spirituality, and each has pursued a constructive and socially useful career. Of this I am most proud.

We continued to go to the Adirondacks each summer. As the children grew up, the camp became a place where our "family values" were severely tested. One summer, my oldest son, Paul, who for several months had been living with the young woman he later married, arrived in camp ahead of us. We had an unwritten rule at the time that our children and their friends slept in different rooms from their lovers when staying with us. When Jenny and I arrived exhausted after a long hot trip from Washington, however, Paul informed us that he and Debra were in the same cabin, and we were too beat to argue. From then on, the rule changed: if they were living together away, they could live together at home. The only trouble was that a few years later George, age sixteen, who had missed the nuances, demanded to share a cabin with his young girlfriend. I said, "No way!" He replied, "Pop, we aren't screwing, we are just going to sleep together! S-L-E-E-P! What's your problem?" I stood by my guns, but George would stamp across the grounds at seven in the morning to get dressed in Danny's cabin, where he pretended to have spent the night. It was a losing game in the 1960s. The upshot of our permissiveness came a few years later, when I heard a phone ringing and burst into my daughter's room to answer it. There she was, in bed with her boyfriend. I was flustered, to say the least. He just turned toward me, waved, and said, "Hi, Bish!"

Our philosophy in bringing up the children was to give them as much freedom as possible. We would send the younger ones away to camps in the summers and the older ones on trips to Europe. I rarely helped them with their homework, and when I did I often got it wrong. The new math was bad enough, but as an English major from Yale I was humiliated when one of them received a D in a composition I had supervised.

When they grew older and the freedom began to include sex and drugs, the conflicts grew serious. We absolutely forbade hard drugs, although I think some of the kids tried them. We had read authoritative articles that said marijuana was not harmful, and, given the smoking going on among their friends, we felt that too rigid a policy would backfire. But we did counsel moderation. One summer, Danny suddenly displayed a great interest in plants and asked us to buy him a window box. We were delighted. A few weeks later, I saw these spindly plants growing in profusion. I looked more closely . . . marijuana!

Sex was something else again. I believe our culture still suffers from puritanism, and the overemphasis on sex in advertisements, movies, and the like represents a backlash against this. I believe that the morality of sex should be judged like other human activities. If it is loving and does not hurt anyone, and if it is not breaking marriage vows, I do not think sex outside of marriage is sinful per se. The New Testament teaches otherwise, but the Bible came out of a very different culture, where sex was tied up with property rights, where birth control was not reliable, and where women were treated as inferior beings. When dealing with adolescents, other considerations come into play. Most teenagers cannot handle a full sexual relationship, and it can cause grave emotional damage. We taught the kids about birth control but urged restraint, and all of us muddled through the murky waters of their adolescence as best we could. Since seventeen years separated our youngest from our oldest and those were the 1960s and 1970s, years of violent cultural upheaval, it was a bumpy passage to say the least. (Thank God, those were the days before AIDS.) Rightly or wrongly, we had come a long way since the 1950s.

Adapting to the changing mores without sacrificing our own strongly held beliefs in the family, in loyalty, compassion, and truthfulness was a problem everyone with children faced in those days. Families like ours, however, also had to deal with the disruption of moving every so often, moving not only geographically, but from one culture to another. Think of the differences between life in Jersey

City and life with my mother, surrounded by every luxury imaginable. Think of the change from the politics discussed around the kitchen table in Jersey City and the politics of suburban Indianapolis.

Cleveland Park, the part of Washington near the cathedral, was a perfect place for our family: good public schools, a playground nearby, children in the neighborhood.

No longer was there a conflict between our family's progressive beliefs and the other children's; no longer did we have to be careful about what we said. We always took the children to demonstrations and rallies. On Danny's first paper route, he delivered the news of Bobby Kennedy's funeral and talked about it with his friend Teddy Mondale. During the peace marches, hippies slept all over the living room floor. We were in liberal country on the edge of "radical chic." We did have occasional crises. Two of the kids were caught shoplifting at Sears within months of each other. They had just read *Steal This Book*. Once I gave George a BB gun for his birthday. Always the one to do things a little differently, he shot at passing cars from the driveway, delighting in the *ping*. When the pellet hit a hubcap, however, one of them broke a windshield. The cops came and arrested this juvenile delinquent. I, who had been vocal about juvenile delinquency as a social problem, was humiliated, to say the least, as I appeared before the precinct captain in my bishop's purple shirt with my dangerous son. When I took George to task for a messy room and long hair, he said, "No one ever told Jesus to cut his hair."

The antiwar movement caught us up but did not threaten our personal lives until Paul had to make a decision about the draft. He and my future son-in-law Tom Gerety (now president of Amherst College) were among the leaders of the antiwar movement at Yale; in fact, Paul was the organizer of the movement and drafted its demands. In response, one memorable night in 1969, President Kingman Brewster called an informal referendum on the primary issue on campus: whether Yale should continue to host an ROTC chapter. The trustees—of whom I was one—were summoned to the hockey rink where a huge meeting was to take place. We sat solemnly in a row on either side of the president, looking frighteningly Establishment. Meanwhile, on the floor, Paul, Tom, and their friends were busily organizing. Occasionally I wandered down, we had a smoke, and caught each other up on what was going on. Meanwhile, speeches were made, protest songs were played, and the tension rose. Finally, a secret straw ballot was called for. Student activists and faculty of unimpeachable integrity counted the ballots. Professor Dahl, who was chairing the event, came to the mike. Silence fell over the assembly. "It is hard to believe," he said, "but the vote is 1,286 to 1,286. A tie!" Everyone gasped, then roared with laughter and went home. Thus ended student rebellion over ROTC at Yale. The trustees did decide to eliminate ROTC.

But Paul was literally worried sick about the terrible choices he was facing: enlisting, which he was categorically against; fleeing to Canada and possibly never coming home; or going to jail. (In those days, it was hard to be acknowledged a conscientious objector.) He was under such strain that he was hospitalized with a serious ulcer his senior year and almost died of tuberculosis after graduation. Paul and thousands like him did not fight in Vietnam, but the scars of those years will never leave them. Their courage was every bit as genuine as the courage of men I saw under fire in the 1940s. Moreover, moral courage is a rarer quality than physical courage, because it often brings condemnation rather than praise.

Patience tells me the Washington years were good years for her, but even her memories as a little girl are full of politics. She remembers flower-shaped McCarthy stickers all over the house; the first busing of black kids to her school; our going on an austerity diet to show how hard it was for a welfare family to live on its allowance.

The children, while they attended, learned a great deal at St. Stephen's under the courageous, imaginative, quirky, and amusing ministry of the rector, Bill Wendt. Some of the social actions Bill organized had comic, not cosmic, dimensions. For instance, he led a demonstration to urge turning over Bolling Air Base to public housing by gathering a fleet of boats, landing at the base, and placing a flag there claiming the island for the people of the city. He also organized a celebration of the Eucharist at the Pentagon. The clergy, including a visiting bishop, drove to the Pentagon in a VW with a cross and the bishop's crozier sticking up through the sunroof. They all were arrested, including my son George, age sixteen, my daughter Marian, age fourteen. Whenever a march was held in Washington, word passed among the participants that they could always spend the night on the floor of the St. Stephen's parish house. Whenever there was a civic crisis, Bill would dream up an appropriate event. During the long hot summer of 1968, with Washington on tenterhooks, the radical black leader H. Rap Brown was organizing nearby, and the city fathers were terrified that he would come to the district and start a conflagration. No one would give him a hall; even the black churches were afraid. But not Bill Wendt. Rap spoke at St. Stephen's, and the police thanked Bill for keeping him off the streets. There was no riot.

The most dramatic moment at St. Stephen's was the time after Martin Luther King was assassinated. I was at a meeting of an interfaith program meant to connect the new black leadership with white power structures in the cities of America when someone burst in and told us that Dr. King had been killed. We were speechless. Then someone offered an impromptu prayer, followed by silence. We adjourned the meeting and the religious leaders scrambled to telephones to organize a response in their own congregations.

At St. Stephen's, Bill Wendt had planned a Mass for that evening; would I celebrate? As the day wore on, cities across the nation exploded in anguish and despair—including Washington, which until then had been spared large-scale violence. Dr. King had been a symbol of all the hope and idealism of the movement. His insistence on nonviolence had up to now channeled the rage of black Americans. Now he himself had been shot down in cold blood.

By evening, the ghettos of Washington were overwhelmed by rioting and arson. Somehow we got ourselves to St. Stephen's, on the edge of the ghetto at Fifteenth and Newton Streets. I made my way to the sacristy and found a Jesuit, Father Richard McSorley, vesting to concelebrate Mass with me—an unheard of thing in those days. He was a beautifully independent radical who taught at Georgetown. The church itself was so full that people coming in could hardly find a place to stand, yet when the prayers began a reverent silence enveloped the congregation, and we could plainly hear the wail of sirens, the sound of gunshots, and the fearsome sound of men running as fast as they could, soles beating on the pavement. At the time of intercessions, Bill Wendt asked if anyone wished to speak, and several people did: they prayed for Dr. King's family, for the repose of his soul, for the movement, for the cities of the nation, for racial justice. Then, in the back of the church, a man stood up and shouted in a slurred voice, "Why don't you motherfuckers stop this crap of prayers and get out in the street and fight with the brothers!" In the shocked silence, Bill came to the mike and replied, "Johnny, you go on out and do your thing—we are staying here to do our thing." A good-humored "Amen" rose from the crowd and we proceeded.

Once more, the Eucharist picked up the massive, conflicting emotions of the moment in its cosmic embrace and somehow made sense of the terror and devastation of the spirit we all felt. Death, yes— the martyrdom of a great Christian leader with all its agony and tearing grief—but also Resurrection. Tears streamed down the cheeks of many as they received, and yet it seemed to me that they were as much tears of joy as tears of grief: joy that a great Christian soul had made a gift of his life; joy that in Christ we could find new life after his death. I recognized in the congregation people from every part of the city: some just off the street, dirty, sweaty; government officials still in their suits and ties; clergy of all faiths; faces black, white, young, old, a cross section of the suffering city there to make an offering and to receive the sacrament of new life. Even Senator Ted Kennedy, though a Roman Catholic, came up to receive Communion. I thought of the tragedy he had been through. (I did not know what further tragedy awaited him: Bobby would be assassinated within two months.)

Holy Week followed soon after. We celebrated the Palm Sunday Eucharist on a makeshift altar on Sixteenth Street, behind St. Stephen's, and we must have fed a thousand people with the bread and wine as we reenacted the triumphal entry of Jesus into Jerusalem, where he would be betrayed and crucified. The symbolism was all too apt: King's march on Selma, not many months before, had been a triumph in which thousands had joined, but when he was about to lead another march, in Memphis, he was shot down.

On Good Friday, we made the Stations of the Cross where various tragedies had occurred during the preceding year: a boy murdered on this corner, a police beating on another, a store arsoned in the rebellion, a homeless mother found dead from starvation beneath a street lamp. Never have I had a Holy Week like that one nor sensed so intensely the timeless immediacy of the Gospel.

At such moments the terror and horror of violence can be seen in the context of transcendent meaning. Not only did we find strength and a semblance of sanity in the symbolism of a plain wooden cross bobbing along in the midst of the crowd as it passed the places of human tragedy; we also understood, in faith, that somehow what seemed senseless and wasted was caught up in the great sweep of the redeeming of the world. This chaos, this pain, this despair were part of the despair and pain and chaos of the first Good Friday. A new order of reality could be seen emerging from the devastation; the City of God could be glimpsed shining through the City of Man. And that is why some of the tears of that Holy Week were tears of joy and peace. I do not mean that a new and decent America emerged from the blood of such a day. After all, I am looking back from the perspective of nearly thirty years, from a time when our land is even less just, and our hearts even less compassionate. No, I am speaking of something deeper: the belief that all suffering, especially the suffering of the innocent, becomes part of the suffering that redeems the world. The shadow of the cross falls forward through the centuries, the flesh Christ took on is our flesh, and so the suffering he underwent he still undergoes in our writhing bodies. I had learned something of these mysteries during the war, but as the years went on and I saw further pain and tragedy the reality of the cross became certain to me.

Since early 1963, the world had been in turmoil: riots, revolutions, assassinations. Older people of goodwill tried to understand and identify with the aims of the young, yet the methods of mass movements and community organization were strange and often shocking to them.

The presiding bishop of the Episcopal Church, John Hines, was one such sympathetic older person. He came from Texas and had strong social views, which he acted on with courage and imagination. He saw the Church as an instrument that could bring the resources of the Establishment to the assistance of the poor. To do this, he organized an interfaith group whose members included the Roman Catholic archbishop John J. Wright, the eminent and prophetic rabbi Abraham Joshua Heschel, and several black church leaders, including Marion Wilson, chairman of the National Committee of Negro Churchmen. The goal of Operation Connection, as the group was

called, was "to help mobilize and release the resources of the community toward economic power for the poor, especially the black
poor."

John Hines asked me to be the executive director. I was honored
and excited. Bishop Creighton, with his usual generosity, gave me a
six-month leave of absence. Soon after, I was having a drink with my
childhood friend Bob Potter, a prominent New York lawyer who numbered *The Wall Street Journal* among his clients. He had gone to St.
Mark's School and had belonged to the Porcellian Club at Harvard.
His Establishment credentials were unsurpassable. Even so, he took
the gospel seriously and enjoyed teasing his fellow directors on the
Dow Jones board with his theories about redistribution of wealth. I
have rarely known a person for whom all kinds of people showed such
affection. On that particular afternoon he was telling me how upsetting it was for him to look out of his office window, high above
Manhattan, and know that the country was in a struggle for its soul,
that the issues of justice and peace were being fought out on the
streets while he felt impotent and immobile. "What can I do, Moore?"

"Do you really want to know?"

"Yes, I really want to know."

"Take six months off and join me on Operation Connection," I
said, then explained what we had in mind.

"I'll do it," he said, without a pause.

"Don't you have to ask your partners or your wife?"

"Hell no." And we were on.

We were soon joined by Lucius Walker, the head of the Interre-
ligious Foundation for Community Organization (IFCO), and some
of his colleagues. Milton Zatinsky, a veteran of the labor movement,
was to run the office.

Walker was young, black, and respected by the young black leadership that was springing up around the country. Our plan was to
target several cities and make connections there between the white
power structure and the new black leadership. When we found out
the black agenda, we would present it to the white leadership, get
the groups together, and leave them to work things out.

It did not take long to ascertain who ran Detroit (Henry Ford and
his friends), or Cincinnati (Proctor and Gamble and its affiliates).
Nor did it take Potter and me long to make contacts with the lead-

ership through school, college, legal, and church connections. One day in Detroit, we spent the morning with Bishop Albert Cleague of the Church of the Black Madonna, a storefront church guarded by two fierce-looking armed men in fatigues. Then we had lunch with Henry Ford III, whom I had known in college, in his penthouse office. Before long, the black community and the white business community were working together again. The reason was clear: the black leadership trusted Walker, Walker trusted us, and the white leadership trusted us. Trust, the breakdown of which had caused the breach, was reestablished.

In the Bay Area, we met with some Black Panthers, whose chaplain was Earl Neil, an Episcopal priest, as well as with William Knowland, a reactionary former senator and publisher of the *Oakland Tribune*. In Houston, a long dinner with George Bush was most productive.

We had a great time bouncing from one side of town to the other, and gradually I lost some of my cynicism about what business leaders would do. They set up management training, facilitated loans, helped gain support from the Small Business Administration, and so forth. These efforts were more successful, I think, because the business leaders were genuinely afraid of what might happen to their cities and were looking for help. The excitement of the times reached even into the boardrooms. This was one of the first organized efforts to assist black economic development.

The Church was most fortunate to have had John Hines as its presiding bishop during the 1960s. His toughness, his willingness to go forward on an issue of justice whatever the cost, made him the perfect leader for the times. Now, Church leaders are so concerned about unity that they put justice in second place, not realizing you cannot have true unity, true peace, without justice, particularly in the Church, whose very being is founded on the principles of justice.

In the early summer of 1967, with every city in the country on tenterhooks, John was attending a meeting of the World Council of Churches in Cyprus when his staff sent him a cable to come back to New York immediately. On his arrival, he visited some of the smoldering cities and made a historic decision. He would turn over major resources and leadership of the Episcopal Church to the new black and Hispanic leaders of the inner cities, who were seeking redress for the grievances that sparked the rebellions. The General Convention met in Seattle in the early fall. Hines gave an impassioned speech, and the carefully prepared budget was scrapped to provide massive funding for the General Convention Special Program. Led by a black layman, Leon Modeste, the program appropriated money for local community organizations, whether they were affiliated with the Church or not. This caused enormous controversy, because groups that were tagged as radical or even Communist were being funded in dioceses without the local bishop's permission. Hines was embattled, but he stood his ground. By and large, the program was successful in two ways: it assisted powerless people to organize and exert economic, social, and political influence on the local level, and it gave the Episcopal Church an image of justice and courage with this new leadership.

However, the rumbling in the Church over this program and over the war in Vietnam was such that Bishop Hines called a special convention to meet at Notre Dame in the late summer of 1969. The discussion over black empowerment became so heated that Mohammed Kenyatta, of the Black Economic Development Conference, grabbed the mike to demand $200,000 in reparations from the Episcopal Church for all the wrongs the Church had committed against black people over three hundred years. To everyone's surprise, the convention approved an appropriation for this fund. Clearly, this was not the way the dignified Episcopal Church usually did business. Part of me recoiled at what appeared, from one perspective, to be blackmail, but on balance I applauded our Church's making this symbolic gesture in recognition of the ancient wrongs we had perpetrated on the black community over the years. Blacks had been excluded from white churches, they had had little access to positions of leadership, and white Episcopalians, in their secular roles, had been part of the racist structure of America.

Another climax was in store. One evening, the convention was given over to a session on the issue of Vietnam. Bishop Kim Myers of California, my old colleague from Jersey City days, put together a demonstration with other leaders of the peace movement in the Church. The demonstration began, some speeches were made, and those of us in the know awaited a procession, which was to enter the hall. I was sitting in the back when someone rushed up to me and said that the security people were preventing the procession from entering. They had been told no sticks or other weapons would be allowed in. On these grounds, a guard had forbidden the cross and candles to come through the door. Given that we were at Notre Dame, I found it hilarious but hurried to the door and persuaded the guard to open it. The procession worked its way to the podium, and Kim Myers took over. "Here before you," he said, "are two splendid young Americans who have left the Army because they can no longer support the war." The two clean-cut soldiers stepped forward. "Do you support them in their stand?" A chorus of yeas rose from the crowd. "Raise your hand if you support them." This was harder than a voice vote. A few timid hands went up. People looked around to see if anyone was watching them. More and more hands went up. "Those of you with your hands up come down and stand with them on the platform." This was really hard, because now everyone who voted would be seen to have supported deserters from the Army.

Well, the rally continued, and those of us who responded to what was a sort of altar call joined hands around the two men and sang "We Shall Overcome."

I went to a meeting after the rally, and when I reached my room about midnight there was a message to call Father Robert Varley, a friend of mine who had a room upstairs. When I reached him, he told me to come right up; there was a crisis. I grabbed a bottle of bourbon (always handy for any crisis) and went up to his room. There were the two deserters, looking pale and scared to death. They had been followed home from the rally, they thought by the Ku Klux Klan or the FBI. They had driven faster and faster in a car chase all over South Bend and finally come back to the campus, jumped out of the car, run into our hotel, up the stairs, and into the first room with an open door. It turned out to be the room of a Jesuit, Father Ryan, the official Roman Catholic observer to our convention. He got hold of Father Varley next door, and they were trying to decide what to do. Bishop Myers had claimed that the deserters should be given sanctuary by our Church, but no official word had been given. It was too late to do anything that night, anyway, so one slept in Varley's room, and I took the other, whose name was Buff Parry, to mine.

Massive anticlimax: it turned out that the car that had chased them was driven by a reporter from the college newspaper who wanted a story. The young men took off the next day, and Parry, I know, went to Canada. I am still in touch with him.

What a contrast to my first House of Bishops meeting, in Montana in 1964, where they dressed the presiding bishop in a feathered Indian headdress and gave him a live steer as a gift, amid roars of laughter. I sensed the humiliation of the Native Americans who had to go through this farce. The main orders of business at that meeting were the budget of the Church newspaper and Bishop James Pike's claim that a deaconess in his diocese was really a deacon, with the prerogatives of a deacon's ordination, which horrified many of the brethren. I was so fed up with the pettiness of this business and the acrimony against my friend Jim Pike that I seriously thought of resigning. Luckily Bob DeWitt of Pennsylvania caught me in the hall, and with the assistance of the familiar bottle of bourbon he put me back on track.

One of the social liturgies of official Washington was the Georgetown dinner party. Hostesses vied with one another to gather together as many powerful people as possible, and orchestrating such a gathering was a fine art. It was important to invite good friends who would enjoy one another's company but also those who did not see eye to eye and whose conversations might light up the party with polite conflict. Or perhaps a senator wished to have an informal conversation with another member of the government and would ask the hostess to set it up. From time to time I'd see such a pair draw aside, perhaps on a bench in the garden, and lean forward, with furrowed brows, apparently settling the affairs of the world—and they may well have been.

Of course, Jenny and I were fascinated to have a chance to meet and talk with prominent members of Congress and the government, but for newcomers it could be embarrassing. I once asked a familiar-looking gentleman what he did. He said he worked for the government. I pressed him, and after a bit of verbal sparring, he said he was the senator from Maryland.

It was at such a party, given by Liberty Redmond, that I changed my views of the Vietnam War. The Redmonds were old friends; I had supervised Woody (or tried to) at St. Paul's, and Liberty was the younger sister of Mary Aldrich, whom I visited in Maine long ago. Their parties were less formal than most, and they tended to have more social friends than government luminaries. Woody was in business. In any case, McGeorge Bundy was there that night. I also had grown up with him on the North Shore. We went to the same outing class, and since we both despised baseball, we were sent to the outfield, where we would crack jokes and hope that no one would hit the ball our way. Mac was extremely bright and knew it. I am sure he was not surprised when President Kennedy chose him as his National Security Adviser. He had been dean at Harvard and had worked with former Secretary of State Henry Lewis Stimson.

When I was in Indiana and read that so many old friends were in positions of responsibility, men who had had the same upbringing as I, who had attended the same kind of private Church schools and gone to Harvard or Yale, I felt the government was in good hands: Bundy, Vance, Meyer, Pittman, and others, like Robert McNamara, whom I only knew slightly but respected. I assumed that if they thought we were doing the right thing in Vietnam we probably were. However, a few nights before this party, I had spent the evening with Bill Wendt and some black friends who had serious misgivings about U.S. involvement there. Now I thought I had a chance to find out from the source what the administration's rationale was. As a former Marine, I first wanted to know the military strategy, for we had been taught that the objective of any military mission must be clearly defined before the strategy and tactics of the operation could be determined. Well, on the terrace after dinner, I asked Mac what our military objective was in Vietnam. He began to speak about the cold war, the danger of Communist China, and so forth. I said I was not asking about the political or geopolitical objectives; I merely wanted to know what the military objective was. I was astonished when he had no answer.

I began to have severe misgivings about President Johnson's policy and the wisdom of his advisers. I listened more intently to my radical friends. The seeds of doubt that eventually led to my taking a trip to Saigon had begun to grow.

How could decent, dedicated men, many of whom had known the horrors and ambiguities of war firsthand, have been so wrongheaded?

I believe it had to do with a combination of patriotic arrogance based on the fact that the United States has never lost a war; a conviction that the Vietnam War was a war for freedom against Communism; and the inability of men of that stature to admit when they were wrong. Besides this, President Johnson's Texas machismo gave energy to the operation. Here was a strange intellectual and cultural mix: a Boston Brahmin (Bundy), a Detroit businessman (McNamara), a Southern professor (Rusk), and a Texas cowboy (Johnson), who could not allow the United States to be defeated while he was President.

In some ways, I do not blame him. We had all been brought up believing in America's omnipotence, omniscience, and righteousness. Any President that leads the country into war must persuade himself that it is a crusade. But Bundy, McNamara, and Rusk should have known better, and if they could not persuade the President, they should have resigned.

I soon decided the war was wrong and joined the peace movement. Our house became a center of people who were against the war. We hosted a fund-raiser for the moratorium, with Shirley MacLaine and Warren Beatty in attendance.

Another, more subtle dynamic was at work, however. We had been in the heat of the civil rights struggle, and the movement had become part of our faith and part of our lifestyle. But ever since the James Meredith march in 1966, when Stokely Carmichael had declared Black Power, whites were asked to stand aside from civil rights activity and told to work in the white community, because that was where the problem was. True enough, but the necessary motivation to do that thankless job lay in being refreshed by the warmth, power, and camaraderie of integrated actions. Furthermore, it was almost impossible to stay intellectually and morally honest in one's thinking without the constant critique of black sensitivity to racism. Given these frustrations with civil rights, and given that I agreed with Martin Luther King's position, I turned my energies to the peace movement. Many of us believed, as Dr. King did, that the two causes—peace and justice—were so interrelated that no true peace, domestic or international, could come about without justice and that justice could not be effected in a nation intoxicated by war. Furthermore, resources that could have been available to the war on poverty were being hemorrhaged by Vietnam.

The last great peace march occurred on my fiftieth birthday, November 15, 1969. Hundreds of thousands attended. Our house was filled with young marchers sleeping on the floor.

For her part, Jenny wrote a warm and touching book about our time in Jersey City, and then became active in Eugene McCarthy's presidential campain. Life was full, and we thrilled to its fullness.

The diocese was dominated by the National Cathedral, towering above the highest hill in the district, a fitting counterweight to the Capitol on that other hill. As St. John the Divine's massive eclecticism, its presence right on the street, symbolizes New York, so the stately, gleaming white structure of the National Cathedral symbolizes the capital. Surrounded by lawns and gardens, it is a fitting partner to the Lincoln and Jefferson Memorials. But it stands apart, and I always hoped the life of the city could be more a part of its life and that it could come to grips more vigorously with the social movements of the day.

Two attempts at services of social significance turned out to be disastrous. At one, an interracial rally, Malcolm Boyd concluded a stirring sermon with these words, "The only answer to discrimination in housing, to discrimination in jobs, to discrimination in education, is *intermarriage!*" A shocked silence fell over the staid Episcopal congregation. The blacks looked anxious, the whites angry. When the service ended with "We Shall Overcome" many white hands were stuffed firmly in their pockets to avoid the hand clasping and swaying that always concluded that hymn.

Another time, a rainstorm forced an outdoor rock concert into the cathedral. A glorious cacophony of sound bounced off the Gothic arches. The marble sang, the building throbbed. It was wonderful— so wonderful, in fact, that some kids danced and an artful photographer caught them in such a position as to make it seem they were dancing on the altar. *The Boston Globe* ran the photograph, and an irate Bostonian shook it in front of Dean Francis B. Sayre, Jr., when he made a fund-raising address to some Boston Brahmins the following day. Fortunately, the powers that be squelched another photograph of a couple rocking on Woodrow Wilson's tomb. Wilson was Dean Sayre's grandfather.

But I did love the cathedral. The silent beauty of my weekly Eucharist in the Bethlehem chapel gave me graceful steadying in the turbulence of those times.

Looking back on those years crowded with incident—the civil rights crises, which changed the face of America; the beginnings of the anti-Vietnam movement; the radical shift in young people's cultural attitudes; the sexual revolution—I see a clear pattern. World War II began the breakup of the colonial age, and the domestic equivalent of colonialism, namely the domination of society by old established institutions, was being resisted as well. Neither structure could contain the new pressures of technology and the increased education and awareness of great masses of people. Even so, it is unfortunate that our institutions were not flexible enough to deal with them rapidly. If they had, the sacrifices and dedication of those days would have had far more positive results in the United States.

Personally, I learned many lessons during that time: about the federal government, about how to be a bishop, about organizing movements. Part of my vocation was to be a steward of power, to use my office to empower those who were too weak to achieve the modest goals of economic and political justice, and in those years I became even more aware of the constant struggle of the powerless.

THE HEIGHTS

ELECTION

LATE one evening in the spring of 1968, I was in the apartment of the Very Reverend John V. Butler, then dean of the Cathedral of St. John the Divine. I'd been to a meeting in his office with Leslie Lang, another old friend and a prominent priest in New York, and John had asked us to come upstairs for a nightcap. "Paul," John said, in a matter-of-fact voice, "we need to talk to you. Don [Bishop Donegan, then the Bishop of New York] will retire soon, and we want you to be his successor." The adrenaline rushed through my veins as I listened further. "I am positive you would be elected if you ran. We can think of no one with better qualifications. I know Don would be delighted, although of course he cannot express himself publicly.

"The reason for approaching you now," John went on, "is to make sure you do not run for any other election. I know you have been nominated elsewhere. There is no doubt in our minds that you will become a diocesan bishop—but we want you for New York. It is the most important urban job in the Church, and it is your home diocese."

Les Lang nodded his assent and added that he had already sounded out a number of diocesan leaders, who were enthusiastic. And so our life changed again. I told Jenny and swore her to secrecy. She was excited at the prospect; little did we know what dark times lay ahead. Each time we moved, our lives were deeply altered. I have never quite decided about "the will of God" in these matters. I do not think God is a transcendent puppeteer, and yet I have felt, from time to time, that the major events in life are more than chance occurrences, that there is a deeper movement, call it Providence, under which we exercise choice but which somehow points us on the way.

However much God had to do with it, my election as bishop coadjutor unfolded. Finally, the slate of nominees was announced, and I was on it. Of all the positions in the Church, this promised the greatest fulfillment for one who had devoted his life to the work of the Church in the city. Nor was this just a great city: this was New York, where the Episcopal Church went back to colonial times. This was New York, with the largest cathedral in the world. This was New York, whose parishes together had more resources than any other diocese. This was New York, the swirling, wonderful, cruel, powerful, creative capital of the world. It was and is a city I love, for all of humanity comes together here, and here the vision of the Kingdom of God can be seen as nowhere else in the world. Nor was the diocese confined to New York City. Excluding Queens and Brooklyn, we stretched north through the satellite cities of Yonkers, New Rochelle, and White Plains (each with its own urban problems), across the suburban belt of Westchester and Putnam Counties, and over the Hudson to Rockland County. In these suburbs, "country club" parishes were interspersed with less pretentious small parishes. Up the Hudson in Dutchess County, another city, Poughkeepsie, was set in the midst of old, small Hudson River communities, whence came the old families, such as Roosevelt, Fish, and Livingston. A few foxhunting establishments remained east of Poughkeepsie, but the parishes across the river in Orange and Sullivan Counties were less affluent. Our furthest congregation was Calicoon, on the banks of the Delaware River, a three-hour drive from the cathedral.

What a call—to take an old idiosyncratic institution, or really hundreds of interdependent idiosyncratic institutions, and building on the work, its past, help shape it into something resembling the Kingdom even more. I knew I could not come near that goal, but I could not wait to try. What might such a Kingdom look like? Wherever the Episcopal Church hung its red, white, and blue sign, I liked to think, people would know they could find some beauty this way in psalms of holiness, some help, some love, a place that stood for justice. Wherever an institution—a school, hospital, settlement house, home for the aged, or home for disturbed children—called itself Episcopal, a special quality of care would be shown. In this way, the cynical, the broken, even the proud might catch a glimpse of what Jesus is really like. I had an individual ministry, to be sure, but far more important was the daily ministry of thousands of Church members and clergy, which I would support.

I made several trips from Washington to New York to meet with groups from different parts of the diocese. At Grace Church, Millbrook, a little, English-style church in the middle of Dutchess County horse country, I expected Brooks Brothers shirts and tweed jackets. Rather, I found men in windbreakers and women in pantsuits. They were interested in whether I cared for anything outside the city, since my liberal, urban image was all they had heard about. Millbrook was viable, but most of the other congregations nearby were on the edge of going under. To them I spoke of team ministries, maintenance, and fund-raising.

Some High Church clergy invited me to meet with them at St. Mary the Virgin off Times Square. This, the most famous Anglo-Catholic parish in the country, was in financial trouble, yet these priests in their pitch-black suits and high round collars were interested in whether or not I was a true-blue Anglo-Catholic. After I had talked a bit about social responsibility, pastoral care, and urban issues, Bob Terwilliger turned to me and asked, "Paul, exactly what *is* your theology?" I burst out laughing and said I was a card-carrying Anglo-Catholic.

Bob Potter had a cocktail party in his apartment on the East River. I met a lot of other old friends and renewed my Ivy League ties. To climax it all, my principal rival, John Krumm, and I were asked to speak to a large gathering of clergy. The subject was something like "Theology Today," and we were joined by a Dr. Bennett of Union Seminary so that it would not look like a contest between us. No one was fooled; the room was jammed with at least two hundred curious clergy. I learned later that the choice of subject and indeed the whole event were set up by Krumm's backer, Bob Terwilliger, to make me look theologically uninformed in front of two theologians. John Krumm, who was a good friend, was brilliant, far more competent theologically than I, and he had a great sense of humor. Unfortunately for him that day, he read verbatim from a prepared text, and his talk never got off the ground. For my part, I was excited and spoke extempore from notes with great enthusiasm about what the Church could do in New York, basing my ideas on a theology of the Incarnation, on the Church as the Body of Christ expressed through social action, and on developing our parishes into true communities of love.

I am not a theologian, in the sense that I do not have academic credentials in theology. I do not teach theology, as some of my more academic Episcopal colleagues have done, by giving lectures. On the contrary, I believe theology is best taught by bishops and parish priests through action accompanied by the spoken and written word. I believe you teach the meaning of the cross by encouraging people to share in the sufferings of the sick, the poor, and the persecuted rather than by promulgating theories of the Atonement from the lectern. I believe you teach about God's justice as spoken through the prophets by leading movements for justice rather than by analyzing the books of the Old Testament. I believe you teach the meaning of the Eucharist by celebrating on Riker's Island or in the killing fields of Mississippi rather than by encouraging research on ancient liturgies. The words of Jesus were not as important as his death and resurrection; in fact, his words would not be remembered had he not given his life on the cross. I see the likes of Martin Luther King and Desmond Tutu as the real teachers of theology because of their courageous action, and it is they who are my role models.

In any case, that day the clergy of the Diocese of New York seemed to agree. I received a standing ovation.

The day of the election itself I was having lunch at a meeting of the trustees of Berkeley Seminary in New Haven when I was summoned to the kitchen for a phone call. It was Bishop Donegan: "Paul, you were elected on the second ballot." This was the fall of 1969.

When the family heard the news, there was much rejoicing; we were a political family, and we had won the election. Going-away parties were thrown; excitement about New York and what lay ahead was the subject at supper every night. It dawned on the kids only gradually that they would be leaving their friends and their home— for the younger ones the only home they had ever known. Furthermore, all was not well with my marriage.

In June 1969, we took our annual family outing to the Blue Surf

Motel at Bethany Beach, Maryland. It was there that our conflict came to a head. I arrived late from a conference in New York, and that night, in the motel room, Jenny told me that she no longer loved me. I was dazed; I staggered back and sat on the edge of the other bed, my head in my hands. I heard the waves on the beach, the muffled laughter of the children next door—everything perfect but this. It had finally come. I knew Jenny and I had been growing apart—among other things, she had become estranged from the Church—but felt it was a phase we could get through. Even now I do not know what came between us.

We had had so much fun together. As one of the children put it, Jenny would light up a room when she entered. She was always up for adventure. Her mind was sharp, and she had a genius for friendship with all kinds of people. And yet deep depressions would come over her, especially after childbirth. Every spring she became depressed, and these were times of great suffering for her, but she bore up gallantly. I kept hoping things between us would improve. I loved her, I loved the life we had, and I would have done anything to bring us back together.

In the Adirondacks later that summer, the children gave us a crazy fancy-dress party to celebrate our upcoming twenty-fifth wedding anniversary. The agony of the pretense we had to show that day made us decide to tell them how bad things were between us. The next morning, we gathered the older ones in our cabin on the huge double bed, where so many stories had been told, so many teary children comforted. They knew something was up, even though we had tried not to show hostility toward each other in front of them. It was a hard decision: whether to pretend all was well, hoping it would improve, or to let the children know our true feelings with all the anxiety and even fear that such information brings. Well, we let them know.

When I was elected bishop coadjutor of New York, we both felt a new start would help. But we never had a chance, because on the way home from the airport in Washington, Jenny was in a serious accident. A friend of ours gave her a ride from the airport, and they were struck by a car from the side. She did not realize at first that she had been injured, but before long her stomach pains were so severe that we took her to the hospital, where she underwent a critical operation. The doctor told me later we almost lost her. She had to stay in the hospital for several weeks.

The next two years were a nightmare. Jenny seemed to recover from the accident physically, but none of us realized how deep a trauma it had been. The accident had made her even more vulnerable emotionally, and her already severe depressions worsened. She was terrified that she would end up like her mother, who had been in and out of mental hospitals for years. In retrospect, we should not have moved to New York as soon as we did. Jenny was not strong enough for the emotional and physical strain of moving and the burden of bringing the children through the move.

GREETED BY SQUATTERS

The moving vans had been packed, the last farewells said, and I loaded the station wagon with suitcases and odds and ends. As I drove north on the New Jersey Turnpike, my dreams of the future were interrupted by an announcement on the radio: "Squatters have oc-cupied more buildings in New York." I thought to myself: poor John Lindsay, another problem. "The buildings are located on Amsterdam Avenue and 112th Street." My Lord, I realized, that is across from the cathedral! Thus began an endless struggle that would acquaint me with the tough realities of New York. As I drove onto the cathe-dral grounds, I saw picket lines and police across the avenue. The cathedral guards who met me were nervous. I went right to Bishop Donegan's office, where he gave me the background. An Episcopal old people's home and a Presbyterian facility for the aging on Morn-ingside Heights were to close. They could not afford to bring the old buildings up to the standards required by the city; therefore, an ec-umenical board had been formed to consider building a new home across from the cathedral, two blocks from St. Luke's Hospital. It was a splendid idea. The old tenements across the street were purchased and stood ready to be demolished. In the meantime, the squatters' movement in New York had blossomed as an unorthodox solution to the mounting problem of homelessness. Columbia University, located across Amsterdam Avenue from the cathedral and St. Luke's, had suffered a humiliating defeat at the hands of demonstrating students and local black groups the year before. It had been prevented from building a new gymnasium on the edge of nearby Morningside Park. The anti-institutional bias of the 1960s and the long resentment toward the big institutions on Morningside Heights, coupled with the housing shortage and the presence of impoverished Hispanic families a few blocks away, gave momentum to the squatters' movement. Without anyone at the cathedral hearing even a rumor, over one hundred squatters had occupied the vacant tenements in the middle of the night.

"Paul, this is a mess," Bishop Donegan said, "but you have had a lot of experience with this kind of thing. Would you take it on as one of your responsibilities?" Of course, I said yes, confident that the matter could be resolved easily. I did not know how tough New York could be.

The first thing I realized was that the cathedral was totally cut off from the neighborhood. The fact that no one had heard even a whisper about the squatters' plan proved the point. And so I became the representative of the Establishment in their eyes. Their slogan was "No more institutions north of 110th Street." The fact that the new building in question was a facility for old people, many of whom were impoverished, had no effect on their rhetoric. It was suggested that we call the police to evict them, but the chairman of the board and I felt this might incite a riot like the one Columbia had suffered, but on the steps of the cathedral. I finally visited the buildings and found extremely dangerous electric heaters and hot plates in use there; as I looked out my window on cold fall mornings, I had visions of a fire that might kill some of the families and their children. With great misgivings, we voted diocesan funds to put in a furnace for the squatters. This, of course, infuriated the board and made enemies of them as well.

We had open meetings with the squatters on the steps of the cathedral. We offered them alternative housing nearby. We ran through innumerable schemes. The city, in the person of Eleanor Holmes Norton, commissioner of human resources (and later a good friend when we served together as Yale trustees), promised to bail us out if we did not evict them. She was never able to fulfill her promise.

The climax came a couple of years later, one evening in the spring of 1972, when I was alone with two of our little girls in our apartment. The windows were open, and we heard shouting in the distance. We thought nothing of it until the shouting drew close, coming from the street. "We want the bishop! We want the bishop!" The doorbell rang, and a guard told me a large crowd of demonstrators had entered the close. Before long, he came again to say they had broken in downstairs and were on their way up to my apartment. With some trepidation I left the two frightened girls and went down to the meeting room below to face the demonstrators. The scene was rowdy, with much shouting and posturing. I felt right at home, except that for the first time I was on the receiving end. Many later said it served me right.

Finally, the demonstrators agreed to have their leaders join me at a meeting in two weeks, to which I would invite some housing experts to see if there was a way to legitimize their occupancy, because by that time, the old people's residence had been established in the Bronx.

The evening came, and I waited in my office with the housing types for the leaders to arrive. I heard shouts outside and was told that over a hundred squatters had come. I saw placards, women with baby carriages, the works. We met in the auditorium next to my office. The squatters took over and read a manifesto denouncing me as a rich person who was a friend of the Rockefellers (which I wasn't) and the brother of the chief executive officer of Bankers Trust (which I was)—in short, as a symbol of the rich institutions on Morningside Heights, which were oppressing poor people and denying them housing. When I finally got the floor, fuming inside, I said I could not work things out with such a crowd and left the room.

I gave up trying to solve the problem after that, although others did succeed in renovating the buildings for occupancy some fifteen years later. In New York, I had learned, they play hardball. As my successor said to me, "In Kansas City, people meet in good faith to sort out problems. In New York, they start screaming before you even see them." Exactly right!

INSTALLED AS BISHOP COADJUTOR

The squatters began my initiation to New York, but I was formally installed as bishop coadjutor on May 8, 1970, in the cathedral. Bishop Donegan, God bless him, preached a sermon about the social activism of my predecessors, lest my style seem unusual for a Bishop of New York. He spoke of Bishop Horatio Potter, who had been involved in the destruction of the Tweed ring; Bishop David H. Greer, a pacifist in the days when that had taken great courage; Bishop Charles K. Gilbert, who had been considered a left-winger because he was on the side of labor and received emissaries from the patriarch of Moscow. "Bishop Moore is yet another in the great tradition," he said. "He stands for everything to which this diocese is committed."

Bishop Donegan himself had spoken out time and again on social issues. At the installation service, I asked that prayers be said for the Kent State students who had been shot down a few days before and called on all people to put pressure on the President and Congress to reaffirm and protect the right to dissent. "Today, in my former city," I said from the pulpit, "young people from all over the land are converging with cries of rage and grief. The streets echo with the sound of marching." Things were tense in New York. The day before, Trinity Church, the ancient Episcopal parish at the head of Wall Street, had become an aid station for students beaten up by construction workers because they were demonstrating for peace.

Mother came to the service, proud and gallant in her wheelchair. She had suffered a stroke. Jenny and the children filled the front row. For a few moments, in that huge and holy place, I felt all would be well.

PEACE RALLY

The timing of events rarely seems right, though. One of my favorite sayings, attributed to John Lennon, is "Life is what happens when you are busy making other plans." I had hoped to begin my ministry in New York by assuming a low profile, using the two years as co-adjutor to get to know the people of the parishes in the Catskills, Harlem, the Bronx, Fifth Avenue, and Westchester. Instead, a few weeks later, an anti–Vietnam War group asked if they could use the cathedral for a rally. I was delighted, but asked Canon Edward West, the acting dean, to screen them carefully. He found that Dotson Rader, a friend and biographer of Tennessee Williams, was in charge. "A fine young man," Eddie reported.

On the night of the event, I found myself in the midst of a noisy and altogether unpeaceful peace rally. Antiestablishment speeches had been made, and Norman Mailer's dramatic skit *Why Are We in Vietnam?* was being staged in the crossing. I could not believe what I heard and saw. The scene was a locker room in Texas; the dialogue was pornographic—talk of erections, orgasms, and masturbation with accompanying gestures. The idea seemed to be that we were in Vietnam because of the macho spirit of the American psyche, best revealed in the ambience of a locker room. Tennessee Williams, hardly a prude, was so shocked that he got up and left (he later sent me a note apologizing for Mailer). Canon West was away; the cathedral security people, used to caring for fainting old ladies, were helpless. By the time the skit was over, the crowd of several thousand had grown rowdy. No thurible was being used, but a smell vaguely like incense began to permeate the place. A guard rushed up to me and said, "They're drinkin' beer and smokin' joints in the rear of the nave. I tried to stop 'em and they got nasty. If I try to throw them out, we might have real trouble."

"I think we better cool it," I said. "Keep me posted."

Even though I had been at large, unruly assemblies many times, I grew uneasy. I had no idea what the dynamics might be in this huge churchly space. I felt the anger out there, the pent-up emotion of those young people who had struggled so long and so fruitlessly against the horror of Vietnam. They easily could get out of control. But there was a sponsoring group in charge, and this was not my show. "Well, I guess if they aren't worried, there is no reason for me to worry," I tried to persuade myself. Although dressed in a bright-purple cassock with a large peace cross dangling on my chest, I was trying to be as inconspicuous as possible. But at that point, Dotson Rader pushed his way through the crowd to where I was standing, a look of panic on his face. "Bishop! Bishop! The Vietcong are rushing the podium. You're the only one who can stop them! Come! Quick!"

He grabbed me by the arm and dragged me up onto the stage. I looked down the long aisle of the nave. Storming up the center toward me were about thirty shirtless young men carrying what looked like spears, with flags (Vietcong flags it turned out) attached to the points. The crowd was yelling "Right on!" or "Stop those crazies!" Everyone was on his feet. The outrage of the nation seemed to be all focused here, rushing at me. By now the "Vietcong" were only thirty feet away. The spotlight turned on me. I stood up to the mike, lifted both arms, looking like a huge purple scarecrow, and yelled at the top of my voice, "Stop! In the name of Almighty God, Stop! Stop! Stop!"

They stopped dead in their tracks; to this day I do not know why. A hush fell over the place. I said quietly, "We will now go on with the evening in a spirit of peace." And they did.

We felt the aftershocks of that evening for a long time. The newspapers had a field day: "New liberal bishop sponsors peace rally—beer drinking, pot smoking in the cathedral," and so on. Obviously, this was no way to further peace! But we all felt so powerless in those days, as the bombing increased, the body counts rose, and fine young men were going to prison or leaving the country, that I'd have done almost anything to stop the war.

THE CLERGY OF THE DIOCESE

Despite the uproar over the peace rally and the squatters, I was determined to get on with the pastoral side of my job. Since the most important part of a bishop's ministry is being a pastor to the clergy, I began a series of small, two-day clergy conferences. I had been told that the clergy's morale was low, and I needed to find out why.

The relationship of a bishop to his clergy is a special and delicate one. The bishop is their pastor; they come to him with problems of the parish, finances, vestry dissidents, their own marriage problems, personal financial binds, all sorts of things, depending on how much trust they have in him. I have been told the most intimate secrets by some, while others are frightened even to say hello. They are frightened because the bishop has great power over their lives. Although he does not have the authority to hire and fire, unless they are on his staff, he can directly affect their career through references to prospective employers, by supporting them or not in their parishes, by appointing them to committees, and by suggesting their names to vestries when it is time to move. So a priest needs a bishop's trust; having the bishop's support makes all the difference to a priest's morale.

A generation or two ago, the role of a parish priest was clear and his tenure secure until retirement. He (there were no women priests in those days) took services on Sundays and holy days, visited the sick, performed baptisms, marriages, and funerals, counseled parishioners, and visited his people. He served on charitable boards and from time to time dealt with crises in the community. As the social life of America became more complex after World War II, however, so did the vocation of the clergyman. Expectations were thrust upon him for which, in most cases, he had not been trained; even the traditional roles of pastor, teacher, and preacher became more difficult. As pastor, he needed to be acquainted with psychiatric principles so that he would know when someone was too ill to be helped by counseling and needed referral. As preacher and teacher, he had to communicate with a more educated congregation than those of previous generations and therefore needed not only a traditional knowledge of the Bible, but a grasp of current affairs, new intellectual movements, scientific discoveries, economics, and so forth. Furthermore, his people had less knowledge of Scripture and doctrine than their forebears and so were easily bored by an old-fashioned sermon and would seek another church if the sermons did not hold their interest. Fund-raising was supposed to be the vestry's responsibility, but if the rector (the clergyman in charge of a parish) did not preach about "stewardship," and be particularly nice to big givers, the parish might face financial problems. Even the role of community leader had become more difficult and stressful as explosive issues such as peace or war, public housing in the neighborhood, and condom distribution in the schools erupted with frequency. The pastor needed skills by which to draw reluctant young people to church programs. He also was expected to continue calling on his people and to know by extrasensory perception when one of them was sick.

At one clergy conference I attended, the leader went around the room and asked each of the parish clergy how many hours each week he should spend in calling, sermon preparation, prayer, study, parish administration, and so on. He added up the hours to a one-hundred-hour week!

The clergy face subtler and more interesting problems as well. The priest is a symbolic figure onto whom a member of the congregation can project a desired persona. He can be father, son, little brother, older brother, mother, sex object, schoolmaster, moral policeman, Jesus, God, or any of the above, so that the priest does not always know what he represents to a particular person. With neurotic individuals, many of whom are drawn to the Church, this projection can even become dangerous. Now, twenty-five years later, lawsuits against clergy and the diocese have increased to the point where insurance companies have insisted on rigid guidelines for pastoral relationships and have instituted training sessions to guard against allegations of sexual harassment. This trend undermines the clergy's relationship to the people.

A rector needs to have a sense of group dynamics, so that he can figure out what is going on in the parish and how to make any necessary changes. Why did the giving go down last year? Why is the vestry surly? How can I persuade *some* people to teach Sunday school? How can I fire the organist without having the entire choir resign, and if I cannot fire the organist, how can I persuade him or her to play the kind of hymns I feel are appropriate?

Then there is the matter of the priest's personal life. How on earth can he balance the demands of his family against the demands of the parish? You plan to take your wife to the movies; then a parishioner calls to say her mother was taken to the hospital with a heart attack. If you do not go, the old lady may die without the benefit and comfort of prayer. If you do go, you may find out that she merely fainted from a gas attack and your wife will not speak to you for a day. How many nights a week can you avoid "important" meetings? When you are excited about a call to another parish, your children break down in tears at the thought of moving.

Family finances are an eternal worry. Clergy salaries are low (considering that most of us have graduate degrees), and yet if the parish pays you more, it may go bankrupt and you lose your job. If you are in an upper-class neighborhood, how can you keep up appearances when you make about half of your parishioners' income? If you are in a poor neighborhood, how can you keep your comparatively high salary from being resented? The public schools in the city are inadequate, but you do not have the money for a private education for your children. If you are single, your social life is monitored by the parish gossips.

Carrying such burdens without adequate support leads clergy to suffer from stress or depression. It is easy for clergy to blame their troubles on the bishop—and why not? They do not dare confront the vestry. Such problems, expressed or unexpressed, were brought to me at the small clergy conferences I held as bishop coadjutor.

At that time, the diocesan conference center was an estate left to the diocese by the Mortimer family in Tuxedo Park, an exclusive residential community in Rockland County. (The tuxedo was invented there as an informal evening dress.) My colleagues from other denominations enjoyed teasing me about that. The entrance to Tuxedo Park is adorned with iron gates, and a guard still stops each entering car to inquire who is in it and what brings them to the town. Once through the gates, you follow a winding road past châteaus, chalets, and Tudor mansions to a marble palace overlooking the lake. Very few of the clergy would have been invited there in those days, except for the rector of the local church, which was, of course, Episcopal.

We gathered on a Thursday evening for drinks and dinner. As we sat in one of the grand drawing rooms, sloppily dressed, racially mixed, the social history of our Church was reflected, and, in a sense, the dilemma of today's clergy set forth. Our Church was no longer the Church of the gentry, in which budget deficits would be made up by one or two families at the end of the year. The pipe-smoking Anglophile rector, steeped in interesting and esoteric books, was not now the image most Episcopalians looked for.

Underneath the talk on those evenings were the questions posed privately by each priest: "Who am I? Who do they expect me to be? Who does God expect me to be?" However, the conversation usually began on a fairly positive note, as I asked them severally to say a word or two. "Things are going okay, but we are losing the old guard and the few new people who come in do not pledge as much." "The neighborhood is changing. A lot of Jewish people are moving in, and that hurts us as far as new members are concerned. However, the church is in good shape and the member canvas was the best ever."

"The drug problem is critical. In the abandoned building across the street, sales go on all day. Some of my people are afraid to come to church." "We're doing just fine. The housing project for the elderly is about to be funded next door, and plans for enlarging the church are progressing. I hope the diocese can help. My only problem is taking care of hundreds of people without much help." "The parish is going fine, but, Bishop, a lot of my people are upset about the peace rally in the cathedral. They simply don't understand how you can sympathize with people who are killing our boys."

I would try to respond to each one briefly, then open the room to general conversation. Little by little, the reality beneath the brave opening statements was revealed. The conversation became more troubled. "The vestry just doesn't understand. I try to enliven the service to attract more young people, and the older members complain. They worry about the possibility of having women priests. Whenever I preach about a social issue, I get clobbered, and usually by the same old crowd with the same old arguments, like religion shouldn't get mixed up with politics." Others around the room would nod their heads.

"How can I attract new members? George, your church is growing, how do you do it?" I saw George, young, attractive, enthusiastic, witty, charming, full of evangelical fervor, au courant with the latest movie and its theological implications. And I saw the speaker, a man in his late fifties who had been in the same parish for years, who looked tired, who was not particularly attractive or bright, who did not have a sense of humor. George did his best to be helpful, suggesting an evangelism committee, special programs advertised in the paper, a weekend retreat with the vestry led by a spirited priest and committed layman from another parish. They talked more, others chimed in.

As the evening wore on, the conversation grew more personal, and some men described their loneliness and disillusionment. Some said they wanted to speak out more about social issues and to support my controversial statements but that their laypeople were so conservative they simply could not get away with it. Others, usually older priests worn down by parish duties, complained bitterly that they had not had an inquiry about another position for over ten years and that the diocese seemed not to care. I asked them if they had done anything, like updating their résumé at Church headquarters, or writing and visiting other dioceses, but in my heart I knew that there was little likelihood of their moving, because of their age and temperament.

We went to bed depressed. I prayed hard that night and tried to think of what I might say the following morning.

The chapel at the conference center was small but in exquisite taste, delicate, a holy place. We said Morning Prayer together with times of silence between the lessons. I said a word or two, recalling our ordination vows and asking us all to remember that we were never promised an easy time in trying to follow our Lord. True, none of us had suffered martyrdom, but the slow tedium of the pastoral ministry was harder, in a way, than the excitement of action or danger.

After breakfast, we gathered informally again, and I spoke for a while about some of my experiences with difficult vestries, with family pressures, with depression, with doubting my faith. And I did speak about prayer: how in my case it always took a long time to admit I was beaten, to realize I could not pull myself out of the situation I was in. When I finally got down on my knees and turned the wretched business over to God, things seemed to change. Sometimes the particular problem would go away; more often I was given the strength and wisdom to deal with it. In any case, things *always* changed for the better after I gave up control and let go, as it were. However, no matter how often I had that experience, the next time I was just as stubborn and took almost as long as before to admit that only God could get me through the bad time. I mentioned my physical exhaustion, depression, and pneumonia in Jersey City. I described the continual badgering of the conservatives in Indianapolis, and how, when I finally realized I could not reconcile our differences and gave up, they miraculously faded from the vestry one way or another. I spoke of the illness of my wife, some problems we had with the children when we moved. Something began to happen as I spoke. It was not so much what I said but that we were meeting on a deep personal level. Tears came to my eyes occasionally (I cry easily), and I could feel the response around the room as I looked into their eyes.

As we talked further that morning, the mood began to change, and we started to think of specific ways we could make things better. Several suggested we have more conferences like this. I said I could not have them very often, given the size of the diocese, but suggested they form groups of their own.

We concluded the conference with an informal Eucharist right where we had been talking. This service, which can be so grand and solemn, can also be intimate and a way of bonding people together, especially after they have heard and felt the deep places of one another's lives. We listened more carefully to the Word of God in the Scripture reading; we spoke the Creed, our faith, with greater intensity; we prayed for one another, our families, our parishes, the sick (mentioned by name), the peace of the world, the suffering of our cities; we offered ourselves anew in our priesthood; we exchanged the kiss of peace with true affection, expressing our love in warm embrace, uniting with one another; we sensed the presence of Christ as we heard the words, "This is my Body. This is my Blood." We were sent out into the world with the words "Go in peace to love and serve the Lord" sounding in our ears and in our hearts. It was brought home to us, once again, that, whatever the pain and frustration, we were here to serve the Lord and had been given the precious gift of caring for his people. We were part of their lives and part of a struggling, flawed, broken institution that represented his Body here on earth.

In response to the conferences, I tried having a wise and sympathetic priest available to give the clergy advice and support. Very few clergy called him. They wanted to see the bishop, not a deputy. Accordingly, I told my secretary never to turn anyone away, even if it meant I'd have to cancel another appointment. This was a difficult discipline but necessary. Some pastoral work cannot be delegated. Later, we established area archdeacons, who picked up much of this work as they gained the clergy's confidence. Those conferences had bound us together as nothing else could; at no other time did I feel more like a bishop, like I was doing what I was sent to do. I also worked on clergy compensation. It took a while, but gradually we were able to set up a diocesan minimum.

GLORY AND TRAGEDY

THE day finally came for me to be installed as the thirteenth Bishop of New York: Saturday, September 23, 1972. This was a most solemn occasion, because I was being inducted into a line of bishops going back to Samuel Provoost, of Dutch descent, installed on February 4, 1787, as first bishop of New York. It had been twenty-two years since my predecessor's installation; I intended to make the occasion not only memorable but symbolic of my vision for the diocese. In the morning, we began by joining the cast of *Godspell*, the hippie Jesus and his ragged band, under the great Gothic arches of the cathedral. It was a medieval moment, reminiscent of the ancient symbolism of Jesus the Clown, setting the mood for the surprises by which God could be present in our lives, of how Christian love could be found in ways we had never dreamed of. I planned, in my sermon, to set before the people the vision of an invigorated diocese, in which every parish and institution would be a shelter of love and peace as well as a command post for social justice pursued in an ecumenical style. To implement this vision, I inaugurated a program we called Mission '72. Each parish was to survey the human needs of its community and construct a plan whereby it could begin to prevent or alleviate the suffering of its neighbors. The diocese would then help fund each parish's plan. I would hold a rally in each of the thirteen interparish councils to introduce the plans, and our professional adviser, Bob Duke, would coordinate the work that was to follow.

A mammoth picnic was served on the lawn, minstrels strolled through the crowds. The Indian summer sun shone down. Joy, affection, and vitality filled the air. We were ready for the solemnities.

I stood before the great bronze doors of the cathedral in resplendent cope and miter. They opened to the brilliant sound of trumpets, and I entered, greeted by over three hundred clergy whom I followed up the long aisle to the crossing. After resounding hymns, readings from the Scriptures, and my taking a solemn vow, my dear friend, Horace Donegan, with tears in his eyes, handed over to me the great gilded crosier of the Bishop of New York. I felt a weight, a heavy weight, but it was a weight of glory.

My whole family was there, enjoying the celebration, but as I looked down on them in the midst of that joy, my heart sank, for I knew all was not well with us.

The Christmas issue of *Newsweek* featured me on the cover in full vestment in front of a stained-glass window. My children teased me mercilessly and hung twenty of the pictures on our Christmas tree.

A LONG SLOW DYING

When we had arrived in New York, two years before, we had tried to pick up the pieces of our lives. We moved into the third floor of a gloomy old French château. No other kids lived on the cathedral close, and Jenny was not herself. She tried everything she could think of to escape the growing imprisonment of her depression. To be sure, we had some good times seeing old friends, enjoying the city. A high point was a dance given for us by John and Mary Lindsay in Gracie Mansion. But most of the time we all were miserable. There we were, going through the motions of living a normal life. The children were attending new schools and were having trouble getting used to life without their old friends. On Saturday we went on family outings, but they were not much fun. I remember sitting with Jenny and some of the children in Riverside Park one gray day, amid discarded beer cans and old newspapers. If we had been in Washington, the kids would have been at the neighborhood playground with friends, and

Jenny and I would have been playing tennis or sitting on the porch talking to neighbors.

Beneath these normal adjustment problems lay Jenny's deepening depression. She struggled courageously against it, traveling to California with Danny to see friends and going to a health spa in New Mexico. We even looked at apartments on the East Side, thinking that living off the Cathedral grounds might lift her spirits. We went to a psychiatrist, who was not much help. (Those were the days before antidepressant medications.) Finally Jenny could stand it no longer, and decided that she would have to move back to Washington if she was going to regain her equilibrium. Accordingly, we bought a house in Cleveland Park, across from where we had lived, and the family settled down in their old neighborhood. The children were delighted. Jenny improved. I did my best to adjust to commuting once a week from New York, but I felt like a visitor in my own house. I slept in the guest room, and naturally the children turned to Jenny, not to me, when they were making plans. Returning to New York on the deserted shuttle flight Saturday night to be ready for Sunday's visitations to parishes was a dismal business. I would come up the stairs of the gloomy château to be greeted by the mournful meow of Poochai, our ancient Siamese cat, standing at the head of the darkened stairs.

Jenny and I were even more estranged by now, although we tried to keep up a front at home. She bought a small cabin in Virginia. We furnished it simply and began to enjoy the countryside from time to time. One night we went out there by ourselves. Jenny felt sick with what seemed like a bad case of intestinal flu and could not sleep. We sat up all night talking, and for the first time I felt we were beginning to rebuild our love. Hope flickered in the dark of the cabin.

In the morning, we went straight to the doctor, and he admitted her to the hospital. A biopsy was performed, and the next day I went over to be with Jenny when she received the results. I was standing in the corridor when Dr. Bremer came toward her room. He had treated her after her car accident, and they had become good friends. When his gaunt figure drew near, I could see the bad news on his face. "I need to speak to you," he said.

"No," I said, "you will speak to us together."

"No. No. I want to speak to you by yourself."

"I insist," I replied. "No secrets."

So Dr. Bremer and I entered Jenny's room. He sat down, leaned forward in the chair, looked her in the eye, and said, "Mrs. Moore, I wish I had never met you." With this devastating opener, he explained that she had cancer of the colon, which had metastasized to the liver. He added that he did not suggest chemotherapy and that the prognosis was terminal. After he left the room, we sat in stunned silence. There was nothing much that could be said.

Jenny stayed in the hospital, and I drove to the office of a friend, Philip Newell. Thank God he was there and alone. I sat down and wept uncontrollably.

By this time in my life I had gone beyond blaming God for pain and grief, but part of me could not help crying out, "Why Jenny? Why me?"—the age-old cry of Job, of humanity, the terrible *why* of indiscriminate suffering. There is so little you can do about pain, your own or another's. All I could do was to cry for help to Christ on the cross and feel his compassion. The words of the old hymn "Earth has no sorrow that heaven cannot heal" resonated in my mind. Sometimes God seemed not to be there. I tried just to take life a day at a time. I leaned on the love of friends, asked for advice, tried to be strong for the children. I was not able to pray very well; I was hurting too much. But I did try to give my hurt to God, to "offer it up," as that religious cliché puts it. And I did find real comfort in the Eucharist, where I did not have to think or even believe, just go through the familiar act of throwing myself on the altar and being fed, as a child is fed, with hands and heart outstretched.

There were also little tricks to play—to imagine myself in a large bubble of time and space, where all the bad stuff was outside and I could enjoy an hour or two completely away from it, to have a drink with a friend and talk of other things.

After the initial shock and pessimism of the doctor's report, Jenny regained her courage, and although she decided against chemotherapy, she was determined to try every other way to overcome the cancer. She and I had had a long-standing agreement that if either one of us became very ill there would be no secrets between us. I believe this is sound. As the illness progressed, I always told her the truth of what the doctors said when she asked but never volunteered bad news. Sick people can deal with only so much bad news at a time. Likewise with the children: we gave them as optimistic a report as we could in all honesty and, of course, tried to temper the information to their age and ability to accept it. They handled the situation in different ways. The older ones helped out whenever Jenny wanted them to. Rosie's boyfriend, for instance, had a special touch for massaging her feet.

During the weeks that followed, I had a hard time disentangling the meaning of the events that had crowded in on us in the last two years. I could not say, "It is the will of God." People often deal with tragedy by blaming God or, rather, by thinking that some heavenly good must lie behind the calamity. "Why did my baby have to die? It must have been God's will." This is a way of saying it is not one's own fault or a way of avoiding looking into the dark abyss of human suffering in a universe created by a loving and omnipotent God. I become upset, even angry, when I hear such a comment. The god in whom I believe does not willfully kill babies or wives.

As far as God's having some direct role in my Episcopal election, I do not know, but I did feel that my becoming Bishop of New York was providential. Jenny's illness and the children's suffering seemed somehow connected to our move, though. Indeed, I think some of the children felt, on some level, that my ambition had been a cause of their mother's tragedy.

I could answer the dilemma of suffering theologically: God created a world in which we would have freedom of choice so that we could freely choose to love God and one another and thus be fulfilled as human beings. Without such freedom there cannot be love, because love can only be freely given. (You cannot *make* someone love you.) But a world fashioned in such a way as to provide this freedom is a world in which there also will be sin and pain. Even modern physics confirms an indeterminate universe. Christians believe, then, that God cannot prevent all suffering, but that in the passion of Christ on the cross God shares the suffering. In the midst of seemingly meaningless events we can discern the presence of grace, which is a way of saying that God can and does enter into the unfolding of events in subtle and mysterious ways, the rationale and dynamics of which we do not comprehend. But often we experience this grace, this unexpected tenderness, this unforeseen divine assistance in the very depths of pain and terror.

Such dry theological explanations are all very well for the seminary classroom, but in the midst of suffering, intellectual answers do very little good. Like Job, we can only look up and ask, "Why me? Why Jenny?" and throw ourselves on God's mercy. When Job asked God this question, "Then the Lord answered Job out of the whirlwind, and said, 'Who is this that darkens counsel by words without knowledge? Gird up now your loins like a man; for I will demand of you. . . . Where were you when I laid the foundations of the earth? declare, if you have understanding. . . . Where were you when the morning stars sang together, and all the sons of God shouted for joy?' " (Job 38:1–7). These answers are found only at the far reaches of eternity and cannot be understood by us who are prisoners of time and space. But sometimes, when in prayer you touch eternity, the answer comes in a language beyond reason. Somewhere among the singing of the morning stars there is joy to be found, even when the darkness is descending. I do not speak of pleasure nor even of happiness, but of a joy that transcends pain or pleasure, the joy Job heard from the creator of the stars.

In the spring of 1973, as Jenny's condition grew worse, I asked for a leave of absence and returned to Washington to live full-time. This was to be a harrowing but loving deathwatch. Jenny took on the whole business as a project. We became acquainted with the cancer underground, and Jenny put an anti-AMA bumper sticker on her wheelchair. Evans Woollen, one of our close friends from Indianapolis days, volunteered to smuggle in from Switzerland laetrile, a medication that had not been approved for use in the United States. He accomplished this with éclat by putting some contraband Cuban cigars on the top of his suitcase. The customs officer was so delighted to confiscate them that he looked no further. We grew wheat grass sprouts on trays and gave Jenny hundreds of vitamins under the supervision of a naturopathic physician. We interviewed a Chinese doctor about acupuncture. At Jenny's urging, I even took a trip to Arizona with another priest, my old friend John Wing, to see a New Age healer who used a sample of Jenny's hair and a pendulum as an alleged means of bringing about a long-distance cure. You see, we tried everything.

I occasionally took a service in New York. One afternoon, way up in Tivoli on the Hudson, word came that Jenny had taken a turn for the worse. Elliott Lindsley, the rector, drove me to the Newark airport; when we missed the flight he drove me all the way to Washington. Friends like that make it possible to survive.

The last months of Jenny's illness were not only a time of pain but also a time of love and wonder. Friends, children, and dogs came by as she held court on the front porch. It was a happy time, if you can believe it, even though we were locked in a losing struggle with cancer. Jenny talked with her usual humor and style, reaching out with her gifts of friendship and understanding. Her face grew thin but even more beautiful. She wore her wedding ring, too large for her finger now, around her neck, and the familiar jingling of the nine gold bracelets I had given her at each birth accompanied every gesture. Her fascination with other people's lives continued; she made out her will with great care, leaving a rocking chair to her doctor and an etching to Bob Amory, who had been driving her home from the airport when she had her serious accident. We planned the funeral together, choosing pallbearers as we had once chosen ushers and bridesmaids for our wedding. We talked about all this in a most comfortable way. She insisted that the children and I go to the Adirondacks for a vacation; she needed the time to wrestle through her own demons so that at the end she could be at peace with herself.

In August 1973, she began to deteriorate physically, and her condition became more uncomfortable and painful. Her sister Margie and a few very close friends took turns coming to care for her. The last few days in the hospital were loving days, when all the children were there surrounding her, holding her hand, hour by hour. Our daughter Adelia was able to tell her she was pregnant with our first grandchild. One of the last things Jenny said was "I love everyone so much." She and I had a beautiful moment when our estrangement faded away and we could hold each other in a loving goodbye. Toward the end, she slipped into a coma, and the wheezing of the machine that was breathing for her was the only sound in the room.

That last evening, I had a strange experience. I knew we were coming to the end, but I had not cried at all for a very long time. I looked down at Jenny through the plastic envelope of the respirator, and I looked at the children, five or six of whom were there, standing sadly and silently by the bed, hands hanging at their sides. Then I felt a tingling sensation in my toes that began to climb up my legs, and I knew I was in for a violent sobbing spell. I walked over to the waiting room next door, and the flood of sobbing broke forth. So intensely did it fill me that I entered a kind of dream state. I found myself standing on the edge of a dark, unfathomable abyss with Jenny at my side. The abyss was death. I had to let her go, but it seemed as if Someone else took her by the hand to guide her over. I gradually recovered from this vision, went next door, and motioned to the children to come out. The night nurse, a marvelous old warrior of a woman who had dealt with death so often that they were on most familiar terms, told us all to go home. "I will take care of her, my dears. She will not wake up again. There is nothing more you can do."

At four-thirty the next morning, the phone rang; we were summoned to the hospital. Jenny was dead—no more mechanical breathing; her room was completely silent. What extraordinary peace! The children stood around the bed for the last time as I read the prayers for the dying, those great, strong prayers and Psalms. "My soul fleeth to the Lord, before the morning watch, I say before the morning watch. . . . Out of the deep have I called unto Thee. O let thine ears consider well the voice of my complaint. For there is mercy with Thee, therefore shalt Thou be feared. . . . I will lift up mine eyes unto the hills, from whence cometh my help? My help cometh even from the Lord who hath made heaven and earth. . . . The Lord is my Shepherd, I shall not want. . . . Yea, even though I go through the valley of death, I shall fear no evil for Thou art with me. . . . Depart O Christian soul out of this world . . . may your dwelling place be in the paradise of God."

It was over. People came by the house. Love flowed around us and among us in a mighty stream. There were many tears and lots of laughter, too.

Jenny had chosen a phrase from Eudora Welty's *Losing Battles* for her tombstone: "The loneliness and hilarity of survival." There had been loneliness, but the Lord, or someone with an equally good sense of humor, attended to a bit of hilarity: the family was gathered for the formal reading of Jenny's will by our friend and lawyer, Steve Pollak. The room was silent. Steve opened his mouth to speak, at which point our son Danny burst into the room, shouting, "Lucy just had puppies!" We rushed upstairs, last will and testament forgotten, and there, on Patience's brand-new, dainty flowered bedspread, was Lucy, sheepish but proud, licking three little objects of black fur squirming beside her.

Bill Wendt, our old friend and priest, gave us a plain pine box, which he purchased from a Jewish undertaker, the only one in town who sold plain coffins. (This experience, incidentally, started Bill on a ministry to the dying.) Jenny rested in the dark and glistening beauty of the Resurrection chapel in the crypt of the cathedral.

The funeral, in the Washington Cathedral, was Jenny all the way. Hundreds of people came. Just before we began, Jenny's mother, late and dramatic as usual, arrived and wheeled up the long aisle in her wheelchair. The family and friends serving as pallbearers entered the cathedral's great crossing as we sang the joyful strains of "Praise my soul the king of heaven." There were readings from the warm humanity of James Agee's A Death in the Family, and Gene McCarthy read an ambiguous and slightly ribald passage from Yeats. Steve Chinlund, an old friend and priest, gave a eulogy of exquisite understanding, humor, and warmth. Then our children's friends passed unconsecrated bread and wine throughout the congregation in an agape, the ancient name for such a celebration, which began solemnly and grew in joy and affection as talk and tears, laughter and loving embraces again bound us together in that great Gothic nave. Jenny did not want a Eucharist, because it would have excluded our Jewish friends, but I am sure that in the Lord's eyes a Eucharist we had. The closing prayer and blessing were given as we stood in glorious disarray, and with Jenny's favorite hymn, "Once in Royal David's City," the celebration came to an end.

Many friends came to the cemetery where she was buried beneath a tree looking down a grassy hillside. In the distance, we could see some backyards with laundry flapping in the breeze, and I thought of Jersey City.

The final coming together at the house turned into a real party as the older people left and Jenny's young friends turned on the record player and danced. They literally swung from the rafters. Jenny would have liked that.

NEW LOVE, NEW LIFE

W HEN Jenny died, I was faced with one of the hardest decisions of my life. Should I resign as Bishop of New York and move back to Washington or uproot my children once more? The older kids were more or less on their own. They needed support, God knows, in their grieving, but they were away at college. The four youngest, however, were still with me. Marian and Danny were becoming more and more independent, but Susanna and Patience still relied on home as a place to be secure. We had done over two snug rooms with slanting gabled walls on the third floor. With their flowered wallpaper and fluffy bedspreads, shelves for stuffed animals, and favorite pictures on the wall, these were warm and cozy places where they could nurse their grief. Their mother had chosen the wallpaper and chintz with them. Being there was like still being with her. How could I rip them away again to live in the drafty old cathedral house where they had spent a terrifying year?

Morning after morning I woke up with this question before me. I felt in the core of my being that being Bishop of New York was God's will for me. But I was now the only parent of nine children. My heart broke as I remembered their faces when Jenny died. I felt that care of the family was even more important than my work. However, if I resigned and returned to Washington I could not continue as a bishop (a new suffragan had been elected), and probably it would not have been appropriate for me to function in the diocese as a priest. I would have had to find some role in the government or with a social agency. That did not seem right.

I consulted several family therapists and a few close friends. Ev-

eryone insisted I go back to New York. They said children were flexible; they would adjust. I decided to take their advice, but telling the
girls we were leaving was painful. I can still see their faces, still feel
their tears as we held each other through this additional blow, one
that could have been prevented. I was hurt, torn, guilty.

The die was cast, arrangements were made. Danny wanted to finish
his school year, and Marian also wished to stay. Bishop John Walker,
the new suffragan in Washington, and his wife, Maria, kindly welcomed them into their warm home. A singular piece of good fortune
entered our lives when I found Elsie Walker to take care of the children during this transition. By sheer coincidence, she turned out to
be the niece of my dear friend George Mead, and I had lived with
her grandmother in Georgetown for a brief time during the war. Elsie
was in her late twenties, only a year or two younger than Honor. She
came in as a sort of older sister, rather than as a mother. She was full
of energy, good sense, and a splendid resilient humor. Underneath
her good cheer, however, she carried her own grief: her fiancé had
been killed in Vietnam. When the children cried, she could cry with
them.

Elsie took care of things in Washington. I commuted as best I
could. When we moved, Elsie moved with us to oversee the horrors
of packing and unpacking.

We settled into the main floor of the apartment, because the upstairs was a hostel for an assortment of people, including an African
priest and a young Yale alumnus, Philip St. George, who worked in
our urban homesteading program. A couple also on that staff had
converted an old attic into an apartment.

Despite all these people and the children, despite the demands of my
work, I was lonely. It was 1974; Jenny had been gone almost a year,
and although the wounds of her dying were still there, I was ready to
find a new person to love. The grieving process is different for each
person. When someone takes a long time to die, you begin grieving
when you first realize the stark reality of terminal illness. Also, at
some point in your sorrow, you wish to share your hurt with someone
close to you. I began to go out, looking, unconsciously and then
consciously, for someone to love. I felt a bit odd, a fifty-five-year-old

bishop shining his shoes and making a dinner reservation for my "date." But it was a new adventure. I had been married for almost thirty years, and now I was on the loose. But I had to be discreet. Being six foot four, being known by hundreds of Episcopalians, and having had my picture on television and in the paper from time to time made anonymity something of a problem, even in New York.

I spent time with a number of women and liked them all, but I did not fall in love. On a visit to Indianapolis, I met an old friend, Alan Nolan, who had lost his first wife and had married again, and over a long lunch in a fancy downtown restaurant I let my hair down and asked Alan whether you could fall in love again. Alan, as was his wont, was clear and definite. "Absolutely," he said, "and don't settle for anything less."

Before Jenny's death, I had married a friend, Vernon Eagle, then the director of the New World Foundation, to Brenda Campbell. Jenny and I went out with them a couple of times. One evening, Brenda and I ducked out at the intermission of a play and had a drink together. She was great, but of course at that point we were both married. Brenda had lost her first husband, John Campbell, a brilliant young foreign-service officer, a couple of years earlier. Now she was happy again, because she had found Vernon. Then the blow came. On their first wedding anniversary, Brenda and Vernon learned that he had cancer. By this time, I was back in New York, and every week I'd go to see Vernon in the hospital. Brenda was always with him. Because of what I had been through with Jenny, I felt especially in touch with their feelings. These social visits became more and more pastoral, as this tough, funny lapsed Catholic turned to God again. He even asked me to bring him Communion. Brenda's courage, stamina, humor, and sheer beauty touched my heart. I embraced her in a friendly way on one of these visits and, as I look back, began to fall in love with her then.

One night I was away with the children in Connecticut when Brenda called to say that Vernon was not going to last much longer and that if he were to receive Communion I had better come down right away. I drove to the city and brought Vernon the Sacrament. As I began to speak, he came out of a semi-coma, recognized me, and put out his hand. I began the prayers. After he received Communion, he looked at me with a smile I shall never forget, a clear smile of peace that shone as a light in his eyes. I went into the other room to pray with Brenda and his children. Vernon overheard us and asked the nurse to bring us into his room. We all prayed together there. As I left, Vernon lifted up his hand and, with a broad grin, made the sign of the cross. How I treasured that blessing.

We celebrated Vernon's life with simple grandeur as he lay in front of the high altar in the cathedral where I had married them such a short time before.

Naturally, I called on his widow shortly after the funeral. We had a pleasant, somewhat formal chat. I thought she was splendid. She is fairly short, has full brown hair, a round face, and arched eyebrows over green eyes that can twinkle with humor or grow hard with anger. Brenda laughs a lot, especially when she is poking fun at solemnity. She is one of the brightest and most able people I have ever known. When the car breaks down, she fixes it. She is a computer whiz. Her knowledge of art is encyclopedic, and she writes well. I love to dance with her and watch her smile. I love to hear her laughter coming from the other room or across a crowd at a dinner party. When she enters a room, the atmosphere quickens, and she has the ability to make friends with anyone, whoever they may be, whether a be-leaguered Roman Catholic bishop in East Timor, a Park Avenue ma-tron, or a kid in Harlem.

A week went by, and I phoned to see if I could call again. She said not to bother, that she was fine. I insisted. She said okay but told me later she thought I was raising money or proselytizing. I asked her to come to a clergy picnic in Westchester, but it rained so hard we had to turn back. We ate at a cheap Japanese restaurant on the West Side, and as we walked along the sidewalk looking for a cab, something happened. Alan Nolan was right: you can fall in love again.

Jenny and I had a custom of taking the children to Europe for their first visit, and that summer I went with the two youngest children, Susanna and Patience. An old girlfriend of mine was on the ship. Later, I visited her in Switzerland. We had a grand time, but I felt that she and I should not pursue our relationship further. When I came home, I called Brenda, who was on Martha's Vineyard in an apple tree. I waited impatiently. She came to the phone, and when I heard her voice I knew I was in love. The following winter, we were sitting in front of the fire in my apartment after a long drive home from skiing with the children. I had been planning in my own mind to meet Brenda in Paris the following spring and propose to her after a beautiful dinner in the Bois de Boulogne. Hoping to begin planning for this, I asked Brenda what she was going to do in the summer. She said, "I'm going to Morocco."

I blurted out, "You can't!"

"Why not?"

"We're going to get married."

"We are?"

Then I said sheepishly, "Will you marry me?" She paused. I held my breath.

She said, "Sure."

So much for a romantic setting in the Bois de Boulogne.

We were married on May 16, 1975, in the cathedral garden. It had rained all day, but just before the time for the ceremony the sun came out and shone on the glistening azaleas and dogwood. My old friend Eddie West conducted the ceremony with great aplomb. Susanna and Patience were acolytes, Danny my best man, and Brenda's sisters were maids of honor. Brenda's parents came up from Richmond. Some of my family were there, including my mother, who, since her stroke prevented her from speaking, stood up and gave a touching toast in pantomime. Brenda looked splendid. I was so happy, after all the dark times we had both been through.

Life settled down. Brenda worked on film editing and later took a course in appraising. She also drove me to my Sunday visitations for the first few years, and the diocese was delighted with her. The people who lived and worked on the close found her a warm, thoughtful, and funny friend.

My mother died a few years later, having lapsed into a coma. I found her Bible on the bedside table; folded within it were several passionate love letters from my father, written when they were engaged.

DISCERNING VOCATIONS

With some difficulty, I picked up the strands of my work as a bishop. In our churches, parishes and dioceses rise and fall depending on the quality of the clergy. The laity do most of the ministry, but without effective support, leadership, and training it is almost impossible for them to carry out the mission of the Church except in their individual lives. Therefore, one of the most important responsibilities of a bishop is screening men and women for ordination. Although there are many checks and balances, the bishop ultimately decides on the number and qualifications of those who are to be ordained, as well as making the final decision about each individual. Given the complexity of the priestly vocation, I agonized over the decision of whom to accept. Among other things, I wanted to protect those who seemed unfit from the bitterness of a failed priesthood: not finding a job or breaking under the pressure.

Once the bishop's hands are laid on your head, you will never be the same. Catholic theology calls this the "indelibility" of ordination. Psychology would call it a traumatic experience. I have known men who lost their faith, resigned from the priesthood, went into secular life, and yet still never quite got over their sense that somehow they had betrayed God, even if they said they no longer believed in a god at all.

Before an interview with the bishop, the aspirant must be approved by his or her rector, be interviewed by a suffragan bishop, attend a screening weekend, and have a physical and psychiatric interview (the results of which only the bishops see). After this obstacle course, you can imagine how nervous the young man or woman is when he or she arrives in my office. I too am anxious to be as sensitive and alert as possible, because the whole life of a human being will be affected by our time together. I pray silently before the door opens, holding the person before God, thinking of how he or she must feel, and asking earnestly for the guidance of the Holy Spirit.

The interview is unstructured. After a few pleasantries and some nervous laughter, we move to two easy chairs by the fireplace. Then I ask him or her to begin at the beginning, to tell me a little about childhood, family, time at school and college. Is he or she married, or hopes to marry some day? Has he ever been in love? Does he have close friends? And finally we seek to uncover the first intimations of a vocation to the ministry.

I remember the ways aspirants have told me they were called. "I was sitting in the train one day thinking about nothing in particular, and I suddenly began to think that God wanted me to be a priest." "I always wanted to be a priest, ever since I was a boy. I used to have a little altar in my room and dress up and pretend to celebrate Mass." "I honestly don't remember exactly when I first thought about it, but over a period of a few years the idea grew stronger and stronger." "I was in business and doing fairly well. However, after one extremely frustrating day, I thought to myself, do I want to spend my life like this? And the next Sunday in church it occurred to me that maybe I could be a priest. I told my wife, and she said, 'You, a priest, you got to be kidding.' " "I was in an exchange program in Nicaragua and met some of the priests who were working with the poor and who were committed to liberation theology. I got hooked then and there."

There were as many different stories as there were interviews, and I suppose I have screened at least three hundred people over the years. As they spoke of their lives, I watched and listened intently, not only to what they said, but to how they said it. Did their body movements fit their words? Were they a little skeptical about visionary moments? Did they say, for instance, "God spoke to me," or, rather, "You know this may seem a little far-out, but it felt that God was really getting through to me directly." Did they have a sense of humor about themselves? Did the accounts of revelations in prayer or by chance seem healthy or neurotic? When you are exploring the emotional and psychological aspects of religion, you are on delicate ground. Often a strong religious faith is a cover for neurotic tendencies. Sometimes a person is looking for a lost parent. Sometimes he or she is seeking emotional security. Sometimes the person is overly dependent or has passive-aggressive tendencies. People who have had a problem with addiction are sometimes superb pastors, but often they see their work only in terms of the twelve steps of Alcoholics Anonymous. In these areas, the psychiatric exam is useful and often guides my line of questioning.

I am also interested in their politics, not so much as to whether they are liberal or conservative, but whether they see any connection between the Gospel and the affairs of the world. And then there is the issue of sexuality, increasingly important in this day and age. I try not to invade the person's privacy unnecessarily, but rather to give him openings to talk about it if he wishes. I feel more comfortable with those who can open up. However, this is often a cultural matter. A middle-aged West Indian woman is far less likely to discuss her sexuality than a single man who has always lived in New York. In our interviews, I am frank about the problems of sexuality in the priesthood. I emphasize the closeness of the emotional roots of religion and sex. I speak of the lack of privacy. Those who talk openly about being gay I ask whether they have had a steady relationship and try to see whether they have handled their sexuality in a healthy way. I make them aware that even in a liberal part of the country many parishes would not ask a gay or lesbian priest to serve in their congregation. I talk of loneliness, of frustrations, trying to deromanticize the priesthood.

Sometimes one interview is enough, other times I may see someone three or four times. Often I accept them but suggest they explore problem areas with a therapist.

At the conclusion of the interview, we pray together, I give them a blessing with the laying on of hands.

Before they leave, I tell them that if they are ordained I will assure them of a ministry but not necessarily a paying position and that they should be able and willing to support themselves in a secular job if they cannot find a position in the Church. Nowadays, in our denomination, there are many more clergy than paid positions. Most of those applying have had experience earning a living. In fact, I insist that they take at least two years in secular employ before they apply for the ministry. Even so, it is hard to think that someday they might have to go back to their old jobs. Time and again, a crestfallen priest will become bitter and angry if he or she does not secure a paid, full-time position in the clergy.

In our diocese alone, we have had over one hundred so-called worker-priests: teachers, bankers, lawyers, social workers, taxi drivers, headhunters, psychologists, psychiatrists, physicians, stockbrokers, bureaucrats in public or private organizations, fund-raisers, artists, a prison warden. Many of them were happy to be making, usually, more money than they would have made in full-time ministry and, more importantly, to be financially independent from the Church. For some, this arrangement does not work, and they slip away from the ministry. For others, a steady relationship with a parish keeps them involved in priestly ministries.

PASTORAL CARE OF THE DIOCESE

Carefully choosing new priests was important. Equally important was placing the right priest in the right parish. This involved long search processes and negotiations among bishops, archdeacons, and vestries.

We worked out different strategies for dealing with diminishing resources. In depressed rural congregations, we gradually replaced older priests with team ministries. In the city, we trained laypersons and clergy in community organization under the tough tutelage of the Industrial Areas Foundation. We organized parishes to receive block grants and found other ways to distribute the funds in order to induce cooperation and to avoid favoritism on the diocesan level. Every time I visited a parish, I would hear of some new project. The dream of Mission '72—that every parish sustain a vigorous ministry to its neighborhood—was becoming a reality.

The ministries to communities multiplied. In Orange and Sullivan Counties, a retired layman, Richard Barnett, began helping migrant workers who came to the area to work on the large farms and apple orchards. When I visited them, I was received as if I were the pope. They had been so forgotten that to be noticed by a bishop was cause for rejoicing. These were black and Latino people for the most part, bending, day after day, over the long lines of lettuce or cabbage in the fertile fields beneath the Catskills. We could have been in California or Africa, not eighty miles from New York City. Volunteers brought them food and clothes, parishes made donations, and, after a few years, thanks to the encouragement of Archdeacon Robert Willing and the total commitment of Richard Barnett, the project had grown into an ecumenical ministry with two full-time priests and several social workers on the staff. These migrant workers had no permanent home, no insurance policies, no voting rights, no union. Only the twenty-year struggle of someone like Cesar Chavez could change the underlying causes of their suffering. We could only apply Band-Aids. And yet a touch of humanity made a great difference in their daily lives. I was amazed that the total dedication of one layman could be the catalyst for such a program.

When I visited them, we celebrated the Eucharist in the evening on a picnic table in the yard. The shadows lengthened over the fields, the beautiful children lifted their eyes, the rough, scarred hands of the men reached out for the Sacrament, some of the women wept for joy.

St. Philip's in Harlem had developed several large housing projects. Our Savior, Chinatown, offered music lessons, English as a second language, and computer training. With skillful financing, the Rev. Albany To and some competent laymen tore down the old building they had outgrown and built a new church attached to an apartment house they called Bishop Paul Moore Tower. Long lines of shivering men and women waited for meals at Holy Apostles, a small, poor parish in Chelsea. They served thousands of meals each month and had a residence for ex-convicts upstairs.

St. Clement's, in Hell's Kitchen, used its church for off-off-Broadway plays and took care of homeless families who were billeted in a rundown hotel nearby. I brought our presiding bishop there one day. We visited a mother and three children who lived in one ten-foot-square room. As we sat, hunched over on the lower bunks of the children's beds, their mother poured her heart out. She had been there for almost a year awaiting placement. Conditions in the hotel were so dangerous because of drug dealing that she could not allow her children to go outside the room to play even in the hallway. A man had been murdered on their floor just a few weeks before.

I was so upset by conditions like these that in the early 1980s I asked for an appointment with Mayor Ed Koch. He and I had been friends at the beginning of his administration; in fact, I had given the invocation at his first inauguration. Over the years, however, he seemed to have sold out to real estate interests. Granted, they had saved him when the city was on the verge of bankruptcy in the mid-1970s, but now the problem of homelessness had become overwhelming. I had preached about it and written an op-ed article in *The New York Times* saying that we were becoming the Calcutta of the West and that soon businessmen with briefcases would be stepping over sleeping bodies in Grand Central Station (a prophecy that, unfortunately, came true). About that time, the phone rang one night. "Hello, Paul. This is Ed."

"Ed who?"

"Ed Koch."

"Oh. What's up?" This was a strange call for ten at night.

"I want you and all the churches in New York to take in ten

homeless families and put them up in your churches. If you do that, we will not have a problem."

"But how will we get them?"

"Oh, just send some of your ladies down to the Bowery in their station wagons, and we will provide a pickup center."

I could not believe my ears. How about fire? How about security? How about sanitary facilities? A few weeks later I heard President Reagan make the same suggestion, claiming it came from Billy Graham.

It was against this background that we met in Koch's office several years later. By now homelessness was a national phenomenon. One of the root causes was the reduction in housing funds from the federal government; another was the deinstitutionalization of mental patients. There was much that could be done on a local level. In fact, the churches had begun a program of sleeping the homeless, and other private initiatives had taken place. However, I believe that food, shelter, and health care are rights for every citizen in an affluent country and that the government must be responsible. There are always plenty of works of mercy for the churches to perform over and above such rights. (For that reason, I always resented George Bush's Points of Light program and Bill Clinton's volunteerism conference in Philadelphia.)

In any case, when we visited the mayor, I understood that money was available for a long-range housing program. When we came into his office, he pulled a tired old trick. He sat my colleagues and me on a low sofa, while he and his staff sat on upright chairs facing us. We got nowhere. He said he was doing all he could but that the funds we spoke of were not available for housing. I found out later that he resented my criticism. In fact, a year or two after that, we were selling the hostel for sailors of the Seamen's Church Institute, in order to serve the changing needs of the sailors on container ships. The mayor went public, calling me hypocritical for not giving the building over to the homeless. This would have been unethical if not illegal, since the funds for the building had been donated for a ministry to seamen.

This story illustrates the close tie between programs of social service and programs of social action. I became involved again and again in advocacy because our parishes uncovered human suffering as they ministered to those in need. Our cathedral started a self-help housing program called "sweat equity," because people gave their work to rehabilitate old buildings so as to have them as places to live. Jesse Jackson led a march for the homeless after a cathedral rally about the issue. I met with the Ford Foundation and President Bush's coordinator of volunteers to no avail. Gradually, some good housing was made available, but the problem is still with us. (I do not think Mayor Koch would have done even what he did do had a lawsuit not been brought against him declaring it illegal for the city not to provide shelter.)

Trinity, Wall Street, started a drop-in center for the homeless and built a residence for old people. St. Mark's in-the-Bowery employed local teenagers to renovate the cemetery where Peter Stuyvesant is buried. St. Luke's in the Fields in Greenwich Village and St. Peter's, Chelsea, as well as many other parishes, conducted vigorous ministries for people with AIDS, gaunt young men in their final hours, tenderly cared for by a friend or lover, who in turn was supported in his sorrow by the parish family.

In the Bronx, St. James joined with Fordham University to stabilize their neighborhood. St. Ann's in the Bronx, a historic parish where Gouverneur Morris (a signer of the Declaration of Independence) is buried, became a center for community action against the arson and deterioration that were killing that borough. St. Paul's had a huge youth program; St. David's battled valiantly against a crack trading den across the street. All in all there were probably four or five hundred community programs throughout the diocese.

In addition, our institutions were active. The Episcopal Mission Society took care of the elderly in several locations, ran residences for mentally retarded children, monitored chaplaincies in city hospitals, ran a summer camp for children, and established groups for ex-convicts. The Seamen's Church Institute ran a hostel for seamen for many years, but when that no longer was a need it developed a vigorous program for seamen's rights, based in the container-ship port of Newark. Our people might find a bewildered and beleaguered African who had been picked up with golden promises in some far-off port, or an Indian who had not been in touch with his family for months, or a Malaysian who was not being paid what he had been promised. The container ships can unload and load in twenty-four hours. Many

Newsweek

Civil Rights
and the
Church Militant

FREEDOM
FREEDOM
FREEDOM
FREEDOM

HOW
MANY
MORE
MURDERS
?

Bishop
Paul Moore Jr.

Washington: Calling for protection for the Selma marchers in a rally in front of
the White House, and in a meeting with Vice President Humphrey, 1965

The family, mid-1960s: Jenny and I with (from left) Abdillahi Haji, Honor, Paul, Adelia, Rosemary, George, Marian, Daniel, Susanna, and Patience

At the Cathedral
in Washington

Marching for D.C. Home Rule with Martin Luther King, Jr. (far right), and the Rev. Walter Fauntroy (near right), 1968

Tear-gassed in Saigon, 1970

Arriving in high winds for Jenny's funeral

With Brenda on Martha's Vineyard,
1976; gone fishing on the Beaverkill

Speaking before an audience of a hundred
thousand people on Mar Thoma, India,
1978

The plaque at the Cathedral dramatizing
my struggle to ordain women

Discussing nuclear disarmament in
Moscow, 1982

With Archbishop Desmond Tutu and friends outside Johannesburg, 1986

The Blessing of the Animals on St. Francis Day at the Cathedral
(Dean Morton is at the far right)

Preaching my last sermon as
Bishop, 1989

With Mayor Dinkins and Osborn Elliott en route to the Save Our Cities march
on Washington, D.C., 1992

With Bernard McVeigh at his abbey (*left*); with my brother, Bill (*above*); and with all my grandchildren (*below*)

men go for over a year without shore leave; thus an important part of the program was correspondence courses. St. Luke's Hospital is an Episcopal institution, and I insisted that it remain Church affiliated after it merged with Roosevelt, another Manhattan hospital. It maintains an active chaplaincy and a clinical training program for seminarians and was one of the first hospitals to establish an AIDS ward and a hospice program.

Serving the community had always been a part of diocesan life, but the impetus of Mission '72 enlarged this side of our ministry considerably. Although the number of communicants did not grow during this time, the number of people of all kinds touched by the Church increased dramatically. Thousands of people in need were reached by our diocese in the name of Christ. I once tried to find a vacant space for a weekday program in Manhattan and discovered that there was not one vacant room available.

I have been talking about the life of the institution, and I suppose that the chief executive officer of a corporation could talk in the same terms. Our "product" is different, but we are subject to the same stresses and strains. I remember saying to my brother that I envied him his power, as CEO of Bankers Trust, to open and close branches, which I could not do with parishes. "Are you kidding?" he replied. "Just try to close down a branch of the bank, and the whole neighborhood is after you, as well as city hall. And they all love the old nineteenth-century buildings."

A closer model might be the university. When I became the senior fellow of the Yale trustees and talked through the president's problems with Benno Schmidt, again and again I found they resembled my own: budgets, warring constituencies, ideological biases, tenured personnel. In the diocese, we always faced budget agonies, but instead of alumni, students, faculty, trustees, and administrative personnel colliding for the president's sympathy and support, we had rectors with tenure, laypersons with strikingly different points of view, diocesan staff, seminarians, institutional leaders, seminary faculty, vestries, cathedral trustees, and so forth all seeking the bishop's ear. The poor parishes were crying for financial support, while the rich parishes resented having to pay large assessments to programs over which they had no control.

Administration is a cold word, but it has the same root as *ministry*, and I enjoyed orchestrating this amorphous mass of heterogeneous institutions. Sunday by Sunday, I would venture forth to briefly become part of their life.

A TYPICAL SUNDAY

It is a beautiful Sunday morning. Brenda and I get up early and set out, Brenda driving, I reviewing my sermon notes. The Hudson Valley is bursting with the yellows and light greens of early spring. The country parish we are to visit has a new young priest, and I understand things are going well. As we drive up, we see people clustered around the door in their Sunday best—boys in blue suits with boutonnieres and girls in white, lacy dresses. As we enter the parking lot, I see a place reserved for the bishop. A vestryman in a dark suit and white collar rushes up to take my suitcase; one of the women of the altar guild is there to welcome Brenda and show her to her pew. I find the rector in the sacristy, vested in a white alb. We embrace as old friends; I had ordained him a few years before. This is his first parish, and he is proud to be the rector.

"Let's look at the church and go over the service. Would you like to sing the sursum corda?" he asks.

"Not my strong suit, but I'll give it a try if you'd like," I reply. "And I would like to tell the children a story at some point. When should I do that?"

He looks confused. He had everything all planned out, and I was about to mix it up. Gallantly, he says, "Oh, anytime you'd like, Bishop."

The bell starts ringing; people begin to stream into the church. We retreat to the sacristy. I put on a white alb with a purple cincture indicating I am a bishop, then the cope, an elaborate cape, and the miter, a large golden hat indicating the bishop's authority. I take my staff, shaped like a shepherd's crook and symbolizing the bishop's pastoral role. We line up on the lawn outside. The children are awed by my outfit. I must say, at six foot four plus another six inches of miter I do look pretty impressive. On the other hand, sometimes I think to myself that I look silly! But the ancient symbolism of the vestments has its importance.

The bishop connects the parish to the wider Church—the diocese, the Episcopal Church, and the Anglican communion throughout the world—and symbolizes our ties with the past, going back almost two thousand years to the twelve apostles, the first bishops. Most people see a bishop only once a year and see the diocesan bishop, myself, only every three or four years. There were two hundred parishes in the diocese, and the two suffragan bishops and I took turns visiting. In accordance with Church canon law, a bishop must visit a parish at least once every three years; customarily, one of the three of us visits once a year. Only a bishop can confirm; only a bishop can consecrate a church; only a bishop can ordain a priest or deacon. Parishes like a bishop to be there to celebrate anniversaries, to baptize the rector's child, to dedicate a new parish house. Besides these liturgical events, the bishop should assure himself of the parish's solvency and take the pulse of the place as best he can.

As we enter the church, I am at the rear of the procession, according to protocol, and when I reach the front of the church I stand in full view before the bishop's throne, which is placed in front of the altar. After a rousing hymn, I pronounce, "Blessed be God, Father, Son, and Holy Spirit." The people reply, "And blessed be his Kingdom, now and forever."

Readings from the Old Testament and from an Epistle follow. I turn to the organist to delay the next hymn, ask the people to be seated, and motion the children to come forward for a story.

When I was a little boy, my Scottish nurse took me to the Presbyterian church; the pastor told a children's story. I told Mother I wanted to be a Presbyterian, which startled her. In any case, I resolved always to tell a story when children were present. Church is so *boring* for kids. No wonder they quit as teenagers.

One of my stories has to do with the lost sheep and my dragging a hidden child from behind the pulpit with my pastoral staff. Another has to do with why bishops wear funny-looking clothes. I enjoy hamming it up, it loosens the atmosphere, and I love looking into the wide wonder-filled eyes of the children.

After the gospel is read, I preach. What to preach about is always a question. First, I want them to feel that the bishops and the diocesan staff are there to serve them and that we value them, appreciating the hard work they do in caring for the parish. If possible, I use the Scripture of the day as a starting place. I always mention some social issue so that they realize I feel that working for justice and peace is part of the Church's ministry. I also make sure that some part of the sermon is of comfort to anyone who came to church carrying a sorrow, or was suffering, or was afraid. And I conclude with a special word to those who are to be confirmed that day, that the gift of the Spirit will not only comfort them over the years, but is to be brought out into the world.

I always say a silent prayer before preaching. When you look out on those faces, waiting expectantly for the Word of God, you feel unworthy and privileged. A sermon is a dialogue, even though the people do not speak; they communicate with their eyes, their expressions, their body movements. If they start reading the bulletin, they are saying you are boring; if they fidget and look away, you have said something that irritates them; if they look at their watches, you have gone on too long. However, I know of no deeper thrill than when you touch a congregation and the church grows still. People lean forward on their seats, all eyes and ears; you know that what you say in the next few moments may change someone's life.

When the sermon is over, I move to the bishop's chair and begin the rite of confirmation. The questions: "Do you reaffirm your renunciation of evil?"

They say together, "I do."

"Do you renew your commitment to Jesus Christ?"

"I do."

We repeat the Creed together, a prayer is said, and then the candidates come forward and kneel before me. I place my hands heavily on each head and say, "Strengthen, O Lord, your servant *John* with your Holy Spirit; empower him for your service; and sustain him all the days of his life." Each head is different: the warm, moist scalp of a teenage boy, the lace over the golden hair of a girl, the formal coiffure of a matron (be careful of hat pins), the smooth bald head of an older man. Some kneel with eyes downcast, some are shaking with nervousness, some meet your eyes with a piercing stare, as if they are searching for a glimpse of God there. I wonder about their lives —what suffering they may face, what this gift of the Spirit may mean.

After a concluding prayer, the kiss of peace is exchanged. This is a break in the formality of the liturgy, a chance for people to greet one another. I go down and exchange the peace with the confirmands. We then settle down to the celebration of the Eucharist: the bishop, as father in God, presides over the family meal at which, we believe, the risen Christ is present.

The visitation is not over with the hand shaking at the door. At the coffee hour, sometimes we have a forum at which the people can ask questions and I can discuss matters not appropriate for a sermon. I also meet with the vestry to thank them for their work and answer whatever questions they may have. If I have done something they feel to be outrageous, such as going to Saigon or ordaining a lesbian, I hear about it in no uncertain terms.

Brenda, meanwhile, has been circulating among the people with her wonderful smile and easy laughter. She is much loved in the diocese. Occasionally, however, things do not proceed according to Hoyle. One time, as I was walking down the aisle, the rector went over to ask her to come out and greet the people. Unfortunately, Brenda was fast asleep. I guess she had heard me preach once too often or had got up far too early. When the rector touched her shoulder, she jumped what seemed like a foot in the air. Another time, she went unescorted to the coffee hour, approached three young men, and introduced herself. "I'm Brenda Moore," she said. Not recognizing who she was, one replied, "Madam, none of us is looking for a date," and they walked away. Another time, I was in the sacristy of a small inner-city parish and overheard a warden ask, "Who is that fox in the rear of the church?" It was Brenda.

When all is over and my vestments packed up, we adjourn to the rectory, where the rector's wife, having been warned of my predilections, furnishes me with a nice stiff vodka on the rocks (Brenda is driving). This is an enjoyable, relaxed time, when the priest and his family can let their hair down, show us their children, tell us their problems.

At two-thirty or three, we drive off for a similar event at another parish. Finally, at ten o'clock or so, we wearily ascend the long stone stairs of the French château and collapse.

These were exhausting but exhilarating days. Sometimes we found depressed little places with a rector who had been there too long and felt a failure, and the parish, struggling to keep afloat, wished the rector would move along. Sometimes, a major row was afoot between the rector and the vestry, not dissimilar to the warfare of an unhappy marriage.

We visited parishes in a burned-out section of the Bronx, Hispanic congregations, a church in Chinatown. In the Haitian parish and in a white, French-speaking congregation remaining from Huguenot days, I would celebrate in schoolboy French; in the Latino parishes, I'd use my very broken Spanish. Over the years, in Washington and New York, I have made over two thousand visitations. These have been the foundation of my ministry.

THE ISSUES

THE NEW PRAYER BOOK

A S bishop, I was drawn into many issues outside the boundaries of the diocese. Some were expressly religious, others only implicitly so, but as our people were affected by these problems in their daily lives, they sought my action and counsel.

For most people, the main function of a church is to have services on Sunday morning. Whatever programs a parish sponsors, whoever its priest is, Sunday worship is at the heart of the whole enterprise. It is small wonder that a change in the prayer book would cause consternation.

When the Church of England broke off from the papacy in 1534, the liturgy remained in Latin. The first prayer book in English was issued in 1549, and since then there have been numerous versions in many languages. Each independent Church in the Anglican communion has its own prayer book. However, each is consistent with the basic Catholic liturgy that binds us all together. Our first Book of Common Prayer was composed in 1789, after the United States became independent of England and the American Episcopal Church was formed as an independent Church but one still in communion with the Archbishop of Canterbury. Since then we have had several editions. In the late 1960s, the church began to plan a new prayer book to replace the one then in use, which had been issued in 1928.

Because our people are so steeped in the liturgy, which they have prayed through Sunday after Sunday, the Church took great care in introducing the new book. Several trial liturgies were promulgated and criticisms and suggestions received. The final edition was approved by General Convention in 1979, replacing the 1928 book as the official liturgy of the Church. Since Anglicanism does not have any doctrine except what is contained in the Bible, the Creeds, and the General Councils of the early Church (we have no Anglican "Confession" nor papal encyclicals), the prayer book carries the weight of doctrine as well as the weight of liturgy. We believe in the old saying *lex orandi, lex credendi*: the doctrine of prayer becomes the doctrine of belief. Thus for us the Book of Common Prayer is a supremely important document. The authors of the new revision struggled for years under pressures to modernize—to include the insights of contemporary liturgical scholarship—and counterpressures to retain the old language, with its *thees* and *thous* and its beloved familiarity. The sonorous language of the 1928 book held beauty cherished by many, and yet others felt strongly that more contemporary language should be used.

The book was also influenced by the liturgical movement, an ecumenical trend that began just before World War II and had a great impact on all the Churches. The Roman Catholic Church, for instance, forsook the ancient Latin Mass as a result. In order to enhance the participation of the congregation in the Eucharist, the movement urged every parish to have the Eucharist as the principal service on Sunday; to provide alternative forms of the prayers; to emphasize the theme of Resurrection more than Crucifixion, of forgiveness rather than guilt; and to enhance the corporate nature of the liturgy. New liturgies of baptism, marriage, burial, and other services were introduced. For the most part, the changes were efforts to reach back to the liturgical forms of the early Church, abandoning medieval accretions.

The change to more contemporary language blurred the wall separating the sacred from the profane, making the Church less mysterious, less a place in which to escape from the world. When they come to church on a Sunday morning after a hard week of work and worry, most people wish to be soothed, healed, comforted by a loving God who communicates with them through familiar prayers, hymns, and sermons. The new service was unfamiliar, and understandably people resented it. Similarly, the new book caused a furor. The old words had entered the very souls of the people—they were felt to be

God's words. Liturgical changes brought about by the new book were upsetting to conservatively minded people: more prayers had to do with social concerns; baptisms were held at the main service on Sunday morning rather than privately; the new informality often gave rise to other musical forms, guitars rather than an organ. Oddly enough, the introduction of the kiss of peace was the most upsetting of all. This is an ancient rite of the Church, whereby members of the congregation greet one another at the time of the offertory to symbolize our being in "love and charity with our neighbor" before offering our gifts to God. The "kiss" consists of a formal handshake and the words, "The peace of the Lord be with you" and the response, "And also with you." That is, Episcopalians now have to touch one another in church, a most radical idea! In church, one is spiritual, not physical. Underneath the resistance to the kiss of peace is a denial of the doctrine of the Incarnation, that God took on *flesh* and dwelt among us. As the years have gone on, many parishes have begun to celebrate the kiss of peace with embraces, conversation, and laughter, a healthy break in the solemnity of the Liturgy.

THE ORDINATION OF WOMEN

The ordination of women was a great struggle. Here we were dealing not only with radical change, but with a phenomenon that touched the very depths of the psyche. The Church has always taught that God is beyond gender. Traditionally, however, it has used the male pronoun to refer to God. In our prayers, we say, "Our Father, who art in heaven." Jesus called God his heavenly father. Psychologically, then, we have attached the emotions we feel toward our fathers to God rather than those we feel toward our mothers. The cult of the Virgin demonstrates the longing people have for femininity in their worship, but it has been suppressed in Protestant theology.

The feminist movement advanced the cause of women priests. At first, I could not accept the idea; it struck me as outlandish. Then, over a period of years, I came to realize that I was against it for purely emotional reasons, and I became one of its leading advocates. To be sure, my wife and six daughters hastened the process! We finally won the day and now have over a hundred women priests in our diocese alone, occupying every position, including suffragan bishop.

As it happened, the ordination of women was approved in 1979, the year the new prayer book was introduced. Understandably, the same people who were against the new book were also against the ordination of women. Soon the church was polarized—liberals versus conservatives—just as it had been during the civil rights struggle and the peace movement.

GAY RIGHTS

A sample of this conservative resistance was the publication of a scurrilous article in *Harper's* magazine by one Paul Seabury, whose sole claim to credibility was his being a descendant of the first Episcopal bishop. The gist of the article, titled "Trendier Than Thou," was that the leadership of the Church had sold out to the secular world and had jumped on every bandwagon. I was one of the targets. I counted ten errors of fact on one page. It was outrageous. However, it raised an important point: how much should the Church adapt to the zeitgeist?

I believe that the Holy Spirit moves in the world as well as in the Church, an obvious but often forgotten truth. Therefore, if a movement of justice or a trend, such as the feminist movement, is of God, the Church should become part of it. In Western culture, so immersed in Christianity and Judaism over the centuries, many movements that appear to be secular in reality have their roots in Judeo-Christian moral principles, such as justice, the sacredness of every individual, and a reverence for Creation. This is true not only of feminism, but of the peace movement, the ecological movement, and even the demands for gay rights. The problem, of course, is that people differ strongly in their discernment of what is of God and what is against his will.

Of all these controversies, the one that has caused the greatest anger has been gay rights.* I was involved in fighting discrimination

---

* I wrote a book about the ordination of women, gays, and lesbians and the accompanying events titled *Take a Bishop Like Me* (Harper & Row, 1979).

against homosexuals since the 1950s as a member of the board of the George Henry Foundation, a social agency that helped homosexual men with their problems. I learned of the entrapments, police brutality, suicides, and despair of many gay people. Also, my mentor at St. Paul's School, Frederick Bartrop, was a priest who was dishonorably discharged from the Army and deposed from the priesthood for making a pass at a young soldier when under the influence of alcohol on a beach in New Guinea. His hospitalization for addiction and long years of difficulties taught me more about the issue.

In 1980, shortly after the church admitted women to the ordained ministry, I ordained a lesbian to the priesthood. The outcry was tremendous. The ordination of women had drawn the attention of the press. They were hungry for another story. The ordination of Ellen Barrett in Holy Apostles Church, a tiny parish on Ninth Avenue, was blown up way out of proportion to its importance. A blizzard covered New York that night, but all three major television networks sent camera crews to the ordination. Luckily, Holy Apostles ran a hostel for released convicts in the parish house, and two or three of them volunteered to keep order.

Ellen Barrett had come to see me seeking ordination several years earlier. I said neither the standing committee nor I could approve her, since she was publicly known to be a lesbian, having written some articles for a gay magazine. I knew that we already had many splendid clergy who were homosexual in the diocese, and over the centuries clergy who were gay had been an important part of the life of the Church. The Church had been run on the "Don't ask, don't tell" principle for years. It was Ellen's openness, not her sexual orientation, that was the problem. In other words, the question really was, "Is honesty a bar to ordination?"

Meanwhile, the gay rights movement had hit its stride, more and more thoughtful discussion of the issue had taken place, and some ordained clergy had come out of the closet. In 1978, Ellen applied again and was approved. I ordained her a deacon without much controversy. But when I ordained her to the priesthood, I had to hire a special secretary to answer all the mail. Several parishes withheld their assessments (their required annual payments to the diocese) in protest. When people said I was courageous, I replied, "That is like saying you are courageous when you are standing in a road and get hit by a truck!" There was even an attempt to censure me in the House of Bishops.

The issue still is causing disruption in the Church. In 1996, Bishop Walter Righter was threatened with a heresy trial for ordaining a gay deacon. When Ellen Barrett was ordained, she was not known to be sexually active—only her orientation was at issue. Now the controversy is over the ordination of sexually active gay clergy and over the blessing of gay relationships.

Throughout the 1980s I lobbied continually for a city ordinance banning discrimination against gays and lesbians due to their sexual orientation. John Cardinal O'Connor, my Roman Catholic counterpart in New York, waged a strenuous campaign against the ordinance. Those of us who favored the ordinance finally won the day after stormy hearings in city hall and my openly criticizing the cardinal on television at the time.

This is not the place to elaborate on the pros and cons of this issue. Suffice it to say that I believe sexual orientation is a given, not something chosen, and that a human being has a right to express him- or herself sexually. I believe homosexuals are developing a sexual morality at least as authentic as that of heterosexuals. To strengthen this development, the state and the Church should recognize their relationships on the same basis as marriage.

The black civil rights struggle touched deep emotional chords, which from the beginning had sexual overtones ("Would you want your daughter to marry a Negro?"). The gay rights movement carries an even heavier sexual freight. When religion and sexuality swirl around an issue, it becomes explosive.

THE FREEZE

Other controversies arose. We had a moving ecumenical service in the cathedral at the time of the huge antinuclear freeze rally in Central Park. On a television panel I denounced the Christian Coalition, which had come out against the freeze. I also debated Jerry Falwell on television. Brenda and I and our cairn terrier arrived in the studio. A few minutes later Falwell marched in, surrounded by bodyguards and clothed in smiles. The interviewer insisted we sit close to each other on the sofa. I had distanced myself at the other end. As we chatted in this artificially cozy setting, I became more and more frustrated at his God-and-patriotism rhetoric. I could not resist pointing out that I had been wounded in combat. That did not slow him down at all. His final statement summed it all up: "When the Russians invade New York," he said, "I will be in the trenches to defend this great city." I did not have a chance to ask him which war he was talking about.

Because of the national coverage of these television appearances, I received a letter threatening my life. I was not a bit worried; I had had other such threats before. But when I reported it to the police, they took it seriously, since President Reagan had been shot a few weeks earlier. They insisted that I have a bodyguard and that I disguise myself when I left the cathedral. I donned dark glasses and a beat-up trench coat, left my round collar at home and walked the streets with a six-foot, two-hundred-fifty-pound cathedral guard following me. Brenda christened me the Morningside Flasher. After two uneventful weeks, I resumed my normal style.

DEEPER MEANINGS

When I looked out at the city and the diocese, I saw more than an institution: I saw the Body of Christ acting out, however inadequately expressed by the very human Church, Christ's ministry in the City of Man, as St. Augustine called it. When the Church is not true to this vocation, people receive a distorted image of God and either reject him as unworthy of their attention or worship a god far smaller and pettier than God's true reality. My responsibility was to shape the Church, as best I could, so that it reflected the image of Christ —the suffering servant, the crucified innocent convict, the tender shepherd, the sovereign of heaven, the risen, glorious Lord, still bearing the wounds on his hands and feet and in his side. One of our great Advent hymns has it that, even at Christ's Second Coming: "Those dear tokens of his Passion / Still his dazzling body bears."

Not only is it important that the Church be seen as serving God's people, but also Christ must be authentically experienced in what goes on in the Sunday worship of the churches. The mystery of being

whom we call God is so overwhelming, so loving, so full of power
that the usual experience in church on a Sunday morning does not
do God justice. It belittles God. Sometimes it almost feels like an
American Legion meeting, with bake sales and special events; sometimes like a second-rate concert; sometimes like a cute children's pag-
eant. Often the mystery, the numinous, is not apparent—not the
Being who dwells beyond the furthest light-years as well as within
the infinitesimal quark; nor the wild beauty of the sea and the sky
and the wind and the mountains; nor the call to sense the world's
agony as it was taken on by the infinite suffering of the cross. The
suffering servant is dismissed with the dropping of a bill into the
collection plate or a mumbled phrase of intercession; the numinous
is dispelled by sloppy liturgy.

Many live happily with an undemanding "Now I lay me down to
sleep" God. Then something happens in your life—death, pain, di-
vorce, addiction, mental breakdown; reality comes crashing down,
and you reach out to a god not large enough or deep enough to
respond to the horror and terror of your life. You pray to this Sunday
school god and nothing happens. This cozy god should make things
better right away but often does not. However, if you are deeply acquainted with God, you are not frustrated. You open your agony to
the agony of Christ hanging on the cross, you know that God cannot
always relieve pain, but you know too that God is there with you in
the midst of your pain and that on the other side of this death of
pain will be new life and resurrection.

The great teachings of the faith are a solid foundation for understanding the nature of our lives and the mystery of being. It is the
business of the Church to teach these doctrines, to inspire us in such
a way that not only do we understand them, we feel their strength
in our very bones. Creation is not only the world we know, but the
unimaginable beyond, beyond the borders of space and time; the Incarnation is God's presence through Christ in the flesh of love, the
sweat of work, the swirl of humanity; Atonement is the massive dealing with sin and suffering held up in the cross; death and resurrection
together are the very rhythm of life; the Holy Spirit is the presence
of God in our own depths, bringing us into the very heart of the
Trinity; the Eucharist takes up the great and small events of the world
and of our lives and makes them holy. The principal vocation of a

bishop is to help bring this mystical reality to his people. That was the deepest and most subtle of all the vocations to which I was called.

When I looked at my life honestly and at my fumbling attempts to carry out this noble vocation, I felt inadequate, unworthy. All I could do was to pray that the Lord could use me, and sometimes it has seemed as though he did.

ABROAD

THROUGH the years, I have traveled all over the world on various missions in search of justice and peace and a wider understanding of the people of God in other lands, cultures, and religions. In 1966, the Bishop of Tokyo asked me to give his clergy a seminar on urban ministry. I found myself in a conference center looking through a landscape window at the glistening, holy Mount Fuji, while trying to break through the burden of being translated and the conceptual barriers between us. The bishop wanted me to urge the clergy of the Nippon Sei Ko Kai (the Holy Catholic Church of Japan) to venture forth from their Victorian heritage to participate in the cities around them. Two decades later, the archbishop of the Mar Thoma Church, an ancient Christian body founded by Thomas the Apostle on the southwestern shores of India almost two thousand years ago, asked me to address a multitude of 150,000 as they sat on the hot sands of a dried riverbed about the social implications of the sacraments. In 1970, I went to Saigon to meet with members of the peace movement there; not long afterward, Cyrus Vance, later the Secretary of State, brought together statesmen and religious leaders in a luxurious hotel on the shores of Lake Como to discuss the elimination of hunger throughout the world. Brenda and I found ourselves in Nicaragua at the start of the Sandinista revolution, in Soviet Russia discussing nuclear disarmament during the cold war; in South Africa examining the involvement of American corporations in apartheid. And in retirement, Brenda and I spent two months in the South Pacific, including a harrowing exposure to conditions in East Timor.

Although they doubtless were too polite to say it, I am sure many people wondered why on earth the Episcopal Bishop of New York should do so much globe-trotting. Well, it seemed to me that the search for justice and peace could not be limited to New York or even to the United States. I felt an urge—a calling, if you will—to go wherever the Spirit seemed to be pointing me, feeling that some good would come of it. Throughout the world, even in non-Christian countries, bishops are respected as men of God or, at the very least, men of integrity. This gives bishops access to other religious leaders and often to secular ones as well. Sometimes the respect we are given seems superficial (as if protocol demands it); at other times, we can make an impact. We can give moral and sometimes financial support to beleaguered people, who feel they are fighting against great odds and are forgotten by the outside world. We also can convey a side of American opinion different from, and often antagonistic toward, our government, reassuring those we meet that the U.S. policy now harming them might well change under another administration. In these ways we can bring hope, without which no one can move forward under persecution.

I loved the risk and excitement of these adventures and also felt them part of my calling. When I went abroad, I was inspired by the courage and style of the people I met and came back to New York with renewed vigor. As the years passed, it became more and more clear to me that the same fundamental issues and dynamics were present everywhere: the domination of the ruling establishment, with varying degrees of injustice and corruption; the resistance of those on the bottom, especially the courageous and sometimes too impulsive youth, most of whose leaders seemed to have an innate drive toward freedom; and the intervention of outside forces for good or ill. Of course, some regimes did not allow the slightest show of protest, while in others an unexpected and sometimes misdirected anger bubbled beneath the surface. A youth exhibit in India, for instance, pictured two fat bishops embracing as each plunged a knife in the other's back; blood spurted out, running over the caption "The Ecumenical Movement."

GASSED IN SAIGON

One of the most exhilarating of these trips was to Saigon. Not many days after the disastrous peace rally at the cathedral in 1970, Ron Young, a leader of Clergy and Laity Concerned about Vietnam (CAL-CAV), came to see me. A tall, gangly young man, he flopped down on the sofa and said they had a "big one" coming up and they needed me. My heart sank.

Ron was a child of the 1960s and an effective organizer. He had secured funding from the Fellowship of Reconciliation to bring a delegation of young people and clergy to meet with leaders of the peace movement in Vietnam. I did not know of the peace movement there, but his account of the bravery of the participants was convincing: they had been tortured and imprisoned in tiger cages, and were now becoming the nucleus of a third force for reconciling the enemies. "What would we do?" I asked whether we would take part in demonstrations or civil disobedience. "No," he said, without much conviction. "We will just talk to them, encourage them, and show them that all Americans are not like the soldiers they see. We are calling it a fact-finding mission." His enthusiasm caught me up, and after a long pause, I said I would try to go.

Already I knew that I would wind up going. You see, I am always torn between the desire to avoid trouble and the lure of adventure. Surely, I believe in the cause at stake, but underneath all that genuine commitment to justice and peace is a very simple fact: I love excitement. These mixed motives do not really bother me; in any major decision there are always different forces at work, some conscious, some unconscious. The important thing is to be aware of these so that the less authentic motives do not impede the venture.

A few weeks later we were queuing up at the JFK ticket counter: Sam Brown, an organizer of the Vietnam Moratorium in Washington; Mother Mary Luke Tobin, superior of a large Roman Catholic religious order, the Sisters of Loreto; Charles Palmer, president of the National Student Association; Rabbi Balfour Brickner from New York; Tim Butz, a student from Kent State and a Vietnam veteran; Dorothy Cotton from the Southern Christian Leadership Coalition (SCLC); Bernard Lafayette, coordinator of SCLC's Poor People's Campaign; and David Hunter, deputy secretary of the National

Council of Churches. We were a great mix of ages and backgrounds, and we were to pick up some Dutch, Australian, and New Zealand students on the way.

Our first glimpse of Saigon, so to speak, was in the Paris airport, where we saw a small man, almost lost in the crowd of hurrying Americans, the Buddhist monk, Tich Nat Thanh. He had waited five hours to spend five minutes with us—an intellectual, a poet, an ascetic, and a political exile. His eyes burned with the suffering of his people and his longing for Vietnam. The symbol of the people of Vietnam is a woman carrying a bamboo pole; they say their strength is in their weakness. Tich Nat Thanh, who wrote a book on Vietnam called *Lotus in a Sea of Fire*, radiated that strength in weakness. In the days that followed I thought of his face again and again.

Our sponsors, the Fellowship of Reconciliation, had lined up the cheapest hotel they could find in Saigon, called the Caravel. A scruffy hallway opened up into a small, dingy courtyard with a bar and lounge on one side and some dying palm trees on the other. Although it was the middle of the day, a few overdressed women were sitting at the bar, and the ground rules of the establishment were scrawled like graffiti on one wall: NO PANTS OFF IN HALLWAY; BE SURE ZIP UP PANTS; WASHING GOOD FOR YOU BEFORE GO HOME; NO FIGHTS ALLOWED; NO CREDIT FOR SERVICES. Mother Mary Luke Tobin took it all in stride. That night, as she and I walked into the hotel, one of the women approached me, and I said: "Sorry, lady. I already have a date."

Our high spirits were soon dampened by our meeting with Don Luce, the courageous leader of the Church World Service there. Don's young face was weary. He himself lived in a brothel so the police could not distinguish between people who were customers and people who were visiting him. He said you could not trust anyone. There were some hundred thousand secret police everywhere, and we noticed later that they followed us wherever we went—to restaurants, to the hotel lounge. Don also told us of the notorious tiger cages, built so the prisoner could not stand up straight. I began to have a cold feeling in my stomach. It was fear.

The next morning, we gathered at a student center with some extraordinary young people. Their leader, Mam, was tall, with strong, clear features and long unruly hair. His eyes held us in a direct gaze as we were introduced. They told us their stories. One young woman was beaten repeatedly by police; she showed the ugly scars on her light-brown skin. A young man held up his hand so that we could see the bloody fingertips, where his nails had been pulled out. Another student had spent weeks in the tiger cages, forced to drink his own urine, and shackled day and night.

The students' stories made us fearful and sad, but when they told us that, as they were being tortured, American advisers would come into the room to confer with the Vietnamese police and do nothing, I could feel the anger rising through my body. These young men and women were the same age as some of my own children. Where did their courage come from? It is one thing to have courage for battle; there are so many props for that—comrades in arms, strict military discipline, patriotic songs, uniforms, traditions, and the like. These kids had another kind of discipline and dedication. Why did they trust us, we Americans whose country had supported the very regime that was torturing them? Perhaps their openness rested on the trust Don Luce had built so painstakingly over the months. In trusting us, they took a risk for peace.

A cloudburst of tropical rain splashed down the sides of the shed, and the students began to sing with joy and energy some delicate lilting songs of peace. We cherished them, we trusted them, we came to love them. And we agreed to attend a rally the next evening.

That evening we spoke with some Roman Catholic priests. The strands of the peace movement sprang from many sources within Vietnam: students, intellectuals, Roman Catholics, Buddhist monks, journalists, some businesspeople. They all seemed to come together for the same goal: the recapture of their beloved land by nonviolent means from the forces of the Vietcong and the Saigon government, which in their different ways were tearing it apart.

Nationalism is too shallow a word for their patriotism, Dan Toc; it runs deep and resonates with reverence for the land in a spirituality that springs forth from that special part of the earth. The closest comparison I can think of in the West is Charles de Gaulle's reverence and passion for France.

On the third day we drove to the An Quang Pagoda in Cholon, a poor section of Saigon, where we met with Buddhist monks. In the courtyard we greeted one another with the traditional Buddhist bow. The monks were small men, tonsured, dressed in orange robes. Their faces were solemn, their eyes searching, as if trying to find out our inner intent in being there with them. The press hovered around us with their cameras and microphones. At first, we regretted this, but apparently the monks needed every bit of publicity they could get in order to squeeze their views into the government-oriented press.

A few months earlier, several of the monks had been killed by the police. Their commitment to peace, whatever the cost, was hard for us to comprehend. For all its bluster, the peace movement in the United States produced few martyrs.

The leading monk, Thich Thien Minh (the head of the United Buddhist Church), thanked us for coming and expressed his solidarity with us. He stressed that they were not Communists but only wished to build a country of freedom and democracy. He spoke especially clearly and carefully, lest by one slip of the tongue he be accused of siding with the enemy, labeled a Communist, and thrown in jail or killed. As we were leaving, the monks asked me to lead the group in prayer; we stood in a circle, silent, heads bowed.

The next day we drove to the Mekong Delta through the quiet countryside, where peasants in conical hats tended rice paddies and water buffalo plowed the fields. We were escorted by John Steinbeck, Jr., whose father had just died. Dao Dua, the head of the strange island religious community we were about to visit, had adopted him as a son, a custom of the community. We found Dao sitting on a throne on the bow of a barge, surrounded by monks. He lived on coconuts and had taken a vow of silence until peace came to Vietnam. He communicated through symbols. To us he gave a Taoist ceremonial bell made from an American artillery shell. Just before our trip, on a visit to the U.S. ambassador he had carried with him a covered basket in which he had placed ten mice and a friendly cat. If even a cat and mice could live in peace inside a very small basket, it seemed to say, surely human beings could live together in a small country. At the embassy a marine guard insisted on opening the basket to see if it contained a bomb. Out scampered the mice in every direction. Dao insisted that the Marines catch every last one. So there they were, in full-dress blues, crawling after the nimble mice—itself an apt symbol of the U.S. forces' clumsy attempts to catch the Vietcong.

The night after our trip to the Delta, we attended the rally, of which the young people had spoken earlier, at the Buddhist student center of the university. When we arrived the police had shut off the electricity. We were ushered into a hot, crowded auditorium illuminated by flaming torches.

The climax of the meeting was to be the handing of the torch of peace from the Vietnamese to our students. And so Ron Young of CALCAV took the torch and held it high, not noticing the papier mâché dove hanging above his head. The dove of peace burst into flames and fell on the wooden stage. I was about to kick it off when I saw that it would land on the laps of a row of Buddhist monks.

The evening was not over. We were taken up some dark stairs to the roof of the center. There, kneeling on the floor, their faces lit by candles, the student leaders laid out a map of Saigon to explain to us the plans for the next day. The night before, after an agonizing three-hour discussion, we had decided to join their manifestation. They thought that if we were with them, perhaps the police would not break it up. None of the older members of our group, myself included, felt comfortable about the idea: somehow, demonstrating against one's own country in a foreign land during a war seemed inappropriate. Our younger colleagues, however, were keen to go: "If the Vietnamese students were willing to risk their lives for peace after imprisonment in the tiger cages, how can we stand on the niceties of protocol and refuse to march with them?"

Early the next morning, we gathered at an open-air hall on the edge of the campus. After many speeches and songs, Mam called for silence. Up the aisle came four tiny, wrinkle-faced old women. On their shoulders was a long pole, and swinging from the pole a small casket. When they reached the stage, the people were totally quiet. One of the women spoke to me in Vietnamese and handed the casket to me, as the translator said: "This is our gift to the American people—our dead children." All eyes fastened on me, awaiting my response. I felt like I had received a blow to the stomach. I was unable to speak. Finally, I took the casket and laid it gently on the table. I mumbled something like, "We are deeply ashamed of the pain and sorrow our country has visited upon your people, very, very, sad. May peace come soon."

Mam rose to give a final passionate oration, concluding with directions: proceed out the gate, turn right, pass the embassy. There the Americans would leave a petition; the rest of the marchers would go on to the presidential palace and leave another petition there.

The leaders followed Mam, his fist upraised, down the aisle. As we reached the street, they pushed me to the head of the march: in my seersucker pants and purple bishop's shirt, picket sign aloft, I never looked more like a WASP. I felt ridiculous.

Off we went, leading what must have been more than a thousand people—students, old ladies, Buddhist monks, Roman Catholic priests, and other elements of the Saigon peace movement. As we went through the gates, I saw the soldiers put on their gas masks, and when we reached the embassy, a line of South Vietnamese soldiers blocked the end of the street, crouched behind sandbags in battle dress, their bayonets fixed. How strange it was: the last time I'd faced armed soldiers I'd been leading a platoon of Marines on Guadalcanal.

We had agreed beforehand that we would keep marching until we were physically halted. When we had come within a hundred yards of the troops, there was a command, which brought their rifles to their shoulders. Another command, and they raised them toward the sky. A third command, and they fired projectiles into the air. Rifle grenades—but were they explosives or tear gas? They exploded, and the tear gas burst forth among us. It was suffocating and so thick we could not see for more than a few feet. My eyes began to burn, and I started choking.

We began to retreat in confusion. Then someone shouted, "We can't go back, they've cut us off!" Finally, we discovered a small doorway in one of the walls and began pouring through. I was carrying one of the old women who had presented us with the coffin. (She had tried to wipe the tear gas from my eyes with lime juice—what courtesy!)

I thought the more quickly we all dispersed, the less likely we were to be arrested. Besides, I was frightened and just wanted to get the hell back to the hotel as fast as my legs would carry me.

The old woman was okay, so I left her and hurried down an alley. I looked back and saw I was being followed. Enthusiastic young people, fists held high, were following the American man they thought was their leader: *me!* All I wanted to do was get back to that hotel. The faster I ran, the faster they ran. I motioned them to disperse. They thought I was motioning them to press on.

Finally we debouched onto the square in front of the legislature. There my colleagues began a new manifestation, while another of our group and I, deciding that discretion was the better part of valor, sneaked back to the hotel.

Later that day Ron called a press conference in the bar, ceded to us for the time being by the overdressed young ladies. He read a statement protesting the breakup of the peaceful demonstration and pointed out that the tear-gas grenades had been made in the United States. We had brought two or three grenades with us, and now we produced them, only to realize they were still exuding gas. The reporters started to weep and wanted to end the conference immediately. We insisted they stay to hear our ultimatum: we would not leave the country until the students who had been arrested were released. With the help of the embassy, which clearly wanted us out of there, the students were released.

A week or so after returning to the States, I received a long letter from Lieutenant General Lew Walt, who had been my battalion commander in Guadalcanal. Now he was commanding officer of the Marines in Vietnam, and he wanted to know how a good Marine like myself could have participated in such a subversive, unpatriotic action.

Good question.

Many years later, I went to see the movie *Platoon*, the story of a Marine rifle platoon in Vietnam. On the way out of the theater, I found I could hardly breathe. I staggered into the crowded lavatory, leaned against the white, cool tile of the wall, and hyperventilated for at least ten minutes. I was half sobbing as my breath went in and out. I was sobbing for the men I had lost in Guadalcanal—the movie's jungles and battles could have been my own. But I was sobbing too for Vietnam—for the brave students, for the wrinkled old women, for the crushed beauty of that delicate land—and for those Marines.

I cannot put into words the obscenity of the breaking of nations, the killing of beautiful young men and women, the desolation of despair that we bring upon one another. Is there no way this can ever cease?

Somehow, these two experiences, almost thirty years apart, became one. And in both places, this stranger from America had glimpsed the Kingdom of God and the horror of hell. Nor were these the only such times. Again and again, in moments of grief and sorrow and powerlessness, I have found the presence of God; more so, much more so, than in the quiet beauty of a sunset. I have seen the glory of love so strong that death does not break it; I have felt the power of peace undergirding it all, so that even when the world is wild, I have been able to stay still in the strength of God's presence.

As I grow older and continue to try to unravel the meaning of life, I keep going back to times like these. The Vietnam War destroyed several countries in Asia and tore a ragged gash through our own, a wound that may never heal. Yet in the midst of that unrelieved tragedy shone God's glory in the courage and sacrifice of the people. History is about the interpenetration of the world by the Kingdom of God, unfolding in the patterns of war and peace, of loneliness and love, of youth and age, of male and female, of hatred and forgiveness. One of the vocations of a Christian is to become so familiar with the patterns of God's Kingdom in Scripture and in liturgy that we can recognize it glistening in the most unlikely places and occasions in the world around us. Then, having recognized the Kingdom, we are called to join in its movement.

CRACKS IN THE ICE

At the heart of the cold war, of course, lay the tension and misunderstanding between the United States and the Soviet Union, built up through a series of events going back to World War I, the Russian Revolution, and beyond, feeding on Russian xenophobia and America's strange paranoia of Communism. In 1983, resolving the conflict

seemed almost impossible. Many different groups, however, kept trying to find new ways through the impasse. That May, Brenda and I
were asked to join a delegation to the USSR from the Institute of
Policy Studies (IPS), a liberal think tank in Washington that had
maintained ties with people in Russia. Marc Raskin of the IPS staff
was in charge, and the group included Don Fraser, mayor of Minneapolis; Roger Wilkins, a black scholar; our friends the Potters; and
two or three others. All hands had a sense of humor, and we needed
it.

The Soviet delegation rolled out the red(!) carpet for us, for in
those days we were one of the few American groups willing to listen
to their side of the issues. The Hotel National overlooked the Kremlin
and was decorated in the style of the czars; our living room was graced
by a grand piano of inlaid wood and two enormous mirrors in gilded
ceramic frames. There was no vodka in the fridge, though; and, having been told that the rooms were bugged, we commented on our
disappointment to the chandelier. When we returned to our room
after dinner, the vodka was there. Because of this perceived efficiency,
we only talked shop sitting on the edge of the bathtub with the water
flowing full blast.

Looking out on the massive beauty of the Kremlin from our balcony, we contemplated the bizarre, brutal, and sometimes glorious
history of Mother Russia, and I wondered whether we could even
begin to understand (much less to trust and be trusted by) those with
whom we would speak.

I saw our purpose as twofold. We wanted to show that there was
a wide spectrum of opinion in the United States, that the stereotypes
appearing in the Russian press were no more accurate than our stereotypes of them, and that there were areas to explore that had never
been on the official agendas. In return, we wished to come to know
our hosts as people and to try to understand their emotions as well
as their political views. (One barrier to true communication was that
they were representing their government and we were private citizens.)

Most of our meetings were in the baroque palaces of the ancien
régime, an anachronistic backdrop for conversations with Communists. The first meeting was convened by Madame Kruglova, the chair
of the Association of Soviet Friendship Committees. She was a strong,

massive woman, whom I immediately pictured driving a troika of horses through a blinding blizzard chased by wolves. (Talk about stereotypes!) Like everyone we met during the visit, she spoke of the twenty million Soviet citizens who had died in World War II. Somehow the war dead had become a religious symbol; every bride and groom, right after their marriage ceremony, would pay a visit to the war memorial. In repeating the terrible statistics to us, they seemed to be saying that the war had torn the heart out of Russia and that we Americans had no idea of the suffering they had endured fighting the same enemy as we.

For our part, we asked whether they would join us in planning a conference a year hence to discuss such matters as arms control, international rules of nonintervention, and the implications of the Nuremberg trials on personal responsibility.

Through Thomas Watson, chief executive officer of IBM, I secured a personal interview with Georgi Arbatov of the politburo. He was most likable and open but clearly distressed about how he had been treated when he'd come to the United States for the Dartmouth conference on peace. The State Department delayed issuing him his visa and then made him return right after the conference, forbade him to appear on television or travel within the country, and generally insulted him. If face-to-face visits were a way for the Soviets to test our credibility, surely this treatment would have made him report negatively on the United States when he returned home.

I think most Americans at that time were under the impression that we alone were working for peace and that the Soviets were making reconciliation impossible by their words and actions. However, I firmly believe that a more sensitive approach could have had a salutary effect. But I also remember vividly the smiling face of Stalin in conversation with Roosevelt and Churchill, the smile of a man responsible for killing millions of his own people.

That evening, although we were expected to go to the opera, we had been secretly invited to a seder at a professor's apartment. His small sitting room was crowded with refuseniks—Jews who were seeking to leave the country but had been refused exit. The ceremony of the seder was deeply moving, as the Scriptures reenacted the imprisonment of the people of Israel four thousand years before. Now Leonid Brezhnev, the modern pharaoh, would not let the people go.

Two days later, I received a mysterious message; I was to meet two men from the seder a block from the hotel at 11 P.M. It was drizzling outside; I pulled my trench coat around me and lowered my hat over my eyes. Two men, also in trench coats, greeted me. We started walking and one of them handed me a letter about the plight of the refuseniks. He asked me to have it published in *The New York Times*, which I was able to do. I felt I was in a spy movie.

Among the other leaders we met, I particularly remember Bykov, an academician at the Institute of World Economic International Relations. He omitted the usual propaganda harangue, with which we had been deluged in other meetings. We thanked him for that. As we ranged broadly over the issues, I realized we were talking with a most profound, forthright man. At one point, he discussed the most frightening danger facing our two nations, the new launch-on-warning missile systems, which did not require human intervention to react to an incoming missile. As he spoke, I saw fear in his eyes. At that moment, I felt I had seen the very heart of the cold war; in our paranoia about the Soviets, we were forgetting their terror of us.

In order to find out the role of the Orthodox Church, Bob Potter and I visited Metropolitan Filaret, who was in charge of foreign affairs for the Church. We drove out to his dacha, a modest house in the suburbs. He welcomed us at the door dressed in a cassock, a short, well-built man of about fifty, with close-cropped hair and a full black beard. He gave us a broad smile and a bearlike embrace. We were led into his small chapel, decorated with a collection of exquisite gold, silver, and crimson icons, where we prayed together for peace.

After a vodka or two in his sitting room, the conversation became animated, and I asked him how soon it would be before his Church would have women priests. He threw up his hands and said, "Never! Never! Never!" As we adjourned for lunch, he apologized for the austere Lenten fare, which turned out to consist of caviar, several delicious fish dishes, more vodka, and three kinds of wine. I thought to myself it was lucky this was not Eastertide. During lunch, I asked him if he had problems in being controlled by the state. "Oh, no," he said with a straight face, "we are free to discuss anything except politics and economics. There is nothing different now. The Church has been part of the State for over a thousand years."

That Sunday was our Easter, their Palm Sunday, and we attended Mass at the cathedral. We were escorted behind the iconostasis to pay our respects to the Patriarch, who sat on an elaborate throne in gleaming cope and miter with a flowing white beard. The cathedral itself was packed with worshippers, who, since there are no palms in Moscow, held bouquets of pussy willows with crocuses in the center. Our KGB guard that day was a tough-looking fellow, resembling Khrushchev. When the priest handed him the pussy-willow bouquet, I saw the blood rush up the back of his neck, either in terror or embarrassment. When the holy water was sprinkled on us, he ducked and snorted and sneezed at the incense. He told us afterward that he had never been to church before but that his grandmother would be pleased.

Our last conversation with Arbatov reached the heart of the matter. We agreed that the lack of trust between our nations was the most difficult and threatening element in our relations and that, as a result, the launch-on-warning missiles were particularly dangerous.

We were given a rousing farewell dinner with much champagne. Mr. Arbatov was voluble, as were most of us. Madame Kruglova arrived in a smashing floor-length purple gown; she was not amused when I told her she looked like a bishop.

Since we had begun developing a relationship, both sides enthusiastically accepted Mayor Fraser's invitation to meet again in Minneapolis a year hence. There we greeted one another like old friends. Some new members accompanied each delegation (including William Sloane Coffin, who is fluent in Russian, and Seymour Melman, the disarmament expert), but a nucleus of each previous delegation remained.

We wasted no time in bringing up the substantive issues of arms, discussing SALT II; the issue of parity (should the nuclear power of the Europeans plus the United States be the measure, or should the Europeans be left out of the equation?); the problem of weighing submarines against missiles against bombers; and the doctrine of mutual assured destruction, nicknamed, appropriately, MAD. These were complicated and highly technical questions, but even these came down to a matter of trust: Who is being honest, who insincere? Why does the United States keep blocking, why does the USSR appear so adamant? In the end we agreed on two points: that our goal should be disarmament, not mere arms control; and that the two states should agree to no first use of nuclear weapons.

These discussions seem dusty with age now, but at the time we believed they were relevant to the survival of the human race. This was the era when Khrushchev had said he would bury us and when Reagan described Russia as the Evil Empire.

We continued to build personal relationships too. One evening, Mrs. John Pillsbury, grande dame of Minneapolis and an old friend, then in her nineties, gave a formal dinner for the Soviet leadership. On her first trip to Russia, she had had dinner with the czar, and, after sharing her horror over the way the serfs were treated, she had declared that Russia deserved a revolution. Now Georgi Arbatov responded with a toast, saying how grand it was to be with the rank and file of America. The Russian next to me murmured, "A lot of rank, but not much file."

As the conference drew to a close, Roger Wilkins summed it up: "We do not have to like each other, we only have to figure out how not to blow each other up."

I describe some of the social aspects of these conferences because I believe these may have been more important than the stilted issue-oriented discussions. Meals and toasts, dancing and joking—is it naive to think this would engender the trust our nations needed?

A MOMENT OF HOPE IN NICARAGUA

Not only was nuclear war a terrible threat in itself; the fear of Communism, manipulated by conservative political leaders, became the excuse for a militaristic, business-oriented foreign policy—in Africa, in Vietnam, even in such small and faraway places as East Timor. Nowhere was this more so than in Latin America. The more I read about our policies and actions in Nicaragua, Panama, Guatemala, and El Salvador, not to mention Chile and Grenada, the more horrified

I became. This subject arose again and again in the journals I read
and in conversations with friends. We heard of the assassination of
Archbishop Oscar Romero of El Salvador with horror and unbelief.
A friend of mine, the Reverend Edward Waldron, was serving a parish
in Panama at the time and gave me firsthand accounts of the clumsy
and brutal U.S. military action there. Another friend, the Reverend
Bill Webber, led the Witness for Peace movement, which put volunteers from the United States on the front lines with the Sandinistas
in Nicaragua. Thus, when the opportunity arose to go to Nicaragua
early in 1984, Brenda and I leaped at the chance. The trip was sponsored by the Central America Resource Center and led by its co-
director, Michael Conroy; my son George, his wife, Alice Christov,
a few Episcopal clergy, and some interested laypersons accompanied
us.

We were met at the plane in Managua by the organizers of a local
protest group, who handed me a letter: "We are hoping you will speak
at a rally in front of the United States embassy tomorrow morning at
7:30, stating your opposition to U.S. policy in Nicaragua." I was sympathetic to the group's aims but did not know much about them; and
since I had just arrived, my credibility was dubious. On the other
hand, the group needed all the help they could get. To have an
American bishop speak would improve their image. I agonized for a
few moments, then told them I would speak.

When we entered our small, run-down hotel, we noticed a large
pit being dug on the side of the patio. We asked if they were putting
in a swimming pool.

"No," they said. "That's a bomb shelter."

"Who do you think will bomb you?"

"The United States," they replied.

I felt a mixture of fear, anger, and sympathy: fear that we could be
killed either by such a bomb or by the hatred of some Nicaraguan at
a U.S. citizen; anger that the United States' actions could lead to
such a conclusion; and sympathy for the people of Managua.

Since 1856, when an American mercenary, William Walker, led
an expedition to Nicaragua, the United States had exploited and
manipulated the country's politics to benefit American investments,
especially those of the United Fruit Company. I knew this history
when I arrived, but the sight of the bomb shelter at our little hotel

moved me to act. I showed up at the U.S. embassy the next morning more than ready to speak. A small crowd was waiting outside the gate, mostly Americans who had organized themselves as a local group working for peace. I was given a bullhorn, and soon I was berating the government of the United States in another foreign land. It felt right to say that the United States was *wrong, wrong, wrong* to be arming the contras, who were trying to topple a regime dedicated to justice and in the process murdering thousands of innocent people. As in Saigon so many years before, I wanted the Nicaraguans to know that many Americans sympathized with them.

Later we called on Thomas Borge, the only surviving member of the original Sandinista junta (which had overthrown the dictator Somoza) and the most influential leader in the country, at his suburban home. A burly man dressed in fatigues and accompanied by two armed guards, he spoke of the long domination of Nicaragua by the United States and the corruption of the Somosa regime, and he told us the accomplishments of the Sandinistas in health, education, and welfare. I asked him if he was a Communist and what his attitude was toward the Church. He said, "I am not a Christian, but I have an extraordinary love for the moral principles of Christianity. If being honest, loving others, practicing generosity, not fearing the powers of this world, being loyal to the interests of the poor—if that is Christian, then I would like to be a Christian. If it means going to Sunday Mass with a coin in your pocket to put in the hand of a blind person, I don't want to be a Christian. If I have to beat my breast for sin yet consider it appropriate to oppress others, then I don't want to be a Christian. If God exists and hears prayers, he will hear the poor." He went on to say that theirs was a strange brand of Communism that encouraged the churches, encouraged a mixed economy, rejoiced in pluralism, and was setting up elections. "This must be a new kind of Marxism," he said. "We do not advertise ourselves as Marxists . . . indeed, why don't they accuse us of being Christians?" He said the revolution never could have succeeded without the support of an element of the Church and that Christian teaching had influenced its policies. Borge appeared to be a crude, Castro-like figure, despite his sympathy with the Church. However, beneath this image lurked an unusual integrity. We learned later that he had visited, in prison, the man who had murdered his wife with the express purpose of forgiving him.

With the exception of a few priests who sided with the Sandinistas, the Roman Catholic Church did not support the revolution. I tried in several different ways to secure an interview with Archbishop Obando y Bravo (or even one of his assistants) and was rather rudely put off. He had been against the revolution from the start and had attempted to influence the policy of our government. Obando's posture was visibly supported by the Vatican, and when the pope visited Nicaragua, he publicly rebuked Ernesto Cardenal and shook his finger at Miguel del Scoto, two priests who had joined the Sandinista government.

We drove into the countryside to see the work of the revolution there and attended a meeting of the board of directors of a cooperative farm, which had been taken over from one of the large landowners. On a broken-down porch, ragged farmworkers listened intently as the chairman of the board, also dressed as a peasant, explained the finances and led a discussion of policy. I thought of the boardroom at the Bankers Trust Company in New York.

One evening we were invited to sit in on the meeting of a Catholic base community, one of hundreds across Latin America that form the foundation of the liberation theology movement. I have been fascinated by this most original of theological dynamics of the century, arising, as it did, in Latin America, where the Roman Catholic Church was at its most reactionary and corrupt. The basic idea behind the movement is to return Scripture to the people and to encourage them to apply the revolutionary doctrine of freedom found there to their everyday problems. The explosive force of this simple action had the power of the Protestant Reformation. A few years after it began, the Catholic bishops of Latin America adopted the movement's "preferential option for the poor" at a historic conference in Medellín, Colombia.

Again and again throughout history, the conservative and often corrupt Church is overturned by the radical Gospel that it has forgotten: the Desert Fathers, St. Francis, the Reformation, Wesleyan-

ism, the followers of Martin Luther King, Jr. Nor did liberation
theology stop at the Mexican border: its theme of freedom from oppression has been embraced by Christian feminists, black theologians,
and gay activists.

I was excited at the prospect of witnessing a base community firsthand. The group of a dozen old women, teenagers, and seemingly
illiterate peasants sitting on folding chairs and benches was hardly
impressive, though. A Sister introduced us, then one of the women
read a passage she said had been especially selected for our benefit,
the story of David and Goliath. When she finished reading, I stood
up next to a tiny old man, who reached my waist, and said, amid
much laughter, that I understood who the Goliath was in this parable.
A discussion followed about the enormous power of the United States
in its attempt to crush this small, weak nation, where the people had
risen up after years of oppression, dictated by the commercial interests
of the United States, and now were trying to rebuild their country in
their own way. It was excruciating for us to hear. All we could do
was say "Amen!"

I write these lines with some sadness, because in the years since
that visit many of the people once involved in the revolution have
become disillusioned and others have become corrupt. That spirit of
hope and promise is lost. Was the smashing of the country by the
United States responsible, or was this loss the result of human
weakness?

Not surprisingly, for me the most telling of all our experiences was a
Eucharist in the church of Father Uriel Molina, a priest in Nicaragua.
He had joined the Franciscans, studied in Rome, and returned to his
native Nicaragua to embark on a conventional ministry. His beloved
nephew, an early young Sandinista revolutionary, had been castrated
and had his eyes gouged out and his corpse dragged through the streets
of Managua. In response, this priest had become a leader of the liberation forces. His church was an octagonal building, the walls of
which bore murals of the history of Nicaragua from the Mayans to
the revolution. At the offering of the gifts—the collection and the
bread and wine—a dozen teenagers came forward, then a middle-aged
couple. Father Molina gave the couple a red-velvet cushion on which

had been placed a pair of old army boots. These belonged to a young man who had been killed in the war—the son of the couple, a friend of the young people. Carrying the cushion, the mother and father and friends solemnly processed around the church behind a cross, candles, and the bread and wine. There was something heart wrenching about those wrinkled boots; the young man who had worn them had been killed by the contras. Hanging my head in penance and shame, I heard Father Molina give the peace and was immediately surrounded by Nicaraguans wishing me peace and embracing me, me whose country was responsible for their friend's death. The Liturgy closed with a foot-stomping, militant, patriotic song.

I must say I had very mixed feelings about that service, having been immersed in patriotic and military emotions in the Marines and having seen the havoc the mixture of religion and nationalism has caused around the world and is presently causing in our country at the hands of the so-called Christian Coalition. And yet I saw at that Eucharist the chemistry of redemption again. The horrible death of Father Molina's nephew had in a sense converted the priest when he heard the cry for justice as a cry from God. This changed him into a man who could lead in the struggle and yet preserve the love of God within it.

Now, many years later, the United States, so self-righteous in sending millions of dollars of military aid to the contras in order to "save democracy," is avoiding any major commitment to rebuilding the fragile structures of the government presently in place.

I returned to New York more convinced than ever that our foreign policy was corrupt. Could intelligent men and women in the State Department really believe that the Sandinistas posed a Communist threat to the security of our country? If voting Americans could have visited this small place, they certainly would not have wanted to see their taxes used to fund the murders of women and children.

YALE GOES TO SOUTH AFRICA

In the early 1980s, while I was serving on the Yale Corporation, students who were supporting the antiapartheid movement in South Africa put pressure on nonprofit and government institutions to divest their holdings in any corporation that did business there. This student concern went back to 1968. Yale was in a classic bind between its financial interests and its ethical principles. By this time Bart Giamatti was president. He was brilliant, attractive, witty, and, on this issue at least, stubborn: when the students flouted university regulations and built a shanty in imitation of the housing of South Africa's poor just outside the president's office, Giamatti had it torn down. After many meetings, the corporation established a policy that it would disinvest any holdings of a corporation that did business with the oppressive government itself. The student movement insisted on complete disinvestment, and I agreed, because this was the stand of the African National Congress (ANC) and the antiapartheid clergy like Bishop Desmond Tutu, whom I knew from the Lambeth conference. That was the only time I publicly took a stand against the position of the corporation, since I had already stated my position in other contexts and because I felt strongly that Yale was being morally timid in the face of pressure from the financial community. (The corporation did show courage in disinvesting its stock in J. P. Morgan, many of whose senior officers were prominent Yale alumni. Giamatti was deluged with letters. How could we impugn the ethics of a firm whose officers had supported Yale so generously over the years?)

Still, feeling he had to address the students' concerns further, Giamatti organized a fact-finding expedition of trustees to South Africa chaired by Cyrus Vance. Were U.S. corporations keeping to the Sullivan principles, which outlined equitable policies for businesses there? How much economic harm would their withdrawal visit on the poor of the country? Was there anything constructive that Yale could do to assist the black and colored populations?

Our delegation of twelve stayed in a comfortable hotel in Johannesburg, sallying forth each day at seven in the morning and returning exhausted at about eleven at night. We wished to see university faculty and students, clergy, and business, union, and other significant leaders. Although we were there only a week, we interviewed 275 people and dipped deeply into the mood of South Africa and the views of almost all classes of people.

My first visit was to the University of Witwatersrand. The student body was 16 percent black, the faculty and administrative staff only slightly integrated. The administrators earnestly would tell us how hard they were trying to help the black students, who arrived on campus with no books, no money, and only the rudiments of primary and secondary education. Many would rise as early as two-thirty to catch a bus to school. Sometimes they slept on benches rather than go home at night. Yet peaceful student protests were met by the police with hoses, tear gas, arrests, even torture, and the university authorities were helpless to prevent such incursions.

Later that week, we visited a settlement house in Soweto, a black suburb of Johannesburg, and were told of a boycott on the part of schoolchildren that had turned the already beleaguered school system into chaos. One had the impression of a stormy sea in which a few lifeboats were trying to keep afloat while an SOS was broadcast to the world.

When we visited corporate headquarters—including those of Coca-Cola, Du Pont, Eastman Kodak, Exxon, and General Motors—the managers were generally defensive. In one meeting, we sat stiffly as a top manager told us how hard it was to follow the Sullivan principles but emphasized that labor-management relations were good. When he turned to two black employees, they nodded their heads. After the meeting, we asked to see the black employees alone. When the doors were closed, they told a different story.

The fact that one member of our delegation, Cyrus Vance, had been on the board of IBM assured us a warm welcome from its managers. They said that the sooner conditions improved in South Africa, the better it would be for business and spoke of plans to put computers in poor schools. Outside their posh conference room, though, vast slag heaps towered like misbegotten pyramids over the modern city. All of a sudden we heard a loud explosion, and the building trembled. We rushed to the window, saw nothing, and returned to our seats. After the meeting, we were told a bomb had been set off outside the building.

In the evenings and at lunch, we were entertained by businessmen and met other community leaders, black and white. The conversation was always polite—too polite, it seemed to me. At one luncheon, a Dr. Tjaart Vander Walt was present. He was a Dutch Reformed theologian and one of the major ideologues of the apartheid movement. He was complaining of the difficulty he had with black leaders and that communication was uncomfortable. I exploded and said that no one could be polite to representatives of a group that murdered their children. Dead silence. The subject was changed.

At the heart of these encounters lay the basic conflict that had plagued me over the years: the polite, smooth talk and assurances of sympathy for the poor, which seemed to ignore the great gulf between them and those in power. The situation in South Africa highlighted the problem that underlies capitalism from New York to Indonesia.

While the rest of the Yale delegation went to Capetown, I stayed in Johannesburg to see Bishop Tutu and to preach at St. Paul's, Soweto. I had come to know Desmond at the international meeting of Anglican bishops at Lambeth. His stature, his holiness, and his irrepressible humor won him a position of leadership. One evening, he came to dinner with us in New York with his wife, Leah, and two of their daughters, who teased their father: "Daddy, why do you always preach about the same thing? Justice, peace, reconciliation—boring, boring, boring." Then two of my daughters took up the chorus against me. Desmond was delighted.

Desmond picked me up early Saturday morning in a bright, shiny red car, very nearly the color of his shirt, and we set off on his round of pastoral visits. You could tell you were entering Soweto, or any other black township for that matter, by the cloud of smoke lying over the thousands of matchbox-like houses. Our first stop was at Winnie Mandela's home, which was surrounded by a high, brown clay wall, topped with barbed wire. Ms. Mandela's warm, smiling face and simple dress were not what I had expected, given her imprisoned husband's dangerous legacy. I remarked on her seeming happiness, to which Desmond replied, "You can't cry every day."

In the next township, we called on his archdeacon, recently released from custody. As we visited and watched the children eat their cornflakes, we heard the thunderous noise of a diesel engine; the police had spotted the red car and ordered a monstrous troop carrier to pull up outside the rectory. It remained, engine running, until we left. When Desmond emerged, he was mobbed by laughing children, glad to see their beloved bishop. It was so bizarre to see such military force sent after a tiny clergyman surrounded by children. As it turned out, his power was the stronger.

Before the day was over, we had visited the wife of an imprisoned bishop in her bombed-out rectory, talked with a handsome young curate who had been imprisoned for holding a young people's meeting, and read Evening Prayer by candlelight in a little church where the electric power had been cut off. As we prayed, I could see the children in the dusk, playing as best they could on a dump next door. The words of the Magnificat rang out: "He has put down the mighty from their seat and has exalted the humble and meek." Bishop Desmond Tutu knew how to love his people, and they responded that day; wherever we went, strangers waved at that familiar face.

However, the bishop was not always calm. On the occasion of our formal meeting with him, he took Cy Vance to task for asking questions that seemed to him obvious. "I get so fed up," he said, "with delegation after delegation that insists on seeing me, takes up much of my time, asks questions the answers to which I have given time and again, and leaves without any benefit to us when they return home." The former Secretary of State was not used to being lectured to like that. I saw the back of his neck redden. He kept his temper, but the meeting was concluded before long.

The next day I preached at St. Paul's, Soweto. Hundreds of children giggled as we acted out the parable of the lost sheep, and I spoke about the civil rights movement and its similarities to the antiapartheid movement in South Africa. (The translator had a hard time with the word "Mississippi," and whatever he said brought down the house.) Wonderful singing welled up spontaneously during Communion and sounded like a cross between plainsong and Negro spirituals—an apt combination, I thought.

On the way home, Cy Vance, Leon Lipsom, and I stopped in Zambia to confer with leaders of the African National Congress in exile. A most impressive group of mainly young men and women they were. When asked whether any Communists were members of the ANC, they simply answered that whoever was with them was their ally. They had sharp words for Chief Buthelezi and his organization, Inkatha, whom they believed to be agents provocateurs behind many of the uprisings for which the ANC was blamed.

That evening, Kenneth Kaunda, president of Zambia, gave a dinner in honor of Cy Vance at the presidential palace, the former governor general's residence. We drove down an impressive allée and were ushered into the palace by two immaculately turned out guards. There, in the front hall, was a lion. I stepped back and felt foolish. It was stuffed. Before the banquet, we had a long conversation with the president as we sipped iced tea on the pillared porch. Antelopes nibbled the grass in front of us; monkeys and parrots chattered in the trees. Beyond them stretched the president's private golf course. Kaunda's comments, however, were far from reassuring. He told us that he expected South Africa to blow up and that, if it did, the whole of southern Africa would explode in a racial war. He was a person of great dignity, wisdom, and charm, the dean of African leaders, and we took his words most seriously.

On our return, we gave a press conference and stated that we still did not agree on divestment. In fact, none of the delegation changed position, and Yale continued its policy of divesting only those corporations dealing directly with the government of South Africa. On balance, however, I believe the trip was worthwhile, one more small pressure on the government to change.

As I write this today, it seems miraculous that South Africa has rid itself of apartheid with comparatively little bloodshed.

THE CATHEDRAL

IN Europe, two styles of cathedrals were built in the Middle Ages: the one, typical of the British Isles, was set apart on a hill or in the midst of a large close, complete with lawns and gardens; the other, typical of the Continent, was placed in the very center of the city, where all the activities of society could take place, from mothers nursing their babies, to political rallies, to celebrations of the great holidays. One represented a theology that situated God apart from life, to be reached in quiet meditation; the other suggested that God is in the very center of the hustle and bustle, the joys and tragedies, the filth and beauty of the everyday. The National Cathedral in Washington typifies the former, the Cathedral of St. John the Divine in New York the latter.

When I came to New York and looked out the window at that massive pile of stone, I wondered if it would be possible to give life to the world's largest cathedral in the modern metropolis of New York. The cathedral, despite its glorious history, had become quiescent, except for a regular liturgical life under the inimitable leadership of Canon Edward West, the acting dean; some groundbreaking conferences set up by Canon (later Bishop) Walter Dennis; a boys' choir school; and occasional, great special services, such as the first performance of Duke Ellington's jazz Mass. When I asked for advice as to what to do with that big pile of stone, my friend Bob Potter said, only half jokingly, "Sell it." Even the building itself was in trouble: a recent engineering study declared that the central dome was unsafe and would have to be rebuilt. This would have wiped out whatever endowment was left. We faced a genuine crisis. I needed a most un-

usual dean to give leadership to this venture. I needed someone with
the competence to be the steward of a great architectural monument,
someone who cared passionately about the city and who shared my
liberal, Catholic theology. Most important, I needed someone of great
energy and courage.

The first and only person who came to mind was James Parks Morton. Jim had studied for a career in architecture at Harvard. On a
visit to Cambridge in the early 1950s, I met him and had something
to do with his changing course to the priesthood. After seminary, he
joined our team in Jersey City. He and his wife, Pamela Taylor, lived
and worked with us for five years. Jim went on to run the national
urban program of the Episcopal Church and an ecumenical urban
training center in Chicago. He was known to take risks, sometimes
at the expense of sound financing.

In 1972, at my suggestion, Bishop Horace Donegan nominated Jim
to the trustees to be dean of the cathedral, and he was confirmed
with great enthusiasm. This was the most important appointment I
have ever made, for under Jim's brilliant (if sometimes chaotic) leadership, the cathedral has become one of the great religious institutions
in the world.

As the Eucharist spells out in liturgy the heart of the Christian
faith, so, in its way, the Cathedral of St. John the Divine spells out
that same faith in action: in its acceptance of all peoples; in its involvement in every aspect of the city; in its seamless life of worship,
education, social action, and in the pastoral ministry of compassion.

Come and stand on the northwest corner of Central Park and look
at it. Its great bulk towers on the cliff of Morningside Heights. It
watches over the deep poverty of Harlem, can be seen from the
gleaming skyscrapers of midtown. Behind it stand the institutions of
the Heights: Columbia University, Barnard College, the Jewish Theological Seminary, Union Theological Seminary, Riverside Church,
St. Luke's Hospital, the Bank Street School, the convent and school
of the Community of the Holy Spirit (an order of Episcopal nuns).
Although some New Yorkers think of the location as too far uptown
and wish the cathedral were in midtown, the trustees chose the site
so that the cathedral would be near what they thought would be the
intellectual center of New York, a modern Acropolis. As the city
developed, however, its location on the edge of Harlem became a

different blessing and shaped the kind of place the cathedral was to become, a spiritual home for all the people of New York and a sign of hope for the poor.

When you approach the cathedral, you will notice scaffolding on the south side of the facade. Strangely enough, the most publicized activity of the cathedral has been the work on the unfinished towers. During the financial crises of the 1970s, when the people of the city were losing the confidence, even the arrogance, that has always been the mark of a genuine New Yorker, Jim Morton decided it was time to finish those towers. The nave had been dedicated on the Sunday before Pearl Harbor, and no new stone had been laid since that time. During the urban crises of the 1960s, Bishop Donegan declared (rightly I think) that no more building would occur until the conditions of the city improved. For this reason, I was initially against Jim's idea. But one of his great qualities is stubbornness. Instead of setting aside his plan, he sought to combine work on the towers with works of social purpose that would remove the stigma of spending money on bricks and mortar when so much poverty surrounded us.

Within a year, men and women from the city began training as stonemasons. People were excited by the idea, and money was raised. The image of minority youths being trained by an old English artisan who had last worked on the facade of the Liverpool cathedral was appealing. Furthermore, we declared the project a sign of hope for the city, especially uptown Manhattan. One day an old taxi driver told me, "I remember when I was a kid during the Depression and the cathedral was being constructed, my dad told me that as long as Big John was a-building there was hope for our town."

One of the first apprentices was a former Hispanic gang leader whom we had met through the urban homesteading project. Another was a young black woman who became, as far as we know, the first female stonemason. This training was not just a romantic notion; the ability to work with stone had become more and more valuable as the restoration movement gained momentum in the cities of America. And so, slowly, stone by stone, the cathedral continues to rise, and lives rise with it.

Come up the stone steps and stand before the great bronze doors depicting scenes from the Bible. On each side of them, stern sculptures of Old Testament prophets guard the entrance. Their words of justice and peace often sound forth from the pulpit. Each Easter, dressed in a gold cope and miter, the bishop knocks on the doors with his ornate crosier, and as the doors swing open he cries, "He is risen! Alleluia!" And thousands of voices reply: "The Lord is risen indeed! Alleluia!"

One Easter Sunday in the early 1970s, I was picketed by three groups: one claiming that our choir was not integrated, even as it filed past with several black members; another that we were being unfair to the squatters across the street, even though we had provided them with a furnace; and a third that somehow I was keeping a local settlement house (over which I had no jurisdiction) from being run by the local residents. Being picketed from the left was especially painful—my right side was tough, my left sensitive.

When the doors of the cathedral open and your eyes become accustomed to the gloom, you immediately are confronted on one side by a larger-than-life cross, where hangs a strong and suffering Christ, and red vigil lights burning. Directly in front of you is an iconostasis on which glisten images of Christ the King, Mary Theotokos (God bearer), and other icons of saints revered by the Orthodox. Both Dean Morton and Canon West were deeply influenced by Orthodox spirituality. Thus, as you enter, you see the great symbols of Catholic Christianity East and West, the icons and the crucifix.

When you look up through the opening in the iconostasis, the largest Gothic nave in Christendom stretches before you; your eyes pass beyond this nave and the chancel to the distant high altar, the heart and soul of the place.

The original architects of the cathedral, George L. Heins and Christopher Grant La Farge, designed the sanctuary and choir in Romanesque and Byzantine style, but a later bishop decided the nave should be Gothic. Ralph Adams Cram, the architect who took over the work in 1911, declared it his greatest work. Between the nave and chancel, the unfinished crossing with its huge, round Roman arches of unfinished blocks of stone lends the building a crude strength reminiscent of Durham Cathedral in England. I rejoice in the unfinishedness of the central space, for it symbolizes the restless unfinished city that surrounds it and is an appropriate setting for the variety of productions, some secular, others from different faiths, that are part of the cathedral's life.

As you walk through the opening in the center of the iconostasis, you see on your right an altar made from an enormous, handsome slab of walnut designed by the Japanese-American artist Isamu Noguchi and dedicated to peace. In recent years, peace has been a major concern of our life here. On the afternoon before the great march for peace at the time of the freeze movement, on June 11, 1982, the cathedral was filled with several thousand people, representing every faith imaginable: the Hiroshima maidens (still bearing the scars of the atomic bomb) were there, as were Japanese Buddhist monks, Hindu holy men, rabbis, bishops from the Anglican, Orthodox, Methodist, Lutheran, and Roman Churches, leaders of the black churches, and an ancient Native American chief intoning an eerie chant for peace. There were orphans of war from all over the world who spoke of their loneliness and terror. As each person prayed, it was as if the whole world were screaming to the one god of all to help us cease the murder and horror of war and protect us from atomic annihilation. Never have I felt so proud of that dear place.

Behind the peace altar, on a pillar, is a small bronze bas-relief depicting a dramatic moment in the fall of 1978 during the struggle for women's ordination. Several women in the diocese had been made deacons but were not yet allowed to be ordained to the priesthood. They wished to demonstrate at the service in which the male deacons were to receive priests' orders. I was happy to have them do so, and Eddie West, with his customary aplomb, arranged the demonstration with liturgical dignity. I was seated in my chair, having just ordained the men, when the women came forward and knelt before me. I so wanted to ordain them that I could hardly keep my hands from going forward to touch their heads. Since canon law prevented me, I felt as if my hands were literally tied behind my back. The bronze, sculpted by Florence Dykstra Karns, depicts that symbolic moment.

Across from the altar of peace stands a large cross depicting the agony of the people of Nicaragua, created by a Nicaraguan cartoonist and billboard artist, Carlos Sanchez Arrias, known as "Kalo." The corpus is a woman. At its center a blade pierces the figure, and the blade is adorned by the Stars and Stripes. My son George, an artist, had lived in Nicaragua and arranged for the cross to be lent to the cathedral. When I visited Nicaragua, I became a friend of Miguel del Scoto, a priest who was the foreign minister of the Sandinista regime and had carried this huge cross on his back in a pilgrimage of peace.

On either side of the nave are bays commemorating aspects of the life of the Church, each with its own window. The stained glass shows doctors, nurses, lawyers, sportsmen, soldiers, athletes, artists, architects, authors, and so on. From its very start this great building has recognized the vocation of the laity, and Canon William A. Johnson's Institute of Theology, located at the cathedral for many years, has provided lay persons with superior theological education.

The acquisition of one window provides an amusing lesson in the importance of good manners. One day, Canon Jonathan King was giving a guided tour to some tourists. As he was describing the stained glass, a rather badly dressed tourist in a Harry Truman–style tropical shirt asked, "How much does a window like that cost?"

"Thousands of dollars."

"If I wanted to give one, who should I write?"

The other tourists giggled but not the canon. He politely gave the gentleman the dean's address. The call was made. The dean flew to Miami with a sketch of the only remaining uncompleted window under his arm, nervous that the old gentleman would not want to give a window honoring sportsmen. The dean was ushered into a palatial front hall, adorned with the heads of elk and antelope, a lion's skin, and other mementos. The donor was a retired colonel; the cathedral was given a window and a bequest of a million dollars when he died.

The windows are permanent, of course, but some of the bays depict contemporary subjects. The first bay on the right memorializes the suffering of the Holocaust with a sculpture of a corpse twisted in an agony of death. In the next bay stands a huge cross of burned timbers, constructed by Ralph Felman with Engine 37 and Ladder 40 in Harlem; at its base lie a fireman's helmet and glove. This is a memorial to the twelve firemen who died in the most costly fire in the history of the city.

Underneath the window depicting the medical profession is the AIDS memorial, a book in which one can have the name of a person who has died of AIDS written in handsome script. Several thousand names are now inscribed there. Red vigil lights flicker in front of the book, lit by those who offer prayers for their departed lovers, friends, and relatives. I will never forget the dedication of this shrine, No-

vember 5, 1985, early on in the epidemic when so much shame and
fear was attached to the disease that it was often hard for families or
friends to find an undertaker or a church to hold a funeral. This shrine
was to symbolize God's love for those who had died and to lend them
in death the dignity they had been deprived of in their dying. The
evening of the dedication the names of those who had died of AIDS
were solemnly recited, each echoing through the darkened Gothic
arches as if up to heaven: John, Harry, Bruce, Mills, Matthew . . . At
the conclusion, members of the congregation came forward for a blessing. We clergy laid hands on them, one after the other. I remember
whispered requests that I pray for Ralph or Daniel; tearful words that
the person himself had AIDS but had not dared tell his family, who
did not know he was gay. One man sought absolution for the guilt
he felt; another stood up after the blessing and said, "Please hug me."
He just wanted me to hold his shaking body. This service has become
an annual, and now an interfaith, event. Giving the blessing of dignity and love to those involved in this epidemic is the most important
thing we can do for the thousands of people, mostly young, who feel
rejected even by God at the moment when they most need love.

Nor was the tragedy of AIDS something happening outside the
diocesan family. Early on in the epidemic, one of our clergy, Mills
Omaly, told me, in the strictest confidence, that he was HIV positive
and that he already was having symptoms of AIDS. He was a splendid
priest and had just been called to a new parish, where, he said, he
was happier than he had ever been in his life. He and I agonized over
when he should tell his people. Mills courageously took the matter
into his own hands. A couple of months after our conversation, the
annual diocesan convention took place. A resolution urging compassion and support for people with AIDS was presented. I saw Mills
approach the microphone; my heart sank. Being a quiet person, he
had never spoken at the convention before. I was anxious, because
the diocese had only recently calmed down after the uproar of my
ordaining a lesbian to the priesthood. Mills spoke powerfully to the
resolution, paused, and said, "I am especially moved by this resolution,
because I have AIDS." The convention was stunned. Finally, someone arose and began to clap. Then another and another, until the
whole convention gave him a standing ovation, surrounding him,
hugging him, with tears streaming down their faces. Love had over-

come fear and hostility. Our anger and pain over homosexuality had been redeemed. Mills died a year later, but in that moment in convention he knew he was loved. He was buried out of the cathedral.

Several years ago, I was visiting the AIDS ward at St. Luke's Hospital. The chaplain said he was particularly glad to see me, because the most beloved person on the ward had just died. She was a middle-aged black woman whose faith, humor, and good cheer had kept up the spirits of the other patients, most of whom were gay white men. This wonderful chemistry had created a spirit of hope there, where pain and agony and the near hovering of death would have meant despair. I stopped to see the patients and prayed with them. Some were in tears, others yearning for a prayer and blessing. Some wanted me to hold them for a few moments. When I had finished the rounds, I was exhausted but also strangely exhilarated. The Lord had been present in each room. I was talking with the chaplain and one of our sisters, when a man came running down the hall from the elevator, his raincoat flapping, his hair a wild tangle. He threw himself into the chaplain's arms, sobbing uncontrollably. As they withdrew into a nearby sitting room, where the man could cry himself out, I turned to the sister and asked, "How can you bear up under this strain day after day and week after week?"

She smiled and said, "This is the closest I have ever been to the Kingdom of God." She dwelt in the heavenly city of love, faith, and hope in a place where there could have been nothing but darkness.

When AIDS first became a public controversy, we organized an interfaith press conference to declare that AIDS was *not* God's judgment on homosexuality, as some conservative ministers had pronounced. As a result of the publicity attending this effort, Governor Mario Cuomo appointed me chairman of the first advisory council on AIDS.

The next bay after the AIDS memorial celebrates the ecological movement. A great bronze wolf, sculpted by a member of the cathedral family, Kappy Jo Welles, stands guard, as it were, for endangered species, and a huge fossil seashell is there as a reminder of our stewardship of the ocean. Jim Morton was one of the first people to bring the Church's attention to ecology as a theological issue: he chaired a conference on the subject in Moscow whose panelists included the Dalai Lama, Mikhail Gorbachev, and Mother Teresa, among others.

Many of the great leaders of the movement, such as Carl Sagan and René Dubos, have preached from the cathedral pulpit.

As you reach the crossing, you will see a plaque dedicated by the Queen Mother, a friend of Bishop Donegan's, to commemorate her visit on October 31, 1954.

Pause now at the crossing and look back at the deep blue of one of the most glorious rose windows in Christendom. In its center is depicted a life-size Christ, who looks tiny in the context of this great circle. Then turn and see the blazing red of the east window, which incorporates images from the book of Revelation, whose author is now honored in the name of the Cathedral of St. John the Divine.

Underneath this window is the high altar, on either side of which stand two menorahs, given in gratitude by Arthur Ochs, the publisher of *The New York Times*, for work by Bishop William T. Manning in behalf of the Jewish community. Beyond them, two majestic blue vases, from Emperor Hirohito of Japan, adorn the retable. Benito Mussolini gave two silver candlesticks by the bishop's throne. We are proud of these gifts from the people of Japan and Italy, despite what their leaders later did. President Edvard Beneš of Czechoslovakia donated a crystal chandelier that hangs nearby in the ambulatory, and President Kemal Atatürk of Turkey gave the rug that leads up to the high altar.

The crossing is the largest of any Gothic cathedral in the world and has been the setting for many great moments over the years. Up the long aisle to the crossing comes the procession of the beasts on St. Francis's Day for the Blessing of the Animals: a horse, a camel, a bowl of algae, a golden eagle, a parrot, a python, and an elephant (followed, of course, by two people with shovels). We thank God for these animals and bless them as they lumber into the sanctuary, for in New York, animals grace lonely lives and provide creature companionship to children who long for nature. I remember putting my little finger into the hole of a small cardboard box to bless Jeremy, a white mouse.

Here, during an especially tense time in the Middle East, came the mayors of two towns in Palestine. They had been staging a hunger strike at the United Nations and had told the secretary-general that they would break their fast only if they could do so in a religious setting. He called Dean Morton, who drove down to the UN in his vestments and brought them to the Christmas midnight Mass. When the time came for the kiss of peace, a rabbi (whom we had invited to chant the Old Testament lesson from Isaiah) met them, and they embraced.

There, in the crossing, I was ordained a deacon in the Church of God in 1949. And there, over the years, the bodies of the great and humble have been brought for a last farewell. Some of these services were memorable. The liturgy for Jim Henson, the beloved creator of the Muppets, included Big Bird and Kermit the Frog singing "It's Not Easy Being Green."

It was there that I conducted a memorial service for John Belushi, whom I had come to know on Martha's Vineyard. In his beach house one afternoon, he taught me three chords on a guitar and drafted Brenda to sing. John led us in an hour of riotous rock and roll. He had always hated the *Saturday Night Live* skit in which he and Dan Aykroyd dressed up as bumblebees. The two of them had a pact that whoever survived the other would dance it at his funeral. So Dan did the bumblebee dance in the crossing. I fantasized, in my homily, that John was playing his electric guitar with the heavenly harpists. There were those who disapproved of our having a service for him, because he died of a drug overdose. But John had had a warm heart and had brought joy and laughter to millions.

On Thanksgiving Day, Native Americans and their culture are honored in the crossing. (The Pilgrims take a back bench.) And on Good Friday the Passion of Christ is acted out in solemn beauty. Plays and dances are performed here; even the whirling dervishes have offered their liturgy of dance in this space. Here then, truly, is the crossing of the sacred and the profane, the holy and the broken. Here the Incarnation of Christ in the world is displayed for all to see.

Climb the steps into the chancel and behold, towering above you on either side, the great granite columns that support the arching ceiling, each weighing 130 tons. High on the right is the console of one of the great organs of the world, which has resounded with the classics of the ages—and jazz, too.

One windy day in March, I took my grandchildren on a tour of the mysterious upper regions of the cathedral, climbing an endless, circular stone stairway that begins at the entrance to the chancel. We eventually came out on a balcony overlooking the nave. Far below,

I spied a gaggle of tourists and could not resist the temptation of bellowing down at them in my most thunderous voice: "God is looking at you!"

In the clerestory, we went past the studio of Philippe Petit, the acrobat who walked on a wire between the Twin Towers of the World Trade Center. When we laid the cornerstone for the new east tower, Philippe danced across Amsterdam Avenue ten stories in the air: he stood in the sunshine on the roof of the old people's home, dressed in gleaming white knickers, purple socks, and a purple sash, and flashed the silver trowel used to lay the original cornerstone of the cathedral. Halfway across, to everyone's horror, he genuflected and proceeded to the parapet of the cathedral. There, he presented me with the trowel to lay the cornerstone of the new tower, which I did, my cope billowing behind me in the high wind.

I took the grandchildren to the very top that day and discovered that above the false ceiling of the nave is a roof. Between the ceiling and the roof is an enormous barnlike space, where scores of pigeons fly back and forth to their nests. The greatest thrill of all that afternoon, however, was stepping outside and seeing the whole city of New York spread before us.

There is an ambulatory around the back of the chancel and sanctuary, along which are set the Chapels of the Tongues. The first architects carried out in this way the theme that the cathedral was for all the people of New York, by having each ethnic group then living in the city represented with a chapel designed in the architecture of its native land and named for its patron saint: St. James for the Spanish, St. Martin for the French, and so forth. I particularly love St. Martin's, where the Sacrament is reserved for private prayer. Here, every other week, I celebrated the Eucharist for the diocesan staff before we came together to plan our work, and I believe these gatherings were one of the reasons we remained a relatively dedicated and happy group. It is hard to maintain a hostile attitude to one with whom you have just exchanged the kiss of peace. I have been blessed, over the years, with a loyal and creative staff; our meetings are fully helpful discussions, with mutual support and much laughter.

Moving behind the high altar and along the north side of the chancel, you come upon the baptistery, a small, high-vaulted octagonal space of exquisite Gothic design. On one side, is the columbarium, where ashes are placed with dignity and grace. I baptized my granddaughter Indiana in this font and laid to rest some dear friends in the columbarium. Here is the beginning and the end of a Christian's earthly life.

The ambulatory and the north wall of the crossing are appropriate places for art exhibits. The most widely publicized celebrated Christian women and their contribution to the life of the Church down through the ages. One sculptor, Edwina Sands, a granddaughter of Winston Churchill, depicted a woman on a cross—an attempt to show that God took on the flesh of women as well as men in becoming incarnate and that women as well as men have borne the suffering of the cross down through the ages. Inevitably, the exhibit, opening in Holy Week, caught the attention of the media, some of which incorrectly stated that the female crucifix was on the high altar. On Easter afternoon, I left New York for a Trappist monastery for a retreat. Well, at breakfast Monday morning a monk put the local paper in front of me; on the front page there was a photograph of the sculpture, and the article said both my suffragan bishops had condemned it as heretical. I was both bemused that so many people failed to get the point and angry that my two suffragans had made statements without notifying me. As with most controversies, it provided a fine moment to elaborate on the Incarnation, as well as on the suffering of women, and the equality of the ministry of women in the Church. (In general, over the years the two suffragan bishops have been most supportive. Bishop Stuart Wetmore has taken on difficult administrative tasks and persevered year in and year out with pastoral care for failing clergy. Bishop Walter Dennis has insisted on the rights of the clergy and has sponsored conferences on controversial subjects. Only very occasionally did we have differences.)

Before leaving the east end of the cathedral, I want you to visualize what it was like to stand behind the high altar, looking out over the faces of thousands of people, and realize that their hopes, their fears, their joys, their pains had been set forth on the altar and that in lifting up the bread and wine you were offering their lives to Almighty God. Sometimes celebrating the Eucharist there was so

intense an experience that I could hardly utter the words of consecration.

There were other great moments in the sanctuary, such as the
Maundy Thursday service, commemorating the Last Supper, when
Christ washed his disciples' feet. The congregation acted this out by
coming forward and giving their hands to be washed—the small and
timid hands of children, the wrinkled fragile hands of old women,
the calloused hands of manual workers; black hands, Asian hands;
the caring hands of doctors and nurses, the hands of priests.

After the austerity of Good Friday came the Easter Eve service of
baptism and confirmation, when as many as fifty people were baptized
before the altar amid the joy of the first Eucharist of Easter. Sometimes more water splashed on me than on those being baptized, since
we dealt with lively, squirming children. But I was always deeply
moved by the adults who came forward, often shaking with emotion,
and bent over the font, presenting their gray hair to be wet in the
waters of baptism, presenting their wrinkles to be born again. The
ceremony was always a bit chaotic, but the very chaos gave a vitality
to the wonder that was occurring. After the baptisms, I would move
to my chair in front of the altar and lay hands on many more in the
rite of the gift of the Spirit in confirmation.

We walk down from the altar through the chancel and back to the
crossing, where, on the north side, stands the great marble pulpit from
which is preached the Word of God. At ordination, a priest vows to
preach the Word of God, and theological education is meant to assure
the people, as far as humanly possible, that what they hear is within
the teaching of the Church. No such assurance is present when a
layperson speaks, but both the dean and I feel strongly that there are
laypersons whose words we need to hear—whose words represent
God's presence in the world. Thus we had secretaries-general of the
UN, Vice President Al Gore, Leonard Bernstein, Marian Wright Ed-
elman of the Children's Defense Fund, and many others speaking
from their heart of the hurts and dangers surrounding God's people.

We also invited religious leaders of other faiths. I remember particularly the first time the Dalai Lama came to speak of the sufferings

of the people of Tibet. He is humble and whimsical, a holy and courageous man. Someone must have told him that in America every speech begins with a joke. And so he started off by speaking of a frustration he had experienced. He said, "I was like a man who buys a beautiful car from a dealer and on the way home it stops and he cannot fix it. It makes him throw up!" After a moment's silence, the congregation laughed nervously. No one could believe that this holy man would tell such a silly joke, but you know, it made his later remarks the more believable and profound. He did not exalt himself but was earthy and spoke to us as a humble person.

On another occasion, Jesse Jackson preached on the subject of homelessness, preceding a great rally and march starting at Columbus Circle. Housing has been a subject very close to me since 1950, when I became chairman of the Jersey City NAACP committee on housing. We were concerned with poor conditions and overcrowding, but widespread homelessness did not exist then. Homeless people came to us only once in a while—chronic alcoholics or families left on the street after a fire. By the time I was made Bishop of New York, however, the numbers of homeless had grown, and as the federal government cut back its funds for housing and the state emptied its mental hospitals without providing shelter for the discharged patients, the problem grew worse and worse. I once tried to start a movement to include having shelter as a basic human right. Someday this may occur; until then we have to work for short-term solutions. Certainly, in this country, if you do not have an address, you are deprived of rights afforded other citizens.

Shortly after Jim Morton became dean, the cathedral began a housing initiative called the Urban Homesteading Assistance Board (UHAB), which encouraged local people to rehabilitate vacant buildings and move in. This was called "sweat equity," since their equity in the building was their work, not their cash (for they had no cash). The city cooperated with guaranteed mortgages, and our staff taught the builders about the paperwork and administration involved. Over the years, thousands have made homes for themselves in this way. I used to say to those who claimed homelessness was a complicated problem that indeed it was simple. Provide homes, as the government used to, and homelessness would disappear. The point is that the private sector cannot or will not provide houses cheap enough for those beneath the poverty line, and ever since the Reagan years, the government has held back on subsidy.

Perhaps the most publicized sermon I preached at the cathedral was in the spring of 1976, when New York was on the edge of bankruptcy. Businesses had begun leaving the city for pleasanter and cheaper headquarters in the suburbs, usually not far from where the chief executive officer lived. A couple of weeks before Easter, Jim Morton and Brenda suggested that I give a sermon on the issue. So we called Peter and Ellen Straus, native New Yorkers who owned a radio station (Ellen was one of the *New York Times* Sulzbergers), and Osborne Elliott, then the editor of *Newsweek*. They were quite surprised to be asked to help me prepare my Easter sermon. After some discussion, we decided I should state that corporations with headquarters in New York had a moral obligation to stay in the city at this time of crisis. Ellen suggested I call her aunt, Iphigene Sulzberger, who was still the power behind the throne at the *Times*, and ask her assistance in giving the story prominence. Assist she did: the Easter service was covered in a front-page spread, and the whole sermon printed in the financial section (a first, I think). In it I had said that these corporations owed their very existence to the city and to its people and that even if they moved to, say, Darien, Connecticut, they would still benefit from New York. Therefore, it was totally irresponsible of them to desert the city in a time of need, like rats scurrying away from a sinking ship. This caused a major reaction. My brother told me that his business friends began referring to one another as Brother Rat. Businessmen called me and explained why they had to leave the city. Others called to say they were staying. The question of a corporation's responsibility to its community was debated in New York and other cities. Unfortunately, the power of the bottom line has overcome such moral questioning, and businesses are once again deserting the cities that give them life.

That ornate stone pulpit was a splendid place from which to preach the Word of God, never more so than on Christmas Eve, when, in the darkness, thousands of candles twinkled, held in the hands of thousands of unknown people, each of whom had come to find God, in thanksgiving, or praise, or forgiveness, or for healing.

Going down the side aisle, we pass the white effigy of Bishop Manning, who once erected a tenement at the door of the cathedral so that all who entered were made aware of the slums of New York. Further down, you come to the Poets' Corner, where, year after year, we dedicate memorial plaques to great American authors: poets, playwrights, novelists, whether Emily Dickinson or James Baldwin.

The action of the cathedral does not stop on the steps. Underneath, in the great crypt, two basketball courts are used by the cathedral school and neighborhood children; one office runs a meal program for shut-ins, and another helps homeless people (who may be staying in our shelter) to find jobs. A counselor is kept busy finding work for young people. Several artists have studios there. In a room adjoining the building, a tapestry-repair workshop takes care of ancient, precious tapestries, including the cathedral's own collection of Mortlake tapestries designed by Raphael. An ensemble specializing in the playing of sacred music on period instruments practices in a studio next to one used by the cathedral ballet troupe.

In the cathedral house each Saturday, Canon Johnson holds classes of theology for the laity at the Institute of Theology. There, too, the Instituto Pastoral Hispano began to train Latino church persons for the ministry within the context of their own culture. In the Synod Hall, next to my office, the Big Apple Circus was born.

We have been criticized again and again by so-called orthodox Christians for hosting what they consider secular activities in God's house. Others are enraged that the Dalai Lama, who is not a Christian, has spoken from the pulpit. Images like a female crucifix deeply offend many because they are misunderstood. In my view, however, the inclusiveness of our life there is *true* catholicism. I believe we have symbolized the wounded hands of our Lord outstretched to welcome all of God's people into his house of worship. But we have been scrupulous in maintaining Anglican teaching and liturgy, lest we lose our own identity in welcoming others'.

The cathedral's transcendent beauty, catholic inclusiveness, vitality, identification with the city, and plain human warmth have affected countless people who are not religious in any formal way. A college professor I know was brought back to the faith by a visit there;

the singer James Taylor speaks of it as his church; a skeptical, agnostic friend of mine was overwhelmed by a mystical experience during the Easter Eucharist. Many Jewish people feel at home with us—more so, they say, than in their own synagogues. The life and work of the city goes on within and without those giant walls, and those who walk down the great stone steps, we hope, carry with them into the world the love of God and God's longing for justice and peace.

RETIREMENT

IN the late 1970s, Brenda and I were discussing where we would like to live when I retired. We loved New York and could not think of living elsewhere—but where in New York? I favored Greenwich Village; Brenda, who had lived there with her first husband, was not sure she wanted to go back. One day we called on Lee and Cora Belford. He was a priest of the diocese who taught at New York University, and they lived in an 1840 brick house on Bank Street. "Paul, we are about to move back to Mississippi. Do you know anyone who would like to buy a house in Greenwich Village?" I looked at Brenda. Brenda looked at me. We visited them a week later and said we were interested, and Lee began to expound on the charms of Village life as we stood on the corner in the Indian summer sun.

"Why, Paul, you get to know everybody," he told us in his gentle Southern way. "The Chinese laundryman will do your shirts in a hurry; there's an ever-so-nice travel agency across the street. Neighbors will even keep your dog when you go away. We often sit on the stoop on summer evenings and pass the time with the neighbors."

Just then two young men came down the street holding hands. One was dressed in a turtleneck sweater and tweed jacket, but the other was got up as a juggler, complete with pantaloons, pointed shoes with bells, and a pink-and-white dunce cap. I guess I stared at them a little longer than necessary, because even for the Village this was an unusual sight. As they passed us, the fellow in the tweed jacket looked at me and said, "What's the matter with you, you silly-looking WASP?"

I turned to Lee and Cora and said, "That does it. We'll buy your house. I am finally a member of an ethnic group!"

It is a great house. We rented it out until the time came for retirement.

By 1987, I had decided to call it a day. After some difficult restructuring, the diocese was in good shape financially. The rich parishes were paying their share, a special fund for clergy needs had been established, each area of the diocese participated in the allocation of funds to its area, the clergy's minimum salary, though still far too low, had been brought up, our staff was mature and competent, and even the volatile finances of the cathedral were steady. It was a good time to retire.

ELECTING A SUCCESSOR

On September 27, 1988, the election of a coadjutor took place in Synod Hall, a Tudor banquet hall suitable for any pomp imagined by Henry VIII. Inside it, you can easily imagine yourself in some peaceful cathedral town in England were it not for the police sirens, the roar of buses climbing Amsterdam Avenue up to Morningside Heights, the blaring horns, the occasional shout. (The space is so large that the Big Apple Circus—complete with jugglers, clowns, and Philippe Petite—used to practice in Synod Hall while I conducted my own circus in my office next door.)

But this was the day my successor was to be elected, and Synod Hall was filled with a larger and soberer cast a thousand strong. The only thing they had in common was that they were all Episcopalians.

In the front rows, delegates from prominent Manhattan parishes took their place: clergy in well-cut black suits, laymen in three-piece suits, women in conservative dresses. Other rows were filled with delegates from the black parishes, West Indian in background for the most part. I could spot those from the rural areas of the Catskills, already looking a bit sleepy, for some of them had risen at five a.m. to get there. Then there were younger, more casually dressed people from the scores of small unpretentious parishes and Chinese, Haitian, and Hispanic people in groups. The clergy, almost without exception, wore clerical collars and were obviously enjoying the prestige and excitement of the moment. I sat in a lordly chair beneath the organ pipes, dressed in a scarlet academic gown, purple silk vest, and golden pectoral cross.

We had started the day by celebrating a solemn Eucharist in the cathedral, following a custom as old as the Church itself. Although the politics of the situation sometimes brings out less than godly actions, it was hoped that the Holy Spirit would influence the proceedings, that God's will would be done.

We then adjourned to Synod Hall for the nominating speeches, which spelled out the virtues, accomplishments, pastoral concern, and dedication of the nominees. The first ballot followed. Bishop Walter Dennis, our suffragan bishop, received the most votes, but nowhere near the majority of each order (lay and clerical) necessary to elect.

As the ballot was being cast, suddenly a knot of people rushed together near the stage and bent over someone. Presuming an elderly person had fainted, I clambered down from my throne.

"Bishop, it's Bishop Dennis! Oh, my God! It's Bishop Dennis!" I saw him on the floor, writhing, foaming at the mouth, eyes showing only their whites, and I thought he was dying.

"Call an ambulance!"

"Someone has."

"Step back, give him air!"

"Let the bishop in!"

I knelt down and took his hand. He had stopped writhing, but his eyes were still closed. "Walter!" I said. "It's me, Paul."

His eyes opened, and he looked around with a "Where am I?" expression. I laid my hands on his head and prayed with all my heart that he would recover.

Finally, the ambulance arrived, and Walter was taken out on a stretcher. I told the driver to take him to St. Luke's Hospital, a Church hospital just up Amsterdam Avenue where his doctor was on the staff. The driver said, no, he would have to await orders. I pulled myself up to my full six foot four and shouted, "If you do not go to St. Luke's, I will lie down in front of your damned ambulance!" He was somewhat taken aback and called his boss to say he *was* going to St. Luke's.

What was to be done? Should we cancel the election? Would Walter withdraw? I called a recess and rushed over to the hospital to see how he was doing. Two or three stretchers were along the wall. One had a sheet pulled over the head of the body lying underneath. Could that be Walter? In fact, Walter was in a back room, fully awake.

"You sure scared the hell out of everybody," I told him.

"I'm glad it happened now rather than later," he replied. "It seems as if I just couldn't carry the strain of being Bishop of New York. I guess you could say I'd rather be alive than bishop. I am withdrawing my name."

Like any election, this one was a power struggle. The Diocese of New York had sprung from the parish of Trinity Church. The first Bishop of New York, Samuel Provoost, was the rector of Trinity, and it was he who began the custom of sharing Trinity's largesse with smaller parishes and using its resources for the mission of the Church. Other large and rich New York City parishes wielded considerable influence as well. Although the smaller parishes in rural areas and the poor inner-city parishes appreciated assistance from whatever quarter, they also resented what they felt to be the undue influence on the policies of the diocese of these grand parishes.

As bishop, I had done my best to keep on good terms with the large parishes, for many of the projects important to our life depended on them. I also knew many of them from earlier family, school, and college connections. Yet some of my progressive views and actions were anathema to them, and most of them wanted a more conservative person as my successor.

The black members of the diocese were liberal in their views about race, but they were not of one mind on other subjects. This situation was complicated further by the conservative, Anglophile West Indian influence. They had got Bishop Dennis, who was black, elected suffragan, but there were those who did not trust the small group of black clergy who were the leaders of his caucus.

Perhaps the most ancient antagonism was between the rural northern and the urban southern parts of the diocese. The archdeacon of the northern region, Robert Willing, was a candidate for bishop. And of course there were the differing personalities of the candidates. Historically, New York had never elected a bishop who had not served in the diocese, so it came as a surprise when the Bishop of Kansas emerged as one of the five final candidates. No one thought Richard Grein had a chance, because he had had no big-city experience, was not known to take stands on social issues, and was thought to be less than enthusiastic about the ordination of women and homosexuals, two powerful constituencies in New York (the more so because of my support of them). All the other candidates were from New York, had served the diocese, and were more or less liberal on social issues. Such then was the political mix of the diocese as we reconvened after the recess.

I called the convention to order, and Father Frederick Williams came forward, a handsome man, his gray hair neatly cropped, his black suit well-tailored. He spoke eloquently and carried great dignity, but some felt he had politicked too hard for Bishop Dennis and suggested that he had been promised the deanship of the cathedral were Dennis elected. Now he announced that his candidate had withdrawn his name.

Soon a hand shot up, and a delegate came to the microphone on the floor. "I move the convention be adjourned."

"Seconded!"

This was a delicate issue. Adjourn for how long? We could reconvene on Saturday, but what kind of turmoil would go on in the meantime? If the motion to adjourn were voted down, would this be seen as an antiblack action, since Bishop Dennis was black and no other black candidate had been nominated? Furthermore, was the proper word "recess" rather than "adjourn"? I told the convention I needed to consult with my chancellor, the legal officer of the diocese who always sat at my side in convention. Conrad Harper was an eminent New York lawyer, later to be elected president of the New York Bar Association and appointed counsel to the State Department. He also was black.

"So Conrad, what should we do?"

"Well," he said, and explained that if we adjourned—rather than just recessing for a few days—we would need a new convention and a whole other nominating process.

I called the convention to order: "I will ask the chancellor to explain the parliamentary pickle in which we now find ourselves." The word pickle helped ease the tension, and soon the mover changed his motion from adjourn to recess until Saturday morning. I called the question, "All those in favor of recessing the convention, please say 'Aye.' " A good number of voices said, "Aye." "No?" A roar of noes resounded through the hall. We would proceed to the second ballot.

The balloting continued with no result. We broke for dinner in the nave of the cathedral. (A few years before, no one would have dreamed of eating in a church, much less a cathedral. But in the 1960s, many formalities fell by the wayside.)

Then we reconvened in Synod Hall, and after a time of silence and prayer, the process continued for a couple of ballots with more withdrawals of names. After the eighth ballot, I went to my office. Brenda and several key members of my staff were there. I asked them whether they thought we should keep going, and we discussed the pros and cons. I looked at my watch. It was ten o'clock. I said to myself, we'll go till midnight and then call it a day.

Back in the hall, people were nervous. So I led a couple of familiar hymns, the kind people know by heart. Then everyone queued up at the voting machines. After the tenth ballot, I decided to try to adjourn. We were down to three contenders. Bishop Grein from Kansas was out in front. Archdeacon Bob Willing, from the northern part of the diocese, was not far behind; he had been endorsed by the black caucus. George Regas, a former priest of the diocese and now rector of one of the largest and most successful parishes of the Church, in Pasadena, California, was a distant third.

It now was eleven o'clock. This time, it seemed to me that neither prayers nor hymns would get the group through one more ballot, so I asked them all to stand, and we sang, "I can't give you anything but love, baby." That almost brought the house down.

"All right. Any motions? Well, let's have an election!"

At eleven-fifty-five, the chief teller brought me a slip with the result of the ballot, and I called the convention to order.

"We have an election," I paused, and the silence was intense. "Bishop Richard Grein has been elected the fourteenth Bishop of New York." I saw Bob Willing bow his head amid all the applause. As was customary, I asked them to rise and sing the doxology: "Praise God from whom all blessings flow . . ."

•   •   •

I retired a few months later, taking a leave of absence in June (my official retirement was December 30, 1989). I was truly looking forward to it. I had been a priest for forty years, a bishop for twenty-five, and Bishop of New York for eighteen. Before that I had been in the Marines, at Yale, at St. Paul's. I had always been subject to the demands of an institution. Now I would be free, or so I thought.

Also, for the last few years, I had been afflicted with depressions, some of them severe. Psychiatrists prescribed medication, which helped for a while, but they could not find the cause. When I made a definite decision to retire, the depressions lifted. Apparently, as you get older, you become less able to deal with pressure, and depression reflects the body's struggle to cope. I would say to myself, "Cheer up! You have a wonderful wife, nine fine, healthy children, several grand-children, money in the bank, a summer house on Martha's Vineyard, many friends, a strong Christian faith—and yet you are miserable. You should be ashamed of yourself!" But these depressions had nothing to do with particular events, and depression cannot be argued away. Prayer became almost impossible, except as a cry for help. It seemed to me that when the adrenaline flowed, I was okay, but when I slowed down on my day off, the waves of darkness would come on.

I am sure there are many causes of depression, but for me it was the stress of responsibility. As bishop, I was always on call if a problem came up anywhere in the diocese. Since we had two hundred churches, a huge cathedral with a multimillion-dollar budget, a score of Church-related institutions, and a volatile city, problems arose frequently. In any case, the depressions disappeared as I prepared to retire.

We planned a major service in the cathedral to which everyone could come. Brenda's fertile imagination and sense of style made the planning take off.

Before I knew it, the day had come: June 11, 1989, and my final service as Bishop of New York. I stood before the great west doors, as I had done every Easter morning for eighteen years, as I had done on the day I was installed as bishop. This time, a full-fledged dragon from the Church of Our Savior in Chinatown stood alongside, its head made up of a man standing on the shoulders of another. The doors opened, and this enormous dragon and I lurched through. Chinese drums were beaten, the dragon roared, and the congregation roared in return. The service was off to a splendid start.

My favorite hymns were sung, including "Jerusalem" ("And did those feet in ancient times / Walk upon England's pastures green") and "In Christ there is no East or West" ("Join hands then children of the Faith / Whate'er your race may be"). The lessons were read in English, Spanish, Haitian French, and Chinese, the languages of the diocese. This was followed by short remarks from three people who represented aspects of my work: Benno Schmidt, president of Yale; Ruth Messinger, the Manhattan borough president; and my old and dear friend Mellick Belshaw, Bishop of New Jersey. Then James Taylor sang a hymn he'd written in my honor with the novelist Reynolds Price.

Now it was time for me to preach my last sermon from that amazing pulpit, a time to reminisce a little and to show my love and appreciation to the people of the diocese, with whom I had been through so much. I began at the crossing, thanking everyone who had made the day possible; and then, wearing a portable microphone, I began to wander through the cathedral. I sang the first few lines of "I'm gonna take a sentimental journey," then I took out a list I had of the two hundred parishes of the diocese and read off their names, commenting now and then as I strolled down the long aisle. I began with St. Paul's, Tivoli, the northernmost parish in Dutchess County. When I had reached the very back of the cathedral, I turned around and started up the aisle, reading the names of parishes from the Bronx and Manhattan. We had made a trip around the diocese, and I had timed it so that I returned to the pulpit itself just as we arrived at St. Stephen's, Tottenville, on the very tip of Staten Island.

I then preached a short sermon, charging them to keep up the great work we had all been doing together for these many years:

> I charge you to be a Catholic Church in love with freedom. I charge you to exercise your freedom by having courage. We have been made timid by great dangers; our lives are threatened on the streets by crime and drugs; our world can be destroyed by a nuclear war. But this is not a time to be timid; this is a time to be brave. I charge you to be catholic, universal,

open to all people. I charge you to be free in your mind to push forward the boundaries of theology, to liberate your thinking from the dusty metaphysics of the past to a new dynamic of the Gospel, so that the vigor of its love invades the issues of the day. I charge you to face without flinching the approaching crises in our city and in our land. Dare to look on reality and stare it down by transforming it, whether homelessness, crack, AIDS, or a school system in deep trouble. No way, they say, can these problems be solved. No way, I say, can they remain unsolved.

But how can I help? Start small. Get to know a homeless person. When you see a bad law coming up, write your congressman. If you are young and brave, go to El Salvador. Whatever it is, do it at the behest of Christ, because one act of courageous love, however small, leads to another. When many act together with courage, the power of goodness grows.

You are messengers of God's truth clothed in the beauty of God. Take hope, be strong, be brave, be free, be open, be loving, and hold up the glory of the heavenly city. Without a vision, the people perish. See that vision yourselves; remove the scales from your eyes so that you can see the City so clearly that you will never cease till you have built Jerusalem in our land.

When I concluded, the congregation, three or four thousand strong, gave me a standing ovation. That was one of the great moments of my life, and I savored it. Tears came to my eyes; I was filled with joy. I looked over them all: my family—Brenda, children, and grandchildren in front; old Canon West, who had been there when I was ordained, sitting in a wheelchair below me; clergy, some of whom, like Jim Morton, Ledlie Laughlin, Steve Chinlund, and Davis Given, I had known for more than forty years; the acolytes and choir; and then the people, row upon row, all ages and colors, some very poor, some rich, country people, city people, from the ghettos and barrios, from Park Avenue and the East Village. What a privilege to have been their pastor for so long.

The service concluded with a recessional led by a troop of dancers and drummers from our youth employment project, in African costume, naked to the waist. Brenda and the rest of the family walked out with me down that long aisle once again and out onto the streets of New York.

A fourteen-year-old boy who was there, named Paul Leeming, wrote a poem, which describes that great day better than I can:

Tall man in the cathedral
One last word
Echoing off the stone columns
Off the vaulted ceiling
One last look at his home which he must leave now
Walking for the last time in the procession
Walking toward the doors at the end
The organ plays for him
I follow him with my eyes
As he walks further and further away
In the midst of the procession
In the midst of the candles and the incense haze
I see people gather around him
His followers
He walks through the sad sea of people
Towards the doors which have opened for him
One last time.
A beam of light at the end of the cathedral
At the end of his career
I can see him walking with the people around him
The light coming through the doors into the dark of the cathedral
It flows around him
Weeping silhouette
His tears not dripping on his face
But flooding his mind.

REFLECTIONS

THIS morning is August 6, 1995. It is a Sunday and the feast of the Transfiguration, which commemorates the moment when the three disciples saw Jesus glistening in glory on the mountain. It is also the anniversary of another Sunday morning fifty years ago when the United States dropped an atomic bomb on Hiroshima. I went to church and kept seeing an image, a vision of the transfigured Christ shining forth from the cross against the backdrop of a smoldering city; and above him, in a parody of Renaissance paintings of the Ascension, the mushroom cloud.

This also is the morning when I am to sit down and begin the final chapter of this book: reflections on life's meaning, reflections on my own life. The vision of the transfigured Christ against the radioactive ashes of Hiroshima says it all, for over the years, I have seen more and more clearly the consequences of human sin crush millions of God's children. I also have seen, more and more vividly, the glory of Christ in the love and courage of men and women. And I have felt, more and more deeply, the flesh of Christ in his people. In prayer and meditation, I see and sometimes seem to feel the crucified flesh in the pain of another person, but transfigured, because the suffering is also being borne by God. This terrible but redeeming suffering Jesus endured on the cross is still being worked out in the suffering of humanity through the ages. We cannot understand why a loving God allows pain any more than we can understand the why of Creation itself. This is the way things are. Yet our faith in the paradigm of death and resurrection leads down into the depth of the mystery of pain, through the horrible darkness of it, and out to the other side where new life awaits.

The underlying principle of the Christian faith is that spirit and flesh are one in Creation. Men and women constantly try to separate them or to put them at war with each other. But the Incarnation forever joined the two, when, as John's Gospel puts it, "The Word became flesh and dwelt among us, and we beheld his glory." The cross is the inevitable agony that such joining brings. The Word of God became flesh; the qualities of that mystery of being (love, freedom, justice) were lived out in a human body and confronted the world in its broken, sinful, demonic state; persecution, suffering, and death resulted. When those divine qualities show themselves in human beings today, persecution, suffering, and death result. Yet out of that suffering in the life and death of Jesus came the strange event we call the Resurrection, and out of this collision of love with evil, and the innocent suffering it entails, comes the dynamic of the redeeming of the world. Whether or not you believe in the historical validity of the Christian faith, I ask you to perceive in the death and resurrection of Jesus the intention of love, the projection of love from the heart of the mystery of being some call God.

PRINCIPALITIES, POWERS, AND THE KINGDOM

As recently as ten years ago, the primary fact of history was the struggle between the USSR and the United States. Those principalities wielded sufficient power to destroy each other and the world itself. Fear, fostered by politicians and corporate leaders who stood to profit by the rivalry, turned into paranoia. The fear ran so deep, and its senselessness was so masked, that neither the people of the USSR nor the people of the United States rose up to end it. Now that the cold war is over, and we are left like a wounded rooster crowing on top of the dung heap, the same military-industrial forces gobble up our resources. Quick as a flash, they were able to change the reason for military excess from fear of Russia to an alleged need to fight two full-scale wars at the same time against an enemy no one has named. There are hints that nations that are not part of Western culture may be substituted for the USSR as a needed enemy. The greed of massive international corporations was behind their exploiting fear during the cold war. Now the cold war has ended, but corporate greed has not gone away, and their penetration of our culture is so complete that the arms race continues. Those weapons we do not need ourselves we gladly sell or give to nations who can ill afford them and who sometimes use them not only to kill one another but often to kill American soldiers and civilians. We sell more weapons by far than any other nation.

The result of this greed is catastrophic; nor are we able to control these corporate entities, because they have tremendous power over politicians and often are beyond the law of any particular nation. The power of chief executive officers who earn millions while laying off workers or condoning sweatshops is Dickensian. The money squandered on the arms race alone could rebuild our schools, provide job training for our unemployed, and build decent housing for every American. Such an obscene waste of resources touches the life of every human being on earth.

In other centuries, imperialism, colonialism, and unbridled nationalism brought about great human misery. Corporate greed and lust for power are the demons of our day. I cannot imagine how this cycle of events will end. Prosperity in China could energize another cold war. A rogue state with an atomic bomb could hold the democratic world hostage. Alternatively, a generation of enlightened corporate leaders could see that peace is more profitable than war and organize a mechanism to govern the economies of nations and corporations. A massive movement of young people, as in the 1960s, could insist on universal human rights.

These speculations may seem naive, yet prophecies of the collapse of the USSR or of racial peace in South Africa would have seemed naive twenty years ago. Whatever the future may bring, it is important that people of goodwill be on the alert, sensitive to signs of movement, and ready to mobilize for such a change.

YOUNG PEOPLE OF THE WORLD

I have been encouraged again and again by the young people I have met in so many different places. Several years ago, I was asked to preach at a huge mission rally in Kerala, India, at the ancient Mar

Thoma Church. For six days I preached to 150,000 people. The church traces its history to St. Thomas, the apostle who is said to have traveled to Jewish settlements on the west coast of India. The Christian communities he founded have lasted all these years in a non-Christian land. The Maramon Convention of the Mar Thoma Church, as this meeting was called, took place in a dry riverbed. The sight of thousands of people sitting in the lotus position in the hot sun was like a biblical fantasy.

The archbishop asked me to preach the social gospel, for he felt his church had too infrequently expressed itself on social issues. In that totally different culture, I again found young people longing for justice. Kerala is the only province in India that has had a Communist government, and the young people had picked up its political views. They displayed cartoons critical of the church in their booth. In one, a beggar pleads for food at the sumptuous table of two fat bishops.

I had some sessions with these young people and pointed out that the Gospel, if taken seriously, was even more radical than Marxism. But the important thing to me was that, despite the incongruity and violence of their cartoons, they expressed ingenuous eagerness and clear-eyed zeal.

I see the same clear, young eyes in faces of so many different colors; I hear the laughter between the words of so many different tongues: the boys of Mississippi, the radical youth of the Indian Mar Thoma Church, the teenage teachers of the Sandinistas in Nicaragua, the Buddhist college students demonstrating in Saigon, the high school students seeking sanctuary with the Bishop in East Timor.

Of course, there are also young people who are selfish, cruel, and cowardly, but even in the New York jail of Riker's Island I found reason for hope in the young men. I used to go there every Sunday before Christmas. The last time I went, we held a service in the male adolescent block. I always felt nervous going out there; not afraid of the men, but totally inadequate. Here I was, an old, white-haired WASP of a bishop, brought up in the lap of luxury, comfortably housed in a French château, presuming to preach the good news of Christmas to three hundred mostly black and Latino kids who had grown up in the grinding ethos of New York's inner city, who had been behind bars for months awaiting trial, whose future was nearly hopeless, whether they were convicted or not. A black minister, Carl Flemister, was with me, but he, except for his color, was as far removed as I from the lives of those youngsters.

Was Christmas good news? No—I knew that Christmas for them was bad news, since it was the time when their despair most clearly stood out against the mindless blather of commercial Christmas, the glitter and the Norman Rockwell images. Christmas was white indeed! But I *did* know that the real theme of the Christmas Mass was fashioned for the likes of them far more than for the likes of me. If anything, the gospel of Christmas is bad news for the secure and comfortable but wonderful news for the poor and wretched. "He has filled the hungry with good things and the rich he has sent empty away," Mary sang when she heard she was to conceive the Christ child.

We walked out on the stage in the room that served as a chapel. I said, rather weakly, "Merry Christmas," to which they tried to reply with spirit. We sang "O Come all ye faithful, Joyful and triumphant . . ." Who there was joyful or triumphant? To combat the traditional image conjured by the Christmas lesson of a beautiful pine-bough-covered crèche sheltering fluffy lambs, a nice clean cow, and Mary in a lovely, sky-blue dress, with Joseph standing near her, his long hair just shampooed, I told the Christmas story as it might happen in New York: A homeless black couple up from the South was looking for shelter but intimidated by the Hilton and rejected at one hotel after another, until finally being taken in by an all-night garage in Harlem. A couple of mangy dogs were in attendance and a rat or two. Mary lay down on a workbench, and when Jesus was born they wrapped him in some greasy rags and laid him on an oil drum. The men listened.

I said that, even though Jesus was born in a cold cave smelling of manure, we look back on the scene as beautiful, because of who the baby was. He can make all things beautiful, even a wretched birth, even death on a cross.

We then explained the Eucharist and how Jesus was arrested and condemned right after the first Lord's Supper. He went through death and rose to new life. They can get through what they are now facing and find new life beyond. I told them to try to offer him their lives on the altar, which would be joined to his life and to one another's.

And then they could come up and receive him into their very bodies in the bread and wine. They listened. Few had ever been to Communion before.

The simple, glorious prayer of consecration was said, "This is my Body, This is my Blood"—their body, their blood? And the men came forward, knelt down, and put out their upturned hands like children. As I gave each of them Communion, they looked up with guileless eyes and awkwardly but carefully received the bread and wine.

After I communicated the first row, a strange thing happened. Only a few arose to return to their seats. The rest stayed, transfixed, silent, motionless. I finally leaned over and said gently, "You can go now."

I went to the door to greet them after the service. As the first young man came toward me, big and very black, I put out my hand. He ignored it. For a moment I thought he was refusing to touch me. After all that had gone on in the service, I felt rejected. But then he opened his arms and gave me a huge hug. So did all the rest; and as they drew close, they would ask me to pray for a mother or a girlfriend or a sick child. It was hard to keep back the tears.

Whether in India or Nicaragua or East Timor or Riker's Island, whether among young heroes of the revolution or young men awaiting trial, I felt the reality that each was made in the image of God, I felt the flesh of Christ in the clumsy embraces, I sensed the grace of God, the Kingdom, present.

I have no illusions about the crimes some of these young people have committed nor about some of the other young men and women who have been part of liberation movements over the years. After all, young soldiers took part in the rape of Nanking and were Nazis under Hitler. Young soldiers nailed Jesus to the cross. Like everything else, the fire and courage and sacrifice of youth can become demonic. But still, I have been privileged to see the image of God, latent in every human being, shine forth with special brilliance as young people dedicate themselves to the cause of justice and peace.

INSTINCTS FOR WAR, MOVEMENTS FOR PEACE

Surely an instinct to fight is part of human nature, but so is the instinct toward reconciliation. In 1965, I visited Japan to give some lectures on the Church and the city for the Nippon Sei Ko Kai (the Anglican Church of Japan). I asked my host, Bishop Goto of Tokyo, if he could find a Japanese veteran who had served on Guadalcanal. One of his priests, it turned out, had been in the first battle of the Matanikau. He could not speak English, but by drawing a map on the tablecloth we reached back to the day we'd fired on each other across that jungle stream. Another Japanese came over to translate.

"Yes, we were dug in on that bank right there, our whole battalion. Why did you keep sending men across that exposed sand spit? Were you in some kind of kamikaze outfit?"

I shook my head: "No, we do not think that way—but sometimes it amounts to that. I think our colonel was a bit mad."

Thus were old demons put to rest. We were now fellow priests, friends—and our countries were allies. Within twenty years, allies become enemies, enemies become friends, but because of the manipulation of the Principalities and Powers we are led into war; and if we win, we still must contemplate our bloody hands.

War is a totally unacceptable instrument of foreign policy. How could George Bush, a decent man, lead us into the Persian Gulf for oil? How could Lyndon Johnson, so instrumental in the compassionate war on poverty, insist on the wild and fruitless slaughter of Vietnam? How could we again respond with a certain joy to the sound of bugles, less than twenty years after the publication and the movie of *All Quiet on the Western Front*?

I myself have felt the infantile instinct toward violence. I have a primitive vanity in being a decorated Marine and am proud to have received the Navy Cross and the Silver Star. What is wrong with us? Why can't we pray away this feral instinct? "Testosterone poisoning," my wife calls it, but women have it too: Gold Star mothers, holding their heads high with pride as taps sounds over their sons' graves, Margaret Thatcher blasting away at the little Falkland Islands. As long as the poison, the sin, the instinct lie there undisturbed in the deepest springs of our beings, we will be willing, at the slightest provocation, at the sound of the bugle, to stand, to salute, and to kill.

And strangely enough, this same emotion galvanizes movements for justice and peace. We *march* in demonstrations; we make a peace sign, mimicking the military salute. Many have risked their lives for peace, and when a movement becomes angry and divisive, even if the wrath be righteous, we are on the edge of blood. I long for some cosmic surgeon to slice delicately through human emotion to separate war fever from the emotion needed to overcome it, lest movement after movement disintegrate into violence: nonviolent movements for civil rights turn to rage, right-to-life efforts devolve into clinic bombings, liberation theology become guerrilla warfare.

Very occasionally, a Martin Luther King, an Oscar Romero, a Mahatma Gandhi, a Desmond Tutu, a Carlos Ximenes Belo of East Timor emerges to lead a nonviolent movement with power. Such people are touched with a peculiar charisma, a special grace; each is a man of prayer, which gives him power without a hint of violence.

More often, glorious crusades slip into jealous rivalries and violence, as the young participants lose patience with slow and undramatic progress toward justice. Corruption sets in, leaders burn out. Movements rise, shine, and fade or take on life in another form or as institutions. St. Francis of Assisi would not have recognized his order shortly after his death.

You cannot start a movement. The conditions must be ready. If they are, the slightest spark can ignite women and men into action: Rosa Parks refused to move to the back of the bus, and the civil rights movement took off; tea leaves were dumped in Boston Harbor and the American Revolution began in earnest. This moment in time is called *kairos*, which is Greek for "the fullness of time" into which Christ appeared and the Christian movement began.

In the Bible, we are told of the Remnant who stayed on in Jerusalem during the exile and prepared the way for its rebuilding when the exiles returned from Babylon. I think of William Sloane Coffin and Cora Weiss, who kept the peace movement alive during the 1970s, until the freeze on nuclear weapons gained force, which in turn had much to do with the end of the cold war. How I admire those people who keep the faith when there is no movement, who prepare for the *kairos*.

MY FAMILY

I have observed the work of the Spirit throughout the world, and I have known great wonders and great pains in my own life as well. I am most blessed. Brenda has stuck with me, showing great courage as she endured two years of pain from a riding accident and then an automobile accident in which we almost were killed. We laugh together; we travel together. I am so proud of her ability to be friends with all kinds of people, and I cherish her extraordinary grace and her laughter as I hear it across a crowded room.

I am inordinately proud of my children. Honor is a poet and has written a biography of her artist grandmother, Margarett Sargent. Paul, the father of three, lives in Berkeley, where, at the age of forty-two, he had the courage to begin a new career and has become a psychologist; he also leads a meditation group and lectures—preaches?—every other Sunday. Adelia is also a clinical psychologist and the mother of four sons; drawing on her Jersey City roots, she works with poor and homeless men, women, and children. Rosemary, a creator of whimsical, touching monologues, is working on a play and is the mother of twin girls. George is a painter; he and his wife, Alice Cristov, have founded an institution in San Salvador called Intercambios, where the young people of a very poor district are taught art, computers, forestry, and much else. Marian lives in Minneapolis with her three children, producing concerts and hosting a weekly program on the radio. Daniel is a film critic for *Variety* and produced a prizewinning documentary on the election of Václav Havel as president of the Czech Republic. Susanna, who spent years in Central America, is studying to be a clinical psychologist. (What did I do to have three shrinks in the family?) And Patience is a blossoming country-western singer in Manhattan, with her own band, Patience and the Cowboy Angels.

It means a great deal to me that they all are giving their lives to art and to the helping professions and that they have strong marriages and splendid, healthy children. It seems a special gift of the Holy Spirit that nine children, eight in-laws, and sixteen grandchildren are all well!

GETTING OLD

One of my editors suggested I write about getting old. I do not feel differently for the most part, with some notable exceptions: I lose a lot more golf balls, and I do not run after every tennis ball. But I have energy, good health, interests, friends, a great wife, children, and grandchildren. I still go on fishing trips to faraway places like Belize and Alaska. I write, I preach, I do some informal counseling. I go to church and sometimes celebrate the Eucharist but find sitting in a pew just fine. Brenda and I work on human rights, especially in East Timor, where the opposition leader, our friend Monsignor Carlos Ximenes Belo, has been given the Nobel Peace Prize.

As the years slip by, I lose more and more friends, and often I am asked to take their funerals. This is a sad but fulfilling task. Of course, I try to visit the person before he or she dies. Sometimes this makes a great difference to the dying person and also to the family; even if they are not particularly religious (especially if they are not, in fact), they appreciate your prayers and advice.

At the service, I always say a few words about the person, with a bit of humor fashioned to the kind of congregation that gathers. A good farewell somehow makes it possible for the family to pick up their lives and go forward. Death comes as a terrifying stranger to most families, so it means a great deal to have someone with them, such as a priest, who is both a friend and one familiar with dying.

I have had some rare experiences with the dying. When Sister Rachel, a nun of deep spirituality, was dying of cancer, I asked her what it felt like to die. She said, "It's wonderful, you don't have to make any decisions." She went on to say how she felt buoyed by the love and faith of her friends.

A few months ago I made my last visit to my old and closest friend, Walter McVeigh, at the Trappist monastery in Lafayette, Oregon, where he was abbot for twenty years. Quig, as his friends called him, was bedridden with a terminal blood disease. We talked for hours about old times and mutual friends. I told him how much his life had meant to all of us. Even though we rarely saw him, his presence in the monastery, his prayers, and his letters had become a stabilizing force in our lives. He and I also talked about dying. He had no fear of death. He said, "I can't wait!" (My son Paul, his godson, called him a few days later. "What will I do without your guidance?" he asked. Quig replied, "Prepare to meet me in Paradise.") The morning I left, as has been our custom, we celebrated the Eucharist together. This would be the last time. The altar was the bed tray, covered with a linen cloth and adorned with a cross and two candles. We spoke the prayers together, blessed the bread and wine together, and gave each other Communion. We remained in silence for some time. The presence of the Holy Spirit enfolded us both with a deep joy and wonder. For over sixty years we had been friends. Death surely would not divide us, since we were one in Christ.

Quig died quietly in his sleep. Two days later, a splendid Requiem was celebrated at the monastery. Peter McCarthy, the present Abbot, described the overwhelming affection shown by the three hundred people from the surrounding countryside who attended. Instead of a coffin, the Trappist tradition is to lay the departed on a plain pine board, dressed in the white habit of the Order. All during the night before the funeral, two brothers kept vigil, reciting the Psalms from beginning to end by the light of the candles burning by the bier. The morning of the service dawned gray and damp, but after the solemn Requiem in the chapel, as the procession approached the grave, the sun broke through to clothe those last moments in the glory of a perfect spring day. The people sprinkled flowers over his body and he was lowered into his grave, at the end of a line of white crosses marking the graves of his Brothers who had preceded him on the journey into eternity.

Since none of his old friends could be there, Quig and I planned a service in New York in the Episcopal Church of the Resurrection from which he and I had come when we began our vocation to the priesthood. Fifty or so of the old crowd were there. His brother Charlie read a lesson, and his niece Lynn and Tony Duke reflected on their memories of him. I gave the homily, recalling the old days, including the grand party he gave in his grandmother's marble palace on Long Island. I asked how many of the congregation had been there. Twenty hands went up.

When Quig became a monk, many of his friends asked the big question: Why on earth would a wonderful person like Quig shut himself off from the world? How could a *bon vivant*, the life of the party, put away his precious martinis and Zeus cigarette holder forever? Couldn't he do more good helping people?

I believe, as time has gone on, his sacrificial life, his extraordinary devotion to his old friends and his family, and his influence far beyond the gates of the monastery, made us feel, at the deepest level, that his choice was a glorious one.

It is fitting, in the busy, preoccupied world in which we live, that a few who are so called give themselves completely to the life of prayer, making up, perhaps, for the vast neglect of prayer on the part of so many. It meant so much to me to know that Quig was there, worshipping the Lord, morning, noon, and night, and praying for us as well. He continued to be a presence in our lives, even more of a presence than most other friends, even though he was far away and seldom seen.

When someone dies, there is a surge of love that floats you through the worst of it. Then comes the long and difficult healing time, as people are caught up in other things and you are alone. Here is where prayer helps, as day by day life becomes livable again. Do not expect life to be as it was, but do expect to fashion a new way of life with its own rewards. No sudden decisions should be made for a year or so; it takes at least that long to know what you wish your new life to be like and to feel your way into the new person you are becoming.

I have never yet seen someone die who was not at peace (although I am sure some die with great agitation). In my experience, the closer death comes, the more peaceful people become, as if they felt the Lord coming to take them into his presence.

Right now, I am not afraid of death. Of course, I do not know about the afterlife, whether it is eternal sleep, whether we continue our existence in some unimaginable state of being, whether we meet our departed friends—who knows? But I believe that God is loving and that we continue, and if we do not, it would not be a painful thing, because we would not know.

What about the parable of Judgment Day, when the sheep and the goats are separated? Well, if this should in some way occur, I will take my chances on God's mercy. When someone asks me about heaven and hell, I tend to say that if the latter exists, it is the same place as the former. For some, being in God's presence would be heaven, for others, being in his presence would be hell. It is like a kid being sent to the principal's office in school: if he goes there to be congratulated on a high grade, it is delightful; if he goes there to be reprimanded, it is painful. Same principal, same office; same God, same afterlife.

If there is indeed some kind of Judgment, it will be on how we have loved, not on what we have believed.

These meandering thoughts are far too anthropomorphic and pedestrian, for when we leave this life we will be on the sea of eternity and infinity, enveloped by the mystery of being. Who knows what that dazzling glory might be?

HOLY PLACES

Throughout this book, I have spoken of the power of what we call the Holy Spirit—a discernible spirit, which, because of its grace and power in people's lives, we call holy and believe to be part of the Holy Trinity. I am convinced of God's presence in the world and that from time to time his Kingdom breaks through into the events of history, into the life of the Church, and into the lives of individuals.

There is another sign of God's presence, one even more mysterious: the numinous quality of holy places. Recently, Brenda and I traveled to Turkey, where amid the ruins of Ephesus is the supposed burial place of St. John the Divine. Some believe him to be the young man described as the disciple whom Jesus loved and who leaned on his Lord's breast at the Last Supper. After a wearying day of sight-seeing, we climbed to a rise of ground. A few slim white pillars stood in the soft glow of a September afternoon. I felt a light sense of peace, a buoyancy of spirit, and in my mind's eye I saw a delicate vision of that strange saint. I did not want to leave. Afterward, I asked our friends if they had felt a special quality about the place. None were devout Christians, but all had sensed this numinous presence. I was glad St. John was the patron saint of our cathedral.

I have always felt a kinship to St. Francis of Assisi. Part of me wishes, I suppose, that I had had his courage, as a rich young man, to give all away and follow my Lord in poverty and wretchedness. Part of me loves his humor, his singing, his pleasure in Creation, his joy, which dwelt with him even in the deepest agony. He exulted in his humanity and loved Claire with a passion. When his body got in his way, he called it "Brother Ass." Of all the saints, he seems the most like Jesus.

Assisi is no more beautiful than some other hill towns in that part of Italy, nor are the three churches, one on top of the other, so handsome architecturally. But when I go there, St. Francis's joy seems palpable, whether in the small crypt chapel where he is buried, in the soaring frescoes of Giotto in the spacious chapel above, or in the stone cell on the side of a wooded mountain where he went to be alone and where (it is said) he spoke to the birds. From that beautiful place you can look over the flat landscape far below. The day we were there, the birdsong was everywhere. Francis never sought pain, but when suffering came upon him he knew that it was part of the on-going passion of Christ in his people. The climax of this redemptive pain was the receiving of stigmata, the wounds of Christ in his hands, his feet, and his side. This presence of joy and suffering, this sunny faith, I feel each time I visit that holy town where the spirit of Francis permeates the very stones. Sitting in Francis's stone cell, I could truly imagine that the stigmata he suffered were his greatest joy. I saw, through him, the terrible truth that the deepest love and the deepest pain are intertwined and that if only you can allow the Lord to be intimately with you—*within you*—you can find joy in the very depth of agony.

As Assisi, through Francis, epitomizes the joy and suffering of Christ's humanity, the atmosphere of St. Sophia in Istanbul calls up the Holy Spirit. Western Christianity dwells on the second person of the Trinity, the Christ; Eastern Orthodoxy emphasizes the third per-son, the Holy Spirit. The first time I visited St. Sophia, I felt the Holy Spirit as never before. Somehow, in that great space, you feel lifted into a new realm. The ceiling high above is centered in a great dome, but unlike the Gothic arch, the dome does not lift your eyes upward. Rather, it seems to contain you. The Holy Spirit is not "up there" but down here among her people. Christ is not forgotten; star-ing down at you from the golden mosaics are the piercing eyes of Christ the King, for the image of Christ most used by the Orthodox is not the suffering human Christ on the cross but the heavenly Christ reigning as King of Heaven.

When I first visited the church, Professor Whittemore, a friend of my grandmother's, was uncovering the mosaics. I had the great privilege of standing beside him on the scaffold as he carefully chipped away the plaster with which Muslims had covered the images when Sophia was used as a mosque. He showed me how each glass tile was slanted down toward the floor so that its full glory would strike the viewer below.

In recent years we have become more conscious of the femininity of the Godhead, as expressed in early theology by the concept of the Holy Spirit as wisdom (in Greek, a feminine noun); and this aspect of God was part of the mystery of that great basilica. The West fulfilled the longing of the human soul for a feminine object of worship through the cult of the Virgin; the East also celebrated the feminine Sophia, holy wisdom.

Of all the holy places I have visited, Jerusalem moved me most profoundly. For many years, I avoided going there, as you might avoid going to a movie based on a beloved book. I had visions of crass commercialization, tacky tourism, and all the rest. However, in May 1977, Brenda and I decided to go with our friends the Potters. My first impression of the city was of its limitless strength. In the United States, we are used to subjective religion: what *I* happen to believe, what spirituality appeals to *me*. But when I encountered Jerusalem I knew that it did not really matter much whether *I* believed in God, because the great holy Rock of God, which had endured the battering of the ages, stood strong. "A Mighty Fortress is Our God" indeed! The city is crowned by the golden Dome of the Rock, sacred to Muslims; in the crevices of the Western Wall, Jews have placed notes describing their hopes and hurts and fears. Jesus knelt on stone in the garden of Gethsemane the night he was betrayed, and sweat and tears dropped from his face like blood onto its rocky pavement. Calvary is a rock; there John and the Marys knelt and watched Jesus die. Even the alleged site of the Ascension is a rock on which a footprint is discernible, which local tradition holds to be the last footprint of Jesus as he leaped up to heaven.

I entered the holy sepulchre with curiosity only, not anticipation. Could this really be where they laid the body of Jesus? Did he really lie here? The basilica of the holy sepulchre is a huge church, noisy with the liturgies of three faiths, the prayers of pilgrims, and the murmurings of tourists. In the center is a small building of stone, like a baptistery. I entered and in the dim light saw the narrow opening leading down a few stone steps into the tomb. I stooped low and crept down. The only other person there was an old man kneeling before some flickering candles. Carved into the wall of the chamber is a stone bench, about six feet long. I turned to look and wondered: Could this be where he lay? At that moment I felt tremendous pressure on my shoulders, as if two great hands were forcing me onto my knees. There I was, kneeling, my hands resting on that cold stone bench. I stopped thinking. My consciousness was changed to a dream-world. I felt a giant throbbing, and it seemed that I was at the epicenter of the universe with Christ, buried with him in that cold tomb, but I felt too that indeed he was alive (and that word is too small), that he was the power and energy of all cosmic force. "Through him all things were made."

That, then, was Jerusalem, the center of three major faiths—the center, so it felt to me, of the universe. I did not expect any of this, and when I try to find words to express that extraordinary experience, they fail me. Nor can my skeptical mind account for what happened. Forty years earlier, God broke into my life when I made my first confession—and now he had broken through again, an overshadowing of equal intensity.

Whenever my faith falters, whenever it grows dim, something takes place to bring me back with a rush and to make me know that whatever happens to me, whatever I feel, whatever I believe or do not believe, the mystery of being I call God *IS*.

ACKNOWLEDGMENTS

First, I thank Brenda for her unending patience and encouragement as I disappeared morning, noon, and night to wrestle the book. I have had many editors: I particularly wish to thank Judith Jones, who helped me enormously, and above all Paul Elie, my final and most helpful and sympathetic editor. Jeff Seroy, briefly my editor, pulled me through a difficult time.

I asked my children, and five friends who were acquainted with different periods of my life, to comment on the manuscript: Elliott Lindsley, historian of the Diocese of New York and a fellow native of Morristown; William A. Johnson, Canon Theologian of the Cathedral of St. John the Divine; Robert Moskin, historian of the Marine Corps; the Reverend Philip Newell, a colleague from my Washington days; and Peter Stiglin, who worked with me in the early stages of the writing and who was my assistant for several years in New York. I am grateful for their comments and suggestions.

INDEX